THE VITAL CENTURY

Social and Economic History of England

Edited by Asa Briggs

THE VITAL CENTURY
England's Developing Economy, 1714–1815

John Rule
Professor of History, University of Southampton

Longman
London and New York

Longman Group UK Ltd
Longman House, Burnt Mill, Harlow
Essex CM20 2JE, England
and Associated Companies throughout the world

*Published in the United States of America
by Longman Publishing., New York*

First published 1992

British Library Cataloguing in Publication Data
Rule, John
    The vital century: England's developing economy, 1714–1815.
    – (Social and economic history of England)
    I. Title II. Series
    942.07

ISBN 0-582-49424-9
ISBN 0-582-49425-7 pbk

Library of Congress Cataloging-in-Publication Data
Rule, John, 1944–
    The vital century: England's developing economy, 1714–1815 /
    John Rule. p. cm. — (Social and economic history of England)
    Includes bibliographical references and index.
    ISBN 0-582-49424-9 (csd). — ISBN 0-582-49425-7 (ppr)
    1. Great Britain—Economic conditions—18th century. 2. England–
    –Social conditions. I. Title. II Series.
    HC254.5.R85 1992
    330.941'07—dc20   91-17397
                                                   CIP

Set in Baskerville

Produced by Longman Singapore Publishers (Pte) Ltd.
Printed in Singapore

Contents

List of Abbreviations

Econ. H.R. Economic History Review. All references are to the Second Series

Jn. Econ. Hist. Journal of Economic History

Smith, *Wealth of Nations* All references are to the edition of E. Cannan first published in 1904 and reprinted in two volumes by Methuen in 1961

List of Figures

List of Tables

Introductory Note

This is the latest volume in an established series which sets out to relate economic history to social history. Interest in economic history has grown enormously in recent years. In part, the interest is a by-product of twentieth-century preoccupation with economic issues and problems. In part, it is a facet of the revolution in the study of history. The scope of the subject has been immensely enlarged, and with the enlargement has come increasing specialization. There has also been a change in the approach to it as a result of the collection of a wider range of data and the development of new quantitative techniques. New research is being completed each year both in history and economics departments, and there are now enough varieties of approach to make for frequent controversy, enough excitement in the controversy to stimulate new writing. Interest in social history has boomed even more than interest in economic history since the first volume in this series was published, and debates continue both about its scope and its methods. It remains the purpose of this series, however, to bracket together the two adjectives economic and social. There is no need for two different sets of historians to carry out their work in separate workshops. Most of the problems with which they are concerned demand cooperative effort. However refined the analysis of the problems may be or may become, however precise the statistics, something more than accuracy and discipline is needed in the study of social and economic history. Many of the most lively economic historians of this century have been singularly undisciplined, and their hunches and insights have often proved invaluable. Behind the abstractions of economist or sociologist is the experience of real people, who demand sympathetic understanding as well as searching analysis. One of the dangers of economic history is that it can be written far too easily in impersonal terms: real people seem to play little part in it. One of the dangers of social history is that it concentrates on categories rather than on flesh and blood human beings. This series is designed to avoid both dangers, at least as far as they can be avoided in the light of available evidence. Quantitative evidence is used where it is available, but it is not the only kind of evidence which is taken into the reckoning.

Within this framework each author has complete freedom to describe the period covered by his volume along lines of his own choice. No attempt has been made to secure general uniformity of style or treatment. The volumes will necessarily overlap. Social and economic history seldom moves within generally accepted periods, and each author has had the freedom to decide where the limits of his chosen period are set. It has been for him to decide of what the 'unity' of his period consists.

It has also been his task to decide how far it is necessary in his volume to take into account the experience of other countries as well as England in order to understand English economic and social history. The term 'England' itself has been employed generally in relation to the series as a whole, not because Scotland, Wales or Ireland are thought to be less import or less interesting than England, but because their historical experience at various times was separate from or diverged from that of England: where problems and endeavours were common or where issues arose when the different societies confronted each other, these problems, endeavours and issues find a place in this series. In certain periods Europe, America, Asia, Africa and Australia must find a place also. One of the last volumes in the series will be called 'Britain and the World Economy'.

The variety of approaches to the different periods will be determined, of course, not only by the values, background or special interests of the authors but by the nature of the surviving sources and the extent to which economic and social factors can be separated out from other factors in the past. For many of the periods described in this series it is extremely difficult to disentangle law or religion from economic and social structure and change. Facts about 'economic and social aspects' of life must be supplemented by accounts of how successive generations thought about 'economy and society'. The very terms themselves must be dated. Above all, there must be an attempt to relate society to culture, visual and verbal, separating out elements of continuity and discontinuity.

Where the facts are missing or the thoughts impossible to recover, it is the duty of the historian to say so. Many of the crucial problems in English social and economic history remain mysterious or only partially explored. This series must point, therefore, to what is not known as well as what is known, to what is a matter of argument as well as what is agreed upon. At the same time, it is one of the particular excitements of the economic and social historian to be able, as G.M. Trevelyan has written, 'to know more in some respects than the dweller in the past himself knew about the conditions that enveloped and controlled his life.'

ASA BRIGGS

Preface

The last decade and a half has been an active time in eighteenth-century history. After a longish period of relative neglect compared with the centuries on either side, the 1700s have returned to the foreground of historical scholarship. In social history, interest in social protest and crime not only opened up those specialist areas but posed bigger questions about social relations and the exercise of power. Re-estimating rates of change in output in both manufacturing and agriculture led to a strong challenge to traditional views of economic 'revolutions' but has not, in my view, invalidated the old concepts as completely as some would claim. Especially significant was work using new methods and new data in population history. This confirmed the perception of those scholars who had stressed the key role of fertility in driving the demographic revolution. A new urban history has emerged as something to set against the over-rustication of the 'proto-industrialists'. Trade-union history has escaped the constraints of the Webbs' definitional rigidity, and the bicentenary in 1989 focused attention on 'Britain's avoidance of revolution'.

All these challenges met with responses. That is why this book has been six years in the writing. The thud of the latest *Past and Present, Economic History Review* or *Social History* dropping through the letterbox brought anticipation and a slight sinking of the heart at the near-certainty that yet another article on the social and/or economic history of the long eighteenth century would have to be read! Gone are the days when 'keeping up with the literature' was easier for eighteenth-century historians than for most of their colleagues. By the time this book appears yet more important arguments and findings will have been printed. There has to be a moment to stop. All textbooks are interim, and those on the eighteenth century are, at this time, especially so. Findings have, however, to be assessed and presented to students and to the less specialised world of readers; I tentatively offer a synthesis in this and its companion volume, *Albion's People: English Society, 1714–1815.*

The world of eighteenth-century history is still a smaller one than that of the nineteenth. My debt to around twenty historians on whose work I have relied and from whom great inspiration is gained from occasional meetings at seminars or shared examination duties will be obvious from citations in the text and in the footnotes. Walter Minchinton was supportive and prompt in helping me on several matters, especially on the slave trade. Roger Wells and I have been brought together for various academic purposes in recent years and have been able to find time to discuss many matters of common interest. It has been especially warming to have been once more in contact with Edward Thompson on his welcome return to eighteenth-century history.

Throughout I have offered approximate conversions of pre-decimal prices. Yet converting sums which do not amount to even the smallest coin now in use vividly indicates a problem of comprehension for the post-1970 generation. (Next year we shall be admitting to the universities, polytechnics and colleges many students during whose lifetime no one has walked on the moon!) I will repeat a paragraph from a previous book.

> not only decimalisation separates today's students from the wage and price data of 1750–1850: even more of a problem is the exceptional inflation of recent times. I was once offered in 1962 employment as a clerk at £3.00 for a five-and-a-half-day week. Between me and the skilled wages of, perhaps, £1.50 a week of a craftsman in the early nineteenth century yawns no gap of comprehension equal to that of the modern student on an inadequate grant of perhaps £30 a week . . . in the middle of our period (1795) . . . a farm labourer could expect to earn no more than 8s (40p) in the south of England . . . . Another 20p to 30p a *week* would have very substantially relieved him: a further 80p would have placed him among the well paid.

An apology:

> Thus I set pen to paper with delight,
> And quickly had my thoughts in black and white.
> For having now my method by the end,
> Still as I pulled it came, and so I penned
> It down, until it came at last to be
> For length and breadth the bigness which you see

And John Bunyan did it all without the word-multiplying technology of the Amstrad PCW8256. For the first time I don't have a typist to thank, and only myself to blame! Instead I will thank my patient family, Ann, Geoffrey and Helen and Towan and Ky, two mongrels of determination, whose 'prioritisation' of walks in a nearby wood from time to time got me away from the green screen.

Hampshire, 31 December 1990   J.G.R.

Acknowledgements

The publishers are grateful to the following for permission to reproduce copyright material:

The Academic Press for tables 2.3 and 2.4; Cambridge University Press for tables 2.1, 2.2, 4.2, 4.3, 4.4; Macmillan Publishers for figs 2.1, 2.2, 3.1, 3.4, 3.5 and tables 3.5, 3.6, 3.7 and 3.8; Manchester University Press for tables 7.1 and 7.3; Oxford University Press for table 4.7; Rogers, Coleridge and White Ltd., for tables 9.1 and 9.2.

Whilst every effort has been made to trace the owners of copyright material, in a few cases this has proved impossible, and we take this opportunity to offer our apologies to any copyright holders whose rights we may have unwittingly infringed.

CHAPTER ONE

Introduction

The Vital Century is about the eighteenth-century economy and, inevitably, about the society in which it performed. Fuller treatment of social history is provided in its companion volume, *Albion's People: English Society, 1714–1815*. Historians of this period especially seem to be divided into those who emphasise change and those who stress continuity. It is a truism that any age presents a mixture of both, but the eighteenth century does so in a special way, coming as it does between the seventeenth century, which was hardly 'modern', and the nineteenth century, whose modernity in most respects is not disputed. Sometimes the dilemma has been evaded by cutting the century across the middle. Textbooks have tended to append the first fifty years to form an under-considered extension of the 'early modern economy', or to race through its latter half *en route* to a real concern with the nineteenth century. The eighteenth-century economy has hardly been presented as a whole in a general study since T.S. Ashton's influential book of 1955.[1] Possibly those who stress continuity are conservative in sentiment, while the more radically inclined favour change. It seems more likely that those who come to the eighteenth century from a deep knowledge of the seventeenth recognise different things from those who have travelled back from the nineteenth. A polemical advantage lies with the former, for they can accuse the other group of a 'Whig interpretation' of history, looking back from known outcomes. There is no equally recognisable label for those purblind to change.

Perhaps because I combine my interest in the eighteenth century with an equally strong one in the nineteenth, I am inclined to see change. That does not mean I intend an unqualified reassertion of a once general belief in a *rapid* and transforming industrial

1. T.S. Ashton, *An Economic History of England.*

revolution, still less of a parallel and only slightly less dramatic agricultural one. I have remarked elsewhere that: 'Like most dramatic concepts, that of "industrial revolution" in conveying a major truth, exaggerates the suddenness and completeness of actual happenings.'[2] This caution is even more necessary at the beginning of a book which goes no further than 1815. But while the traditional concept does not have to be fully embraced, total rejection of it dulls appreciation of the significant distance travelled by the developing economy between 1700 and 1815. Quantification may have diminished magnitudes, but it has not removed the cumulating and accelerating importance of interrelated changes and trends over the eighteenth century.

As a starting date 1714 may lack special economic significance, but it is certainly arguable that continuation of a Stuart monarchy, and Catholic at that, would have led to England playing a very different world role with significant economic consequences. It also seems to me that key economic trends had become more evident by the Hanoverian period, even if some of them had dimmer and more distant origins. As well as enabling me to describe my period as a 'century' without excessive licence, ending in 1815 is a well-established and sensible practice among many historians of 'the eighteenth century'. Ending in 1800, in the midst of what was until 1914–18 the 'Great' war, seems inappropriate. There is a case for ending at an earlier date. Professor Malcolmson ended his splendid book a generation earlier: 'I always refer to the roughly 100 years up to the period of the American Revolution.' He excludes the last two decades because:

> This last generation of the eighteenth century with its noticeably
> accelerating processes of social change – the emergence of modernised
> factory production, renewed and very rapid population growth, the
> development of a widespread popular political consciousness, a
> heightened sense of 'agricultural improvement' – is most logically and
> fruitfully reconstructed when it is studied in conjunction with the early
> decades of the nineteenth century.[3]

Yet to stop at a point perceived as one of 'acceleration' is to imply too much of a break and, since that chosen coincides with one popular as a starting point for the industrial revolution, risks distorting the longer profile of economic growth.

Some historians extend the eighteenth century at both ends. It is

2. J.G. Rule, *The Labouring Classes in Early Industrial England 1750–1850*, p. 2.
3. R.W. Malcolmson, *Life and Labour in England 1700–1780*, p. 19.

an increasing practice to write of the 'long eighteenth century', variously dated but usually beginning with the Restoration and continuing until 1820.[4] More controversially, Dr Clark has insisted that politically the English 'ancien régime' did not end until 1828–32, when first the hold of the established Church and then that of the political establishment were broken by Catholic emancipation and by the Reform Act of 1832.[5] Whatever the value of such dating for the political historian, I see no impelling reason for an economic historian to adopt it. I prefer 1815 and remind myself that one of the greatest of historians of the nineteenth century, Elie Halevy, chose it as his *starting* date.

The series in which this book appears presents the economic and social history of *England*. That may have been an easier task for the authors of earlier volumes, but for those who work on periods after the unification with Scotland it is something of an artificial constraint. Wales is even harder to drop, and many statistical series do not even allow its separation. Ireland is another matter. Its economic relationship with England was that of a colony, and even before the end of the 'vital century' it was becoming the base of the 'reserve army of labour'. The matter does not end with Britain. As Professor Rediker has written of England's trade routes: 'These pulsating routes, stretching from one port city to the next, were the most elementary material structures of the Empire, indeed of the entire world economy.'[6]

Protected by her famed naval power, England's maritime hegemony had become well established by the 1760s. Her 'First Empire' fell with the American Revolution, but had done its economic work so well that English manufacturers continued to dominate the North American market for at least another generation. It was an empire of people as well as goods. There was, according to Dr Linebaugh, an 'international working class within England'. Irish, Jews, Scots, Welsh, Huguenot French, Africans and Americans were to be found, especially in London; some of them were common seamen, the archetypal proletariat of the commercial revolution.[7] The British may have been defeated by American rebels in the surprising

4. For example, see E. A. Wrigley, 'The growth of population', pp. 340–54.

5. J.C.D. Clark, *English Society, 1688–1832*. For a thorough critique of this controversial book, see Joanna Innes, 'Jonathan Clark, social history and England's ancien régime', *Past and Present*, **115**, 1987, pp. 165–200.

6. M. Rediker, *Between the Devil and the Deep Blue Sea: Merchant Seamen, Pirates and the Anglo-American Maritime World 1700–1750*, Cambridge UP, 1987, p. 21.

7. P. Linebaugh, 'Laboring people in eighteenth-century England', *International Labour and Working Class History*, **23**, 1983, pp. 1–8.

outcome of an unexpected war, but for four-fifths of the eighteenth century London was the heart not only of a thrusting national economy but also of one of history's greatest commercial empires.

CHAPTER TWO
Growth of Population and Output

George I came from Hanover in 1714 to rule over 5.25 million English subjects; by the time of Waterloo his great-grandson George III had 10.5 million. These hundred years can be termed the 'vital century', for the doubling of population which occurred in them was the beginning of the sustained demographic increase which is the most important feature of modern economic history. The relationship between population and the economy is a two-way one. Economic changes are part of the explanation of population growth, which, once it has gained momentum, itself becomes a cause of further economic and social changes. Over the so-called 'long eighteenth century' from 1680 to 1820, England's population grew by 133 per cent. This not only was without precedent, it was unequalled elsewhere in Europe. The population of France, her great rival of the eighteenth century, grew by only 39 per cent, while that of her major trade competitor, Holland, stagnated.[1]

Population growth was not even paced. Over the latter part of the century there was a great surge, adding 3 million souls by 1800. Growth was less marked in the early Hanoverian era, but it was happening nevertheless. George II inherited 5.45 million English subjects in 1727 and, despite setbacks in mortality crises in the late 1720s and in 1740–1, was ruling over 6.15 million at his death in 1760. Thereafter a stabilising death rate maximised the effects of rising fertility.[2]

This was a demographic transformation over a century which began with anxieties that England was an underpopulated country and ended with the forebodings of Malthus. There has long been controversy over its causes. Some scholars have stressed the role of a declining death rate. Others insist that it was explained largely by a

1. Population figures from Wrigley, 'The growth of population'.
2. Figures from E.A. Wrigley and R.S. Schofield, *The Population History of England.*

Table 2.1 Population: compound annual percentage growth rates over previous decades

1701	0.3	1741	0.5	1781	0.9
1711	0.3	1751	0.3	1791	0.9
1721	0.2	1761	0.6	1801	1.3
1731	– 0.2	1771	0.5	1811	1.3
				1821	1.5

Source: E.A. Wrigley and R.S. Schofield, *The Population History of England 1541–1871*, 2nd edn, Cambridge UP, 1989, pp. 528–9.

rising birth rate. Disagreement persisted because serious deficiencies in the data before the first census was taken in 1801 allowed competing explanations. Recently the publication of a major study has gone a long way towards establishing the primacy of fertility, while still leaving a large question mark over just *why* the birth rate began to rise.[3]

Readers of general textbooks usually wish to be spared detailed discussions of the methodologies employed by their researchers. But no discussion of historical demography can ignore the plodding hours of patiently plotting 'mean' figures. In this field conclusions cannot be scrutinised independently of the methodology which produced them and the data from which they were derived. Wrigley and Schofield's *Population History of England*, first published in 1981, was a new departure. Previous population estimates had usually involved the re-working of the same source: the abstracts from their parish registers at decennial intervals made by the clergy in 1801 for John Rickman, the taker of the first census. Increasing sophistication and compensation for its discovered deficiencies could not change the fact that this was a flawed source. The new approach rejected it and instead used the facilities of the computer age to build up new data. This was provided by an aggregation of the monthly totals of baptisms and burials from more than 400 parish registers, which was then processed with more sophisticated statistical techniques. The aggregated data still allowed the calculation of only crude birth and death rates, acceptable for estimates of overall population size but unable to reveal much about the mechanisms of change. To probe more deeply, the age and sex structure of a past population as well as its size needs to be known. Mortality needs to

---

3. For a survey of the controversy, see the Introduction to Drake (ed.) *Population in Industrialization.*

be age-specific for it matters a good deal whether it is child mortality or that of old people which is changing. Birth rates convey usable information on fertility changes only if they can be related to the 'population' of women at any given time of child-bearing age.[4]

The authors of the new population history developed a method of *back projection* with which they could turn totals of vital events into *rates*. Put simply, they were able to reconstruct the characteristics of past populations by starting with the known population revealed by the 1871 census and working back. Using life-tables to distribute mortality, they regressed at five-yearly intervals, making an allowance for migration. Their assumption is that given the age structure of a population and a knowledge of both the number of births and the ages of those dying over the preceding five years, a population base can be established from which to move back a further five years, and so on back to the beginning of parish registration in 1541. The possibility of error being compounded with each further backward step is real enough, but cross checking with the known populations at the decennial census points back to 1801 discovered a margin of error of only 2 per cent.[5]

The population totals that Wrigley and Schofield provided do not differ much from expectation. They suggest an actual decline for the second half of the seventeenth century with the population for 1701 actually being below that of 1641, but they replace the generally held view of stagnation from 1701 to 1741 with one of modest net growth of 0.3 per cent a year. Their estimated annual 0.71 per cent from 1741 to 1781 is very close to the 0.73 calculated by Brownlee in 1916 on the basis of the Rickman abstracts. However, it is not so much in the enumeration as in the reconstruction of the characteristics of past populations that they have broken new ground. As well as crude birth and death rates, they have provided the *gross reproduction rate* (GRR) and the *expectation of life at birth* (e/ø). These sensitive indicators allowed for more confident claims about the relative roles of mortality and fertility in the demographic transformation. GRR measures the number of girl babies which would be born to the average woman at prevailing fertility rates should she survive to the end of her child-bearing years. It is a 'pure' measure of fertility, as e/ø is of mortality. The latter

4. For a convenient summary of the main findings and methods, see E.A. Wrigley, 'Population growth: England, 1680–1820', *ReFRESH*, 1, Autumn 1985, reprinted in Digby and Feinstein, *New Direction*, pp. 105–116.

5. For a discussion of their methods, see the review article by M.W. Flinn in *Econ. H. R.*, XXXV, 3, 1982, pp. 443–57.

measures the number of years a child will live at prevailing age-specific mortality rates and is unaffected by the population's age structure. The four measures have been graphed in Figures 2.1 and 2.2. These reveal that during the first half of the eighteenth century mortality was as important as fertility in determining the rate of population growth, but that after mid-century fertility became much the more important. Over the extended period 1680 to 1820, Wrigley has argued that fertility changes accounted for two-thirds of the increase. For mortality to have played an equivalent role it would need to have fallen as much over this period as it was to do in that of much greater medical advance between 1820 and the Second World War.[6]

None of this means that what was happening to the death rate can be disregarded. In the first place, rising fertility can operate only to the extent that mortality allows. While rapidly improving mortality could in itself explain demographic growth – and indeed seems to in other countries in the later eighteenth and early nineteenth centuries – slowly improving mortality or at least stabilised mortality is also needed if fertility rises are to have a significant impact. In the second place, fertility and mortality interact and had later-eighteenth-century England had a different mortality regime, it would probably have had a different fertility one too.

MORTALITY

Western Europe lived through an awful moment in 1720. A ship from Syria brought the bubonic plague to Marseille. Tens of thousands died as the 'pre-eminent arbiter' of populations swept through Provence. For two generations western Europe had been spared its pestilential visitation. The Polish outbreak of 1709–13 had not spread beyond Bavaria, and the reappearance of the plague so far west was terrifying. Yet by 1721 the epidemic was over and it had not spread. It was to be the last serious threat, although the prospect of plague epidemics was to hold eastern Europe in thrall until the middle nineteenth century.[7] What had cried 'Hold!' to the sharpest and widest scythe of the grim reaper? Epidemiological historians have offered a range of explanations from a change in the character of the disease itself to a species shift in the rat population,

6. Wrigley, 'The growth of population' pp. 130–1.
7. The phrase is from Flinn, *The European Demographic System*, p. 55.

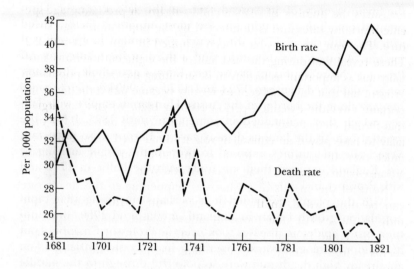

Figure 2.1 Fertility and mortality change: crude birth and death rates

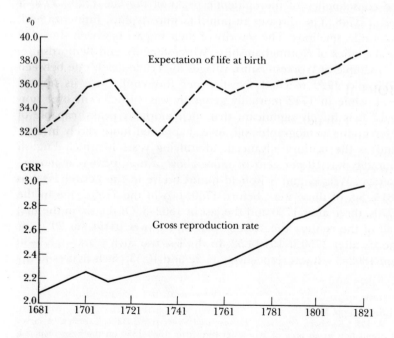

Figure 2.2 Fertility and mortality change: expectation of life at birth and **gross reproduction rate**

the main agency of its spread. Yet, as the late Professor Flinn pointed out, human action was the most important factor. Faced with the outbreak of 1720, the French government mobilised as if for war. A quarter of its cavalry and a third of its infantry cut off Provence. More important for western Europe as a whole, the Habsburgs established between 1728 and 1770 a 1,900-kilometre *cordon sanitaire* along the border of the Austro-Hungarian empire with Turkey, which they maintained in some form until 1873. It was the greatest benefit the famous dynasty gave to Europe. Also important were trade quarantines imposed to prevent the plague arriving by sea. England imposed them on trade with the Baltic in 1711 and with Provence in 1720–2.[8]

With the plague contained it is perhaps surprising that rapid population growth began in England only around 1750. But until then other epidemic diseases took over; as Professor Chambers put it: 'random biological causes operating in successive onslaughts on an already high death rate were so powerful through to the middle of the eighteenth century that they could initiate long waves of demographic depression'. The slow growth before 1750 was largely the consequence of the epidemic peaks of the late 1720s, 1740–2 and 1747–8. The diseases responsible were typhus, influenza and, especially, smallpox. The severity of their impact has been shown in local studies of Nottinghamshire, Worcestershire and Bedfordshire. In a sample of Worcestershire villages the crude death rate between 1725 and 1729 reached sixty-five per thousand, twice its normal level, while in 1742 mortality generally was 40 per cent over normal.[9] It is hugely significant that such mortality peaks, capable of interrupting demographic advance, happened more rarely in England as the century advanced. Identifying years in which English mortality was 10 per cent or more above a twenty-five-year moving average, Wrigley and Schofield found twelve in the period 1700 to 1815. Six of these were before 1750, two in the 1760s, one in the 1770s, three after 1780 and the last in 1802–3. Of the six in the first half of the century the average percentage over trend was 29.7; for the six after 1750 it was 14.52. In the last two such years – 1779–80 and 1802–3 – it was respectively 11.22 and 10.53. Such figures justify

8. *Ibid.*, pp. 58–61.

9. J.D. Chambers, *Population, Economy and Society*, p. 87; D.E.C. Eversley, 'A survey of population in an area of Worcestershire from 1660–1850 on the basis of parish registers', *Population Studies*, X, 1957, pp. 253–79, reprinted in Glass and Eversley, *Population in History*, pp. 394–419.

writing of a 'stabilising of mortality' after mid century, for it was the peaks rather than the plateau that were lowered.[10]

What, as well as the disappearance of the plague, explains this crucial stabilisation? One suggestion is that there was a significant shift towards mass diseases of a more benign character. Greater integration of the population acted to reduce previously epidemic diseases affecting all groups into endemic childhood ones, like measles. It is also the case that some of the serious diseases which became prevalent in the eighteenth century had a different epidemiology from the plague. Tuberculosis took life gradually, although it became a major killer over the eighteenth century. Typhus had epidemic potential but never attained the dreadful momentum of the plague, although it was endemic in crowded, insanitary places as its other names, such as 'gaol fever' or 'workhouse fever', suggest. It contributed much to the crisis of 1741–2, but then its epidemic ravages subsided.[11] Smallpox reached its apogee in the earlier eighteenth century. In towns it ravaged chiefly the young, with adult immunity tending to be high. In Manchester over 90 per cent of smallpox deaths between 1769 and 1774 were of under-fives. In smaller towns and villages its impact on adults, especially young ones, was high. Pregnant women were particularly susceptible. Evidence from the epidemics of the 1720s suggests a mortality range from 11.6 to 50 per hundred births. This varied impact depended on different immunity levels, with isolated villages suffering the most. Given this impact and its tendency to attack the young adults crucial for maintaining the birth rate, it follows that any significant control of smallpox would have had a major demographic effect. Dr Razzell has gone so far as to suggest that inoculation against it could possibly account in itself for the magnitude of eighteenth-century population growth.[12] Inoculation with matter from infected persons had been introduced in England as early as 1721, but because of the high risk of contracting the disease through it, had little impact before a safer virus was introduced in the 1740s. After further improvements in the 1760s inoculation became widespread in villages and small towns. Many historians have been dismissive of its effectiveness, arguing that it was only with the development of

---

10. Wrigley and Schofield, *Population History of England*, pp. 332–5; K.F. Helleiner, 'The vital revolution reconsidered', *Canadian Journal of Economics and Political Science*, XXIII, 1, 1957, reprinted in Glass and Eversley, *Population in History*, p. 85.

11. Flinn, *European Demographic System*, pp. 62–4.

12. P.E. Razzell, 'Population change in eighteenth-century England' in Drake (ed.), *Population in Industrialization*, pp. 128–56.

vaccination with cowpox by Jenner in the early nineteenth century that smallpox was brought under control. Razzell has produced impressive evidence to argue that the significance of Jenner's work has been exaggerated. Not only was inoculation less dangerous and more effective than has been supposed, but with supplies of the new vaccine being exclusively propagated by arm-to-arm passage and commonly supplied from hospitals, contamination probably reduced the advantages it might have had over inoculation.[13]

There is contemporary testimony to the effectiveness of inoculation before Jenner: 'the increase of people within the last 25 years is visible to every observer. Inoculation is the mystic spell which has produced this wonder . . . before that time it may be safely asserted, that the malady, added to the general laws of nature, did at least equipoise population' wrote a contributor to the *Gentleman's Magazine* in 1796, while Howlett claimed in 1781 that in 'provincial towns and villages' inoculation was resorted to by 'all ranks' whenever smallpox threatened, with deaths being reduced to a tenth of previous levels.[14] In the 1750s rural parishes began to pay for mass inoculations, but the practice did not penetrate the larger towns. In London both the number of deaths attributed to smallpox and its proportion of all deaths recorded in the Bills of Mortality remained constant through the eighteenth century. Yet smallpox seems to have declined in other places where inoculation was hardly practised, such as Manchester. There is, however, some point to Razzell's comment that most of the population did not live in large towns, and the case for inoculation in the rural districts seems strong. He has certainly established that some reduction at least in smallpox mortality is likely to have occurred before Jenner's popularisation of vaccination. However, since both the contribution of smallpox to overall mortality and the possibility of changing virulence are matters of dispute, it is perhaps wisest to regard its conquest as a contributory factor in the stabilisation of mortality rather than as being largely responsible for it.[15]

Following Thomas Malthus, historians have tended to regard famine and fever as acting together to produce the 'classic' mortality crisis. However, English evidence seems to confine hunger to a lesser role by the eighteenth century. Chambers noted that epide-

---

13. *Ibid.*, pp. 147–54.
14. *Ibid.*, pp. 148–50.
15. T. McKeown and R.G. Brown, 'Medical evidence related to English population changes in the eighteenth century', *ibid.*, pp. 50–1; see also B. Luckin, 'The decline of small pox and the demographic revolution of the eighteenth century', *Social History*, II, 6, 1977, pp. 793–7.

mics were capable of wreaking havoc in years of normal or even low food prices, while in the food crisis year 1799–1800 the death rate was below normal. Flinn pronounced western Europe as a whole 'very largely' famine free in the eighteenth century, and England was especially noted for the improvement in its output and distribution of cereals. During the death-rate peaks of 1727–30 and 1740–2 grain prices were high, but not notably so. High food prices do seem, however, to have had muted effects. In twenty parishes during the 'hungry' year 1766 mortality levels averaged 10 per cent over normal, with a similar fall in the conception rate. Although this is less extreme than the soaring mortality and sharp decline in conceptions which define the 'crises of subsistence' identified by the demographers, it is still worth remarking.[16]

If hunger had only a limited role in explaining peaks in the death rate, nutritional improvement may well have made a contribution during some periods to the overall decline in mortality in so far as it improved the general health level. Expectation of life at birth had been high in the epidemic-free years at the end of the sixteenth and beginning of the seventeenth centuries when mortality was less severe than at any time before 1815. This mild regime degenerated until the last years of the seventeenth and the early eighteenth centuries, when there was a sharp but short-lived improvement. At only 27.9 years in 1731, it was at its second worst level of the whole period 1558 to 1871. Thereafter expectation of life at birth improved fairly steadily, though with lapses in the early 1740s, 1760s and early 1780s. Then began a period of diminishing fluctuations through which expectation of life increased from 35 to 40 years from 1780 to 1826. This gradual and erratic eighteenth-century improvement, paralleling a fall in the crude death rate from 30.7 per thousand in 1670–89 to 24.5 in 1810–29, cannot be wholly explained in terms of the decline of epidemics. In seven of a sample of twelve parishes, infant mortality was higher from 1700 to 1749 than in the periods on either side, and its decline after 1750, although it has been exaggerated in some discussions of the towns, played a significant role in the overall mortality decline. Better standards of nutrition almost certainly contributed. Indeed, McKeown and Brown argued in a seminal article that given the lack

16. Chambers, *Population, Economy and Society*, pp. 95–6; Flinn, *European Demographic System*, p. 97; D.E. Williams, 'Were hunger rioters really hungry? Some demographic evidence', *Past and Present*, **71**, 1976, p. 73; Wrigley and Schofield, *Population History of England*, pp. 325–9.

of evidence for substantial medical improvement, better living conditions must have been the main cause.[17]

Even for the towns Dr Corfield has brought together evidence to suggest a 'slight but significant' fall in the death rate in the later eighteenth century. Chambers noted that in Nottingham the death rate, never below forty per thousand from 1720 to 1730, was under thirty by the late 1740s and felt that 'the age of massacre by epidemic' was over. From some point after mid century in several towns which have been examined, the birth rate began to exceed the death rate. It did so in Exeter from 1770, Leeds by 1740–70, but not in Norwich until 1800. Towns were ceasing to be the great devourers of population, which they had hitherto been through history when only immigration from the countryside had allowed them to grow.[18]

Population historians must often present their findings in terms of national trends and levels, yet the urban/rural differential, which may well have widened again in the early nineteenth century, serves only as the most vivid reminder that death rates were far from uniform. Even in rural districts low, marshy parishes were notoriously unhealthy, while the dominant occupation like mining or knife grinding gave the men of some communities a shortened life. On balance it seems wise to allow mortality improvement, becoming distinctly more perceptible after 1780, to have had at least a positive impact in the second half of the eighteenth century, though less critical than its negative impact had been before 1750.

FERTILITY

In claiming to have resolved the 'conundrum' of population growth in eighteenth-century England, Professor Wrigley has displayed strong confidence in the results of the 'new' historical demography. The great rise after mid century was, he insists, due overwhelmingly to rising fertility. This was anticipated by some earlier historians. Professor Krause, for example, stressed the importance of a rising birth rate after rejecting the evidence for a marked mortality drop. Professor Habakkuk's insight and instinct led him to the same con-

17. Wrigley and Schofield, *Population History of England*, pp. 236–7.
18. The evidence on urban mortality is summarised in Corfield, *The Impact of English Towns*, pp. 99–123.

clusion, but he lacked the new data to establish his view.[19] The ability to calculate the gross reproduction rate as well as the crude birth rate has produced a new confidence. Wrigley and Schofield calculate that GRR rose steadily over the long eighteenth century, from two to three girl babies per woman, while the expectation of life at birth increased by only 20 per cent from 32 to 39 years. If fertility had stayed constant, mortality improvement would have produced an annual demographic rate of 0.5 per cent. If mortality had been constant, rising fertility could still have produced one of 1.5 per cent per annum. Against a background of stabilising and steadily improving mortality, fertility rates soared and powered a population increase by 1821 over 1751 of 99 per cent.[20]

Why were there so many extra births? There is no evidence of any change in marital fertility: women once married had the same number of babies from Elizabethan through to mid Victorian times. The presumption must be either that the marriage rate increased, that is fewer people stayed unmarried, or that the age of women at first marriage fell, or that both trends featured. Nuptiality seems to have been the key. Drawing on the evidence from the few detailed family reconstitution studies that have been completed by demographers, Wrigley and Schofield have shown both tendencies at work. The proportion never marrying fell rapidly from around 16 per cent in the 1690s to around 7 per cent towards the end of the eighteenth century, while a significant fall in the age at marriage was also indicated.

Table 2.2 Mean age at first marriage: means of twelve reconstitution studies

	1600–49	*1650–99*	*1700–49*	*1750–99*	*1800–49*
Males	28.0	27.8	27.5	26.4	25.3
Females	26.0	26.5	26.2	24.9	23.4

Source: E.A.Wrigley and R.S. Schofield, *The Population History of England 1541–1871*, 2nd edn, Cambridge UP, 1989, p. 255.

19. Wrigley, 'The growth of population' p. 126; H.J. Habakkuk, 'The economic history of modern Britain', *Jn. Econ. Hist.*, 1958, reprinted in Glass and Eversley, *Population in History*, pp. 147–58; J.T. Krause, 'English population movements between 1700 and 1850', in Drake (ed.), *Population in Industrialization*, pp. 118–27.

20. These data are summarised by Wrigley in his article, 'Population growth: England 1680–1820', *ReFRESH, 1*, 1985.

If these figures do represent the national picture, then they strongly suggest that a fall in the age at marriage has to be considered a likely, if not certain, cause of the rise in fertility. But are they representative? Family reconstitution is a long and laborious process and so far only a few parish studies have been completed. The argument of Wrigley and Schofield in this respect is based on twelve parishes, unlike their aggregate analysis which is based on more than 400. Professor Flinn pointed out in a review that the addition of just two subsequently completed reconstitutions would have made the trend far less clear. The evidence for a fall in the age at marriage is growing but, until more reconstitutions have confirmed it, can hardly be described as firm. It could explain a great deal, for a lower age at marriage not only increases a woman's child-bearing potential by adding a number of highly fertile years, it also over time shortens the gap between the generations. Nor does there seem to have been any significant interference in this effect from deliberate family limitation. David Levine in a study of the Leicester village of Shepshed found that over a period in which the age at marriage fell, average completed family size rose from 3.62 to 5.29. A study of a group of parishes in the west of England has shown that whereas in the farming parish of Steeple Ashton the mean age of women at marriage rose by a year from 1751 to 1790, in the nearby village of Timsbury, situated on the rising Somerset coalfield, it fell by 3.25 years. This was not the only difference, for Timsbury also saw a significant decrease in the intervals between births, so that when the age of the woman at the birth of her fifth child is considered, the women of the mining village were on average almost five years younger than those in Steeple Ashton.[21]

PROLETARIANISATION AND REPRODUCTION

A strong and growing body of scholarship has suggested that the momentum if not the initiation of the great population surge can be explained by a major shift towards wage dependency on the part of the lower orders. Proletarianisation is not here meant in the special sense of the creation of the factory labour force, but as a broad

21. Wrigley and Schofield, *Population History of England*, pp. 254–6; Flinn's review article, p. 451; D. Levine, *Family Formation*, p. 64; S. Jackson, 'Population change in the Somerset–Wiltshire border area, 1701–1800: a regional demographic study', *Southern History*, **7**, 1985, pp. 128–9.

description of the protracted process by which working for wages, characteristic of perhaps a quarter of England's population in the reign of Henry VIII, became the condition of more than 80 per cent by the mid nineteenth century. Figures in an area where problems of definition compound those of measurement are never more than guesstimates, but it seems reasonable to suggest that over this period, when the population as a whole increased seven-fold, the proletariat did so twenty-fold. This had demographic significance because the proletariat tended to reproduce itself more quickly than did the older society of peasants and independent craftsmen. A combination of motive and response over time changed a demographic regime with a late marrying age and high celibacy ratio into a new proletarian one with earlier and more frequent marriage.[22]

John Hajnal, in a seminal article, defined the 'European marriage pattern' of the early modern period. Late marriage 'lost' around ten female fertile years, as couples had to wait until one of the limited opportunities to establish a new household arrived. In the case of the farming majority this meant a land-holding, usually through inheritance, but for craftsmen it meant a workshop and a foothold in a sufficient market. In so far as the development of capitalism over time both reduced the numbers of peasant cultivators and independent artisans and increased the numbers dependent on rural manufacturing, or on waged farm work, then it broke a traditional constraint on early marriage. Looking forward to neither land-holding nor self-employment, the wage-earner when he reached an adult wage was as capable as he ever would be of supporting a family.[23] In England the process of proletarianisation was especially marked. In agriculture the landless farm labourer was increasing rapidly in numbers, especially in the south, while in urban manufacture a class of permanent journeymen was expanding in an increasing number of trades where the traditional road from apprentice to master was becoming blocked. Historians have recently paid most attention to the demographic effects of the spread of rural manufacturing under the 'putting-out' system. This has been labelled *proto-industrialisation.* Merchant capitalists, beginning to operate in the expanding international market, drew on the spare labour to be found in some districts of pastoral agriculture to produce in greater volume and at lower wage cost than they could have

22. The most forceful case for a 'proletarian demographic regime' is made in D. Levine, 'Industrialisation and the proletarian family'.

23. J. Hajnal, 'European marriage patterns in perspective', in Glass and Eversley, *Population in History*, pp. 101–43.

done in the guild-controlled towns. By the early eighteenth century this mode of production had become widespread, not only in textiles but in the manufacture of nails, cutlery and other metal goods. Under it merchant capitalists put out materials to be made up in their workers' cottages at what were in effect piece-rated wages. Several of them employed out-workers in numbers larger than the labour forces that were to be assembled in the early factories. Villages became communities of weavers, of miners, of cutlers or nailors, and with their changing occupational structure came a changing demography which represented a significant break with the past.[24]

Hans Medick has pointed out that a rising population in the seventeenth century provided the first condition for proto-industrialisation by offering large numbers of underemployed country people as a source of cheap labour. But the way in which that labour source responded to the nature of this employment generated a further and crucial demographic momentum. The key lay in the dependence of rural manufacturing on the *family* as the unit of production. Research has discovered rural manufacturing households to have been larger than those of farm workers and that this was due to a younger marrying age as well as to the greater likelihood that teenage children would remain working in the household until marriage. (Previously they had left to become living-in servants in other households.) This was less a matter of conscious calculation than a response to a situation where available labour rather than amounts of land determined what the family was capable of producing. As the importance of inheriting land holdings receded it was replaced by the new possibility of founding a family primarily as a unit of labour. In such a situation there was no effective sanction by which parents could control the marriages made by their grown-up children. High levels of endogamous marriage among groups like weavers and knitters reflect the necessity of securing the work output of both partners. Proto-industrial workers not only *could* marry younger, they *needed* to since the family, not the individual, was the basic production unit. A new demographic response emerged of early marriage and a premium on children who could work from a young age. In order to ensure income there was a tendency to increase labour supply beyond the immediate demands of the trade.

---

24. For the formation of an agricultural proletariat in the south see R.A.E. Wells, 'The development of the English rural proletariat and social protest 1700–1850', *Journal of Peasant Studies*, 6, 1979, pp. 115–39. The literature on proto-industrialisation is critically surveyed in L.A. Clarkson, *Proto-Industrialisation: The First Phase of Industrialisation?*, Macmillan, 1985.

This amounted to an element of self-exploitation, with the family keeping the price of its labour low through the imbalance between fluctuating markets and the constant process of demographic expansion. Once trodden, the treadmill kept turning. There was no step-off back to the old demographic pattern.[25]

Such explanations linking rising fertility to the changing household economy of the poor in manufacturing villages are indeed plausible, even likely, but as yet they rest on few detailed case studies. So far as England is concerned, they depend heavily on the research of David Levine on the Leicestershire framework knitting village of Shepshed. He has demonstrated that the arrival of hosiery manufacture in what was an agricultural village precipitated a rapid population increase after 1750. Between 1680 and 1750 the inelastic demand for agricultural labour together with the long waiting period before a family holding or workshop could be inherited had necessitated a prudent approach to marriage which had maintained a balance between population and resources. After 1750, however, a slow population rise gave way to what Levine calls a 'radical demographic discontinuity'. The hosiery manufacture had created a demand for a class selling labour power. Severing the link with land-holding as a condition for economic independence freed the villagers from the old constraints and a distinct fall in the age at marriage was a consequence.

Table 2.3 Mean age of women at marriage in Shepshed

1600–99	1700–49	1750–1824	1825–51
28.1	27.4	24.1	22.6

Source: D. Levine, *Family Formation in an Age of Nascent Capitalism*, Academic Press, 1977, p. 61.

Manufacturing also brought a slight worsening in mortality, but with women having a longer married/fertile span, the gap between generations narrowing and the increasing frequency of marriage

25. Hans Medick, 'The proto-industrial family economy: the structural function of household and family during the transition from peasant society to industrial capitalism', *Social History*, **3**, 1975, pp. 291–315.

from the larger number of children, the effect on the population was startling, as Table 2.4 shows.

Table 2.4 Years needed to double the population of Shepshed at the rate of reproduction for each cohort

1600–99	1700–49	1750–1824
250	200.6	40.1

Source: D. Levine, *Family Formation in an Age of Nascent Capitalism*, Academic Press, 1977, p. 74.

As a control, Levine examined the neighbouring village of Bottesford, where the population was of the same size but where the hosiery industry had been kept out by the single landowner, the Duke of Rutland. Here the population *declined* after 1750 before beginning a rapid rise after 1800. This rise was the consequence of a shift, not towards manufacturing but to a more labour-intensive form of agriculture. The later change in marriage patterns in agrarian economies will be discussed below; for the moment the point to note is that Shepshed's neighbouring village, lacking the novelty of industrial employment, experienced no demographic transition in the second half of the eighteenth century. The age of women at first marriage was still 26.5 in 1800; it then began to fall as the agrarian employment pattern changed.[26]

Wrigley and Schofield are reluctant to accept either proletarianisation in general or proto-industrialisation in particular as the explanation of the marriage variable. They accept that the spread of manufacturing employment did lower the age at marriage in some villages and permit a population expansion which could continue for a far longer period before outrunning its economic support than was the case with a purely agricultural village. It was not, however, a final escape from the Malthusian trap – that had to await the industrial revolution. Proto-industrial communities could suffer both temporary and permanent decline. Their very rapid expansion would sooner or later lower real wages and eventually make the earning of a subsistence wage difficult, even with increasing hours

26. Levine's work on Shepshed is contained in D. Levine, 'The demographic implications of rural industrialization; a family reconstitution of Shepsted, Leicestershire, 1600–1851', *Social History*, **2**, 1976 and in *Family Formation*.

of work. That rural manufacturing communities could decline to the point of desperation is well enough demonstrated, both by the experience of handloom weaving and framework knitting villages in the nineteenth century and by regional shifts in prosperity in the eighteenth. De-industrialisation certainly happened, especially in the south of England, and frequently led to depopulation, mostly through out-migration.[27] However, the demographic consequences of industrial decline do not seem to have been an inevitable return to the earlier regime of late marriage. Levine has suggested that something like this may have happened at Colyton where out-work for Devonshire serge manufacture dried up in the later seventeenth century and where the age of women at marriage rose at the same time. There is, however, some uncertainty about this link. Colyton was far from being a mainly manufacturing parish like Shepshed, and changes in the birth rate there can be explained in other ways.[28]

In Shepshed the age of marriage did not revert. The new reproductive aspect of the manufacturing economy did lead to an increase in labour supply beyond the demands of the trade, keeping the price of labour low; but there was little sign of a fresh adjustment, apart from some small signs of deliberate family limitation in the second decade of the nineteenth century. Overpopulation with its low wages and overcrowding did have an effect on mortality. Of children born 1825 to 1850 only 614 per thousand reached fifteen years of age, compared with 724 for 1750–1824, and there was a slight deterioration in adult expectancy of life. These effects had little impact on the rate of population increase which remained three times greater than it had been in the pre-industrial village.[29]

Proto-industrial communities may be special cases, but they were far from rare. Rural manufacturing workers were a fast-growing section of the population. In the eighteenth-century economy there was a distinct shift towards those occupational communities which tended towards a lower marriage age, although, as expected in an age of transition, communities with different demographic regimes existed side by side. To manufacturing villages must also be added mining ones and the growing towns now beginning to show a capacity for natural population increase. A study of parishes in the

27. See Wrigley, 'The growth of population', p. 144; Wrigley and Schofield, *Population History of England*, p. 463.

28. Levine, *Family Formation*, pp. 108–13, but see also Wrigley, 'Mortality in pre-industrial England: the example of Colyton, Devon, over three centuries', *Daedalus*, **97**, 1968, pp. 546–80.

29. Levine, *Family Formation*, pp. 77–8.

Somerset and Wiltshire border area in the eighteenth century has shown how within a region population shifted from agricultural and, in this case, stagnant manufacturing parishes to rising mining and urban ones. The out-migration from the former group consisted primarily of young adults contributing directly to the superior fertility of the latter group.

The demographic consequences of the growth of non-agricultural employment were subsequently amplified by changes which began to become noticeable after 1780 in the nature of agricultural employment itself. An agrarian proletariat was being formed and with it came a fall in the age at marriage in many agricultural parishes. Levine contrasted the demography of Bottesford in Leicestershire with another agricultural parish, Terling in Essex. In the former, pastoral farming in the eighteenth century was related to a low demand for labour and, as we have seen, there was no fall in the age at marriage and no increase in population. After 1800 a new emphasis on dairying increased the demand for labour, the age at marriage fell and the population increased by 71 per cent over the first half of the nineteenth century, while small-scale peasant farming ceased to be of any importance.[30]

Terling, however, was only 35 miles from London and the pull of the City's food markets had led to an early transition to a capitalist form of agriculture in which a few farmers employed a mass of agricultural labourers. In the sixteenth century the landless labourers had probably been made up of the younger sons of the middling peasantry, but their numbers expanded over the sevententh century and social mobility largely ceased. An employing elite had come to dominate the village. Men and women began to marry relatively young, for prospects of land-holding were faint and there was accordingly no incentive to postpone. High mortality and a strict operation of the settlement laws controlled population growth up to the last quarter of the eighteenth century, but then Poor Law changes, improving mortality and a shift towards a more labour intensive form of farming, produced a rapid rise in population from 1780 to 1850. According to Levine, Terling lends 'impressive support to the Malthusian argument by showing the great reserve of prolific power that was unleashed when traditional social norms, prudential checks on reproduction, were rendered obsolete'. Precocious in the seventeenth century, the Terling experience became typical of southern and eastern English agricultural villages in the

---

30. S. Jackson, 'Population change', p. 127; Levine, *Family Formation*, pp. 94–6.

late eighteenth as a wage-dependent landless labour force became the norm.[31]

This shift had long been under way by 1780, but what became especially significant was a change in the way wage labour was hired and its relationship to the increasing enclosure of commons and wastes. In the early modern economy young persons hired on a yearly basis had lived as 'farm servants' in the houses of the employing farmers. Teenaged children left their homes of origin for these posts, to make up 'a large and distinctive part of the labour force, differing from adult wage earners in the nature of their contracts and their marital status'. Farm service filled a life-cycle stage for huge numbers of the rural population between childhood and full adulthood: 'No one was born a servant in husbandry, and few expected to die as servants.' They supplied between a third and a half of the labour needs of the early modern agrarian economy, but although they also worked for wages they exhibited a marked difference in their marriage practice from the living-out labourers who were to displace them in many regions over the late eighteenth and early nineteenth centuries. In the south and east their decline had become a rout by 1815, but in other regions where they remained important they delayed the arrival of the proletarian demographic regime. A tract of 1766 refers to farm service as a 'covenanted state of celibacy'. For the years that they offered themselves as living-in servants, young men and women were postponing marriage. That they did so reflected not just the constraint of servanthood but the possibility of accruing savings that would give them a partial independence when they did leave service to marry. As Howlett noted in the 1780s, a man could save perhaps £20 or £30 from a series of hirings and in his mid twenties find 'a young woman possessed with nearly an equal sum'. A cottage with a small acreage could be obtained and, crucially, some beasts kept on the unenclosed common. From this basis of 'independence', income could be supplemented by taking waged day labour. It was a marriage pattern which widespread enclosure of the commons and wastes disrupted. Newly enclosed consolidated farms were the first to dispense with living-in hands. Farmers found it more profitable to draw on cheap day labour and by the late eighteenth century were also being deterred from subsisting workers by higher food prices. There is evidence that enclosures in the south and east led to a significant decline in the need for women's labour, leaving little but early marriage as a

31. *Ibid.*, pp. 119–26.

prospect for the village girls. Enclosure of the commons had, then, a dual effect. As Dr Snell has put it: 'when they were ploughed up, there was certainly less motive to save, and the decline of farm service left . . . little means to do so'. Arthur Young wrote of the 'series of years of great industry and most economical saving – to become independent, to marry a girl and fix her in a spot they can call their own'. He lamented that enclosure had removed this incentive to sobriety, thrift and industry.[32]

Diminishing farm service accentuated the rise in rural population which, by increasing the labour supply, had begun the decline in the first place. It is therefore a distortion to imply that the rural proletariat was created simply by the increase in population in the countryside. In agriculture, as in manufacturing, proletarianisation and population growth were interrelated. Pauperisation was also to add its weight in some villages through the operation of Speenhamland-type systems of poor relief linked to family size. Their precise demographic impact is disputed, but rate-paying farmers were clearly disposed to give employment priority to married men whose families they would in any case have had to support through the poor rate. Because of this, high unemployment among single labourers encouraged rather than discouraged early marriage, while the contraction in female employment on the land, aggravated in the south by the parallel loss of cottage manufacturing, made sure there were 'potential wives in doleful abundance'.[33]

Among craftsmen apprenticeship was the institution which paralleled farm service in filling a phase in the life cycle between childhood and marriage. 'He shall not commit fornication, nor contract matrimony' states the typical indenture binding a fourteen-year-old for seven years to a watch-maker. In the Sheffield cutlery districts a decline in apprenticeship was blamed for the increasing number of 'improvident marriages' among young cutlers. We know rather little about the rate and timing of the decline in apprenticeship generally, as opposed to its history in some individual trades. It has been suggested that outside London it declined sharply over the second half of the eighteenth century, especially so in the south-east in the 1780s. In the old guild towns it had begun its decline a generation earlier. Without occupationally specific marriage studies it is impossible to confirm that earlier marriage among artisans became widespread as apprenticeship declined. We can at least note the at-

---

32. A. Kussmaul, *Servants in Husbandry in Early Modern England*, Cambridge UP, 1981, pp. 4–9, 112; K.D.M. Snell, *Annals of the Labouring Poor*, pp. 67–103, 212–14.
33. For the Poor Law, see J. Rule, *Albion's People: English Society 1714–1815*, Ch. 5.

tenuation over the later eighteenth century of yet one more traditional constraint on early marriage. In so far as the decline of apprenticeship was in itself an indication of decreasing upward mobility in the trades and of the search for cheaper and more flexible labour, this too was part of the old demographic regime giving way before the prolific reproductive momentum of the proletariat.[34]

Though they regard a fall in the age of marriage as the crucial mechanism behind population growth, Wrigley and Schofield do not see it as having been brought about by the arrival of a new proletarian demographic regime. Wrigley has suggested that the fact that the downturn in fertility after 1815 came at a time when proletarianisation was going forward steadily is fatal to that explanation. This is to confuse the consolidation of the proletariat into its classic nineteenth-century urban/industrial form with the longer protracted process by which a wage-earning labour force emerged. Indeed, Levine has suggested that the expansion of machine production after 1815 was the beginning of a 'second phase' of proletarian demographic response during which the gradual emergence of the 'male-as-breadwinner' norm replaced the family basis for earning and production and new family and fertility strategies developed.[35]

They propose instead a theory of 'dilatory homeostasis' – as hard to explain as it is to pronounce. Relating nuptiality to a real wage index, they note that there is a 'fit', although with a time lapse of around thirty years. This suggests that marriage was sensitive to economic crisis in the long as well as in the short term. That fewer couples took the plunge in years of high food prices and scarce employment has long been known, but Wrigley and Schofield also believe nuptial trends followed the longer-term secular movements of improvement or deterioration in real income levels. But why was there a time lag before marriage tendencies adjusted themselves to significant changes in the standard of living? It is perhaps an indication of the fact that cultural adjustments do tend to be slow, with customary expectation continuing to influence the age at which people expect to marry.

There were three main turning points in the real wage index: the ending of a period of falling wages in 1610; the termination of a

34. Quoted in J.G. Rule, *Experience of Labour*, pp. 100, 104; Snell, *Annals of the Labouring Poor*, Ch. 5.
35. Wrigley, 'The growth of population', p. 144; Levine, 'Industrialisation and the proletarian family' generally argues for a two-phase proletarian demographic response to the industrial revolution to accommodate the nineteenth-century fertility decline.

century and a half of improvement around 1750; and from 1805 when the combined effects of agricultural and industrial growth began to show. The three main turning points in the fertility measure, the gross reproduction rate, point the same way, but with a lag; that is, they occurred in 1660, around 1815 and in the 1840s. Such is the argument: changes in marriage practice took place when a generation came to view its circumstances as significantly better or worse than those of its parents, whose situation they wanted to equal. Accordingly marriage was delayed in worsening times and hastened in improving ones. There is no assumption of knowledge of trends or of conscious adjustment, but mediated by conventions on the timing of marriage, the impact of real wage shifts on marriage patterns over a period of time matched that which would have been produced by conscious calculation. Applied to the period of our interest, the argument suggests that towards 1750 accelerating population growth began to exert downward pressure on real wages which became more malign as the later eighteenth century progressed. When fertility nevertheless continued to rise, even though it was further reducing wages, this was because it was still responding to the behaviour of real wages fifty years earlier. From this perspective the lower living standards of the working classes between 1765 and 1815 are seen to be as much the consequence of a sluggish nuptial adjustment as a result of the impact of war and early industrialisation.

As an explanation, this is ingenious but somewhat contrived. The pessimism of parents might have had some effect, and popular attitudes towards early marriage might be expected to have changed when a perception grew that the economic situation was the result of changing times rather than a temporary blip. Even so, the posited time lag is a long one and it is difficult to feel confident about the causal linking of two separate indices over it. Further, as Professor Flinn pointed out, the Phelps Brown and Hopkins index of real wages is not one which inspires confidence when precise turning points have to be identified, for it is acknowledged to be 'a terribly frail foundation' for an ambitious hypothesis. It also seems to imply a standard demographic response when there was a marked regional variation in the experience of economic change and its impact on real wages. The theory cannot easily accommodate the divergent trends in agricultural wages after the 1760s when they began to fall in the south but continued to rise in the north, yet both regions saw the age at marriage fall. Up to about 1770 rising wages in the south may have created an optimism about marriage which survived the downturn, so that early marriage persisted through some very difficult years. But there seems no inherent reason to prefer this complicated explanation to one which points to the impact of the changes and pressures associated with proletarianisation, increasing enclosure of commons and wastes and the rapid ending of farm service.[36]

THE GREAT ESCAPE?

Around 1800, according to Professor Wrigley, came a turning point which was 'one of the most fundamental of all changes in the history of society'. Up to the end of the eighteenth century the general Malthusian proposition that a growing population would in time mean higher food prices, decreasing employment, lower wages and falling living standards seems to have held true. Periods of demographic growth could not produce *sustained* economic growth, for they provoked the very changes which in the end prevented it. However, in the early nineteenth century rapid population growth was actually accompanied by improving national income per capita. This was not marked until after 1820, but even before then it is clear that a pronounced deterioration in living standards was no longer the inevitable sooner-or-later consequence of increasing numbers. There was a relatively short period around the final decade of the century which seems in retrospect to have been dark with Malthusian menace, but then the real-wage index turned up before there was any adjusting change in levels of nuptiality or any severe mortality crisis: 'By an ironic coincidence Malthus had given pungent expression to an issue that haunted most pre-industrial societies at almost the last moment when it could still plausibly be relevant to the country in which he was born.'

Looked at in this way, the old idea of coinciding industrial and agricultural 'revolutions' still carries a dramatic message, however much this usage has become restrained in recent years. Aided to what was still a small extent by food imports, runs the traditional view, English farmers fed the growing population without spiralling

36. The argument is most fully expressed in Ch. 10 of *Population History of England*; however, a significant refinement of the supporting data has been presented in the introductory note to the 1989 paperback edition. This shortens somewhat the time lapse between real wage turning points and those in the age at marriage. Flinn's review (pp. 454ff) is representative of a widespread scepticism among specialist reviewers on this argument. Up to now I have seen no reaction to the 1989 modification.

food prices save in exceptional years of harvest failure, while thanks to the growth of manufacturing, output and aggregate employment increased. Clearly no period of stagnation was to set in. Population growth never attained a rate so high as to bedevil any chance of economic progress in the way it has often done in the twentieth-century underdeveloped world. Marriage remained relatively late, while the living conditions of the new urban populations meant that mortality improvement was slight. The outcome was a doubling of the English population over the first half of the nineteenth century which nevertheless allowed income per head to increase two and a half times between 1780 and 1860. Wrigley has suggested that 1800 marks the start of a period when, 'for the first time in history', poverty 'for the mass of mankind became not a necessary part of the lot of man, but a preventable evil'. We can agree at least that potentially it had become so for most English people.[37]

THE GROWTH OF OUTPUT

Between 1680 and 1820 the population of England grew at more than twice the rate for western Europe as a whole. If output per head had remained only constant, then the growth of national income would still have been correspondingly more rapid than that of her competitors. It did more than remain constant. According to most economic historians, somewhere in the eighteenth century there began a transformation of production so that output per head was to rise to new heights and the economy revealed a new ability to sustain this growth through successive generations. England not only got richer, it stayed richer.

Output data for the eighteenth century present problems of scarcity and of reliability. There was no official mechanism for the systematic collection of information. It is a reasonable estimate that there was at least a three-fold increase in total output between 1700 and 1815 during the period of population doubling. Historians have found the point of departure at various points in the 'vital century'. As Phyllis Deane has put it, whereas around 1700 the economy was almost stagnant, 'within the next hundred years some-

37. Wrigley, 'The growth of population', pp. 147–8; Wrigley and Schofield, *Population History of England*, pp. 404, 412–14, 450; D.S. Landes, *The Unbound Prometheus. Technological Change and Industrial Development in Western Europe from 1750 to the Present*, Cambridge UP, 1969, p. 41.

thing happened to turn it into an expanding economy'. The appropriateness of the traditional label 'industrial revolution' is much disputed by recent historians. Certainly, as a concept it exaggerates the suddenness and completeness of actual happenings, but it still conveys an essential meaning. In any case the significant debate is not over whether the economy was transformed by the middle of the nineteenth century, but over the growth profile by which this was achieved. The idea of an industrial revolution implies a turning point not so much between an era of near zero growth and one of rapid growth, as between one of a potential-creating modest growth – beginning perhaps, as Charles Wilson has persuasively argued, around 1660 – and one in which there was a dramatic acceleration. This turning point has sometimes been located in the middle of the eighteenth century. To R.M. Hartwell it was in the hundred years after 1750 that a 'great discontinuity' divided a world of slow economic growth, in which output and real incomes could rise only slowly if at all, from one of much faster growth capable of outpacing the population growth which it in part stimulated. It is not at all easy to find a point where preconditioning changed into dramatic growth. In a much-discussed work in the 1960s, Professor Rostow attempted to do this with his famous concept of a 'take-off', but few scholars were convinced by his schematicism. His suggested date of around 1780 had, however, long been popular. In 1955 Professor T.S. Ashton asserted:

> [The] roots of modern industrial society can be traced back
> indefinitely into the past. If however, what is meant by the industrial
> revolution is a sudden quickening of the pace of output, we must move
> the date forward, and not backward from 1760. After 1782 almost every
> statistical series of production shows a sharp upward turn.

More recently Professor Mathias has suggested that the end of the American war in 1783 marked a point of sharp increase in the economic growth rate related to new developments in transport, banking and technology. From then on total output began the increase of around 2 per cent a year (1 per cent in per capita terms) which has been the underlying measure of the sustained economic growth of the modern era.[38]

38. P. Deane, 'The Industrial Revolution and economic growth: the evidence of early British national income estimates', (1957) reprinted in R.M. Hartwell (ed.) *The Causes of the Industrial Revolution in Britain*, Methuen, 1967, p. 85; C. Wilson, *England's Apprenticeship*, pp. 385–7. Hartwell used the phrase several times, but see especially his article 'The great discontinuity' in his collected essays on the theme, *Industrial Revolution and Economic Growth*, pp. 42–57; Ashton, *An Economic History of England*, p. 125; P. Mathias, *First Industrial Nation*, p. 16.

In their pioneering work of quantitative economic history, Phyllis Deane and W.A. Cole also favoured the 1780s but found an additional earlier turning point. The economy reached an annual expansion rate of around 2 per cent only from the 1780s, but it had begun to grow at 1 per cent from around 1745. The difference between the two phases was not simply one of magnitude. Two decades of growth followed 1745, but from the mid 1760s to the mid 1780s the growth rate fell, although, importantly, not back to pre-1745 levels. A sufficient base had been established for the growth surge which began in the 1780s. This could be interpreted as suggesting that through increasing output and employment the economy first held off the Malthusian threat and then, over the final two decades of the century, outran it: 'It is in the last two decades that the expansion appears to be sustained by forces of quite a different order to any that had emerged in earlier centuries.'

According to Deane and Cole, economic progress before 1745 had been modest and such as there was had taken place mostly before 1725, after which there followed a twenty-year check, associated, as we have seen, with a demographic crisis. Once this had been survived, there began a 'much stronger, many sided wave of expansion' which had sufficient momentum to carry through the relative stagnation of the later 1760s and the 1770s to the upsurge of the 1780s. This profile presents some difficulties. It is as likely that the upturn around 1745 is a short-term recovery point following some difficult years as that it was the beginning of a distinct growth trend. Although one historian has described the second quarter of the eighteenth century as a period of 'deceleration', it seems that although some sectors of the economy were in short-term difficulties, the underlying trend of the earlier eighteenth century was upward, if very modestly so. Agricultural output seems to support this view. It has important implications, for if growth over the first half of the eighteenth century was more substantial than Deane and Cole estimated, then their later eighteenth-century surge needs to have been correspondingly less dramatic in order to reach the levels of output recorded for the early nineteenth century.

More recent estimates of eighteenth-century growth have certainly flattened its profile. They point to a gradual increase in output taking place over the century as a whole. If there was an acceleration of growth from 1780 it was considerably less dramatic than the one suggested by Deane and Cole. Professor Crafts has estimated growth between 1780 and 1801 at 1.32 per cent a year, compared with the 2.06 per cent of Deane and Cole. (In per capita terms the respective figures are 0.35 per cent and 1.08 per cent.) For 1801 to 1831 Crafts reduces per capita improvement to 0.5 per cent from Deane and Cole's 1.61 per cent, suggesting that the industrial revolution had only marginally raised output per head before the second quarter of the nineteenth century. This, while it severely dents some optimistic views of the impact of early industrialisation on living standards, still means that the balance between population and its supporting resources had tipped positively by 1800. We do not have over-eagerly to anticipate nineteenth-century improvements in living standards to appreciate the historical significance of that.[39]

The pioneering work of Deane and Cole has served as the basis for all subsequent discussions of eighteenth- and nineteenth-century economic growth. Although not in a crude form, their assessment of the 1780s still allowed for a shift which could be termed an eighteenth-century industrial revolution. Later writers have been less permissive. In order to review the implications of their work, we must look beyond overall growth into the separate sectors of the economy.

AGRICULTURE

The estimates of agricultural output do need considerable revision, especially for the earlier eighteenth century. There was an overall increase from 1714 to 1815 and although the change from being a net exporter to being a net importer of grain around 1750 is a significant moment in British history, it is so as an indicator of a future position rather than of a serious deficiency. Up to 1815 the contribution of imports remained small. Professor Jones has calculated that in 1800 around 90 per cent of the population were being fed from home production compared with 101 per cent in 1700. He suggested that there was an increase in agricultural output of around 61 per cent over the century: twice the increase over the two preceding centuries. Since the agricultural labour force re-

---

39. P. Deane and W.A. Cole, *British Economic Growth*, pp. 49–50, 57–8, 79–80; A.J. Little, *Deceleration in the Eighteenth-Century British Economy*, Croom Helm, 1976; N.F.R. Crafts' work appeared in a series of articles, but is now conveniently brought together in *British Economic Growth*. See also his summary 'The Industrial Revolution: economic growth in Britain, 1700–1860', *ReFRESH*, 4, 1987, pp. 1–4, reprinted in Digby and Feinstein, *New Directions*, pp. 6–75.

mained constant at around 2 million between 1714 and 1815, this amounts to a considerable productivity gain. Growth from 1790 to 1815 was impressive enough to hold imports level over the first decades of the nineteenth century despite rapid population increase. It owed much to increased land inputs, themselves partly enabled by the extension of improved farming to more marginal soils.[40]

Deane and Cole found little increase in output before 1740, but then an acceleration through the rest of the century (1700 = 100; 1750 = 111; 1800 = 143). Although qualified in impact and relatively modest in dimensions, this profile still retains something of the old idea of an 'agricultural revolution' roughly contemporary with the industrial one. Few later historians, however, have found any short period of unusually rapid growth. Instead a gradual process is indicated beginning even before 1700. Indeed, the ability of agricultural output even to keep up with demographic increase has recently been questioned, and doubt cast upon the degree to which English agriculture merits its traditional plaudits.[41]

The method used by Deane and Cole is seriously flawed. They took the best population estimates available to them, those of Brownlee, and multiplied them by a constant consumption factor, adjusting for net exports and for seed corn. On this basis they portrayed output growing slowly and unevenly before 1740 and then increasing more rapidly. This so closely reflects the pattern of demographic growth that one critic has pointed out: 'For the purpose of long-run analysis [their] index of eighteenth-century agricultural output *is* the Brownlee population series.' It is not simply that the newer population estimates of Wrigley and Schofield suggest revision, but that any method of calculation which is based on an assumption of constant consumption per head cannot assist investigation of the relationship of population growth to the food supply. Further, since Deane and Cole also derived their rent and service estimates from the population series, there are serious implications for their calculation of overall growth in national income.[42]

Professor Crafts has presented significantly different estimates for agricultural output, especially for the period before 1760. For 1700 to 1760 he posits a decennial growth rate of 6.2 per cent compared with Deane and Cole's 2.3 per cent. For 1760 to 1800 he is closer, at 4.5 per cent compared with 5.6. The revision is significant, for

40. E.L. Jones, 'Agriculture, 1700–80', in R. Floud and D. McCloskey, *Economic History*, pp. 66–86.
41. Deane and Cole, *British Economic Growth*, pp. 62–75.
42. R.V. Jackson, 'Growth and deceleration', pp. 334–5.

32

what appeared as a doubling of the rate of increase in the latter part of the century now becomes a distinct slowing down in food production at the time of increasing population growth. Evidently if agricultural output was increasing at 4.5 per cent per decade from 1760 to 1800 against a demographic rate of 8 per cent, it seems likely that both output *and* consumption per head fell.[43]

Crafts rejects the assumption that consumption remained constant and argues that its level was much affected by changes in the relative prices of agricultural to other goods and by changing levels of real income. The former were falling from 1710 to 1745 and rising from 1760 to 1800. Real wages were rising for much of the eighteenth century, while the income elasticity of demand for agricultural output was quite high. On these assumptions, he presents a picture of a near-stagnant agriculture from 1760 to 1780; he is a little more sanguine for 1780 to 1800 but less so for the period 1801 to 1831.

Table 2.5 Estimates of agricultural output growth (per cent)

	Crafts	*Deane and Cole*
1700–60	0.60	0.24
1760–80	0.13	0.47
1780–1800	0.75	0.65
1801–31	1.18	1.64

Source: N.F.R. Crafts, *British Economic Growth during the Industrial Revolution,* Oxford UP, 1985, p. 42.

The newer estimates are consistent with the empirical evidence available from regional case studies of agrarian change and crop productivity. Jones suggested that crucial new cropping systems were being introduced more quickly before 1760 than afterwards. Turner also thinks the main improvement in cereal yields came before 1770. A subsequent pick-up in the 1790s is suggested by Feinstein's showing of real investment in agriculture to have been twice as high by then as it had been in the 1760s. Perhaps there is an emerging consensus on impressive growth before 1760, surpassed by even faster growth as agriculture became more capital intensive in the early

43. Crafts, *British Economic Growth*, pp. 38–44.

years of the nineteenth century. In between there was a period in which output failed to keep pace with the increase in population. Ironically it is in these intervening years that the traditional 'agricultural revolution' was commonly placed.[44]

It has even been suggested that Crafts is himself too optimistic on the matter of growth after 1760 and that in choosing that date as a dividing point he obscures a real trend change in the movements of population, real incomes and agricultural prices which set in around 1740. Dr Jackson suggests two long-run phases over the period 1660 to 1790: strong growth up to 1740 and then a fifty-year period of much slower growth and possibly stagnation. A fall in per capita consumption and output, which is possible even on Deane and Cole's figures, now seems quite likely given that imports did not rise sufficiently to provide full supplementation. The contrast with the period up to 1740 when, except in individual years of bad harvest, output safely outpaced population growth is striking. It at least suggests that there was some point to Malthusian gloom over rapid demographic increase, near-stagnation in real wages, increasing cereal imports and the onset of an agrarian price trend which seemed to indicate that demand was outrunning supply. Such features make it hard indeed to accept calculations based on constant cereal consumption. Jackson is even more pessimistic than Crafts in concluding that whereas total agrarian output increased by 40 per cent between 1660 and 1740, it did so by only 14 per cent over the next fifty years. This does not suggest anything so dramatic as a food crisis, but a fall in per capita consumption seems most likely. The inability to increase land inputs remained a constraint, even though it was partly overcome when the high prices of the war years 1793–1815 gave an incentive to cultivate more marginal lands.[45]

Agricultural output increased much more slowly than did that of manufactured goods; their rate was three times as fast. Professor O'Brien has suggested that this provides a context not only for the pessimism of Malthus but also for that of Ricardo and his followers among the early classical economists who argued that the early industrial economy might flounder on the supply constraints of the agricultural sector. Impressive as were the achievements of agriculture in the late eighteenth and early nineteenth centuries, it was the emergence of Britain as the 'workshop of the world' which was to provide the answer. Food imports might have increased even

44. See E.L. Jones, 'Agriculture, 1700–80', *op. cit.*, especially his conclusion.
45. R.V. Jackson, 'Growth and deceleration', pp. 339, 349–51.

more quickly if they had not been restrained by war and, artificially, by the Corn Laws. Historians, too, have tended to ignore the growing role of Ireland well before the end of the eighteenth century, especially in supplying animal products. All this pointed towards the time when, as Professor Brinley Thomas has put it, Britain found the way out in endowing itself with the equivalent of a 'vast extension of its own land base'. In becoming the first industrial nation, it was able to exchange increasing manufactured output for cheap food and give improved support for numbers of people beyond any eighteenth-century projection.[46]

MANUFACTURING

Here, too, re-measuring has significantly modified views of the pattern and pace of eighteenth-century growth. Dr Harley allocated very different weights to the separate industries and found that growth over the key period 1770–1815 was a third lower than suggested by Deane and Cole. They, it seems, gave too much weight to the small number of technologically transformed industries like cotton, iron and steam power. These certainly did grow rapidly, but even by 1841 had a combined output of less than a quarter of the manufacturing total. Older, less transformed industries like wool, leather, linen and silk generated more income. Although cotton ouput increased by 2,200 per cent from 1770 to 1815, most industries did so by between 40 and 200 per cent. Using his corrected weightings, Harley does not greatly differ from the much-used Hoffman index for 1815 to 1841, but he does for the period of the *early* industrial revolution. His estimate of the annual growth in industrial output from 1770 to 1815 is a full 1 per cent below that of Hoffman, for which he compensates by suggesting that pre-1770 rates were 50 per cent *higher*. On this basis the idea of a truly dramatic growth surge in the late eighteenth century is seriously diminished.[47]

Weighting apart, he suggests that Deane and Cole too readily assumed that the performance of manufacturing exports was a near proxy for total output. Much exporting was, however, demand led,

46. P.K. O'Brien, 'Agriculture and the Industrial Revolution', pp. 172, 179–80; Brinley Thomas, 'Escaping from constraints: the Industrial Revolution in a Malthusian context' in R.I. Rotberg and T.K. Rabb (eds), *Population and Economy*, p. 171.

47. C.K. Harley, 'British industrialization before 1841', p. 267.

for example by the growth of population in North America. Certainly since markets expand and contract, open and close for a variety of reasons external to the economy, turning points in the export of manufactured goods are not bound to coincide with those in the growth of output. Freeing the output from the trade curve, Harley concludes that industrial production grew much more slowly from 1770 to 1815 than Deane and Cole suggested. Further, if, as seems possible, the pre-1770 manufacturing sector was larger than they supposed, the later acceleration was presumably less spectacular.[48]

Crafts has also paid special attention to the earlier part of the century in putting forward a less dramatic growth profile. Accepting recently revised social tables, he sees England as already more of a manufacturing economy in 1700 than has been represented in traditional accounts of the industrial revolution. Deane and Cole allocated national income shares of 43 per cent to agriculture and 30 per cent to industry and commerce combined. Crafts maintains that even by 1759 the share of agriculture had fallen to 26 per cent and the combined share of industry and commerce had reached 48 per cent. Like Harley, he emphasises that the early contribution of the technologically advanced industries was modest and that the period from 1770 to 1801 was marked by a wide dispersion of growth rates. The median sectoral growth rate shows a steady rather than spectacular advance of 0.67 per cent per annum from 1700 to 1760, varies from 1.32 per cent to 1.65 per cent through 1760 to 1800 and then climbs steadily to 3.03 per cent between 1821 and 1831. In Table 2.6 his estimates for industry and for industry and commerce combined are set against those of Deane and Cole for industry and commerce.

Effectually he replaces the dramatic surge beginning around 1780 with a much smaller one, and overall offers a picture of a gradual, widespread advance over the period. Cotton did not typify the general experience.[49]

In a recent textbook Dr Maxine Berg has brought wide-ranging evidence together to demonstrate that manufacturing growth was, if slower than assumed in the classic accounts of the industrial revolution, more steady and widespread. It was also less dependent on

48. *Ibid.*, pp. 267–8, 285–6.
49. Crafts, *British Economic Growth*, pp. 17–34. The social tables were revised by P.H. Lindert, 'English occupations 1680–1811', *Jn. Econ. Hist.*, **40**, 1980, pp. 685–712. Although it seems probable that the extent of manufacturing in 1700 has been underestimated, Lindert cannot satisfactorily allow for the prevalence of mixed employment, and may well have overstated his case.

Table 2.6 Growth in industry and commerce, per cent per annum

| | Crafts | | Deane and Cole |
	Industry	Industry and commerce	Industry and commerce
1700–60	0.71	0.70	0.98
1760–80	1.51	1.05	0.49
1780–1801	2.11	1.81	3.43
1801–31	3.00	2.13	3.97

Source: N.F.R. Crafts, *British Economic Growth during the Industrial Revolution,* Oxford UP, 1985, p. 32.

spectacular technological progress and on the factory system. It developed in the country as well as in the towns and exhibited many different forms of organisation and levels of technology side by side. If productivity gains over much of manufacturing did not approach those gained in cotton or in iron, the aggregated weight of their impact was nevertheless greater.[50] Professor Feinstein's calculations of domestic investment as a proportion of national income point in the same direction. Gross domestic investment was approaching three times its 1700 level by 1821, but it had got there through steady increase, not through dramatic surge.[51]

Table 2.7 Gross domestic investment as a percentage of GNP

1700	4	1801	7.9
1760	6	1811	8.5
1780	7	1821	11.2

Source: N.F.R. Crafts, *British Economic Growth during the Industrial Revolution,* Oxford UP, 1985, p. 73.

What can, with difficulty, be estimated for the service sector does not much alter the picture of national income change derived from physical output. Expanding financial and commercial institutions,

50. M. Berg, *The Age of Manufactures,* especially Ch. 1.
51. C. Feinstein's figures are considered and adjusted by Crafts (pp. 72–4), but Crafts has himself been recently criticised for his handling of public expenditure data by R.V. Jackson, 'Government expenditure and British economic growth', pp. 217–35.

the growth of towns and the related expanding of the middle-class professions suggest an unusually strong contribution compared with other countries and that growth at least matched that of the population.[52]

Table 2.8 Growth of the tertiary sector, per cent per annum

	Government and defence	*Rent and services*
1700–60	1.91	0.38
1760–80	1.29	0.69
1780–1801	2.11	0.97

Source: N.F.R. Crafts, *British Economic Growth in the Industrial Revolution*, Oxford UP, 1985, p. 35.

Much has been lost of traditional presentations of the industrial revolution – so much so that some historians urge the abandonment of the concept. True, the profile of manufacturing growth has been flattened by recent research, but it remains the case that in Britain there was an unprecedented structural shift in employment away from agriculture, a marked shrinking of the value of agricultural output relative to that of manufacturing, a unique increase in urbanisation, and, above all, an ability to increase total output ahead of what was by some margin Europe's most rapidly increasing population.

52. The importance of the growth of the service sector is clear enough. It has been especially stressed by, for example, C.H. Lee, *British Economy since 1700*, who argues that the emphasis on the manufacturing sector has been misguided.

CHAPTER THREE
The Agricultural Economy

If few historians now cling to the old idea of an 'agricultural revolution' transforming English farming in step with an 'industrial revolution', *improvement* nevertheless remains a key concept in any discussion of development and change over the eighteenth century. It draws attention to the extent, pace and diffusion of better farming methods. Although, under the scrutiny of researchers digging ever deeper on small allotments selected from the wide fields over which an earlier generation of historians ranged, any suggestion of dramatic change has crumbled away, it is still the case that over our period the aggregate effects of changes in farming practice and of the extension of the cultivated acreage by the reclamation of wastes and uplands were very considerable.

New agrarian techniques were introduced rather than discovered. Most of those in the vanguard of progressive farming in eighteenth-century England had originated in the Low Countries in the preceding century. As they diffused, their effect was modified by contact with traditional knowledge and with practices justified by their appropriateness for local soil and climatic conditions. In the best cases regional agriculture became a productive blend of the new and the known.

It might be expected that to the extent that new methods depended upon increased investment, they would have spread most rapidly under the stimulus of high prices, perhaps under long-term influences such as the pressure exerted on the food supply by population growth after 1750, or under short-term influences when wartime conditions brought large farming profits. In fact depressed prices, such as those which prevailed from 1730 to 1750, could also be linked to innovation if they preserved profit levels by lowering costs. The assumptions in either situation are that English agriculture was market responsive and that its pattern of land-holding and occupation was suited to improvement. This latter assumption is fundamental. Our analysis of English agriculture must begin with it.

LAND OWNERSHIP AND OCCUPATION

By the early eighteenth century, according to Dr Porter, 'the tide was flowing in favour of the magnates'. There is general agreement that Professor Habakkuk's thesis that the 'drift of property in the sixty years after 1690 was in favour of the large estate and the great lord' is correct in outline. On no other assumption could the hold of the aristocracy on all the vital sinews of political and social power be fully explained. The minimalist position would have to be that the great landowners at least held their place. Of course, 'aristocracy', 'peerage' and 'great landowners' are not wholly synonymous. This is not unimportant when the details of political influence are under consideration, but in an analysis of land-holding the larger landowners can be considered as a group irrespective of title and dignity. After Domesday no systematic survey of English land-holding took place for 700 years, so historians have to depend upon sources which are local and indirect, such as land tax or tithe assessments. Little has emerged, however, to contradict a general picture of a slight proportionate shift towards the large landowners in the seventeenth century, preceding a more pronounced one in the early eighteenth. After 1750 there was a slowing down but no reversal of this trend. The process, as Professor Thompson has pointed out, was very gradual and there is a need to distinguish between the fortunes of the group as a whole and those of individual families within it. In the face of fickle fortune, profligacy and above all of the dealing of the random cards of demography, a large amount of land was transferred through marriage, inheritance or even through sale within the group. Thompson has suggested that the rate of shift towards those holding 3,000 acres or more never exceeded 5 per cent over a century. At such a pace it was a happening more evident in nineteenth-century retrospect than in eighteenth-century perception. To contemporaries it probably seemed as if little was changing (see Table 3.1).[1]

1. R. Porter, *English Society*, p. 70; Habakkuk, 'English landownership', p. 28; F.M.L. Thompson, 'Social distribution of landed property', p. 512.

Table 3.1 English land-holding, per cent

	1690	1790
Great owners: 3,000 acres	15–20	20–25
Gentry: 300–3,000 acres	45–50	50
Small owners: less than 300 acres	25–35	15

Source: F.M.L. Thompson, 'The social distribution of landed property in England since the sixteenth century', *Econ. H.R.*, XIX, 1966, pp. 510–14.

The most significant feature was that the small shift was not at the expense of the middle group but at that of the small land-owner. The absence of a small-holding peasantry was becoming the distinguishing structural characteristic of English agriculture. This can be left for later consideration. We need first to investigate the methods by which the large landowners not only maintained but slightly aggravated their hold on the English land. A stagnant, or even an especially slow land market is not indicated. The contours of ownership can be preserved in outline, while within them a brisk exchange of land is taking place. Furthermore, the situation may have differed sharply between groups. It is possible that within the group of great landowners transfers were regular but internal; some players did better than others, but few were invited to join the game. In the gentry group there were perhaps more frequent exchanges of land and a more evident turnover of players. In his pioneering work on the great estates, Sir John Habakkuk explained their success through the way in which inheritance practices and marriage settlements acted both to restrict the pressure on the large landowners to sell and to advantage them in the acquisition of further land. At the heart of the matter lay the legal device of *strict settlement* and the custom of primogeniture in the event of intestacy. Through the heir-binding intent of strict settlement, linked to the development of trusteeships to safeguard contingent remainders, landowners were able to treat their heirs as prospective tenants for life, bound to leave the estate intact for the next generation. As for marriage, the increasing availability of mortgages meant that those landowners encumbered with daughters could avoid handing over land with their hands in marriage. Instead they could raise cash portions. These in turn, as Habakkuk ingeniously argued, could then be used by the son-in-law to purchase more land. In his much-quoted phrase, the landowning class was 'pulling itself up by its own bootstraps'. To work in the fullest sense the argument also needs to show that there was little competition from outside the ranks to purchase such land as did become available. Habakkuk offered a number of reinforcing factors: the fall in agricultural prices from the mid seventeenth century; the burden of wartime land tax levels in the wars against Louis XIV; and the increasing proclivity of the gentry to assume a life-style beyond their means, which brought much of *their* land on to a market in which potential competition for the magnates from the monied men of the City was lessened by the increasing availability of attractive alternative investments. In such a configuration the general trend in favour of the great land-owners reflected both the constraints on their selling land and their advantages as purchasers in a market which was not noticeably competitive. Accordingly, the years from the Restoration saw a land market which was brisk enough from gentry sales but within which the magnates were able to secure their position. If there was a lessening of the volume of land available for purchase after 1750, it was partly a reflection of their success in restraining inheritors through strict settlement, consolidating a position more dynamically and dynastically forged between 1660 and 1750.[2]

The Habakkuk thesis has found its critics, especially of the importance it gives to strict settlement. The argument is logical and it is sound in terms of legal history. However, that courts came to accept a form of entailing they had previously frowned upon tells us nothing directly about the extent to which it was actually practised. Further, strict settlement binds only the immediate heir, so for it to have worked in the way Habakkuk suggests there would need to have been a regular process of renewal. There was also a clear procedure through which such settlements could be broken by private act of parliament. As for Habakkuk's 'bootstrap' argument, there can be doubts about how general was the practice of sons-in-law expending marriage portions on land, as opposed perhaps to discharging existing debts. That strict settlement lasted for only a single generation would not matter if it became normal for fresh agreements to be drawn up at the marriage of the prospective heir. But this is an 'ideal' solution, which in the period before 1760 was very often wrecked on the rocks of demography.

Hollingsworth has shown that in the century after the Restoration one in six fertile peerage marriages did not produce a male

---

2. Habakkuk, 'English landownership', but see also his later reconsideration in *Trans. R. Hist. S.*, 1979, 1980 and 1981.

heir and that the generational replacement rate was below unity. Fathers frequently did not survive until the marriage or coming of age of their heirs – the points at which settlements tended to be remade. Only three of ninety-three Yorkshire baronets' families managed successive resettlement over the seventeenth and eighteenth centuries. Bonfield's conclusion, that the correlation between the use of strict settlement and the building up of the great estates is weakened by the demographic evidence, seems justified. Ill-timed mortality co-existed with deliberate entail-breaking. Estate Acts averaged around twenty to thirty a year between 1700 and 1850 and by this means alone a flow of estate land came on to the market. Even in the best of demographic circumstances land was still sold. Continuity was sometimes possible only through the contortion of special remainders and through the enforcement of name changes on collateral heirs or sons-in-law. Holding the family seat together was the objective of most substantial families. To this end they planned and plotted with whatever was available. Strict settlement was a help, but only with extraordinary luck could it guarantee long-term success. The quite widespread failure to produce male heirs probably did not much harm the magnates as a group. It meant that a relatively large proportion of estate land changed hands through marriage before 1760, and it has been reasonably argued that the unusually large population of substantial heiresses then available were mostly acquired by the sons of large landowners, who would have been not only more attractive in terms of status and prestige, but in a position to offer better jointures to their brides.[3]

After 1760 strict settlement was better favoured by demographic trends. If, as has been suggested, this reduced the amount of land coming on to the market as well as consolidated the pattern of landowning, it could have been a supply-side cause of increasing land prices. These had risen slowly, but steadily, from around twenty years' purchase in 1700 to twenty-five years' by 1750. From the 1760s to 1790s they were around thirty years' (that is to say, the anticipated rent yield for that number of years). But the demand side was also changing – perhaps even more significantly. Very large estates hardly ever came on to the market, but parts of them did

3. The debate is carefully reviewed in J.V. Beckett, 'The pattern of landownership' and, especially 'English landownership'; see also the discussion in his *Aristocracy in England*, pp. 58–64; Bonfield, 'Marriage settlements and the rise of great estates', pp. 485–6, 491; Bonfield's view is disputed by B. English and J. Saville, 'Family settlement and the rise of great estates', *Econ. H.R.*, XXXIII, 1980, pp. 556–63; Clay, 'The price of freehold land', p. 183; Clay, 'Marriage, inheritance and the rise of large estates', for a thorough discussion of the role of marriage.

alongside lesser estates and smaller holdings. For these there were competing purchasers, and large owners seeking to expand bid along with new wealth from mining, manufacturing and banking, successful squires, clergy, graziers and yeomen, as well as from rising professionals such as lawyers and land agents. For plots of ten to a hundred acres there was still an active demand from small far-mers. Holderness has stressed that a 'peasant market' remained a significant feature in Lincolnshire throughout the eighteenth century, making it still possible to 'rise': 'The number of farming families who by dint of careful investment, sometimes over several generations, rose to the ranks of the minor gentry in eighteenth-century Lincolnshire is impressive.' The difficulties of the few who did seek to purchase a large estate confirms the slightness of the pressure to sell on those who held them. That is not to say that the great landed did not often sell holdings detached from their main estates. Samuel Whitbread I accumulated his 5,600 acres by buying where he could in eight counties between 1760 and 1785 and leasing property in two others. But when the estates of the 4th Viscount Torrington came on the market in 1795, he seized a rare opportunity and consolidated so that by the end of the year 10,500 of his by then 12,300 acres were in Bedfordshire.[4]

Dr Beckett has pointed to a marked regional variation in the pattern of land acquisition. In some counties the magnate share was consolidated, especially where distance from London lessened the interest of City wealth. In others small and medium estates survived well, though one or other of the two patterns usually predominated. In Cumbria between 1680 and 1750 peers sold more land than they purchased. Beckett and others have pointed to the urge to consolidate holdings. Marriage and collateral inheritance sometimes brought holdings far removed from the family seat, while demography ensured that inheritance went often to an absentee landholder. If not sold in the short term, for they were often excluded from any strict settlement on the main estate, they were sold subsequently after securing Estate Acts. Opportunities to purchase land adjacent to the seat were not to be missed and it made sense to sell outlying property to finance this. There was a resulting tendency for large landowners to dominate land purchases in counties where there was a severality of great estates. In Northamptonshire, for

---

4. For land prices generally, see Clay, 'The price of freehold land', and for the land market the most valuable study is B.A. Holderness, 'The English land market', but see also the analysis of Clay in his contribution to Thirsk (ed.), *Agrarian History of England and Wales*, part I, pp. 170–98; Beckett, *Aristocracy in England*, p. 65.

example, between 1690 and 1740 half of all land changing hands came to families who had been long settled in the county. Professor Stone has contrasted Northumberland, where there was little challenge in the market to the great landowners, with Hertfordshire, where newcomers moving out from London broke up the existing pattern and the cohesion of traditional landed society. In Cumbria, Yorkshire, Lincolnshire, Devon and Cornwall magnate interest was slight, although in Sussex and Essex it was evident until the late eighteenth century.[5]

Successful merchants and bankers hardly ever sought large estates. They lacked a full commitment to land and were content with the advantages in terms of power, position and prestige which more modest country seats could bring. Most historians seem to agree that it was the social rather than the economic value of land which motivated purchase. Land was safe enough, but its returns were not spectacular. Holderness has aptly termed it a 'form of conspicuous investment'. Other forms of investment such as government stock and mortgages were becoming safer than they had been and offered better returns than land. Men of business for the most part made a controlled investment in land as a basis for gentility, while keeping most of their resources in better-paying places. They left it for the following generations to creep, if they wished, along the barriered path to the narrow circle of the elite. As a generalisation, those who came into the world of the landed knew what they were after and costed for venture rather than adventure.[6]

As a group the great eighteenth-century landowners had not washed the sting of bursting South Sea bubbles from their eyes, but the interest of monied men in land purchase was nevertheless sufficient to establish a link between land prices and the rate of return on stocks. Since the borrowing needs of government were highest in times of war, a shorter-term pattern of fluctuation disturbed the steady upward trend of land prices from time to time. George Grenville wrote in 1753:

> If peace continues two or three years longer I am persuaded I shall make more of the estate than I asked of you for it, and if a war, which God avert, should break out the price will fall in Norfolk as well as in

5. Beckett, *Aristocracy in England*, p. 64; 'The pattern of landownership', pp. 18–19.

6. Beckett, *Aristocracy in England*, pp. 69–70; Clay, 'The price of freehold land', pp. 183–5; Holderness, 'The English land market', pp. 563–4; N. Rogers, 'Money, land and lineage: the big bourgeoisie of Hanoverian London,' *Social History*, IV, **3**, 1979, pp. 448–9.

Oxfordshire, and my only reason for selling in the one is to purchase in the other.[7]

When government stocks slipped at the end of the Seven Years War in 1764, land prices soared so that thirty-five years' purchase was deemed 'no uncommon price'. By contrast, in the middle of the American war in 1779 a Warrington attorney wrote: 'Lands are so much on the decline that one's afraid to purchase.' Dr Clay's researches support Arthur Young's contemporary contention that the drop at that time amounted to ten years' purchase from the previous peak. With peace in 1783 land prices began a hesitant recovery. Thus, not only were newcomers to the land market likely to intend sinking only a part of their fortune into land, they would have been variously inclined to do even this according to the state of war or peace. In short, in holding on to their giant estates over the eighteenth century, established landowners were hardly fighting off a full-scale challenge from the parvenu, but demand was at least sufficient to allow a steady inflation of land prices on trend. This underlying appreciation has led Dr Allen to challenge the accepted view that land was not much sought for economic reasons. Although his argument is not wholly convincing in its confidence that increased rentals could normally be expected, for this depended much on the system of tenure and the input of capital, he is correct to point out that appreciating values could be partly realised through mortgaging and thus help to reduce the 'systematic tension' which strict settlement sometimes imposed between the financial interest of the life-tenant and the dynastic interest of the family. Mortgaging against rising values for consumption purposes was 'an indispensable tool of prudent estate management'.[8]

Ultimately it is the pattern of landowning which determines that of land occupation and hence the type of farming practised. Whatever the concentration of a quarter or so of the land into the hands of the magnates meant for the exercise of political and social power, what matters more for the agrarian outcome was the small and diminishing share over the period of the small owners with 300 acres or less. This shrank from between a quarter and a third of the land area at the beginning of the eighteenth century to around a seventh by its close. In contrast, the demand for gentry-sized estates ensured that the overall holding of the middle group, 300 to 3,000

7. Beckett, *Aristocracy in England*, p. 83.
8. Clay, 'The price of freehold land', pp. 178–9; R.C. Allen, 'The price of freehold land and the interest rate in the seventeenth and eighteenth centuries', *Econ. H.R.*, XLI, 1, 1988, pp. 33–4, 49.

acres, did not decrease, although there was a very considerable change of personnel *within* it.

The land-holding small peasantry was not wholly extinguished in England, still less in Britain. Their ways and means of scraping a living from the land persisted into the nineteenth century, but their share of the acreage was small. The fact that the surviving nineteenth-century peasantry mixed its earning activities, as Dr Read has shown, was a reflection of the inadequacy of their holdings. With perhaps 70 per cent of the land held by the gentry and magnates in 1700 and over 80 per cent by 1800, it is clear that the vast majority of English landowners depended upon rentals and that the triad of owner, tenant and labourer was an entrenched and peculiar feature of English agriculture.[9]

THE IMPROVEMENT OF AGRICULTURE

To William Marshall writing at the beginning of the nineteenth century the most impressive quality of the half a million sheep which were 'the basis of Wiltshire down husbandry' was neither the fineness of their wool nor the sweetness of their mutton; it was the hardiness which enabled the animal 'to walk two or three miles for its food and carry its dung back to the fold'. Dung was the essence of the improvement of seventeenth- and eighteenth-century agriculture. The severest limitation on medieval agriculture had been the inability to maintain, let alone much improve the quality of the soil. Only by resting a proportion of the arable land as fallow could the exhaustion of successive cereal cropping be reduced. The circle was vicious. Although all sorts of local fertilising stratagems were employed – for example night soil near the towns, sand and seaweed near the coast – before the industrially produced fertilisers of the later nineteenth century, only a very appreciable increase in the supply of manure could offer a way out. This in its turn required an increase in the animal population, which depended both on improved winter feeding extending the natural pastures of summer and on finding a means of improving the quality of the pasture so that it could support more beasts.

In places the use of water-meadows had increased the possibility of cutting hay for winter feeding, but the significant breakthrough

9. M. Reed, 'The peasantry of nineteenth-century rural England', pp. 53–76.

came with the introduction of fodder crops. Much more important than the over-lauded turnip (itself soon to be replaced by the swede) were the sown grasses: sainfoin and trefoil on the lighter soils and clover on the clays. These had come from the Low Countries and were already making progress in England by the third quarter of the seventeenth century. They spread outwards from Kent and East Anglia and by the second quarter of the eighteenth century were known 'by some farmers in every part of England', and in some districts their cultivation was already usual. By that time, too, the field cropping of turnips was not uncommon in East Anglia, Hertfordshire and Kent. They were not as yet especially associated with new crop rotations, such as the four-course one so famously developed in Norfolk. Up to 1750 farmers grew them in small quantities as winter feed for cattle. The fodder grasses allowed a new balance between grass and arable land in lowland England. Significantly, the lighter soil areas now pushed to the fore. Previously they had been too infertile for permanent tillage, but they drained well enough for stock, especially sheep, to be kept on the land all winter and fed fodder. In return the grateful sheep bestowed upon the ground the fertility necessary for a following cereal crop.

As well as in Wiltshire, William Marshall noted that the practice of shepherding sheep over downlands by day and folding them on the arable at night was crucial in the agricultural systems of Berkshire, Essex, Somerset (where it was 'unremittingly pursued') and Dorset (where 'wether sheep are folded all the year round, running over the ewe leas by day, and are penned on the tillage by night') at a concentration of 1,200 to 1,300 an acre. Professor Jones has shown similar developments in the Hampshire chalklands in the first part of the eighteenth century. The lighter soils were easier to work than the heavy clays which were also handicapped by a shorter working season and a poorer performance from root crops. Over the eighteenth century a notable extension of corn growing into formerly barren uplands was paralleled by an increasing tendency for the clays, especially in the Midland counties like Leicestershire and Warwickshire, to be put to grass and to specialisation in stock rearing and dairying, although only over a long period of overlap.[10]

---

10. W. Marshall, *Review and Abstracts of the County Reports of the Board of Agriculture from the Several Agricultural Departments of England*, Vol. V., *Southern and Peninsular Departments*, 1818, reprinted Newton Abbot 1968, pp. 229, 58, 165, 239, 253; Holderness, *Pre-Industrial England: Economy and Society from 1500–1750*, Dent, 1976, pp. 61–9

Where demonstrated, the advantages of the new fodder crops were sufficiently discernible. Farmers could notice effects without understanding principles. These were hardly understood even by advocates of the progressive methods. The only 'science' of the eighteenth-century improvement was botany, and then only as a matter of observation and practical experiment rather than knowledge. What the eighteenth century largely contributed was the further development of methods novel in the seventeenth century, especially their insertion into farming systems and crop rotations. Planned sequences of cropping, integrated with the growing interdependence of arable and animal husbandry, were the motor of improvement. Mixed farming on permanently tilled fields dispensed with the fallow, offered weed control by ploughing, and, by conferring the grand desideratum of maintaining soil fertility, extended the corn frontier into the lighter soil regions. Agrarian historians have been somewhat obsessed with the celebrated Norfolk four-course rotation involving turnips, clovers, wheat and barley and have diverted attention from the fact that mixed or 'convertible' farming could take a variety of forms responding to local soil, climatic and marketing conditions. Its total effect is impossible to assess, but claims that a third of the increase in arable production in northern Europe between 1750 and 1850 can be attributed to legumes such as clover seem justified. Diffusion was slow and steady. Although half the farmers in Norfolk and Suffolk were growing root crops by 1720, the average acreage was only 9 per cent for turnips and 3.5 per cent for clover; by 1850 both exceeded 20 per cent. Clearly it took a while before they were consciously used as part of a system to raise grain yields, rather than considered simply as valuable fodder crops *per se*. Overton has accordingly suggested that improved output before the mid eighteenth century was as much due to the regional and local specialisation brought about by the widening of the market.[11]

At the height of the Tudor enclosures, the sheep, seen by Sir

provides an excellent succinct account of the diffusion of new methods up to 1750. E.L. Jones, 'Agriculture 1700–80' in Floud and McCloskey, *Economic History of Britain*, pp. 78–81 is a masterly compression which stresses the greater importance of the period before 1760. The regional contributions to Thirsk (ed.), *Agrarian History of England and Wales*, reveal the varied pattern of diffusion and their findings are reviewed in R.B. Outhwaite, 'English agricultural efficiency from the mid-seventeenth century: causes and costs', *Historical Journal*, **30**, 1, 1987, pp. 201–9. A useful summary is provided by M. Overton, 'Agricultural revolution? England, 1540–1850', *ReFRESH* **3**, 1986, pp. 1–4, reprinted in Digby and Feinstein, *New Directions*, pp. 9–21.

11. *Ibid.*, pp. 2–3.

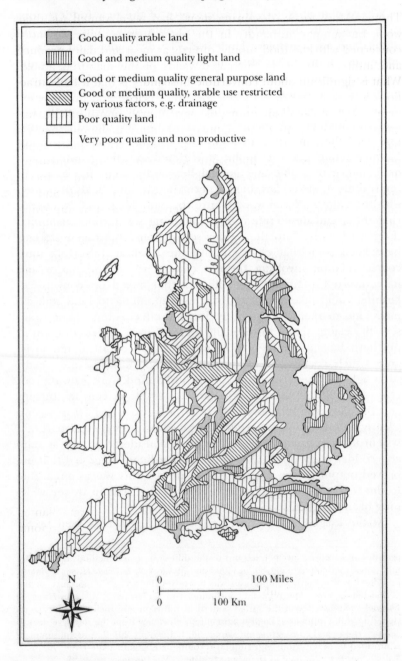

Legend:

- Good quality arable land
- Good and medium quality light land
- Good or medium quality general purpose land
- Good or medium quality, arable use restricted by various factors, e.g. drainage
- Poor quality land
- Very poor quality and non productive

N

0   100 Miles

0   100 Km

Figure 3.1 Land classification map of England

Thomas More to be 'devouring men', had been wanted for their wool, but animal husbandry in the eighteenth century was more concerned with the food supply: directly as meat and dairy produce and indirectly from the increased yields of the manured arable. What is significant about convertible husbandry is that it had attractions in times of both high and low grain prices, and this may explain why some momentum of agricultural improvement was maintained throughout the eighteenth century including the first half when cereal prices had been depressed. When more rapid population increase set in around mid century, the demand-induced rise in cereal prices, especially for wheat, produced an inevitable supply-side response both in expanding acreages and in improving productivity. But why was there an interest in improving agriculture before the upturn? In the first place, the underlying demand for cereals had been stagnant rather than falling. If this did not produce high profits, neither did it produce widespread ruin. Government bounties encouraged exports, while irrespective of the demographic situation, changing economic and social structure exercised a decisive influence on the development of the market.

It was not chance that it was in the Low Countries and in England that new crops and farming methods took hold. In these countries the growth of the non-food-producing population by 1700, through urbanisation and the spread of rural manufacturing, had placed the emphasis on the supplying of food markets and accelerated the decline of subsistence agriculture. Transport developments carried things further and with the increasing activities of middlemen, local markets widened into regional or even national ones. It was a process which had long been under way, but by the beginning of the eighteenth century few English farmers were outside the reach of the market and although that is not the same as to say that all were fully oriented towards it, farmers depended increasingly on cash returns. Not all farmers had both feet firmly planted in this world of exchange and money, let alone thought of national or distant rather than local markets. Professor Pounds has shown that surprisingly little corn was marketed even from some large Cornish estates in the first half of the eighteenth century, and that which was travelled only locally. Yet the far West Country was still within reach of the tentacles of the London food market in years of poor harvest. Its ports offered the opportunity and in 1737 a letter from a Falmouth corn factor to some London merchants mentions three others as well as himself who were engaged in buying corn for trans-shipment. Adam Smith considered that by 1776 the prices of butchers' meat and of bread were very nearly the same throughout the country, and a study of wheat prices has suggested that their movements in the early eighteenth century do indicate a well-developed market transcending regional determination. It seems that other cereal prices, for barley and oats, do not conform to this pattern, but it would be surprising if meat prices were more subject to local market autonomy than wheat prices. Meat had less relevance to subsistence needs and had the capability of being moved on the hoof over long distances.[12]

Norfolk turkeys were used by Defoe as a spectacular example of the reach of the London food market by the beginning of the eighteenth century. He reported that they were driven from Norfolk and Suffolk every August in hundreds of droves each of a thousand birds, feeding on the post-harvest stubble as they passed through Essex. His famous *Tour* is as much a celebration of emerging regional agrarian specialisation as it is of the spread of manufacturing. London drew its wheat and malt from its neighbouring counties, especially Bedfordshire and Hertfordshire, and from East Anglia. Cattle were fattened in large numbers in the Midlands, while on the Essex marshes large numbers of sheep from Lincolnshire and Leicestershire were kept for fattening. It was these merchant graziers, not sheep farmers generally, who persuaded parliament to make sheep stealing a hanging offence in 1741. The great Weyhill sheep fair near Andover was supplied from nine counties. Cheese, bacon and malt were barged from Gloucestershire and Wiltshire and butter could come from as far away as Yorkshire and Newcastle. These are simply illustrative; as Professor Wrigley has put it:

> The steady growth in demand for food in London as population there increased, necessarily caused great changes in the methods used on farms over a wider and wider area, in the commercial organization of the food market, and in the transport of food . . . as larger and larger fractions of the year's flocks and crops were consumed at a distance from the areas in which they were produced.[13]

12. N.J. Pounds, 'Barton farming in eighteenth-century Cornwall', *Journal of the Royal Institution of Cornwall*, NS. VII, 1973, pp. 53–75; PRO State Papers Domestic, 36/42; Adam Smith, *Wealth of Nations*, I, pp. 166–7; C.W.J. Grainger and C.M. Elliott, 'Fresh look at wheat prices and markets', *Econ. H.R.*, XX, 2, 1967, p. 262.

13. For a survey of the movement of agricultural produce, see J.D. Chambers and G.E. Mingay, *Agricultural Revolution*, pp. 21–33, and for development of marketing up to 1750, J.A. Chartres, 'The marketing of agricultural produce' in Thirsk (ed.), *Agrarian History of England and Wales*, pp. 410–502; Wrigley, 'A simple model of London's importance in changing English society and economy 1650–1750' in P. Abrams and E.A. Wrigley (eds), *Towns in Societies*, Cambridge UP, 1978, p. 229.

London was the greatest market, especially before the mid eighteenth century when its growth much outpaced a generally slow population increase, but other commercial and manufacturing towns as they grew also began to exercise a 'pervasive and far-reaching influence over local agricultural specialisation'. Northern farmers began to buy Scottish and Irish cattle to fatten for their growing markets. Large parts of Westmorland, Cumberland, Lancashire and parts of Yorkshire were given over to this trade. On the other side of the Pennines, Cheshire and Lancashire dairying, while still much concerned with London, found an additional swelling demand nearer to home. Arthur Young was so impressed with Bristol as a food market in 1769 that he excepted the area from his generalisation that food prices fell as the distance from London increased. All in all the England described by Defoe at the beginning of the eighteenth century is far from a 'traditional' economy dominated by self-sufficient peasant agriculture lubricated by marginally relevant local markets. A commercial ethos is unmistakable and, as a recent survey concludes, 'if a national market was not in existence by 1750, it was strongly emergent'.[14]

Good harvests and slow population growth in the first half of the eighteenth century made the period not only one in which the general population was better fed, but also one in which farmers faced low cereal prices. They were to some extent aided by official encouragement of exports and of gin distilling. The period was not one, however, in which agricultural innovation ceased, rather one in which it took a different form from periods of high prices. Dr Thirsk has pointed out that:

> Markets by the first half of the eighteenth-century had developed a prodigious appetite for agricultural produce that was highly varied in quality and price. It was to move in the century after 1750 towards satisfying demand of another kind; for quality and uniformity . . ..
> But until 1750 innovation multiplied individuality and the pace of this process was probably as rapid in the years 1640 to 1750 as at any time before or since.

She has stressed that while 'a multitude of farmers adhered to the ways of their forefathers', others responded to low cereal prices by growing different cash crops, some of which were aimed at the industrial rather than the food market. There was an increase in the output of hops, vegetables and dye-crops. Professor Jones, on the other hand, has pointed to the premium that falling prices place on

14. Chartres, 'The marketing of agricultural produce', *op. cit.*, p. 501.

efficiency and cost saving if profit levels are to be maintained, and also to the advantages convertible husbandry offers at such times. Not only do improved yields offer some compensation for lower prices, but the products of animal husbandry bring in alternative income. Hampshire chalkland farmers had the wool clip from the same sheep which improved their soil, while low bread prices, given the usual elasticities of food consumption, encouraged the wider consumption of meat. Farmers on the lighter soils did not much prosper in the agricultural depression of 1730 to 1750 and hardly thrived over the longer period of low prices in which it is contained. Even in Norfolk on the model Coke estates, rent arrears were equal to a third of gross rental in the 1730s and 1740s. They did, however, do markedly better than farmers in the Midlands. Here the open field system was still widespread and combined with heavy soils to lessen the capacity to adapt. Even so there was some tendency to put land unsuited for corn into permanent pasture, notably in Leicestershire. In the longer term the depression, through its marked impact on the number of farms, began the consolidation of holdings which was a basis for recovery after 1750.[15]

Before the mid eighteenth century the agrarian changes cumulating over a hundred years amounted to a 'quiet revolution'. The leading edge was a sufficient number of farmers in the parts of the country less remote from London or other urban centres responding to changing marketing opportunities. After 1750 the so-called agricultural revolution became much noisier. It entered the age of propaganda, even of polemic, and it acquired a force which brought a degree of social casualty to set against economic growth. Landowners became increasingly conscious of rising cereal prices and concerned to turn farmers' profits into higher rents. To do this they needed to find progressive tenants who would respond with efficient production and to ensure that these were leased farms of a sufficient size to employ improved methods profitably. Many also began to see the benefits of investing in the improvement of stock, soil and buildings, or at least in sharing the burden with their tenants. To these ends parliamentary enclosure was a major enabling process. E.L. Jones has remarked that it is difficult to discern much fresh agricultural innovation after 1750 except in stock breeding, and that the rate of improvement in productivity per acre slowed

15. Thirsk, 'Agricultural innovations and their diffusion' in Thirsk (ed.), *Agrarian History of England and Wales*, I, pp. 587–8; E.L. Jones, 'Agriculture and economic growth in England, 1650–1750: agricultural change', in Jones (ed.), *Agriculture and Economic Growth*, pp. 159–68.

down. Extra output came now from increasing the sown arable acreage, especially after 1793 when rocketing grain prices led to an extension of the arable at the expense of the pastoral in some areas, while in others, like the heavy clay lands, it allowed cereal producers to postpone a shift to pastoral farming. This cost some farmers dearly when cereal prices fell again after 1816.[16]

Much parliamentary enclosure after 1750 was concerned to enclose the commons and wastes. The area under cultivation increased over the war years from 1793 to 1815 to a remarkable extent for so short a time. Perhaps a third of the acres enclosed by parliamentary acts during the war was previously uncultivated, compared with a pre-war level of a fifth. If privately enclosed land is added to a million acres of untilled land also enclosed by act, perhaps 5 per cent of wartime cultivated area was a net addition to the stock of land in production. Extensive solutions to agricultural production are rarely unconnected with intensive ones, for many of the new acres in regions of the lighter chalks, limestones and sands yielded sufficient grain only when cultivated with new techniques. However haltingly and fitfully, the years from 1750 to 1815 were ones in which the methods already known to progressive farmers began to spread more widely. Meat prices generally held up well, and levels of output are unlikely to have fallen even if permanent pasture was ploughed for arable. More marginal soils repaid only those farm systems in which animals remained of fundamental importance. On the Hampshire Downs the extension of grain production was accompanied by an increase in store beef and mutton output. In short, the decline in pasture was offset by an increase in the number, weight and speed of fattening of beasts fed from the arable.[17]

In the second half of the eighteenth century the possibilities demonstrated by improving farmers combined with the incentive of rising prices and took off within a structure of land-holding and occupation which was at least propitious for their success. It is to that link between progressive farming and the English agrarian structure that we must now turn.

16. E.L. Jones, 'Agriculture, 1700–80', *op. cit.*, pp. 85–6.

17. G. Hueckel, 'Agriculture during industrialisation' in Floud and McCloskey, *Economic History of Britain*, pp. 184–5; M. Overton, 'Agricultural revolution? England, 1540–1850', *op. cit.*, pp. 1–4; A.H. John, 'Farming in wartime, 1793–1815' in E.L. Jones and G.E. Mingay (eds), *Land, Labour and Population in the Industrial Revolution*, Arnold, 1967, pp. 31, 37–8.

LANDLORDS AND IMPROVEMENT

The role of the larger landowners in forwarding agricultural development has been noted by historians of all persuasions. Edward Thompson, for example, has written of an important 'moment of transition' around 1750, when:

> more and more of the gentry (including the great aristocratic magnates) ceased to conceive of their function in passive terms (as rent collectors and as park keepers with a more or less stable revenue), but took up instead, a far more aggressive agrarian posture, both in their capacity as substantial farmers in their own right and in the stimulation of those improvements among their tenants upon which their hopes of an expanding income must be founded. A glance at that most remarkable of trade journals the *Annals of Agriculture*, in whose pages, noblemen, clergy and commons engage in discussion of the merits of marling, enclosure costs and stock-breeding, serves to impress upon one the profoundly capitalist style of thought of the class – zestfully acquisitive and meticulous in attention to accounting.[18]

The landed classes were politically dominant. Professor Perkin has maintained that only they could act politically as a class. They were parliament and their available instrument for enforcing agrarian change was parliamentary enclosure. Historians have become much more cautious in assessing the contribution made to overall agricultural growth by this last act of the long-running enclosure drama. This problem will be given detailed consideration below, but for the moment we can note both that it has been demonstrated by Dr Havinden that the open-field system was not incompatible with progressive farming, and that, given that so much land had already been enclosed by the beginning of the eighteenth century, let alone its mid-point, a large proportion of the extra output must have been coming from farms not affected by parliamentary enclosure.[19]

It is far from the case that the generality of landowners were strongly interested in agricultural development. More probably acted on an opportunity to increase rents than from a passionate interest in farming. At its peak the *Annals of Agriculture* sold only around 400 copies. The cynic might remark that this was perhaps just as well, for its propaganda for the four-course Norfolk rotation

18. E.P. Thompson, 'The peculiarities of the English' in *The Poverty of Theory*, Merlin, 1978, p. 44.
19. M.A. Havinden, 'Agricultural progress in open-field Oxfordshire'; for the chronology of enclosure, see J.R. Wordie, 'Chronology of English enclosure', but note the qualification offered by M.E. Turner, 'Parliamentary enclosures: gains and costs', pp. 5–6.

amounted to a polemic for the extension of a regional system to unsuitable areas. Many landlords lacked the energy, interest or inclination to practise or project new methods, while still others were strongly constrained by the nature of the tenancies on their estates from any attempt to substitute progressive for backward farmers. The first advantage of enclosing was not so much that it was a precondition for improved methods, but that it called in existing agreements and enabled the landowner to consolidate and re-let. Historians have sometimes been a little too eager to view increased rent rolls following enclosure as an evident demonstration of the benefits of improvement. In the shorter term they rather reflected the grasping of opportunity.[20]

A significant proportion of estate owners were absentees. The quality of farming on their lands depended on their being able to entrust management to an efficient agent. Although, as Professor Mingay has shown, this was assisted in the second half of the century by the emergence of a class of professional land stewards, the supply was not infinite.[21] Neither was that of good tenants, although improving prospects of profit after the earlier period of depression obviously increased the willingness of good farmers to take on larger farms at higher rents. The alternative suggested by Arthur Young was to increase rents to existing holders and force them to become good farmers.

> Of so little encouragement to them is the lowness of their rents, that many large tracts of land that yielded good crops of corn within thirty years are now overrun with whins, brakes and other trumpery. . . . If I be demanded how such ill courses are to be stopped, I answer, Raise their rents. First with moderation, and if that does not bring forth industry, double them.[22]

Young himself was a failure as a practical farmer! This advice, given in 1771, is indicative of the changed atmosphere once cereal prices began to rise. Earlier in the century increasing rents would have resulted in abandoned farms impossible to re-let. In 1733 the agent

20. Beckett, *Aristocracy in England*, Ch. 5, 'The aristocracy and the Agricultural Revolution', considers all aspects. P.K. O'Brien, 'Quelle a été exactement la contribution de l'aristocratie britannique au progrès de l'agriculture entre 1688 et 1789?', *Annales ESC*, Nov–Dec 1987, 6, pp. 1391–409, is the most searching critique of traditional views.

21. See Mingay, 'Eighteenth-century land steward' in Jones and Mingay (eds), *Land, Labour and Population*, pp. 3–27; but for a more serious view of the problems of absenteeism, see O'Brien, 'Quelle a été exactement la contribution', *op. cit.*, pp. 1395–6.

22. A. Young, *Northern Tour*, II, Strahan, 1772, pp. 80–3.

on the Earl of Uxbridge's Nottinghamshire estates could persuade some tenants to continue only by promising to reduce their rents if prices did not improve. After the cattle plague hit Lancashire in 1750 a steward advised that several tenants now unable to pay their rents should nevertheless be kept on, otherwise 'their farms must lie to the crows'. Even on the celebrated Coke estates in Norfolk, arrears at this time amounted to a third of the gross rental. 'More experiments, more discoveries, and more general good sense [were] displayed in the way of agriculture than in a hundred preceding ones', was Young's hyperbolic comment in 1770 on the preceding decade. It was, of course, monstrously unfair to the progress of the post-Restoration era, but remains a fitting comment on the more rapid and wider diffusion of new methods when prices were buoyant and profits appreciable.[23]

An emerging feature of English agriculture was the sharing of investment by landowner and tenant. Many landowners lacked the capital to invest in improving farms in the hope of higher rents. Others had no inclination to dispense their estate revenues in that way. Just what was the landlord's contribution to agricultural investment? To that central question agrarian historians have been able as yet to offer only incomplete answers. It is not an easy area to research. Few surviving estate records employed a method of accounting sufficiently sophisticated for capital investment in farming to be distinguished from other estate outlays, and the form under which landlords did finance improvements was often by allowing rent reductions in recognition of capital improvements carried out by tenants.

Especially after mid century an increasing share of the value of the agricultural product was being transferred to the landlords as rents having largely broken free from the long undervaluation imposed by customary forms of tenure in some regions, began to increase at a rate comfortably in step with rising prices. It was a process which had long been under way, although the inability of landlords to find tenants willing to pay higher rents through the years of the depression had hidden a power which the return of

---

23. Clay, 'Landlords and estate management in England' in Thirsk (ed.), *Agrarian History of England and Wales*, part 1, pp. 211, 230–1; Chambers and Mingay, *Agricultural Revolution*, p. 41. For more information on low rents in this period, see Mingay, 'The Agricultural Depression, 1730–50' in E.M. Carus Wilson (ed.), *Essays in Economic History*, II, Arnold, 1962, pp. 310–15, but see the important reassessment stressing regional variations by Beckett, 'Regional variation and the agricultural depression, 1730–50', *Econ. H.R.*, XXXV, 1, 1982, pp. 35–51; quoted in A. Toynbee, *The Industrial Revolution*, Longman, 1908 edn, p. 20.

high cereal prices once again released. Parliamentary enclosure was a culminating rather than an initiating process in this respect. But perhaps historians have too readily accepted that a shift in favour of the landowners was automatically favourable for the process of capital accumulation. Adam Smith was only one of the contemporary economists who doubted this. Contemporaries were well enough aware of the competing claims on the purses of landowners. Many a hard-working tenant farmer must have cast a disgruntled eye at the diversion of the rent he had created into country houses, libraries, grand tours or parks, or even its removal to support an extravagant urban life-style or political career. Thomas Coke, later Earl of Leicester, was exceptional even for progressive Norfolk in ploughing back 18 per cent of his gross rental into his estates in the 1790s as he embarked on more than a score of building and improving projects. Those estates had been absorbing 8 per cent of gross rental as far back as 1722–59. In East Anglia Holderness estimated that landlords' capital investment did not fall below 7 per cent of rentals between 1750 and 1870, on a general upward trend with peaks in 1776–85 and 1806–30. There were, however, special reasons in the agricultural practice of that region due to an unusually large expenditure on buildings. In general the 5 per cent level prevailing in Lincolnshire in the 1780s was hardly ever exceeded (except in enclosing) and very often not reached, even after 1750. Between 1 and 5 per cent of gross rents were returned by the Duke of Kingston to his Nottinghamshire estates, and the Earl of Darlington's outlay on repairs was less than 1 per cent. Others spent on the home estate farms but neglected more distant holdings. Counties like Cumberland, with many absentee landlords, suffered in this respect. In his farming manual of 1775 Nathaniel Kent stated that an estate in good repair could be kept so for an expenditure of 7 per cent of rental in the case of large farms and 10 or 11 per cent for smaller ones (because of the higher relative cost of buildings). The evidence might therefore seem to indicate a degree of under-investment or even disinvestment in some cases, but this does not necessarily follow.[24]

Agricultural investment still provided almost a quarter of gross domestic capital formation in 1815 – much below the 37.5 per cent it had provided in 1770 but close to the 27 per cent in 1790–3. So, despite the special needs of the war and the growth of manufacturing,

24. Clay, 'Landlords and estate management in England', *op. cit.*, p. 249; Holderness, 'Landlords and capital formation in East Anglia 1750–1870', *Econ. H.R.*, XXV, 3, 1972, pp. 442–6; Beckett, *Aristocracy in England*, pp. 178–9.

agriculture maintained its relative share of total investment throughout the French wars.[25] In absolute terms investment in agriculture had probably increased by three times over its 1780 level by the 1810s. Expressed as a percentage of gross rentals, Feinstein suggests the pattern shown in Table 3.2.

Table 3.2 Investment in agriculture as a percentage of gross rentals

1761–70	6	1791–1800	11
1771–80	7	1801–10	16
1781–91	8		

Source: Based on Feinstein in M.M. Postan and P. Mathias (eds), *Cambridge Economic History of Europe*. Vol. 7 *The Industrial Economies. Part I: Britain, France, Germany and Scandinavia*, Cambridge, 1982, p. 49.

The question is, how much of this investment effort was supplied by the landlords and how much by their tenant farmers? It is impossible to know with any certainty. The distinction of the landlord supplying fixed capital (buildings, fences, drainage, etc.) and the tenant the working capital (stock, seed and fertiliser) was seldom clear. In practice tenants took a large and increasing share of investment in building and improvements such as drainage – in some cases, it was suggested, to an extent not justified by the security of their tenure. Relative investment shares changed over time. Holderness suggests that even in East Anglia the landlords' share fell during the war years 1793–1815: 'In general the war years appear as a period in which farmers were required to take more initiatives, for while rent rolls were inflated, outgoings, except on enclosure, were kept to a minimum.'[26] Landlords in general were more likely to take a greater share in times of low prices like the 1730s and 1740s in order to attract and retain tenants, by renovating or replacing buildings. In times of high prices they could leave more of the burden to their tenants.

Averages over long periods are, however, more than usually distorting in the assessment of the contribution of landlords to the capital requirements of 'improved' agriculture. In the history of individual estates a critical moment of landlord investment came with

25. C.W. Feinstein, 'Capital formation in Great Britain' in P. Mathias and M.M. Postan (eds), *Cambridge Economic History of Europe*, vol. VII, *The Industrial Economies: Capital, Labour, and Enterprise*, I, 1978, pp. 31, 48–9.
26. Holderness, 'Landlords and capital formation', *op. cit.*, p. 440.

enclosure, especially in its parliamentary form after 1740. Although smaller landowners contributed their share, the major input came from the estate owners. Here was a concentrated burst of expenditure which cannot be sensibly expressed in terms of percentages of gross rentals, for it most often involved the bringing in of other resources from outside, or realised from the sale of more distant holdings.

Piecemeal and difficult evidence can support only tentative conclusions. All in all the contribution of the landed classes to agricultural investment over the 'vital century' cannot be dismissed as negligible. However, it is not unequivocally clear that the economic, political and legal developments which increased their share of the rising agricultural product particularly advantaged the economy in terms of the level and facilitating of agrarian investment. Judgement depends on what is considered the alternative. Counterfactually we may be able to construct a model in which the middling land-holders, the celebrated yeomen, increased their share of the cultivated acreage and, imbued with sterling qualities and eschewing conspicuous consumption, produced a different capitalist outcome in which the proportion of the value created by farming returned to the soil was significantly higher. That is speculative. That the different political systems, land-holding patterns and legal contexts of other European countries did not produce so significant an agricultural development before 1815 is history.

Perhaps the large proprietors deserve their traditional presentation more as the pioneers and promoters of agricultural improvement than as investors. There was little pioneering to be done in the eighteenth century, for there was little in the way of novelty. Assisting diffusion was the area in which landlords could make a signif-icant contribution. Agricultural writers stressed the demonstration effect of the well-run estate with a progressive home farm at its centre. Dr Holderness is probably justified in his view of the influence of Norfolk's great improving family, the Cokes, at a peak of landlord interest in 1776–85: 'When the Cokes had no shortage of applicants for their farms the message was clear for their neighbours.'[27] The retired statesman Lord Rockingham returned to his West Riding estate and found there a great opportunity for using energies displaced from politics.

> It was disgusting to him to view so vast a property cultivated in so slovenly a manner. Large tracts of land, both grass and arable yielded

27. *Ibid.*, p. 440.

but a trifling profit, for want of draining. The pastures and meadows were laid down in ridge and furrow, a practice highly destructive of profit and detestable to the eye. The culture of turnips was become common, but without hoeing, so that the year of fallow was the most capital one of slovenliness and bad husbandry.[28]

The miracle of transformation he wrought earned him a hymn of praise from Arthur Young, but the ex-Prime Minister was hardly the typical northern aristocrat, let alone representative of the local squirearchy. The lords and gentry of Somerset, south Lincolnshire or Devon, if the reports to the Board of Agriculture are to be believed, were not setting much by way of example either to their tenants or to their neighbours. The Duke of Somerset was an improver in Sussex, but not on his Cumbrian estate. Essentially the purpose of the home farm was to supply the household, and, according to a recent historian of the aristocracy, it was, celebrated examples apart, 'a dubious means of leading by example'. Indeed, in so far as exemplary farming was an important part of the diffusion of improved practice, the active role was more likely to have been taken by larger tenants, whose methods landlords or their agents might *then* expect others to follow. These farmers in cases where the landowners were meeting fixed capital requirements could, after all, devote their own capital to improved stock and seed. So far as the landowners were concerned it seems reasonable to expect a more active concern with farming methods from the smaller country gentlemen, who did tend to manage their own estates and commonly farmed some of their own land for profit rather than as a house-supplying home farm. A great proprietor need not have been a muddy-booted practitioner to have played a part in the emergence of an atmosphere conducive to agricultural progress. Promotional endeavour could take other forms. Landlord paternalism in the sponsoring and support of local shows and societies was not unimportant, while at the national level, when the Board of Agriculture was set up in 1793 its thirty places for ordinary members were all filled by regularly attending aristocrats.[29]

Over the substantial part of agrarian England where the large landlords had broken free from the restrictions of customary tenures and could determine lease length and conditions as well as rent levels, one obvious way of improving the farming practices of tenants was to insert 'husbandry clauses' in leases requiring that certain farming practices be followed and disbarring others. In

28. Young, *Northern Tour*, I, p. 245.
29. Beckett, *Aristocracy in England*, pp. 161–3, 165–7, 204–5.

general, however, agricultural historians seem to agree that surprisingly little use was made of the improving lease. The practices set out in leases were essentially conservative, literally so in soil terms, designed more to prevent tenants racking their farms, especially by taking too many corn crops, than to require novel husbandry practices from them – although in the case of Devon at least, there does seem a connection between landlords freeing themselves from older forms of tenancy and the introduction of improving leases. The rarity of specific 'improving' clauses in leases does not, however, mean that landlords and their agents did not consider the form of leases important in other respects. The matter of length was much debated, and in general improvers favoured longer leases. Tenancies-at-will or from year to year offered the advantages of readily increasing rents in times of rising prices, which explains a resurgence in their popularity over the French war years. They also allowed for the speedy removal of bad farmers and by replacing holdings more often in landlords' hands removed an impediment towards the consolidation of farms into larger units. However, they did not encourage the tenant's best efforts or input. When the historian Edward Gibbon granted a thirty-year lease on his Hampshire estate in 1772, he saw it as 'giving the tenant a durable interest to use my land like his own'.[30]

It has become almost axiomatic that improved efficiency and greater proportionate output derived from increasing farm size. Given that the landlord's ideal was the leasing of a large farm to a good tenant, can it be shown that the concentration of so much of English farmland into the hands of large proprietors favoured a reorganisation into larger holdings? Unfortunately the tendency towards an increase in farm size is one more easily asserted than measured. Although only about 15–20 per cent of the farmed acreage of England was left to owner-occupiers by 1790, it is they rather than the tenant farmers who have absorbed the attention of historians anxious to trace the 'disappearance of the peasantry' or the 'decline of the yeoman'. Tentative statements are made – 'in the course of time, there was some tendency for smaller tenancies to be amalgamated in the hands of large farmers' – or qualified views expressed that whereas there was, considering the country as a whole, a general increase in average farm size from 1720 to 1830, it

30. R. Stanes, 'Landlord and tenant and husbandry covenants in eighteenth-century Devon' in W.E. Minchinton (ed.), *Agricultural Improvement: Medieval and Modern*, Exeter UP, pp. 41–64; Chambers and Mingay, *Agricultural Revolution*, pp. 46–8; Clay, 'Landlords and estate management in England', *op. cit.*, pp. 217–18, 228–9.

was insufficient to decrease the numerical dominance of smaller farms by much. Practice varied from estate to estate and the only really clear trend is that larger farms came to occupy a much greater share of acreage in the south and in East Anglia than in the north and west.[31]

Whatever the intrinsic advantages of increasing farm sizes, there were many countervailing pressures. In the depressed years 1730–50 there was hardly a sufficient supply of fit and willing tenants to justify substantial reorganisation of estate arrangements. Even if a commercial ethos was increasingly determining landlord attitudes, social obligation was still intrinsic to the landlord's local standing and position. It was all very well for Arthur Young to scorn those who valued their popularity above an extra five shillings an acre, but there were strong inhibitions in the way of turning out a family who had lived on an estate for generations. Although by the mid eighteenth century much the greater part of English agricultural land was let for rack rents to tenants on lease or at will (and this had been overwhelmingly the case in the south, east and Midlands for some time past), in the west and north forms of customary tenure giving security at near-fixed rents to tenants who could, for practical purposes, regard their holdings as inheritable were still widespread. In the south-west when life-leases expired on other than small holdings, they were much less likely to be renewed after 1750. In Cumberland and Westmorland, however, customary copyhold tenures remained predominant and seem to have prevented some landlords from either increasing their share of the increasing profits of farming through raising rents, or from reordering their lettings. In any event, small farmers usually paid a higher rent per acre, and in some forms of farming, for example in the dairy farming districts of the south and north-west where families could usually meet labour needs and equipment costs were low, they were not noticeably disadvantaged. The greatest opportunity for farm consolidation and enlargement came, of course, with enclosure, but even here the evidence is not unequivocal for in some counties, such as Nottinghamshire, the most rapid increase in average farm size seems to have occurred in the early eighteenth century prior to enclosure.[32]

31. See, for example, Chambers and Mingay, *Agricultural Revolution*, pp. 92–3. Outhwaite has pointed out the inconclusive regional evidence on farm size in the *Agrarian History of England and Wales* ('English agricultural efficiency', p. 207).

32. For tenures, see Clay, 'Landlords and estate management in England', *op. cit.*, pp. 199–214; Beckett, *Aristocracy in England*, pp. 183–9. For the persistence of customary tenancies in Cumberland and Westmorland, see C.E. Searle, 'Custom, class conflict and agrarian capitalism: the Cumbrian customary economy in the eighteenth century', *Past and Present*, 110, 1986, pp. 106–33.

Dr Wordie has provided us with a detailed reconstruction of the changing pattern of tenant holdings on the Leveson-Gower estates which were located in Staffordshire, Shropshire and the North Riding. These were already enclosed and so the process of consolidation was operating independently of enclosure.

Table 3.3 Tenant holdings on the Leveson-Gower estates

Acres:	0–20 %	20–100 %	100–200 %	200+ %	Av. size of farms 20 acres+
1714–20	6.3	46.1	28.8	18.8	82.9
1759–79	6.2	26.6	35.0	32.2	103.5
1807–13	6.5	16.7	25.1	51.7	139.0

Source: J.R. Wordie, 'Social change on the Leveson-Gower estates, 1714–1832'. *Econ. H.R.*, XXVII, 1974, p. 596.

These percentages reveal a steady rise in the popularity of lettings of 200 to 400 acres, bringing about a significant increase in the mean size of farms over 20 acres. Dr Wordie points out that although the share of very small holdings (less than 20 acres) did not decline, those who occupied them can hardly be considered proper farmers. For the most part their land simply supplemented earnings from industrial employment. There does seem to have been a marked decline in the groups who could be properly described as small farmers. Confusion over terminology has perhaps tended to exaggerate the numbers of very small farmers persisting throughout the eighteenth and into the nineteenth centuries. Professor Pounds has shown, for example, that by the mid eighteenth century those who occupied the smaller holdings on Cornish estates depended for the most part on wage labour on those same estates.[33]

To Arthur Young, 'Great farms' were the 'soul of Norfolk culture' and their rise in the eastern and southern arable districts, alongside the survival of smaller farms, both tenanted and owner-occupied in the pastoral districts, imparted a pattern to English farming which has persisted into the twentieth century. The observation by a reporter on Wiltshire agriculture in the 1790s that small farmers had declined rapidly on the corn–sheep chalklands but still

33. Wordie, 'Social change on the Leveson-Gower estates', p. 604 for his conclusion; Pounds, 'Barton farming', *op. cit.*, p. 74.

predominated in the dairying districts would have been as true a hundred or more years later. What happened to small farmers in the process of parliamentary enclosure will be considered in detail below, but generally speaking there is as yet little evidence that a trend towards larger farms was much accelerated through a deliberate change in letting practice on the part of a large number of landowners.

There remains one area in which the aristocracy and better-off gentry were perhaps better placed to foster improvement through an active involvement than were most working farmers. This is livestock improvement, which needed large investment and had a lengthy gestation period before it was repaid. The improvement of horses had been an interest of the upper classes well before 1700. Those of their rank who turned to the breeding of cattle and sheep in the eighteenth century could pursue something as a business activity which had much of the aura of a gentleman's hobby, and the prestige attached to success is confirmed by the number of gentlemen who had the likes of Stubbs and his school preserve the imposing images of their favourite beasts in oil paint.[34]

As with the other vaunted agricultural pioneers, the Leicestershire squire Robert Bakewell attracted an attention which perhaps exceeded his achievement. He was much in the public eye – after all, he was a professional breeder who, unlike a grazier concerned to lift the quality of his stock, needed to be noticed. He began his activities in 1745 and drew from earlier stock improvements made by Midland breeders, although we know little detail of stock breeding before his time. There were regionally predominant types of cattle – hardy black longhorns in the west; red and brown middle and short horns in the south, east and Midlands; and the dun-coloured dairy cattle of East Anglia – but generally speaking the fattening and dairying areas both contained mixed types. Sheep too followed a regional typing, but two main types were significant; the long-fleeced sheep of the chalk and limestone downs of Lincoln, Leicester, Kent and the Cotswolds contrasted with the short- and middle-wool varieties of the south-west, south and Midlands. In sheep raising the better wools are produced by the less well-fed sheep. Fodder feeding when it was introduced worsened the fleece while it increased the mutton. Unlike the enclosures of an earlier era, sheep farmers as the eighteenth century developed increasingly responded to the food market. They wanted heavy quick-fattening

34. Thirsk, 'Agricultural innovations and their diffusion' in Thirsk (ed.), *Agrarian History of England and Wales*, p. 578.

beasts, as did the graziers of beef cattle. At the beginning of the eighteenth century fat stock put on weight slowly, a bullock taking around four years to be ready for the market. By way of an illustration of the targets of the stock improvers, Bakewell's New Leicester sheep were literally reshaped to produce meat quickly and in quantity.[35] Arthur Young, describing him in 1771 as 'famous throughout the kingdom' for breeding cattle 'as fat as bears', set down the principles he followed.

> the old notion was, that where you had much and large bones, there was plenty of room to lay flesh on; and accordingly the graziers were eager to buy the largest boned cattle. This whole system Mr Bakewell has proved to be an utter mistake. He asserts, the smaller the bones, the truer will be the make of the beast – the quicker she will fat – and her weight, we may easily conceive, will have a larger proportion of valuable meat; *flesh* not *bone* is the butcher's object. The shape which should be the criterion of a cow, a bull, or an ox, and also of a sheep, is that of a hogshead, or a firkin; truly circular with small and as short legs as possible; upon the principle that the value lies in the barrel, not in the legs.[36]

His New Longhorn cattle fattened well from a modest fodder input but gave poor milk and, disastrously from his point of view, had low fecundity. The mutton from the New Leicesters was too fat for the prime market. John Ellman, a Sussex breeder of the 1780s, had more success in producing a breed of sheep which gave good mutton and usable wool, while at the same time the Colling brothers developed the short horn into a breed useful for meat and milk, showing Bakewell to have taken a wrong turning with his obsession with long horns. Bakewell was a pioneer – not a very successful one in terms of lasting influence – turned by Arthur Young and his ilk into an icon, but what he symbolised was significant. There were, of course, backward regions. Improved animal husbandry diffused no more rapidly than did improved arable husbandry, but the improved size and shape of English farm animals and above all the improved speed with which they converted fodder into meat had become by 1800 a major feature of agricultural development.

---

35. Breeding improvements are thoroughly and critically assessed in Chambers and Mingay, *Agricultural Revolution*, pp. 65–9.

36. Young, *Farmer's Tour through the East of England*, Strahan, 1771, pp. 110ff.

PARLIAMENTARY ENCLOSURE

Leaving fuller consideration of the economic and social effects of the phase of parliamentary enclosure from the mid eighteenth century to 1815 to the end of this chapter does not now seem as surprising as it would have done twenty years ago. Till then practically every discussion of the so-called 'agricultural revolution' centred on the enclosure movement, making it causal in any discussion of improved farming methods and the increased output of cereals and animal products. It would also have been made crucial in explaining the decline of the small farmer, the demise of the yeomanry, the replacement of the peasantry by a class of landless labourers and the displacement of many of the latter to form the first industrial proletariat. To many historians from Karl Marx on, enclosing by act of parliament was a form of class expropriation of the land, an exercise of the class power of the landowners' parliament against the interests of the ordinary people of the countryside. Over recent years parliamentary enclosure has been reassessed from many angles. There is a tendency now to see it as a culminating phase in a long process of social and economic change in English agriculture – as much the outcome as the producer of its particular ownership and occupation structure – while the catalogue of 'social evils' for which it was held responsible by generations of social historians following the Hammonds' influential book of 1911, *The Village Labourer*, has been re-examined and revised.

Before its consequences can be properly discussed, it is necessary to gain some idea of the temporal and spatial incidence of parliamentary enclosure, the process of implementing it and the motives of those who initiated or supported it. Professor Plumb defined enclosure as:

> the replacement of two or three large open fields around a village, whose strips were owned individually, but whose crops and stock were controlled by the community of owners (according to ancient rights and practices), by smaller individually owned fields whose cropping and stocking could be controlled by the owner.[37]

More recently a leading scholar has offered this fuller definition.

> [it] mainly refers to that land reform which transformed a traditional method of agriculture under systems of co-operation and communally administered holdings, usually in the large fields which were devoid of physical territorial boundaries into a system of agricultural holding in

37. J.H. Plumb, *England in the Eighteenth Century*, Penguin, 1950, p. 18 (footnote).

severality by separating with physical boundaries one person's land from that of his neighbours. This was then the disintegration and reformation of the open fields into individual ownership. Inter alia enclosure registered specific ownership, adjudicated on shared ownership (for example by identifying and separating common rights). Enclosure also meant the subdivision of areas of commons, heaths, moors, fens and wastes into separate landholdings and again involved the abandonment of obligations, privileges and rights.[38]

In short, enclosure affected the ways in which people farmed and how and in what amount they held land, redefined the relationship between property law and customary rights and changed the very face of the countryside. 'New roads were planned, staked out and made: the line of some older lanes was discontinued. Many miles of new hedges were planned and planted . . . The drainage of the parishes was improved by the cutting of new public drains.'[39] Such changes can be best illustrated by 'before and after' maps of an actual enclosure. Figures 3.2 and 3.3 show the outcome in the village of East Halton on the south side of the Humber Estuary which was enclosed by act in 1801. Prior to enclosure, apart from a block of old enclosures around the village itself, the parish was farmed in two large open fields, with grazing provided by the common and meadowland of the Carrs, Langmere and the Marsh. After enclosure the commons and the open fields alike were divided into fenced fields of varying size and made over to fifty-seven individual owners in allocations ranging from the 500 acres received by the lady of the manor (Harriet Ann Bonell) to the plots of less than an acre received by the bottom five allottees. New roads traversed the parish and six new drains improved the condition of its soil.

The process by which this transformation was accomplished will be examined below, but first we need to consider the chronology of parliamentary enclosure. J.L. Wordie has suggested that the eighteenth century has been given too much prominence in the long history of enclosure and that as much, possibly more, enclosure had taken place in the seventeenth century. Pointing out that almost half of England's farmland had either never been open field or had been enclosed by 1600, he allocates percentage shares for the post-1600 era.

38. Turner, *Enclosures in Britain*, p. 11.
39. R.C. Russell, *The Enclosures of East Halton, 1801–1804 and North Kelsey, 1813–1840*, North Lindsey, WEA, 1964, p. 3.

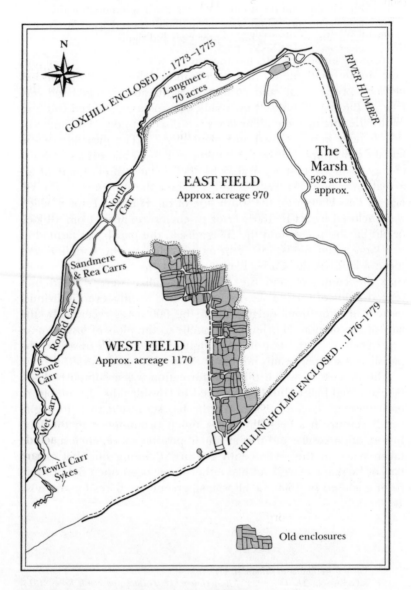

Figure 3.2 East Halton 1801: before enclosure

Table 3.4 Proportion of land enclosed, per cent

1600–1699	24
1700–1799	13
1800–1914	11.4

Source: J.R. Wordie, 'Chronology of English enclosure, 1500–1914', *Econ. H.R.*, XXXVI, 1983, p. 502.

However, as Dr Turner has pointed out, Wordie attributes all enclosures which cannot be otherwise definitely attributed to the seventeenth century, when it would seem as likely that the residual represents private agreements which were spread over more than a century. More seriously, his periodisation is very unhelpful for it splits a major phase of the enclosure movement (that of 1793 to 1815) over two centuries. It is just possible that almost a quarter of England was enclosed in the course of the seventeenth century, but it is certain that 18 per cent of it was enclosed by act of parliament in two bursts of activity, the 1760s and 1770s and the French war years from 1793 to 1815 (see Figure 3.4).

Eric Kerridge considered that only about a quarter of England and Wales remained to be enclosed after 1700. While this and similar estimates are important in indicating that parliamentary enclosure was only one phase in a 500-year process, they also cast doubt on some historians' suggestions that enclosure by private agreement continued to be important throughout the eighteenth century. McCloskey, for example, argued that the some 5,000 acts (in fact the latest count is 5,250) were accompanied by an *equal* number of private enclosures, while Chambers and Mingay thought these were perhaps half as many in number. Even this latter more modest position seems high if we accept that three-quarters of the land was enclosed by 1700 and that to our *knowledge* around one-fifth of it was subsequently enclosed by act. It is not possible to avoid concluding that eighteenth-century enclosure was overwhelmingly parliamentary in form and greatly concentrated into the period after 1750.[40]

Geographical concentration was equally marked (Figure 3.5). The south-west, the border counties and the south-east were hardly affected by enclosure in the eighteenth century. By contrast, the traditional open-field areas in the south and east Midlands, notably Oxfordshire, Northamptonshire and Cambridgeshire, were very

40. Wordie, 'Chronology of English enclosure', p. 502; Turner, 'Parliamentary enclosures: gains and costs', p. 6.

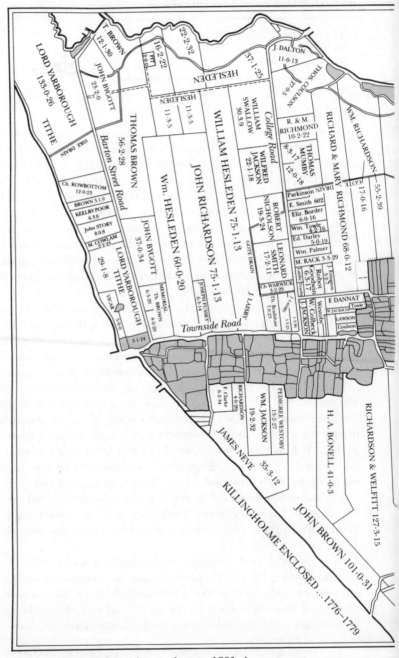

Figure 3.3 East Halton after enclosure, 1801–4

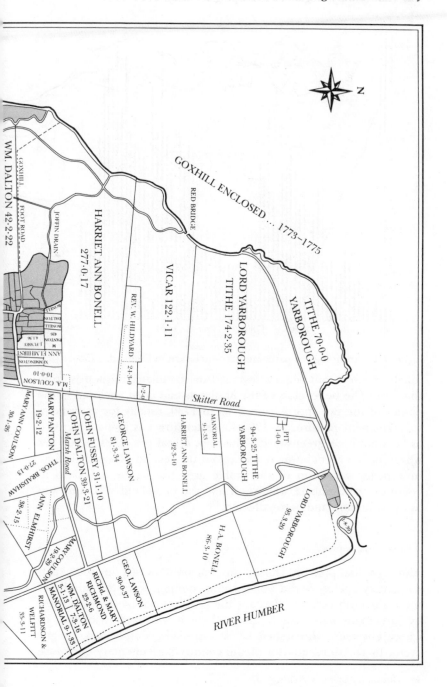

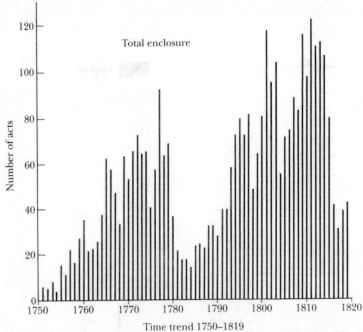

Figure 3.4 Chronology of parliamentary enclosure in England, 1750–1819

much affected, but impact lessened as it radiated outwards from this core. The heavy clays of the Midlands had been enclosed in the earlier of the two spurts from 1760 to 1780, usually for conversion to permanent pasture. By 1790 Leicestershire was being described as 'a continuous greensward'. The high cereal prices, especially for wheat, of the French war years explain the second phase. This time in a major extension of the arable area the lighter-soil areas in counties like Cumbria, which still had the open-field system as well as the common land, were affected.[41]

The enclosure process

Although Radipole in Dorset was enclosed by act in 1604, parliamentary enclosure did not become common until the middle of the eighteenth century. Perhaps the parishes not by then enclosed by agreement were largely those where it was hard to obtain, or where enclosure threatened to be especially complicated. In any event, by the third quarter of the century parliamentary enclosure

41. Turner, *Enclosures in Britain*, p. 33.

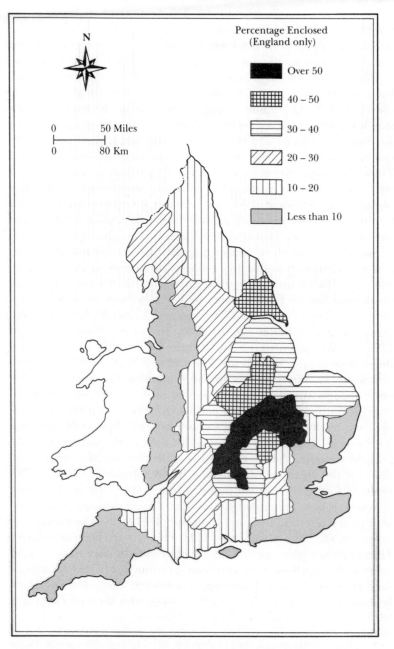

Figure 3.5 Density of parliamentary enclosure in England

had become so frequent that it can no longer have been considered in any way an exceptional recourse. The keynote of enclosing by act was that it could proceed even if a majority of land-holders in the parish did not seek it. As the Hammonds put it: 'suffrages were not counted but weighed', for it needed a two-thirds majority of the acreage, not of the land-holders. It is not difficult to see how this led a succession of social historians from Marx through the Hammonds to E.P. Thompson to the verdict that parliamentary enclosure was a form of 'class robbery', even if it was 'played according to fair rules of property and law laid down by a parliament of property owners and lawyers'. It is, after all, a reasonable position to adopt. Those who made the enclosures made up parliament and made the laws. This certainly makes the enclosure movement during this phase a class offensive. Whether it makes it 'robbery' depends on whether the outcome was that smaller men, landed or landless, lost land and/or rights. That is something to be considered below.[42]

Since the required two-thirds majority was of acres not of owners, it was sometimes possible for a single landowner to start the process. The Hammonds have given the examples of Laxton enclosed on the petition of Lord Carbery in 1772, Ashbury in Berkshire on petition of Lord Craven in 1770, Tilsworth in Bedfordshire on petition of Charles Chester Esq. in 1767, and others from Nylands in 1790 and Westcote in 1765. In several other examples the vicar was the only petitioner besides the lord of the manor. In villages where ownership was more widely spread, including the very many that were oligopolistic in their landowning structure, those seeking to enclose first met to draw up a petition to submit to parliament and decided on the names of the Commissioners who would carry out the process. This was a fairly lengthy task, as the act when it developed from the bill needed to contain very detailed provisions. That for the village of Messingham in Lincolnshire passed in 1798 takes up forty-eight printed foolscap pages. Once the act had been awarded, action moved to the locality. First a detailed survey and plan of the affected area had to be supplied to the Commissioners named in the act – a surveyor would already have been appointed. Then, within a given period all people claiming ownership of land and/or the possession of common grazing rights had to submit their claims in writing. These were considered and evidence in support of them heard by the Commissioners, who then proceeded to

---

42. J.L. and B. Hammond, *Village Labourer*, p. 19; Thompson, *Making of the English Working Class*, pp. 237–8.

value those that had been accepted. They had then to plan the area's roads, drains and land allocations and supervise the fencing of the new plots, which were intended to equal in value the former strips and rights of common. As the process continued the Commissioners assessed the 'public' costs of the work being done, including their own fees and those of the surveyor. Except for the tithe owners who had to bear none of the costs in return for their compensatory allocation, these were raised by levying a rate. When the process was complete a document known as the Enclosure Award was drawn up to summarise the outcome in plan and in writing.[43]

'It may be taken for granted, that the first mover to an inclosure is private interest, rather than public spirit,' wrote William Marshall in 1788.[44] It may be equally taken for granted that 'private interest' was well favoured by the process of parliamentary enclosure. Up to 1774 it was not even necessary for initiators to advertise their intent of seeking a bill, opponents therefore getting little time to prepare an opposing case. Presenting a counter-petition was in any case beyond the means and capabilities of many small owners of land or common rights, as was attendance to give evidence during the committee stage. Nor was it easy for the possibly illiterate poorer people to submit their claims properly in writing to the Commissioners. It was a situation that Young recognised in 1770, a time when he was still a staunch supporter of and propagandist for parliamentary enclosure.

> The small proprietor whose property in the township is perhaps his all, has little or no weight in regulating the clauses of the Act of Parliament, has seldom if ever an opportunity of putting a single one in the Bill favourable to his rights, and has as little influence in the choice of commissioners.[45]

Six out of seven enclosure bills presented between 1715 and 1775 passed into law. Of seventy-two bills which were counter-petitioned, twenty-two failed. While this indicates that *if* a counter-petition could be organised it had a one in three chance of success, in fact many people were not opposed to enclosure in general but objected to particular clauses, for example tithe owners who considered that plates upon which their ill-deserved land allotments

43. Hammonds, *Village Labourer*, p. 35 (footnote 1); R.C. Russell, 'The enclosures of Bottesford and Yaddlethorpe, 1794–7, Messingham, 1798–1804, and Ashby, 1801–1809', *Journal of the Scunthorpe Museum Society*, **1**, 1964, p. 25.
44. William Marshall, *The Rural Economy of Yorkshire*, T. Cadell, 1788, Vol. I, pp. 97–100 describing the Vale of Pickering.
45. Young, *Northern Tour*, I, p. 222.

were to be served were not silver enough. In any case, in allowing a counter-petition parliament was not usually forbidding the enclosure but delaying it for a subsequent resubmission. The amount of undue influence the seekers of an enclosure could bring to bear has been indicated by Dr Martin's work on Warwickshire which shows that in at least half of enclosures from 1730 to 1779 there was a personal connection between the leading petitioners and at least one member of the committee which sat on the bill. As Dr Turner has pointed out, the evidence before the Select Committee of 1800 which preceded the General Enclosure Act of 1801 makes it clear that passage through parliament was not much of a problem once the petitioners had overcome the greater difficulty of securing the support of the necessary 75–80 per cent of the landownership, and here they were undoubtedly assisted by the general fear among the smaller owners and commoners of antagonising the local power of the landed classes.[46]

Few would now go so far as the Hammonds in accusing the Commissioners of being interested, favouring the large owners and inherently indifferent to the claims of the poor. The ink was hardly dry on the pages of *The Village Labourer* before E.C. Gonner began a salvage of the reputation of the Commissioners which was carried on over the years by W.E. Tate: 'the work appears to have been honestly, if not always well done, and to have been marked by a rough and ready fairness'.[47] The Commissioners were, of course, bound by the clauses of the act and had to recognise legal title. But the matter is not that easily settled. Consider these quotations from the standard study of the agricultural revolution by Professors Chambers and Mingay.

> The legal owners of common rights were always compensated by the commissioners with an allotment of land. The occupiers of *common right cottages, it should be noticed, who enjoyed common rights by virtue of their tenancy* of the cottage, received no compensation because they were not, of course, the owners of the rights. This was a perfectly proper distinction between owner and tenant, and involved no fraud or disregard for cottagers on the part of the commissioners.

46. I interpret these figures rather differently from G.E. Mingay in his introduction to the 1978 edition of *The Village Labourer*, p. xxiii. See J.M. Martin, 'Members of Parliament and enclosure: a re-consideration', *Agricultural History Review* **27**, 1979, pp. 101–9; M. Turner, 'Economic protest in rural society: opposition to parliamentary enclosure in Buckinghamshire', *Southern History* **10**, 1988, pp. 94, 98.

47. E.C.K. Gonner, *Commonland and Enclosure*, 1912, pp. 76–7; W.E. Tate, *The English Village Community and the Enclosure Movement*, Gollancz, 1967, very largely expresses the same view.

and

> Most labourers who made use of a common had access not by right but
> by custom. Customary rights to enjoyment of the common were
> sometimes recognised by the Commissioners, but quite often not.[48]

Hidden here is something of vital importance. According to E.P.
Thompson, 'what was at issue was a re-definition of agrarian
property itself'. This redefinition had been for a long time working
its way through into a new concept of property law in the advantages sought by landlords over the terms of their 'customary' tenants, but in the enclosure of the commons it found its most
concentrated moment. What enclosure drastically imposed upon a
village community living by the 'traditional integument of village
custom and right' was 'capitalist property definitions'. According to
one writer in 1700, cottagers on the commons, 'having liv'd Time
immemorial in such places', had 'as good a Title to their Habitations as if they had continu'd there from the Beginning of the
World'. The 'right of commage', asserted Daniel Defoe, was something 'which the poor take to be as much their property, as a rich
man's land is his own'. Of course, the poor man did not own part
of the common; what he owned was a *use right*. Richer men might
have the right to make greater use of the common land but not to
possess it in alienation from the community. Custom was not synonymous with 'tradition'; it was the unwritten law, sanctioned by
usage through the ages. True hustling improvers of the school of
Arthur Young might choose to present a picture of rural England in
which 'custom' had lost its force and relevance, but that was not
how things were perceived either by the poor or by a significant if
diminishing paternalist fraction of the better-off. That the loss of
common land rights was a serious blow to very many of the poor
will be argued below, for now it is to be noted that we cannot pass
by with the simple assertion that enclosures were 'fair' just because
they were consistent with the tenets of an emerging capitalist and
individualist conception of property rights.[49]

The economics of enclosure

We have noted that the two main bursts of parliamentary enclosure
had different farming objectives. Those of 1755–80, mainly on the

48. Chambers and Mingay, *Agricultural Revolution*, pp. 97–98.
49. Thompson, *Making of the English Working Class*, p. 238; R.W. Malcolmson, *Life and Labour*, pp. 142–3.

heavy Midland clays in counties such as Northamptonshire, Warwickshire and Leicestershire although they also involved lighter clay
lands in Lincolnshire and the East Riding, were a response to the
low cereal prices of the century's second quarter. With much better
prices obtainable for animal products, they involved the conversion
of arable into pasture. Even if cereal prices were picking up after
1750, the comparative advantage in cereals of the lighter soils and
the general holding-up of meat and dairy prices meant that turning
the Midlands into grassland still made sense. As Yelling has pointed
out, the Midlands grazing system being based on long grass leys,
because of seasonal restrictions on growing fodder and cereals on
heavy soils, was inevitably linked to enclosure.[50]

The second burst, from 1790 to 1830, came when the upward
trend in cereal prices which set in around 1750 became a spiralling
inflation in the war years 1793–1815. At the centre the quinquennium 1800–5 saw the passing of 547 acts, while the war years as a
whole provided 43 per cent of all parliamentary enclosures. Concern was mainly with completing the enclosure of the remaining
open-field arable in light-soil districts and of extending the arable
into marginal areas – the wastes – as well as with the takeover of the
common grazing lands. In either case it was the near-certainty of
much-increased rent rolls which motivated landlords to initiate or,
since it is sometimes suggested that progressive tenant farmers were
eager, to endorse enclosure proposals. Enclosure was a costly and
bothersome business, but it nevertheless offered to the larger proprietors one of the best investments of the era. Since they rarely
seem to have borrowed to finance it and since the return was as
good and as quick as that on any but the most speculative investment, the influence of the rate of interest on its incidence, stressed
by T.S. Ashton, was probably slight. There can be little doubt that
the landlords were the greatest gainers. The doubling of rents
which usually followed suggests that the net return on their investment was of 15–20 per cent. They may have seen enclosure as an
opportunity of calling in their lands, ending existing under-rented
leases and re-letting. Yelling has suggested that there was a tendency
for rents to freeze in the pre-enclosure period and to thaw in the
renegotiation after enclosure. Dr Neeson has noted that tenants
fearing rent increases were among the opposers of enclosure in
Northamptonshire, while according to Dr Wordie:

One of the great blessings of enclosure acts was they annulled all

50. Yelling, *Common Field and Enclosure*, p. 33.

leases. After enclosure a tenant would think himself lucky to get his farm back at all at a time of increasing pressure on the land and of rapid consolidation of holdings, and if he did get it back, he could expect to pay a much higher rent for his newly enclosed acres.

There is certainly no reason to doubt that landlords would have welcomed a chance to restore the ratio of their rents to an inflating food price level.[51]

From this viewpoint the higher rents after enclosures represented a simple transfer of income from tenant to landlord. However, a large number of historians have followed contemporaries such as Arthur Young in seeing the higher rents as an index of an equivalent increase in output. Indeed, unless the two were at least partly linked, the outcome must have been a relative impoverishment of tenant farmers compared not only with landlords but also with owner-occupiers of equivalent size. There was a relative shift of share in the agricultural product, but tenant farmers, at the least the middling to large ones, are usually considered to have been substantial beneficiaries of enclosure. That farming profits did increase for tenants seems to be indicated not only by their ability to pay higher rents but also by the larger share of fixed capital investment they began to undertake. On one estate the steward complained that eager tenants were expending more in this way than the security of their leases justified.[52]

Nevertheless, caution is justified in considering hyperbolic claims such as that made by Young (on the Vale of Aylesbury): 'the tenants reap bushels, where they ought to have quarters'. Confident anticipation of good prices contributed as much to tenants' optimism as expectations of improved output. In some enclosures, notably where conversion to pasture took place, labour costs fell, as did other running costs, with consolidation. This may have produced cases in which the tenant's profitability owed as much to lower costs as to increased output. It has been suggested that the data which Young collected on grain yields do not support the claims he made for vastly improved output per acre, but in general historians working on the crop returns of 1801 as well as on more scattered sources make a satisfactory case for a measurable improvement in

51. Ashton, *An Economic History of England*, p. 41; Yelling, *Common Field and Enclosure*, pp. 209–11; J.M. Neeson, 'The opponents of enclosure in eighteenth-century Northamptonshire', *Past and Present*, **105**, 1984, p. 132; Wordie, 'Chronology of English enclosure', pp. 504–5.

52. See Yelling, *Common Field and Enclosure*, pp. 211–12; Turner, 'Parliamentary enclosures: gains and costs', pp. 6–7.

productivity. McCloskey suggests a general figure of around 13 per cent. Turner has provided figures which certainly support this for Northamptonshire (Table 3.5). His verdict is that there were productivity gains although they were not always dramatic. Some Oxfordshire parishes, for example, show as much as 25 per cent, others as little as 10 per cent. The Board of Trade crop returns suggest a range of a quarter to a third for cereals but cannot be tested, as a comparison of enclosed with open parishes would have to take account of soil differences and other factors. Barley and oats may have improved more than did wheat, but even so Yelling's analysis suggests a rise which, if modest compared with the exalted claims of some contemporaries, at least confirms that the loss of arable acreage to pasture or convertible husbandry was comfortably offset (Tables 3.6 and 3.7).[53]

So far as livestock is concerned there was probably a slight increase (Table 3.8), despite the increasing arable acreage in the eastern and south-eastern counties. Within the animal population, local evidence suggests that numbers of horses declined, which released carrying capacity for cows or sheep. More importantly, since enclosure undoubtedly assisted stock improvement, increasing weight added to meat supply or at least maintained the total supply (although not in step with population), even during the grain mania of the French wars. After all, if there had been no increase in food production the justifying polemic asserting that enclosure was in the national interest would have fallen flat. According to T.S. Ashton:

> Enclosure was only one aspect of agricultural and agrarian change. The growth of large estates and large farms, the changes in land tenure, increased application of capital, technical innovations, and the growing specialisation of regions to particular crops, might perhaps have taken place without it. But if the growth of population was an independent factor – and not itself induced by these changes – it is hard to believe that in the absence of enclosure, the standard of life could have been maintained. The dearths of 1795 and 1800 were serious enough as things were: if there had been no enclosure to increase the yield of the soil there might have been national catastrophe.

Since Ashton wrote this in 1955, research suggests some qualification of his verdict. The dearths of 1795 and 1800 now appear much

---

53. For a severe criticism of Young's presentation of his data, see R.C. Allen and C. O'Grada, 'On the road again with Arthur Young: English, Irish and French agriculture during the Industrial Revolution', *Jn. Econ. Hist.*, XLVIII, 1, 1988, pp. 93–116; Turner, 'Parliamentary enclosures: gains and costs', p. 7 and *Enclosures in Britain*, pp. 39–41; Yelling, *Common Field and Enclosure*, pp. 203–4.

Table 3.5 Crop distributions, productivity and grain output in Northamptonshire, c. 1801

	(A) *Crop distribution acres per parish*							(B) *Productivity bushels per acre*			(C) *Output bushels per parish*			
	Wheat	Barley	Oats	Total grain	Pulses	Roots	Total crops	Wheat	Barley	Oats	Wheat	Barley	Oats	Total grain
45 parishes in open fields	190.3	164.8	48.9	404.0	178.3	24.8	615.4	17.9	24.0	22.7	3406.4	3955.2	1110.0	8471.6
102 enclosed parishes	141.7	134.5	105.3	381.5	60.4	56.2	509.8	19.5	27.6	27.0	2763.2	3712.2	2843.1	9318.5

Source: M.E. Turner, 'Parliamentary enclosures: gains and costs', *ReFRESH* **3**, 1986, p. 7.

Table 3.6 Wheat acreages before and after enclosure (change expressed as percentages)

Large decrease		Moderate decrease		Little change		Moderate increase		Large increase	
Rutland	− 55	Bedford	− 13	Berkshire	− 4	Wiltshire	+ 8	Lincoln	+ 21
Northampton	− 38	Nottingham	− 11	Oxford	− 2	Huntingdon	+ 8	Yorkshire	+ 58
Leicester	− 37	Cambridge	− 10	Dorset	+ 1	Hampshire	+ 10	Norfolk	+ 77
Buckingham	− 33			Gloucester	+ 1	Worcester	+ 17		
Warwick	− 25			Derby?					

Note: The position of Derby is uncertain because of an obvious error in the statistics contained in the Report.
Source: J.A. Yelling, *Common Field and Enclosure in England, 1450–1850*, Macmillan, 1987, p. 195.

Table 3.7 Barley, oats and pulses before and after enclosure (percentages of replies indicating direction of change)

	Barley			Oats			Pulses		
	Increase	Decrease	No change	Increase	Decrease	No change	Increase	Decrease	No change
Group I	45	43	12	68	22	10	19	75	6
Group II	55	34	11	69	20	11	43	46	11
Group III	61	20	19	79	9	12	25	51	24
Group IV	41	20	39	40	23	20	22	50	28
Group V	46	36	18	53	32	15	54	33	13
Group VI	63	20	17	80	9	10	30	51	19

Group I: Buckinghamshire, Leicestershire, Northamptonshire, Rutland, Warwickshire. *Group II:* Gloucestershire, Oxfordshire, Worcestershire. *GroupIII:* Derbyshire, Nottinghamshire. *Group IV:* Bedfordshire, Cambridgeshire, Huntingdonshire. *Group V:* Berkshire, Dorset, Hampshire, Wiltshire. *GroupVI:* Lincolnshire, Norfolk, Yorkshire.
Source: Yelling, *Common Field and Enclosure,* p. 196.

Table 3.8 Livestock numbers before and after enclosure

| | Percentage of replies indicating direction of change | | | | | | | | | Per cent change in numbers |
| | Cattle | | | Sheep | | | Dairy | | | Dairy |
	+	−	=	+	−	=	+	−	=	
Group I	83	11	6	84	13	2	64	26	10	+ 85
Group II	68	16	16	70	20	10	57	25	18	+ 30
Group III	64	13	23	68	22	10	74	7	19	+120
Group IV	47	33	19	61	24	16	22	56	22	− 25
Group V	44	28	28	54	35	11	28	53	19	− 10
Group VI	53	30	18	61	24	15	33	43	24	− 25

Groups as for Table 3.7.
Source: Yelling, *Common Field and Enclosure,* p. 205.

more serious – witness the fashionable rehabilitation of Malthus. The rate of population growth was more rapid than he supposed and the increase in agricultural output less dramatic after 1760. Study of one Oxfordshire village has put paid to the myth that open-field farming was incapable of 'improvement', and suggests that the gap in potential was slighter than had been traditionally allowed. Nevertheless, few would strongly disagree with Michael Turner's view that investment in enclosure was 'enough to ensure that Britain did not starve, and was not bankrupted by otherwise excessive importation of food'. Essentially the debate over parliamentary enclosure has ever since been conducted within the same parameters as it was in its own time: economic gain versus social cost.[54]

The social costs

The Hammonds presented a trinity of sufferers: the small farmer, the cottager and the squatter on the commons. Successive generations of historians have attended to the first group and pronounced their obituary premature. In the other two cases revision has not gone so far – quite the reverse, for the Hammonds have been considerably rehabilitated. Consideration of the experience of

54. Yelling, *Common Field and Enclosure,* p. 205; Ashton, *An Economic History of England,* p, 48; R.A.E. Wells, *Wretched Faces: Famine in Wartime England 1793–1803,* Alan Sutton, 1988; Turner, *Enclosures in Britain,* p. 60.

small farmers is aided if tenants are separated from owner-occu-piers. A tendency towards the leasing of larger acreages to fewer tenants has already been noted as observable independently of en-closure, as has the fact that its extent and momentum have eluded measurement. The question of whether parliamentary enclosure sig-nificantly accelerated the tendency is accordingly hard to answer. Most probably it did. It certainly speeded up consolidation, for this rather than engrossment *per se* was its primary rationale in respect of the open fields. An advertisement for a farm in East Halton (see Figures 3.2 and 3.3) on the eve of enclosure in 1797 shows how dispersed a holding of 124 acres could be. It consisted of two old enclosures of 5 and 6 acres; 53 acres of arable in one open field and 44 in the other; 14 acres of meadow in one place and 6 in another, as well as extensive rights of common. Consolidation is not the same thing as engrossment, but they are highly likely to have been associated. This, plus the landlords' opportunity to annul existing leases, strongly suggests that it would be surprising if enclo-sure did not reinforce the tendency towards larger tenant farms. Evidence from Oxfordshire and Gloucestershire supports this. Al-though cushioned by the artificially high wartime prices, many small tenants may well have found it difficult to match their steeply rising rents, and if they fell into arrears there were plenty of larger tenants seeking extra land. Further, it has been suggested, although never with any indication of frequency, that some small owners sold out in order to gain the working capital to stock larger tenant farms.[55]

The fate of small owner-occupiers has received more attention. According to the Hammonds the high costs of enclosure doomed them to an ultimate sellout – even if high prices delayed things until after 1815: 'the classes that were impoverished by enclosure were ruined when they had to pay for the very proceeding that had made them the poorer'. They estimated costs to be as high as £5 an acre. Seizing upon this, a succession of self-appointed defenders of the ruling class rushed to insist that costs were not in fact so high. Perhaps they amounted in the average to £2 or £3 an acre with most small owners able to reach this, possibly by mortgaging. It was not so. The 'correctors' had considered only the public costs, levied as a rate to cover the fees of the Commissioners and surveyor and other expenses. To these must be added the private costs, chiefly of fencing. Total costs could rise by the early nineteenth century to

55. Hammonds, *Village Labourer*, p. 58; Russell, *Enclosures of East Halton*, p. 53. Turner, *Enclosures in Britain*, pp. 68–72 reviews the evidence, as does Ch. 6 of Yelling, *Common Field and Enclosure*.

£12 an acre and had to be met within a six-month period. For Buckinghamshire and Warwickshire, Turner and Martin have shown costs to have been fully as great a burden to small owners as the Hammonds had claimed, and both Turner and Neeson (for Northamptonshire) have shown a considerable increase in the sales of small allotments before or very soon after an enclosure. The same phenomenon has been found on the Midland clays. In this important respect the Hammonds seem to have been vindicated. Why, then, was J.D. Chambers able to claim on the basis of Nottinghamshire evidence that far from declining, the number of small owners actually increased from 1793 to 1815? Leaving aside for a moment the fact that his main data source, the land tax assessments, are considered a deficient and precarious source, he himself suggested one explanation. Much of the increase in small owners assessed was due to common-right owners receiving land for the first time in compensation. This paradox of enclosure, initially augmenting the numbers assessed for the land tax, was soon resolved when these too-small plots, burdened by the levy of enclosure costs, contributed to the turnover of small property soon after enclosure. In Buckinghamshire land tax records suggest that within two or three years of enclosure 50 per cent of landowners sold, compared with a normal turnover of around 20 per cent a decade. Naturally the post-war drop in cereal prices, when it came in 1816, was significant but it was not the cause of the decline of the small owner; it simply points out the delaying effect of wartime prices. In some areas an increase in small land-holders, especially tenants, can be linked to manufacturing. These holdings were supplementary to other earning activities, not those of proper farmers. Wordie has indicated this on the Leveson-Gower estates in Staffordshire and Yorkshire.[56]

Where the Hammonds did err was in making the decline of the small farmer fatal. This extreme diagnosis cannot be sustained; the small farm persisted through the nineteenth century. It did so, however, alongside the increasing domination of commercial farming by labour-employing tenant farmers. Dr Reed has castigated histo-

---

56. Hammonds, *Village Labourer*, p. 58; J.M. Martin, 'The cost of parliamentary enclosure in Warwickshire', in E.L. Jones (ed.), *Agriculture and Economic Growth in England, 1650–1815*, Methuen, 1967, especially pp. 143–4; Turner, *Enclosures in Britain*, p. 74; J.M. Neeson, 'The opponents of enclosure in eighteenth-century Northamptonshire', *Past and Present*, **105**, 1984, p. 118; Turner, 'Parliamentary enclosure and landownership change in Buckinghamshire', *Econ. H.R.*, XXVIII, 1975, p. 570; J.D. Chambers, 'Enclosure and labour supply in the industrial revolution' in E.L. Jones (ed.) *Agriculture and Economic Growth in England*, p. 103; Wordie, 'Social change on the Leveson-Gower estates', pp. 601–2.

rians who present England as having become by the nineteenth century a country of *mainly* tenant farmers, with only an 'unimportant minority' of small-holding peasants. The census of 1831 indicated that 40 per cent of all farmers employed no labour outside their own families. Although his article amounts to a major challenge, there are other ratios which need to be considered, notably that of labourers to owner-occupiers. Even by 1700 this was close to 2 : 1 and by 1831 it was at least 3 : 1 for England generally, and much higher in many counties in the south and east. It is to the impact of enclosure on the most numerous class of the agricultural population, the labourers, that we must now turn.[57]

ENCLOSURE AND THE LABOURER

If we understand by landless labourers those who were wholly wage-dependent, or had no expectation of ever acquiring land, then there is no doubt that the enclosure of the commons substantially added to their number. It is generally accepted that there was a link between enclosure and the decline of living-in farm service in many parts of the country (see above, pp. 23–4). In pre-enclosure times there does seem to have been a reasonable prospect of farm servants saving enough to gain some sort of holding which, with common grazing rights, was more or less adequate when augmented by some paid labour for the support of a family. Of more significance was the loss of common rights to existing cottagers and squatters. Chambers and Mingay accept that in this respect there is 'a great deal of truth in the Hammonds' assertion: "before enclosure the cottager was a labourer with land, after enclosure he was a labourer without land"'. On access to the commons a whole way of life depended. Thompson called it the 'scratch-as-scratch-can' subsistence economy of the poor. Professor Malcolmson, who has written the best account of it, writes of the substantial destruction of the 'kind of semi-self-sufficient household economy' for which access to the commons was critical, not only for the keeping of livestock but for the gathering of fuel, and in the case of the squatters for the building of their cottages.[58]

The consequences of the loss impressed themselves, as the true experience of enclosure was revealed, even on such a wholehearted

57. M. Reed, 'The peasantry of nineteenth-century rural England', pp. 54–5.
58. Chambers and Mingay, *Agricultural Revolution*, p. 97; Thompson, *Making of the English Working Class*, p. 237; Malcolmson, *Life and Labour*, pp. 24–35.

advocate of improved agriculture as Arthur Young. To him, and others, the 'loss of the cow' became the symbol of the other side of the coin of parliamentary enclosure.

> by nineteen enclosure bills in twenty they [the poor] are injured, in some grossly injured. It may be that commissioners are sworn to do justice. What is that to the people who suffer? It must be generally known that they suffer in their own opinions, and yet enclosures go on by commissioners, who dissipate the poor people's cows wherever they come, as well those kept legally as those which are not. What is it to the poor man to be told that the Houses of Parliament are extremely tender of property, while the father of the family is forced to sell his cow and his land because the one is not competent to the other; and being deprived of the only motive to industry, squanders the money, contracts bad habits, enlists for a soldier, and leaves the wife and children to the parish? If enclosures were beneficial to the poor, rates would not rise as in other parishes after an act to enclose. The poor in these parishes may say, and with truth, *Parliament may be tender of property; all I know is, I had a cow, and act of Parliament has taken it from me.* And thousands may make this speech with truth.[59]

We are not dealing with a simple and measurable matter of material deprivation. There were those who *intended* to rip away the buffer which stood between the poor and total wage dependency. Thus one zealot for large enclosed farms in 1773:

> Let not the mistaken zeal of well-disposed, but ignorant people, persuade the man of sense that [enclosure] is prejudicial to the Poor. . . . The benefit which they are supposed to reap from the commons, in their present state I know to be merely nominal; nay, indeed, what is worse, I know that in many instances, it is an essential injury to them by being made a plea for their idleness . . . if you offer them work, they will tell you they must go to look up their sheep, cut furzes, get their cow out of the pound. . . . The certain weekly income of the husband's labour, not attended by the anxiety of the little farmer, will procure more real comfort in his little cottage . . . if by converting the little farmers into a body of men who must work for others, more labour is produced, it is an advantage which the nation should wish for: the compulsion will be that of honest industry to provide for a family.[60]

In similar vein the surveyor of Somerset for the Board of Agriculture in 1798 wrote of the keeping of beasts on the common leading to 'a habit of indolence. . . . Day labour becomes disgusting.' Young estimated that the value of a cow to a family was 5 to 6 shillings

---

59. Hammonds, *Village Labourer*, p. 46.
60. Quoted in Snell, *Annals of the Labouring Poor*, p. 173.

a week, but how many kept cows? It is impossible to know. More perhaps kept pigs or geese and, in some parts, sheep. There were parts of the country, like Kent, where common rights had long ceased to be of importance. In some parishes the running of increasingly large flocks or herds on the common grazing by substantial farmers had in any case decreased the value of the grazing. While arguing that the value of the commons to the poor can be exaggerated, Chambers and Mingay accept that: 'The removal of this prop of the labourers' existence was undoubtedly a factor in the increasing poverty which characterised much of the countryside in the later eighteenth century and after.' The loss of the cow is important as a symbol. It stands for the loss of the commons generally for food, for fuel, for recreation and for an important degree of independence.[61]

To an unknowable extent enclosure must have added to the number of those seeking waged employment some small tenants who could not afford higher rents and some small occupiers who were forced to sell. A more important and widespread effect was the reduction of large numbers to total wage dependency. However, wage dependency does not necessarily imply that labourers were worse off; if enclosure brought more and/or more regular employment, they may well have been better off. This is the case for enclosure that Chambers made in an article in 1953 which rapidly established itself as an orthodoxy and became a central plank in the 'optimist' case against the Hammonds. On the basis of the evidence from Nottinghamshire, Chambers argued:

> One important factor contributing to the stability of the agrarian
> population . . . was the high level of employment which was
> maintained both in enclosed and open parishes where the improved
> agriculture was adopted. The explanation seems to be that the new
> agricultural practices had developed in advance of the technical devices
> for dealing with them. Thus the yield of corn per acre went up . . .
> after enclosure but the methods of ploughing, sowing, reaping, and
> threshing were not substantially speeded up until the 1830s and 1840s.
> At the same time the spread of turnip cultivation and green fodder
> crops both in open and enclosed villages called for labour throughout
> the year in field, barn and stackyard; the maintenance of a milking
> herd or fatstock involved continuous fieldwork throughout the year in
> pasture districts as well as in arable, except where the land was too stiff

61. Board of Agriculture survey of Somerset, 1798, reprinted in A.E. Bland, P.A. Brown and R.H. Tawney, *English Economic History: Select Documents*, Bell, 1914, p. 533; Snell, *Annals of the Labouring Poor*, p. 177; Chambers and Mingay, *Agricultural Revolution*, p. 97.

for mixed farming as in south-east Leicestershire; and the hedging and ditching of the new enclosures found winter work for casual labour to a greater extent than the open villages.[62]

In summary, 'in so far as enclosure encouraged the rise of better farming and an expanded acreage it must have greatly increased the supply of rural employment', with the important proviso: 'Only where permanent pasture increased at the expense of arable was the labour requirement likely to fall off.' This hardly needs further exposition. For example in a part of Northamptonshire the number of labourers listed for the militia fell by half following enclosure.[63]

Research findings over the last dozen years have reduced the Chambers orthodoxy to no more than a special case. Martin found that unemployment in Warwickshire villages did increase with enclosure. Chambers used demographic evidence to show that since the populations of Nottinghamshire villages affected by enclosure rose only slightly less quickly in the early nineteenth century than did those of mining and manufacturing villages, no 'general exodus of unemployed rural labour' was indicated. If we keep in mind that the central purpose of Chambers' article was to refute crude Marxist notions that enclosures had driven a dispossessed rural population from the land into the exploiting arms of the factory owners, the point is a valid one. There was indeed no 'rural exodus' of that kind. However, it has been shown by N.C.R. Crafts that there was in fact significant out-migration following enclosure in the Midlands generally, and that the Nottinghamshire case was not typical. The view that enclosure increased employment seems therefore contradicted. Dr Snell has found not only a correlation between enclosure and an increase in the numbers on poor relief, but has shown that in the south and east especially and to a lesser extent in the south-west the seasonal mal-distribution of male employment worsened with enclosure. In Nottinghamshire and Leicestershire, the counties most studied by Chambers, there was a near-continuity in the pattern of seasonal employment before and after enclosure. No improvement in the regularity of employment seems indicated.[64]

62. Chambers, 'Enclosure and labour supply in the Industrial Revolution', reprinted in Jones, *Agriculture and Economic Growth*, pp. 112–13.

63. Chambers and Mingay, *Agricultural Revolution*, p. 99; Neeson, 'Opponents of enclosure', p. 69 (footnote).

64. Martin writes of the 'reduction of the cottager class to beggary' in 'The small landowner and parliamentary enclosure in Warwickshire', p. 343; Crafts, 'Enclosure and labour supply revisited', *Explorations in Economic History*, XV, 1978. Snell's detailed and sustained attack on the 'Chambers orthodoxy', is in Ch. 4, 'Enclosure and employment' of *Annals of the Labouring Poor*.

Hedging and ditching must have increased the demand for some kinds of labour, but this is something of a red herring. The initial demand was very soon over, and in many cases was met by specialist gangs rather than by local labour. All in all the verdict on the relationship of enclosure to the level and regularity of rural employment must be that historians have been rather misled by a special and possibly singular case.

That agricultural productivity measured in output per acre increased more rapidly before 1760 than from 1760 to 1800 may have become accepted by agrarian historians, but considered historically, rates of growth relate to different potentials. It is possible that maintaining a decadal 4.5 per cent increase from 1760 to 1800 was as impressive a performance as achieving a 6.2 per cent one from 1700 to 1760. This would be a reasonable judgement on the basis that the earlier period was one in which improved methods and systems were applied to the better soils, while the latter extended the arable to more marginal lands. What is needed is a better measure of changes in output per worker, for it is generally agreed that the labour required per unit of output fell as a result of enclosure. Yelling argued that reduced labour and other costs may have been as much a factor in enabling farmers to pay the higher post-enclosure rents as was increased output. In any broad consideration of economic structure it is of fundamental importance that the contribution of the agricultural sector towards the feeding of the growing population was made with a declining share of the total labour force. Although in absolute numbers agricultural workers increased up to 1851, in relative terms an agricultural revolution did release labour to industry, not dramatically but crucially.[65]

65. Convincing evidence for the view that crop productivity increased more quickly before 1770 is provided in Turner, 'Agricultural productivity in England'; Yelling, *Common Field and Enclosure*, p. 212.

CHAPTER FOUR
The Manufacturing Economy

England was already a substantial manufacturing economy by 1714. True, the methods by which her growing output was achieved were as yet largely untouched by power technology and the factory system, but that would still be true of much of the manufacturing sector in the mid nineteenth century. Deane and Cole estimated that agriculture was contributing 43 per cent of national income in the eighteenth century and manufacturing and commerce together 30 per cent. That now seems an underestimate. It has been suggested that by 1750 agriculture's contribution may have fallen to a quarter, while manufacturing and commerce had become responsible for a half. That may be an over-correction, but an appreciation of the fact that by 1700 manufacturing involvement already exceeded the level usually associated with economic underdevelopment is fundamental to understanding the eighteenth-century English economy. That there was only a very gradual improvement in income per head reflects the fact that early industrialisation was relatively labour intensive and 'low tech' in comparison with the heavy industry based spurts of later industrialising economies. The capital investment threshold was low and while productivity gains were cumulatively significant, only at the very end of the eighteenth century and then only in a few industries were they dramatic.[1]

By 1801 combined employment in industry and commerce, at 36 per cent of the occupied population, balanced employment in agriculture (37 per cent). The problem is tracing the path to that parity. From Gregory King's famous survey of 1688, it is commonly suggested that by 1700 around a third of the population depended on manufacturing and mining, and that by the time of Joseph Massie's

---

1. Deane and Cole, *British Economic Growth*, p. 142; see the revised proportions discussed in Crafts, *British Economic Growth during the Industrial Revolution*, Chs. 2 and 6, and the discussion in Rule, *Experience of Labour*.

survey of 1759 this figure was perhaps a half. Few scholars would now accept Deane and Cole's suggestion of a 60–70 per cent dependence on agriculture as late as 1750. Indeed, an extreme position recently asserted by Lindert and Williamson on the basis of occupational recording in burial registers is that agriculture employed only 55 per cent as far back as 1688.[2]

The data do not permit precision. Gregory King did not distinguish between agricultural and other 'labourers', and although Professor Mathias has used his figures with great perception, Massie presents similar difficulties. So far as Lindert and Williamson's 'new' data are concerned, burial registers hardly ever give an occupation for women, who may have brought more hands to manufacturing than men, and in the very common cases where men had two occupations they usually record only one. In eighteenth-century reality explicit distinctions would be distorting. The 'putting-out' system was designed to carry manufacturing into the countryside, while many rural craftsmen such as blacksmiths, wheelwrights and others were really part of the agricultural economy, spending more time mending than making.

Historians cannot rigidly separate manufacturing from farming employment for the eighteenth century, because that was not the way in which the economy worked. Dual occupations persisted in many areas throughout the century and in others well into it, even if in some they died out earlier. There is no simple picture of a widespread and equal combining of farming with manufacturing or mining. Regional variation was the keynote. At one extreme a man might be equally dependent on work in both sectors – perhaps even be listed in a parish register as 'tinner-husbandman' or 'weaver-farmer'; at the other a small allotment might be contributing to the well-being of a predominantly manufacturing household. Over time, the first might well have become the second situation. The registers of west Cornwall record the marriages of 'tinner-husbandmen' regularly up to the mid eighteenth century, but less commonly thereafter. By the mid nineteenth century the farming activities of miners were described only as 'collateral aids' to family income. Even within the county the situation varied. Small-holding persisted in the rural mining districts where wasteland was plentiful but declined more rapidly around towns like Camborne and Redruth. Some northern miners were encouraged by the coal owners to take in holdings from the moorland wastes, but Arthur Young com-

2. For example, P.H. Lindert and J.G. Williamson, 'Revising England's social tables 1688–1812', *Explorations in Economic History*, **19**, 1982, pp. 385–408.

mented in 1771 that without direct encouragement, few were willing to give up their leisure time to the scraping of poor soils. Smallholding seems to have been rare among West Country woollen weavers, but common enough among cotton weavers in Lancashire to provoke complaints in 1750 that 'farmer-weavers' were undercutting those who sought to make a full-time living. In the clothing districts of the West Riding the 'alliance of land and loom' characterised the small-farming independent master clothiers who were such a feature of the region.[3] They usually held between 3 and 7 acres, although a sizeable minority had enough to be considered small farmers as late as 1795. Defoe described the district early in the century.

> Every clothier must keep a horse perhaps two to fetch and carry for the use of his manufacture, to fetch home his wool and his provisions from market, to carry his yarn to the spinners, his manufacture to the fulling mill, and when finished to the market to be sold . . . so every manufacturer generally keeps a cow or two, or more for his family, and this employs the two, three or four pieces of enclosed land about his house.[4]

At the end of the eighteenth century the watch and fine-tool makers around Prescott occupied small farms, but according to Arthur Young in 1776, the metal workers of the Black Country hardly ever did so. There, the trend away from the dual economy had begun as early as the 1720s by which time few of those who still held land had more than an acre or two. In part this reflected the growth of the towns like Walsall, Dudley, Stourbridge and Wolverhampton. The last named had 305 houses on 200 acres in 1666, 1,440 houses in 1750 and 2,270 by 1780.[5]

Even if a man was a full-time miner or weaver, he might still head a mixed family economy in which his wife and children filled the labour gap on a family small-holding. Defoe met the wife of a Derbyshire lead miner (living comfortably enough in a cave) and was impressed by the sow and piglets at the door, the lean cow and the barley plot. Seeing to all this and to her five children under ten, she still managed from time to time to earn threepence a day wash-

3. Rule, *Experience of Labour*, pp. 12–14 for a fuller discussion.
4. Daniel Defoe, *A Tour through the Whole Island of Great Britain*, Everyman edn, 1962, II, p. 195.
5. A. Young, *Tours in England and Wales: Selected from the Annals of Agriculture*, London, 1932, pp. 140, 142, 259.

ing ores at the mine and to present herself as a 'tall, well-shaped, clean, and (for the place) a very well looking, comely woman'.[6]

Much occupational mixing was seasonal. Cornish miners took part in the autumn pilchard fishery. Workers of all kinds joined in the harvest. Nor was that simply a matter of a day or two a year. A West Country clothier complained that he lost his weavers to the hay harvest in June and then enjoyed a brief respite before the late-summer corn harvest began, which could last until the autumn apple picking – it was cider country. The earliest of his apologetic letters to impatient customers is dated 15 June and the latest 26 October! Those who put out iron to Black Country nail makers experienced similar problems.[7]

Early nineteenth-century evidence suggests less mixing of employments, although it was still far from uncommon. The shift away from agricultural employment had been increasing over the second half of the eighteenth century. It was not, however, as dramatic as the traditional picture of a mass rural exodus to new industrial towns. It was sufficient to ensure that in the first decade of the nineteenth century the employment shares of manufacturing and agricultural employment were both a third. Over the second decade the trend picked up so that by 1821 manufacturing employed 38.4 per cent – a full 10 per cent more than agriculture.

Table 4.1 Labour force: sectoral growth rates, per cent per annum

	1688–1759	*1759–1801*
Agriculture	–0.05	0.06
Industry	0.51	1.36

Source: N.F.R. Crafts, *British Economic Growth during the Industrial Revolution*, Oxford UP, 1985, pp.15–16.

To juxtapose an urban manufacturing sector with a rural agricultural one would be a major misrepresentation of the structure of the eighteenth-century economy. Town worker versus country labourer would be a false dichotomy. Better sense is made by a three-way division into rural agricultural, rural non-agricultural and urban. The first was shrinking while the other two were increasing.

6. Defoe, *Tour*, II, pp. 161–3.
7. See Rule, *Experience of Labour*, p. 16.

Table 4.2 Populations: relative indices (1800 total = 100)

	Agricultural	Rural non-agricultural	Urban
1700	89	46	36
1750	84	61	51
1800	100	100	100

Source: E.A. Wrigley in R.I. Rotberg and T.K. Rabb (eds), *Population and Economy*, Cambridge UP, 1986, pp. 140–1.

The agricultural labour force increased by only 18 per cent over the latter half of the eighteenth century, while the rural non-agricultural group did so by 64.4 per cent and the urban group doubled. A continued expansion of rural manufacturing is certainly indicated. This was so true of western Europe as a whole that modern historians have made it the defining characteristic of a phase of 'proto-industrialisation' (see below, pp. 140–5). What was exceptional was the growth of England's urban population.

Table 4.3 Percentage of total populations in towns of 10,000+ inhabitants

	1700	1750	1800
England	13.4	17.5	24
North and west Europe minus England	12.8	12.1	10

Source: E.A. Wrigley in Rotberg and Rabb (eds), *Population and Economy*, p. 148.

However fashionable it has become to stress the role of manufacturing in the countryside, it is difficult to escape the conclusion that England's development advantage may have resided in a unique expansion of urban manufacturing. When nineteenth-century steam power brought the textile mills back to the towns, it emphasised but did not create a manufacturing trend.[8]

Manufacturing had urban and rural forms often within the same industry. In wool and cotton there were town weavers and country

8. On the unusual rate of urban growth in England, see E.A. Wrigley, 'Urban growth and agricultural change: England and the Continent in the early modern period' in Rotberg and Rabb (eds), *Population and Economy*, pp. 123–68.

weavers, just as there were town and country framework knitters. In hardware, too, cutlers could be found in both town and country-side. Defoe's *Tour* made at the beginning of the century reveals an industrial geography of populous, active districts. Sometimes these were sufficiently extensive to be considered regions. Within them were sizeable and small towns, villages and hamlets, all engaged in the local manufacture.

> Let them view the County of Devon, and for 20 miles every way round the City of Exeter, where the trade of serges is carried on.
> The County of Norfolk, and for as many miles every way about the City of Norwich, where the stuff-weaving is carried on.
> The County of Essex, for near 40 miles every way where the bay-making trade is carried on.
> The County of Wiltshire through that whole flourishing Vale from Warminster south to Malmsbury north, inclusive of all the great towns of Bradford, Trowbridge, Westbury, Tedbury, Frome and Devizes etc. where the manufacture of the fine Spanish and medlay clothing and drugget making is carried on.
> The Counties of Gloucester and Worcester from Cirencester and Stroudwater to the City of Worcester where the white-clothing trade for the Turkey merchants is carried on.
> The Counties of Warwick and Stafford, every way round the town of Birmingham, where the hardware manufacture and cutlery trade is carried on, as also about Coventry.
> The Counties of Yorkshire and Lancashire, round about and every way adjacent to the great manufacturing towns of Manchester, Sheffield, Leeds and Halifax, where the known manufactures of cotton-ware, iron-ware, Yorkshire cloths, kersies etc. are carried on.

Devon was so full of 'great towns' engaged in serge manufacture that it could 'hardly be equalled in Europe'. So great was the appetite of the Essex clothing district for yarn that 'some whole counties and parts of counties' were engaged in spinning it. Wealthy capitalist clothiers in the West Country sent out raw wool to be spun to 'a great number of villages, hamlets and scattered houses'. Even Lancashire, cradle of the factory system, grew, as its historians have remarked, more from a 'thickening of the population over the countryside' than from the growth of individual towns.[9]

Generally urban artisans made higher-quality goods. Better cutlery was made in Sheffield than in the surrounding villages. Wolverhampton and Willenhall concentrated on locks, while Black Country villagers made chains and nails. Coventry's silk ribbon was

9. Defoe, *Tour*, I, pp. 218, 221, 233, 280; II, 88–9, 189–90; A.P. Wadsworth and J. de L. Mann, *Cotton Trade and Industrial Lancashire*, p. 312.

a cut above that woven in Warwickshire villages, and even before they began to specialise in lace, Nottingham's stockingers produced a more 'up-market' hose than that knitted in the rural east Midlands. It would, however, be incorrect to think of eighteenth-century England as an economy in which a rude peasantry made rough articles as a by-employment in dark and frozen winter hours. Rural employment may have been more mixed than has sometimes been allowed, but this did not prevent a considerable degree of specialisation on the part of what was by then not so much a peasantry as a 'workforce dwelling in the countryside'.[10] This made possible a sustained, if undramatic, increase in productivity even from cottage manufacture. In some districts it is hardly an exaggeration to write of a 'rural artisanry'. Many rural manufacturing workers became skilled through specialised application and passed this on through succeeding generations to gain sound reputations for their particular products. Whatever their origins, over time country manufacturing workers created and confirmed their own traditions, including a defensive labour consciousness and an ability to organise to protect their interests in a similar way to urban artisans. Even where the country districts did produce inferior goods, like the 'knock-ons' forged around Sheffield, these still had their role in national and even international markets.

Between the manufacturing villages and the larger industrial cities was a host of smaller manufacturing towns. Sometimes, as in the cases of Wigan, Preston, Warrington, Burnley, Cole or Oldham, they were integrated into a regional economy – in this case based on cotton, in the same way that Defoe's woollen towns in Devon, Essex or East Anglia had been integrated into regional woollen manufactories. But there were also isolated small manufacturing towns such as carpet-weaving Wilton, Axminster and Kidderminster. Coventry, Banbury, Newbury and Kendall all had localised woollen manufacturing. Bridport made fishing nets . . . the list is illustrative, not comprehensive.

Important as manufacturing in small towns and the countryside was, a special feature of the century was the very rapid growth of some large manufacturing centres. Defoe remarked on several. 'Black Barnsley' was already so described from the smoke of its iron and steel making, and they were 'all smiths that lived in it'. Sheffield too was 'dark and black', while by mid century in Burslem in

---

10. M. Berg, 'Political economy and the principles of manufacture, 1700–1800', in Berg, Hudson and Sonenscher (eds), *Manufacture in Town and Country*, p. 39.

the heart of the Potteries people groped their way even through the midday streets. Over the next two decades its manufacturing continued to grow, amazing the itinerant John Wesley with the inflow of people. At Portsmouth the expanding dockyard had brought into being a 'new town' of Portsea, which by 1800 had three times as many houses as the old town. Smoke from glass manufacturing at Bristol so filled the air with 'noxious effluvia' by 1760 that the well-heeled were fleeing to new homes on Kingsdown Hill.[11]

Five of the ten largest provincial towns in 1775 owed their size primarily to manufacturing: Birmingham (40,000), Norwich (38,500), Manchester (30,000), Sheffield (27,000) and Leeds (24,244). Of the other five only Bath had no really significant manufacturing, for, as well as being ports, Liverpool, Bristol, Newcastle and Plymouth all did. By 1775 other towns, too, had grown rapidly since 1700 from manufacturing: Nottingham by 135.9 per cent from framework knitting; Exeter, even though her best days were already over, by 17.9 per cent from serge making; Coventry by 107.1 per cent from silk weaving; and Leicester by 75 per cent from framework knitting.[12] The growth of Birmingham and Manchester was exceptional even so. Birmingham's 1801 population of 73,000 was a nine-fold increase over the century. Arthur Young reckoned it in 1791 to be 'the first manufacturing town in the world'. Administratively a 'mere village', Manchester (with Salford) housed 19,839 people in 1757, having had less than half as many inhabitants forty years earlier. By 1795 when it was rapidly developing as the world's foremost factory town, the population had reached 27,256.[13]

On a smaller scale, examples of towns growing, or even emerging, as the result of manufacturing or mining can be plucked from all over England. Plymouth's naval dockyard rivalled that of Portsmouth by 1790 and around it the almost separate town of Dock (later Devonport) had grown up, while across the Tamar in Cornwall the satellite town of Torpoint developed. Further west, Camborne grew through copper mining from a small hamlet to a town

11. Hammonds, *Town Labourer*, p. 31; John Wesley, *Journal*, Everyman edn, 1906, IV, p. 202; D. Wilson, 'Government dockyard workers in Portsmouth 1793–1815', PhD thesis, University of Warwick, 1975, pp. 18, 36; P.T. Marcy, *Eighteenth-Century Views of Bristol and Bristolians*, Bristol Historical Association, 1966, p. 14.

12. Figures from P.J. Corfield, 'The industrial towns before the factory' in *The Rise of the New Urban Society*, Open University, 1977, pp. 114–16. The clearest demonstration of the importance of urban manufacturing in the eighteenth century is Ch. 2 of Dr Corfield's excellent *Impact of English Towns*.

13. William Hutton, *Life of William Hutton, F.A.S.S.*, 1817 edn, p. 110; Corfield, 'Industrial towns', *op. cit.*, p. 72; Young, *Tours in England and Wales*, p. 257; Defoe, *Tour*, II, p. 261.

of 5,000 inhabitants by 1801 when it was granted its market. St Helens grew from village to town almost overnight with the arrival of plate-glass manufacture.

London dwarfed them all. A multi-functional capital city and port, it could still claim to be the largest centre of manufacturing in the country. It would not otherwise have grown to anything like its population of 570,000 by 1700, or moved through 675,000 by 1750 to exceed a million by 1811. It was especially remarkable for the range of its artisan manufacturing, which employed an immense army of master craftsmen, journeymen and apprentices. Tailors and shoemakers were numbered in thousands and before the end of the century so too were print workers and watchmakers. Building craftsmen and their labourers abounded and hatters, coopers and the like were not far behind. Shipwrights worked along the Thames and a host of smaller trades like engraving, lock making and spectacle making added to the number. The largest single group of manufacturing workers were the silk weavers of Spitalfields;[14] according to Massie, in 1759 14,000 familes drew support from this employment.[15]

TEXTILES

In all, Massie thought that textiles nationally employed 114,000 familes. In 1759 the great age of cotton was still to come, and wool and worsted manufacture dominated. Cotton closed the gap with astonishing speed after 1770, but wool still outweighed it in 1815, although its rival was steaming at its shoulder. The much-used Hoffman index of manufacturing output (1955) had put cotton ahead with a 12.2 per cent share by 1811 compared with wool's 11.0 per cent, although more recent indices consider that a slight overestimation of the newer textile.[16]

Wool and worsted cloths made up 70 per cent of the value of English domestic exports in 1700 and although this share had de-

14. See Corfield, *Impact of English Towns*, Ch. 5, and Wrigley, 'A simple model of London's importance in changing English society and economy', in *Past and Present*, **37**, 1967, pp. 37–44.

15. For Massie, see P. Mathias, 'The social structure in the eighteenth century: a calculation by Joseph Massie' in Mathias, *The Transformation of England*, Methuen, 1979, pp. 171–89.

16. The major revision of manufacturing output figures is Harley, 'British industrialization before 1841'.

Table 4.4 Weighting of textiles in total manufacturing

	1770 %	1815 %
Wool	15.0	11.0
Cotton	1.0	8.0
Linen	8.0	6.0
Silk	4.0	2.0

Source: C.K. Harley, 'British industrialisation before 1841:
evidence of slower growth during the Industrial Revolution.'
Jn. Econ. Hist, XLII, 1982, p. 269.

clined by 1770, it still stood at 50 per cent. Arthur Young supposed
it in 1776 to be still 'the sacred staple and foundation of all our
wealth'. By 1780 cotton output had increased its 1760 value of £0.6
million ten-fold. By 1813 its value at £28.3 million was fifty-seven
times greater! By such a standard the two and a half times increase
in woollen output seems modest, but its more significant weighting
must be kept in mind, as must the special dynamism of one of its
regions of production: the West Riding. This area on its own accounted for almost the whole increase in taking its share of national
output over the eighteenth century from a fifth to two-thirds.[17]

By 1750 the woollen industry had become increasingly concentrated in three areas: the West Riding, the West Country and East
Anglia. Two other areas were still important but already passing
their greatest days: the Devonshire serge manufacture based on
Exeter and Tiverton and reaching to Taunton, and the stuff manufacture around Colchester. Beyond these localised manufacture
continued in towns like Coventry, Banbury, Romsey and Kendall. By
1800 there was little left in Devonshire of a manufacture which in
1700 had employed four-fifths of Exeter's population and most of
that of Tiverton and the smaller towns and villages of the district.
Its boom years were over by 1720. Its lightweight high-quality serges
had up to 1714 earned around 28 per cent of the £3 million value
of wool cloth exports. By the end of a long period of decline lasting
to 1748 the value of serge exports had halved. New markets in Italy

17. Young cited in P. Mantoux, The Industrial Revolution in the Eighteenth Century,
Methuen, 1961 edn, p. 48. The general pattern of growth in wool output is given in
A.E. Musson, Growth of British Industry, pp. 85–6; for cotton output statistics, see S.D.
Chapman, Cotton Industry in the Industrial Revolution, p. 64.

then underwrote some recovery up to the beginning of the French wars in 1793, but its exports never again made up more than 10 per cent of the national total.[18]

Essex had specialised in light worsteds – the 'stuffs' which, according to Defoe in 1720, clothed foreign 'nuns and friars'. Slow decline from that time accelerated after 1760, punctuated by short-lived booms, to extinction by 1800. As Devon and Essex declined, the main centre of lighter-cloth manufacture moved to East Anglia around Norwich. By 1750 the merchants of that city were selling six times as much cloth in value to Spain as were their Exeter counterparts. The years from then until the end of the Seven Years War in 1763 were the best ones. Around thirty clothier-dyers organised the manufacture, employing 12,000 looms and providing work of all kinds for 70,000 woollen workers. Trade, after suffering in the later 1760s, picked up again in the 1770s, but despite several short periods of promise the drift of worsted manufacture to the West Riding had become unmistakable by 1800 and by 1820 was virtually complete.[19]

Gloucestershire, Wiltshire and parts of Somerset formed the home of the great woollen broadcloth manufacture of the West Country. Over much of the eighteenth century output of its heavy, full woollen cloths stagnated. Its rival was the West Riding, which hardly competed in quality but instead found the rougher, cheaper 'kersies' a better basis for expansion. According to Professor Mann, the doubling in value of West Country output over the eighteenth century represented only a slight increase in output. Extended slumps like those of 1720–70 and 1783–90 brought widespread and severe distress to a population heavily dependent on manufacture. Shorter periods of prosperity hardly compensated, nor did a renewed period of investment in the 1790s which in any event was not sustained into the nineteenth century.[20]

The history of wool cloth production reveals that the industrial geography of eighteenth-century England was altered by the decline of old manufacturing districts as well as by the rise of new ones.

18. The Devonshire woollen manufacture lacks a recent history; the only accessible account remains W.G. Hoskins, *Industry, Trade and People in Exeter 1688–1800*, Exeter UP, 1935 and 1968.

19. Defoe, *Tour*, I, p. 63. For the rise and decline of Essex and East Anglia, see Berg, *Age of Manufactures*, pp. 113–15, and C. Wilson, *England's Apprenticeship*, pp. 293–4.

20. The standard account of the west of England woollen manufacture is Mann, *The Cloth Industry in the West of England*. Its progress is summarised in Berg, *Age of Manufactures*, pp. 115–22.

The arrival of new mechanised and powered technologies affected this only towards the very end of our period. The West Riding began its climb to pre-eminence long before coalfields fixed the location of a factory-based woollen industry. It was a matter of compounding advantages rather than of a single or special one. Cheaper cloths were better suited to expanding markets than were the expensive products of the West Country, which were from 30 to 50 per cent dearer. Dr Wilson has cogently argued that it was not simply a matter of a more marketable product but of a more dynamic approach, especially to the possibilities of the American market after 1770. This market increased its share of total wool cloth exports from 25 per cent to 40 per cent over 1770 to 1800. Yorkshire took practically all of this increase.[21]

At the beginning of the century Defoe had applauded the brisk activity of woollen manufacture in almost all of its main centres, but even so, readers of his celebrated *Tour* feel an extra surge of energy when he comes to the district around Halifax.[22] The eighteenth-century economy offers no better illustration of what Charles Wilson has termed the 'churning vitality' of industry in the period leading up to the industrial revolution.[23] Yorkshire had resource advantages. Coal was not yet needed to power spinning mules or weaving looms, but it heated the combs used in worsted production and the vats for dyeing. The running waters of the hillside landscape powered the fulling mills, while Yorkshire alone of the major districts had plentiful supplies of local wool. Defoe appreciated these advantages: 'There is scarce a hill but you find, on the highest part of it, a spring of water, and a coalpit.' Lower wages helped, but that differential was being rapidly eroded. The manufacture was distinctive in being based on small working clothiers, whereas elsewhere control had long since passed into the hands of putting-out merchant capitalists, separating capital from labour. As a select committee put it in 1806, in East Anglia and in the West Country 'the work generally speaking is done by persons who have no property in the manufacture'.[24] This goes a long way towards explaining the more troubled labour relations in the other districts.

21. R.G. Wilson, 'The supremacy of the Yorkshire cloth industry in the eighteenth century' in N.B. Harte and K. Ponting (eds), *Textile History and Economic History*, pp. 225–46.

22. Defoe, *Tour*, II, pp. 115ff.

23. C. Wilson, *England's Apprenticeship*, p. 288.

24. *Report on the State of the Woollen Manufacture*, BPP, 1806, cited in D. Gregory, *Regional Transformation and Industrial Revolution: A Geography of the Yorkshire Woollen Industry*, Macmillan, 1982, p. 53.

Yet Yorkshire's rise to dominate worsted production in the second half of the century was no less remarkable than its earlier triumph with woollens, and the West Riding's worsted manufacture was organised on a merchant capitalist basis.

Perhaps the reasons lie in the regions which declined. Wool was part of a wider tendency for manufacturing to leave the south and east. E.L. Jones has suggested that this was in part a consequence of the greater potential of these areas for the new agriculture which, by shifting their comparative advantage, drew available capital and energy into farming. Possibly the entrenched traditional attitudes of textile workers in the west and in East Anglia also reduced entrepreneurial inclination to innovate, while their insistence on marketing through London's Blackwell Hall restricted attempts to find new markets. The outcome was that the West Riding, already contributing two-thirds of output by 1800, was to dominate the factory era to an even greater extent. In 1800, however, the factory system so far as woollen manufacture was concerned was still found only in the preparatory processes of carding and scribbling. The stimulus of Lancashire cotton was near by, but wool did not lend itself so readily to machine spinning and weaving. At Benjamin Gott's pioneering mill established at Leeds in 1792, neither of the two main processes was mechanised. Factory mule spinning made little headway in woollen cloth production before the 1830s and power weaving none before the 1840s. Progress was more rapid in the worsted branch. Here, water-powered frame spinning was introduced in 1787 and steam spinning in 1793. By 1800 there were eighteen mills and steam was displacing water power. By 1820 hand spinning of worsted yarn had virtually disappeared from the West Riding, by which time factory weaving had made its entry.[25]

If anything annoyed early eighteenth-century pamphleteers more than England allowing the Dutch to harvest North Sea herrings, it was that despite a suitable climate for flax-growing, linen came second only to 'groceries' in her imports: 15 per cent of the total up to 1740. A consequent levying of protective duties and restrictions first assisted the ousting of foreign suppliers by Scotland and Ireland and then from 1750 brought about a remarkable expansion of English production which by 1775 was four times its level of 1720. At its peak in 1774 linen was producing 8.3 per cent of the total value of

---

25. See the discussion in Berg, *Age of Manufactures*, Ch. 5. On the West Riding generally, see D. Gregory, *Regional Transformation and Industrial Revolution*, p. 53; H. Heaton, *The Yorkshire Woollen and Worsted Industry*, Oxford UP, 2nd edn, 1965, and P. Hudson, *Genesis of Industrial Capital*.

exports. Thereafter progress was less spectacular, but its weighting in manufacturing output in 1815 at 0.06 was still half that of wool and three-quarters that of cotton. Pre-factory production had been widespread but tended towards the north-east, north-west and south-west. Factory spinning was introduced in 1787 with the best-known mill, that of John Marshall, opening in Leeds in 1794. Capitalised at more than £250,000 in 1828, it was an outstanding enterprise but one of only a few flax-spinning mills in England. Scotland and Ireland together boasted 700,000 spindles in 1850 compared with the 265,000 in England and Wales.[26]

Progress in silk manufacture can be measured from its need to import either raw or thrown silk. At the beginning of the eighteenth century these amounted to around £0.5 million a year. By the 1780s the million mark had been passed and by 1815 £1.25 million. Steady and substantial rather than spectacular progress is indicated. In 1770 silk cloth's weighting in total manufacturing was only a quarter of that of wool but four times that of cotton. By 1815 it was a sixth of that of wool and a quarter that of cotton. Nevertheless, to account for 2 per cent of industrial output was a fair performance from a manufacture which was not only specialised and 'up market' but had to compete both with the new product of printed cottons and with established centres of production in France and northern Italy. The 'throwing' stage, producing the yarn from raw silk, precociously entered the factory mode. The waters of the Derwent were powering machinery at Sir Thomas Lombe's famous Derby mill by 1720. William Hutton, who worked there as a child in 1730, was later to curse his luck at having been born in the one place where child labour in a factory could have been his fate. In fact, throwing mills spread quite rapidly to Macclesfield, Stockport and other towns in north Cheshire and south Lancashire. No other stages were mechanised and silk was woven on hand looms. The greatest concentration of broadcloth weavers was in London's Spitalfields district, while Coventry and its neighbourhood dominated ribbon manufacture.[27]

'King Cotton' shoots like a meteor through the growth statistics of the later eighteenth and early nineteenth centuries. Accounting

---

26. For linen, see especially Harte, 'The rise of protection and the English linen trade, 1690–1790' in Harte and Ponting (eds), *Textile History and Economic History*, pp. 74–110, and also Musson, *Growth of British Industry*, pp. 90–1.

27. W. Hutton, *The History of Derby*, 2nd edn, Baldwin, Cradock and Joy, London, 1817, p. 158. For levels of output and progress, see Musson, *Growth of British Industry*, p. 92; Berg, *Age of Manufactures*, pp. 28, 31–5, 224–5.

for only 1 per cent of manufacturing output in 1770, its 8 per cent in 1815 was only 3 per cent behind wool. By 1820 the £29.4 million it was adding to national income exceeded the £26 million of wool.

Table 4.5 Annual growth rates of real output, per cent: cotton, wool and the three fastest-growing other manufactures

	Cotton	Wool	Other manufactures
1700–60	1.37	0.97	Copper 2.62
			Paper 1.51
			Linen 1.25
1760–70	4.59	1.30	Copper 5.61
			Silk 3.40
			Linen 2.68
1780–90	12.76	0.54	Paper 5.62
			Copper 4.14
			Iron 3.79
1801–11	4.49	1.64	Iron 7.75
			Paper 3.34
			Soap 2.63
1821–31	6.82	2.03	Iron 6.47
			Silk 6.08
			Coal 3.68

Source: N.F.R. Crafts, *British Economic Growth during the Industrial Revolution*, Oxford UP, 1985, p. 23.

Table 4.6 Average annual growth rate of thirteen manufactures[*]

1700–60	0.89	1801–11	2.33
1760–70	1.92	1821–31	3.35
1780–90	2.82		

[*] cotton, wool, linen, silk, building, iron, copper, beer, leather, soap, candles, coal and paper

Source: N.F.R. Crafts, *British Economic Growth during the Industrial Revolution*. Oxford UP, 1985, p. 203.

Like silk, cotton uses an imported raw material. Retained imports of raw cotton grew from 8.7 million pounds (lb) in 1781–3 to 99.7 million by 1815–17. The annual gross value of output rose from £0.6 million in 1760, through £4 million in 1781–3 and £10 million in 1794–7 to reach £28.3 million in 1811–13. In percentage terms this represents 1,760 per cent from 1760 to 1790 and 4,616 per cent from 1760 to 1813! Clearly, cotton was overwhelmingly responsible for the doubling of textile output which was to occur between 1800 and 1820. In 1751, 4,531 hand looms were already at work in Manchester alone, with many times that number in south Lancashire as a whole around centres such as Bolton, Oldham and Preston. By 1788 cotton employed 26,000 male weavers and three times as many women and children in spinning. Adding those employed in other processes like dyeing and printing, the labour force reached 350,000. Factory spinning came with Richard Arkwright's water-powered mill at Cromford in Nottinghamshire in 1771. Following Samuel Crompton's invention of the spinning mule, even fine spinning could be done by machine from 1790. Steam power was first applied to coarse spinning in 1785 and to mule spinning in the 1790s. By 1811 there were more than 4 million steam-mule spindles spread over more than fifty mills in the Manchester district alone. Although Edmund Cartwright patented his power loom in 1785, it became established only in the second quarter of the nineteenth century. In the meantime hand-loom weavers increased from 75,000 to 225,000 between 1795 and 1811, by which year factory employees exceeded 100,000.[28]

Recent reassessments of manufacturing progress have not failed to point out that cotton grew from a very low base and that its contribution to exports was greater than its contribution to manufacturing output, which had still not reached 10 per cent by 1815. There is little certainty in estimating eighteenth-century growth but it seems clear that while there was a shift towards more rapidly growing manufactures like cotton and iron in the late eighteenth century, it should not be allowed to overshadow the widely based growth across a range of industries which were both less dramatically transformed than cotton and less export oriented. The three manufactures commonly taken to typify the industrial revolution – cotton, iron and engineering – accounted together for less than a quarter of manufacturing output as late as 1840.[29]

---

28. In addition to Chapman's excellent pamphlet *Cotton Industry in the Industrial Revolution*, for the progress of the cotton industry generally, see M.M. Edwards, *Growth of the British Cotton Trade*, and for the earlier period Wadsworth and Mann, *Cotton Trade and Industrial Lancashire*; Musson, *Growth of British Industry*, pp. 78–85; Berg, *Age of Manufactures*, pp. 205–7; Deane and Cole, *British Economic Growth*, pp. 50–2.

29. For stress on the exceptionality of cotton, see Harley, 'British industrialization before 1841', pp. 267–8, 279; Crafts, *British Economic Growth during the Industrial Revolution*, pp. 33–4, and C.H. Lee, *British Economy since 1700*, pp. 10–11.

Cotton cloth sold well not just because it was cheap and light but also because it could be as brightly coloured and patterned as the much more expensive silks. The branch of the industry usually known as calico printing was crucial for overall success. In the early eighteenth century it was performed largely by skilled male workers who cut and applied the printing blocks. Initially it was based in London, but with the concentration of home manufacture in Lancashire it moved north, taking with it the artisans. Mechanised printing using etched copper cylinders began to de-skill them after 1785, but before then larger employers, such as the elder Robert Peel, had escaped from dependence on the high-paid journeymen by developing simple repetitive hand techniques which employed women and children. 'Picotage' involved patterning the block with thousands of pins or studs and was a more skilled process than 'pencilling' in which the patterns were hand painted. Calico printing reveals how employers faced with high labour costs could attempt to reduce them, not only by employing machinery but also by developing techniques which used cheaper labour.[30]

Statistics do not reveal the full importance of the cotton manufacture which played a leading and strategic role in the modernisation of the British economy. Silk offered the earliest instances of the modern textile factory, and the importance of its example to the early cotton entrepreneurs has been remarked by Dr Chapman. Cotton, however, made the breakthrough into steam power, and as a consequence gave the world the factory *system*.[31]

From the beginning the making of cotton piecegoods was concentrated in south Lancashire, but the building of Arkwright's pioneering mill in Nottinghamshire points to the different location of the cotton stocking branch. These were produced mainly in that county, as woollen ones were in Leicestershire and silk in Derbyshire. Together these made up the great east Midland hosiery manufacture. Yarn was turned into stockings on knitting frames, a sixteenth-century innovation which, after a long delay, had substantially replaced the traditional method of hand knitting by 1700. Defoe attributed the decline of knitting in Dorset to competition from the frame. By then it had become concentrated in the East Midlands, moving away from its original London base to escape guild control and cash in on cheap rural labour. By 1740 around 5,000 frames were at work, and when the famous Luddite attacks on

---

30. The best account of calico printing and its various technologies is Berg, *Age of Manufactures*, pp. 146–8, 216–17, 251.

31. Chapman, *Cotton Industry in the Industrial Revolution*, pp. 14–15.

them began in 1811 there were six times as many creating work for 50,000 persons. Except in the spinning of yarn, the factory appeared only in the mid nineteenth century.[32]

Glove making was less concentrated, but there were several important centres. It employed several thousand in Worcestershire and its surrounding district in the 1770s and perhaps 30,000 by the 1820s. At that date perhaps 20,000 glovers worked in and around Yeovil and 3,000 around Hereford. Severe problems then resulted from the removal of import restrictions on French gloves, and by 1832 production from Worcestershire had fallen by two-thirds.[33] Garment manufacture was more dispersed. London was the greatest centre, with most of its tailors by the early eighteenth century working as journeymen in the workshops of large employers. In other towns independent tailors were more in evidence, but in any of size the trend was towards the workshop. The leather industry may have accounted for a fifth of manufacturing output in 1770 and still a sixth in 1815. At the former date it was easily the largest industrial grouping and at the latter only just second to building. In terms of value added its £5.1 million in 1770 was second only to the £7 million contributed by wool, and in 1801 it was only just beaten by cotton (£8.4 million and £9.2 million).[34] Yet we know very little of the details of its organisation or development. Shoe-makers, like tailors, were to be found everywhere but again were especially concentrated in London. As with tailors, there was a marked increase in the number of permanent journeymen employed in workshops to cater for a widening market. Provincial shoe-making usually supplied local markets, but the putting out of leather to cheap labour in and around Northamptonshire was growing in importance after 1780. Tanneries were to be found contributing smell and smoke in many larger towns, but the largest concentration was on the south bank of the Thames at Southwark and Rotherhithe.

COAL

In its widespread use of coal, English manufacturing led Europe. Because historians have often restricted their interest to its uses for

32. Defoe, *Tour*, I, p. 213; E.A. Wells, *The British Hosiery and Knitwear Industry: Its History and Organisation*, David and Charles, 1972, pp. 48–9; E.P. Thompson, *Making of the English Working Class*, p. 580.
33. Young, *Northern Tour*, III, p. 306; Berg, *Age of Manufactures*, p. 124.
34. Berg, *Age of Manufactures*, pp. 26, 28, 38–9.

steam power and for iron smelting, they have tended to underestimate its importance before the 1770s. Steam boilers are not the only things that can be fuelled by coal, while iron was the last of the major metals to be smelted with it. Energy in the form of heat had as many applications as did steam. Before the end of the seventeenth century coal was widely used to boil, brew and melt. In the brewing industry, Professor Mathias has identified two stages in coal use. Long before the eighteenth century began it was used to heat brewing vats and from the 1780s it was increasingly substituted for real horsepower to grind malt and raise water. Whitbread's bought a Boulton and Watt steam engine in 1786 and considered that by doing the work of twenty-four relayed horses it was well worth the cost of a bushel of coal an hour and an annual premium of sixty guineas for its use.[35] In 1738 parliament received a complaint about the high price of coal from the glass makers, brewers, distillers, sugar bakers, soap boilers, smiths, dyers, brick makers, lime burners, founders and calico printers. A threatened strike by Bristol's local Kingswood colliers in 1792 brought fears of stoppages of 'very numerous and extensive glasshouses, very large copper works, lead works, distilleries and other concerns that consume immense quantities of coal'. None of them did so to fuel steam engines.[36]

The late and fitful spread of coke smelting in the iron industry must be set against its earlier use with non-ferrous metals, as well as against the fact that it was used to forge iron across the country from the village blacksmith to the cutlers of Sheffield and the nail makers of the Black Country. Such usage was the essence of Professor Nef's argument for an industrial revolution in Tudor and Stuart times, but historians have been surprisingly indifferent to later developments before the eighteenth-century industrial revolution. Professor Harris has cogently put things into perspective. He has shown that Britain served an invaluable apprenticeship in the industrial use of coal during this period as one manufacture after another turned to it and as methods of using it became gradually more efficient and economical from the on-the-job experience of skilled workmen. This was a craft rather than a scientific contribution to Britain's technological leadership.[37]

Steam engines, too, were widely used in the economy before the

35. P. Mathias, *The Transformation of England*, Methuen, 1979, pp. 225–6.
36. Mantoux, *Industrial Revolution in the Eighteenth Century, op. cit.*, p. 283; the letter from Bristol is in A.A. Aspinall, *The Early English Trade Unions*, Batchworth, 1949, p. 6.
37. J.R. Harris, 'Skills, coal and British industry', pp. 168–76.

era of Watt began in the 1780s, important as were the fuel economy of his separate condenser and his translation of reciprocal into rotative motion. Steam-powered beam engines had been employed in draining mines from around 1715, when there were seven or eight Newcomen engines operating from Cornwall to Newcastle. By 1733 there were sixty, and by 1780 around 300. In the 1780s, despite the constraints of Watt's patent, other builders continued to supply engines, and if these are added to the Watt engines there may well have been 1,200 steam engines at work in 1800.[38]

Early output statistics are difficult to obtain and usually impressionistic. However, Professor Flinn's recent official history provides a reasonably clear outline of the growth of coal output.

Table 4.7 English coal output ('000 tonnes)

1700	2,430
1750	4,295
1775	7,090
1800	11,195
1815	16,665

Source: M.W. Flinn, *History of the British Coal Industry,*
II: 1700–1830 The Industrial Revolution. Clarendon, 1984, p. 26.

The average annual growth rates between these dates are: 1.5, 2.6, 2.32 and 3.2 per cent. Most coal in 1700 was for household use. Most still was in 1750, but the fact that the annual increase in output between the two dates was more than four times the rate of population increase confirms steadily increasing industrial use, for it cannot be explained by exports. Over the whole period 1700 to 1815 coal output increased almost six-fold.[39]

To write of 'English' output becomes increasingly misleading. By 1800 a quarter of British coal was coming from Scotland and Wales. Even in the first half of the eighteenth century they had been contributing a fifth. Most of Scotland's output was used at home, but Welsh coal was more closely connected with English manufacturing. From only 2.7 per cent of Britain's output in 1750, South Wales accounted for 11.3 per cent by 1800. On its coalfields the tin-plate industry was established and grew after 1750, while ships taking coal

38. Harris, 'The employment of steam power', pp. 137–44.
39. M.W. Flinn, *History of the British Coal Industry*, Ch. 1.

across the Bristol Channel for Cornwall's mine engines returned laden with copper ore for smelting at Swansea.

Table 4.8 Coalfields: share of output, per cent

	1750–60	1811–20
North-east	35.1	22.2
Yorkshire	11.2	10.2
Lancashire and Cheshire	4.5	9.1
Nottingham and Derby	1.89	6.0
North and South Staffordshire	6.0	14.5
Warwickshire and Leicestershire	2.36	1.08
Shropshire	9.0	5.4

Source: S. Pollard, 'A new estimate of British coal production, 1750–1850.' *Econ. H.R.*, XXXIII, 1980, p. 230.

The contributions of the different coalfields varied over the period, although Northumberland and Durham led throughout. Smaller coalfields had local significance. Kingswood, for example, provided Bristol with 600,000 tonnes in 1815, while the growth of the Cumbrian coalfield over the eighteenth century was based on an export trade to Ireland.[40]

Coal getting was a labour-intensive matter and remained so throughout the nineteenth century. Perhaps as many as 15,000 miners were employed in 1700 and a hundred years later hardly less than 50,000.

METALS

The conventional progression of economic historians is from coal to iron. However, in a book which begins in 1714 that great resource combination figures significantly only after 1780. Primacy in the use of coal goes to the non-ferrous metals: lead, tin and copper. Smelting with coal had become normal in England by 1700 and in terms of the value of metal output, if not of final product, lead, tin

40. For regional output estimates and the problems of making them, see S. Pollard, 'A new estimate of Britain's coal production 1750–1850', *Econ. H.R.* XXXIII, 2, 1980, pp. 212–55.

and copper added more than basic iron to the national income for most of the eighteenth century. In the 1750s the annual value of lead output was £496,000, of copper £297,000 and of tin £174,000. Lead alone at least equalled the value of basic iron up to mid century. From then until 1770 it almost doubled, while iron did rather less well. Copper mining and smelting boomed in the 1780s and in 1788 annual output was twice as valuable as that of pig iron. The technological breakthrough into coal smelting had come before the end of the seventeenth century. Fuel economy was achieved through the use of the reverbatory furnace which, by separation of the fuel from the ore, also overcame the problem of pollutants associated with the use of coal. In tin smelting such techniques produced from coal a metal only 10 per cent less pure than that smelted with wood or charcoal.[41]

Copper smelting tended to be located on the coalfields, although one smelting works continued alongside the ores in Cornwall at Hayle, where the health of the labourers was damaged by the arsenic fumes given off. For the most part smelting established itself first at Bristol and then at Swansea. When ores from Anglesey came on to the market in the last third of the century, some were smelted at Swansea although a large proportion went to the Lancashire coalfield. Tin continued to be smelted in Cornwall, where it was mined. This centuries-old industry did not, as did copper, enjoy a boom in the eighteenth century. Indeed, by the end of the century attempts to find new export markets in the Far East were being made, for even the growth of tin-plating after 1750 did not sufficiently absorb excess supply in most years. By the eighteenth century the ores of main centres of lead mining in Derbyshire, the northern Pennines and the North and West Ridings were smelted on local coalfields. Smaller amounts of ore raised in Cornwall followed the copper path to South Wales. Output statistics for the period between 1770 and the beginning of the official series in 1845 seem to be unattainable. But increasing demand from manufactures like glass making, paint making and pottery, from builders for piping and roofing and for its growing use in zinc alloy was met with only marginal imports before the 1820s. Copper was an essential ingredient in the brass-

---

41. Figures for lead production are from R. Burt, 'Lead production in England and Wales, 1700–1770', *Econ. H.R.*, XXII, 1969, pp. 249–68. (See also his more recent *The British Lead Mining Industry*.) For copper and tin output, see J. Rowe, *Cornwall in the Age of the Industrial Revolution*, Liverpool UP, 1953, pp. 58, 76. However, for the last decades of the eighteenth century the output from Anglesey was important and the national data compiled by B.R. Mitchell and P. Deane, *Abstract of British Historical Statistics*, Cambridge UP, 1962 (Ch. VI) can be consulted.

and bronze-using manufactures of Birmingham from coins through buttons and utensils to valves, cocks and pipework for the new mach-inery. Ore output, around 6,500 tonnes in 1750, exceeded 40,000 tonnes by 1795 and 100,000 by 1825. Tin output in 1750 was still under 3,000 tonnes, a level it did not consistently exceed before 1815. A count of the labour force at Cornish copper mines in 1782 indicated 7,196 workers of whom 2,684 were women and children. This suggests from output figures that by 1800 it was probably around 10,000. If workers in tin and lead are added, the non-ferrous metal mines of England employed around 15,000 people in 1800.[42]

The traditional view of iron production was that Britain, through de-forestation, suffered from a growing shortage of the charcoal it used for fuel. More recent scholars have cast doubt on this and suggest that the growing dependence on imports of basic iron was more likely due to the generally higher costs of home production, including labour costs and the unsuitability of British iron for some purposes.[43] Whatever was at work within the industry, the distribution of charcoal furnaces in 1717 reveals a rather different geography from that which later developed, although Professor Court has doubted whether there ever was a fall at any time in the output of furnaces in Staffordshire and Shropshire even before coke smelting favoured them.[44]

Table 4.9 Distribution of charcoal iron furnaces, 1717

Hampshire	1
Weald	14
South-west	16
South Wales and Midlands	13
Cheshire and North Wales	5
Sheffield and north-east	9
North-west	3
Total	61

Source: E. Pawson, *The Early Industrial Revolution. Britain in the Eighteenth Century,* Barnes & Noble, 1979, p. 115.

42. For relations between mines and smelters, see Rowe, *Cornwall in the Industrial Revolution, op. cit.,* pp. 21–2, 63–5.
43. See B. Short, 'The de-industrialisation process: a case study of the Weald, 1600–1850', in Hudson (ed.) *Regions and Industries,* pp. 156–74 and Flinn, 'The growth of the English iron industry 1660–1760', *Econ. H.R.,* XI, 1958–9, pp. 144–53.
44. W.H.B. Court, *The Rise of the Midland Industries, 1600–1838,* Oxford UP, 1953, p. 170; E. Pawson, *Early Industrial Revolution,* pp. 112–16.

In 1806 England's 149,203 tonnes of pig iron constituted 61 per cent of total British output.

Table 4.10 Percentage shares of English pig iron output in 1806

Shropshire	36.8
Staffordshire	33.5
Yorkshire	18.5
Derbyshire	6.1
Northumberland	1.6
Monmouth	1.5
Cumberland	1.3
Lancashire	0.5

Source: E. Pawson, *The Early Industrial Revolution. Britain in the Eighteenth Century*, Barnes & Noble, 1979, p. 113.

The ultimately critical breakthrough into coke smelting made by Abraham Darby at Coalbrookdale in Shropshire in 1709 was not taken on by the industry at large for another fifty years. Recently doubt has been cast on the old myth that this is explained by secrecy and by the fact that the iron produced was inferior. Hyde has shown that for most producers coke smelting offered no cost advantage until the price of charcoal began to rise after 1750, especially since most ironmasters were interested in wrought rather than cast-iron products. Coke smelting thereafter rapidly overtook charcoal smelting. There is some controversy over output levels before mid century, but none over the rapid increase that had set in by 1770. By 1780 output may well have been double that of a generally stagnant level before 1750.[46]

Even had coke smelting diffused more rapidly and readily, Britain would still have needed to supplement her supply of good bar iron. Imports from Sweden and Russia rose from a 1700 level of 15–20,000 tonnes to 50,000 by 1790, then fell away sharply and by 1820 were below the level of 1700. This fall, despite an actual increase in the output of all kinds of finished iron goods, is probably largely attributable to two inventions patented by Henry Cort in

45. The key work of revision is C.K. Hyde, *Technological Change and the British Iron Industry*. See also G. Hammersley, 'The charcoal iron industry and its fuel, 1540–1750', *Econ. H.R.*, XXVI, 4, 1973, pp. 593–613. The technical progress of iron making from the development of coke smelting is concisely described in Mathias, *First Industrial Nation*, pp. 111–14 and in a recent pamphlet by J.R. Harris, *British Iron Industry*.

46. Output figures from P. Riden, 'Iron output before 1870', *Econ. H.R.*, XXX, 1977, pp. 448, 455.

Table 4.11 Pig iron output (tonnes)

1780	62,000
1790	90,000
1800	180,000
1815	340,000

Source: P. Riden, 'The output of the British iron
industry before 1870.' *Econ. H.R.*, XXX, 1977, p. 455.

1784: the puddling furnace and the rolling mill. Previously usable
bar iron had to be made from pig by re-forging with charcoal and
beating with heavy water-powered hammers. Accordingly forges had
often to be located away from smelting works. Cort freed the second stage from dependence on charcoal and water power, and
made possible greater and more efficient output from integrated
sites on the iron and coalfields. Even Hyde, who has pointed out
that a widespread adoption of the potting process brought measurable improvement to bar-iron production over the period 1750–88,
still regards Cort's invention of puddling as a clear advance and
'one of the bases for Britain's industrial leadership'. With the application of Watt's steam engine to the rolling mill, nothing stood in
the way of increasing concentration in Shropshire, Staffordshire,
Yorkshire and South Wales. These regions produced between them
over 90 per cent of the total output of England and Wales in
1806.[47] The only huge enterprise outside them was the giant works
of Ambrose Crawley set up near Sunderland in 1700, reputedly at
the time the largest in Europe. Arthur Young was much impressed
in 1776 by 'several hundreds' of workers on an annual wage bill of
£12,000. He was even more impressed by Darby's Coalbrookdale
works, which he supposed to be 'the greatest in England'.

> Past his new slitting mills . . . the immense wheels 20 feet diameter
> of cast iron were there. . . . Viewed the furnaces, forges etc., with the
> vast bellows that gave those roaring blasts, which make the whole
> edifice horridly sublime. . . . The whole process is here gone through
> from digging the ironstone to making it into cannons, pipes, cylinders
> etc. etc. All the iron used is raised in the neighbouring hills, and the
> coal dug likewise which is char'd. . . . Mr Darby in his works employs
> near 1000 people including colliers . . ..[48]

47. Hyde, 'Technological change in the British wrought iron industry, 1750–
1815', *Econ. H.R.*, XXVII, 2, 1974, p. 200; Musson, *Growth of British Industry*, p. 101;
Court, *Midland Industries, op. cit.*, pp. 177–9.
48. Young, *Tours in England and Wales*, p. 151; *Northern Tour*, I, p. 115.

From the last quarter of the eighteenth century the iron industry had taken on a scale of operation and, by and large, a pattern of location which were largely to persist until the second half of the nineteenth century.

HARDWARE MANUFACTURE

By the late eighteenth century the legion of hand nail makers in the Black Country consumed around half of the iron output of the Midlands. Iron rods were put out to workers' homes where they were cut to length on anvils and headed with a single hammer blow. It was a simple occupation but carried out at lightning speed. It was also a humble occupation, performed by women and children as well as men. There was some regional specialisation according to nail type, but in the Midlands, just as in its other centre around Sheffield, it was the bottom rung of a ladder of hardware manufacture which climbed through chain, scythe spur and lock to the huge range of metal products produced by Birmingham's artisans from copper and brass as well as iron. The skilled labour which was the basis of the higher rungs had been developing in the area from the seventeenth century. By 1660 manufacturing parishes were already noticeably more populous than agricultural ones and special skills were becoming locally concentrated: lorimers produced their spurs in Walsall and locksmiths their locks in Wolverhampton and Willenhall, while the higher branches filled out Birmingham, displacing the cruder ones into the Staffordshire countryside.[49]

By 1800 practically all of the iron output of Staffordshire and Shropshire was being made up in the forges and foundries of the district. And not only iron: from around 1700 braziers and coppersmiths began to increase in numbers, so that by 1720 a single brazier capitalist was putting out his metal to be made up in more than fifty cottage workshops. Artisans trained in iron work could easily change into an out-working population of brass and copper workers applying their skills to these metals, which were produced in far greater amounts than could have been consumed by the small number of large establishments. Before the eighteenth-century changes in iron making, the development of iron founding was slow. Only a

---

49. As well as Court's *Midland Industries*, for the period up to the later eighteenth century, see M. Rowlands, *Masters and Men in the West Midlands Metalware Trades before the Industrial Revolution*, Manchester UP, 1975.

few articles such as chimney backs and garden rollers were cast directly as molten metal into fine sand. But with the development of coke smelting, large concerns like that of the cannon maker John Wilkinson rapidly emerged. He could produce heavy castings up to boilers and cylinders of 7 feet in diameter. The use of copper in large castings fell away, but the lighter 'hollow wares' could not be cast from iron until after 1815, and copper and brass continued to dominate a wide range of household utensil production as well as finding many new uses in Birmingham's coin, button and 'toy' trades. Matthew Boulton minted the first copper coin in 1797 and within two years had produced 45 million of them.

Although it owed so much to the application of power – first water then steam – to the rolling and slitting mills, providing a material (wire, rod or plate) which was itself semi-manufactured, hardware manufacture was dominated by what Professor Court has called a 'vast multiplication of small producers'.[50] Even by 1851 the average metal-working business employed less than six men and many none at all.

'A fine large town of manufacture of all sorts of toys, and implements in the iron way, and some in brass, and they japan also and enamel to great perfection, and cheap.'[51] This traveller's description of 1751, if not the manufacturing understatement of the century, is at least a most concise description of Birmingham, already the greatest centre of hardware manufacture in the world. It was noted for its multiplicity of small metal workshops at which quasi-independent craftsmen made an amazing range of items from iron, tin, bronze, brass and copper: buckles, cutlery, spurs, candlesticks, toys, guns, buttons, whip handles, coffee pots, inkstands, carriage fittings, snuff boxes, lead pipes, jewellery, lamps, tools, kitchen items, coins and medals. Most of the small items were known together as the 'toy trades' and varied from a few pence to many guineas in individual value. Characteristically the patterns of such items changed with great frequency. The eighteenth century was their time. They were not much known before, but there is evidence of a significant export trade by 1712. In the mid eighteenth century they employed around 20,000 hands and had a value in excess of £500,000.[52]

50. Court, *Midland Industries, op. cit.*, p. 180; Musson, *Growth of British Industry*, pp. 104–6; Berg, *Age of Manufactures*, Ch. 11.

51. J.J. Cartwright (ed.), *Travels through England of Dr Richard Pococke*, II, Camden Society, 1889.

52. Berg, *Age of Manufactures*, pp. 288–9.

Frequent changes in fashion and form did not suit mechanised mass production. Arthur Young in 1791 expressed surprise at the

> small or no use that is made of water; in the town there are no mills, and the number in the vicinity, for the direct operations of a fabric, are inconsiderable; the number of little and distinct forges for works performed by a single hand, surprised me; I had conceived that machinery was carried much further . . . so many operations yet remain performed by the re-iterated strokes of the hand. . . . I saw no machines comparable to a cotton mill or a stocking engine.[53]

His reaction was fundamentally correct, but requires qualification. Powered machinery was needed to provide the semi-processed raw material, especially the sheet metal, tin and copper plate. The rolling mill had done this for some time but more cheaply and in greater amount after the rotary steam engine was employed to drive the heavy rollers in the 1780s. Sheet metal was provided, from the thin plate needed by the toy makers to half-inch-thick iron for boiler making. The enormous increase in Birmingham's population in the 1780s and 1790s owed as much to developments in iron making, rolling, slitting and wire drawing as it did to changes in the processes of manufacturing finished goods. The latter, however, did not stand still.[54] In the second half of the seventeenth century the turning lathe, stamp and press gradually took over in manufacturing from sheet metal those items which had previously been cast from solid metal and finished with hammer, anvil, file and grindstone. The new tools were generic types which were rapidly adapted by craftsmen to suit their particular specialisms. It was this which led to Birmingham being noted for inventiveness rather than for the application of power technology. Young conceded 'some tools of beautiful invention', while Lord Shelbourne noted in 1766 'an infinity of smaller improvements which each workman has and sedulously keeps secret from the rest'.[55]

He especially noted the advent of the stamp which, by forcing the die on the metal, made possible the continuous production of impressed goods like coins, buttons and medals. The stamp worked on blanks now produced by the press, which could itself, where less than momentary force was needed, impress the less sharp designs for cruder work as well as producing percussion caps and heading pins. These two complementary machines were not confined to a

53. Young, *Tours in England and Wales*, pp. 254–5.
54. Court, *Midland Industries, op. cit.*, pp. 241–2.
55. Cited in Berg, *Age of Manufactures*, pp. 300–1.

small number of trades. They were, as Professor Court has put it, adapted to make the output of a whole range of metal items, 'cheap, swift and large'. The stamp and the press underpinned Birmingham's spectacular eighteenth-century growth. Even where a more precious metal was involved, London's silversmiths rightly feared competition from Matthew Boulton's candlesticks which by 1773 could be made from one sixth of the weight of metal compared with those cast in a traditional manner.[56] By this time he was producing a range of goods including coffee pots and jugs. Less of a 'craft' product than those made in the old way, they were in effect a new product creating as much as responding to demand.

The adaptability of Birmingham's artisans is well illustrated by the expansion of metal button making after changing fashion in shoes reduced the demand for buckles. There was a short period in the 1790s when wearers of the new-fangled buttoned shoes risked insult and injury in the streets, but then button making quickly absorbed the slack in skill and in raw materials. In general the division of labour was as significant as the development of new techniques and products. In gun making, for example, the 'gunmaker' whose name was eventually stamped on the finished firearm in fact bought in semi-finished parts and gave them out again to specialised craftsmen: barrel makers, lock makers, sight stampers, trigger makers, ramrod forgers, gun furniture makers and bayonet forgers. From such manufactures, produced from product specialisation and shop-floor technical adaptation, Birmingham contributed very strongly to the rise of metal goods from 7 per cent of manufactured exports in 1722–4 to 14 per cent by 1772–4.[57]

It is difficult to date the origins of so many varied and changing branches of hardware manufacture. Japanware is one, however, which can be dated. This highly popular form of decorative enamelling was introduced in the 1720s and was at first confined to small and much soldered tin-plate articles. With the advent of larger stamped tin-plate articles, the product range extended remarkably. Around 1750 papier mâché offered a new cheap material capable of taking the japanning process. By this time the production of cheap decorative knick-knacks like tea trays and snuff boxes had spread to Wolverhampton and Bilston.[58] Although Birmingham manufacturing was in general dominated by small workshops, there were exceptions. John Taylor, who specialised in japanned paper boxes, was

56. Court, *Midland Industries, op. cit.,* pp. 244–5.
57. Berg, *Age of Manufactures,* pp. 288–9.
58. *Ibid.,* p. 289.

the town's largest concentrated producer before the arrival of Matthew Boulton; his method of stamping on pictures and rapidly drying in ovens was described in 1766. He combined japanning with button making, as did Clay who in 1772 introduced a new method of pasting layers of paper as a base instead of the pulped papier mâché. At his peak he employed 300 people.[59] Boulton's great Soho Works commenced operations in 1765 using a source of water power to the north of the town. The uncertainty of the water flow was a potent reason for going into partnership with James Watt in 1775. For the next twenty years, until the opening of the Soho Foundry in 1791, Soho was not only one of the most celebrated of steam-powered factories, it was the largest supplier of steam engines to the Midlands, surpassing even Coalbrookdale. Its triumph did not signal a radical transformation of Midlands hardware manufacturing, however. At Watt's death in 1819 the use of steam power was still very limited, and its most important contribution remained the transformation of the supply of wrought iron, sheet metal and wire on which the metal-workers practised their skills, rather than the making of the finished product.[60]

Tool making was widespread in the west Midlands, but was not confined to that region. South-west Lancashire and adjacent Cheshire had long been noted in this respect. Peasant tool makers in and around St Helens produced chisels, pliers, vices, gauges, small lathes and files to be used by whitesmiths, clock and watch makers and, later, machine makers. The area was also known for making watch parts, as well as locks and hinges. By 1750 most British watch makers whose names appeared on the finished product and whose final stages of manufacture were concentrated in London or Coventry bought their rough movements from Lancashire. The area around Warrington was noted for its files and although there were some eighteenth-century makers who made them from start to finish, more usually one forged, another cut and a third hardened.[61]

Files were an important manufacture in Sheffield, but that city was best known as the great centre of edged steel tool making. A directory of 1797 shows 40 firms engaged in file manufacture, while 134 made pocket knives, 81 table knives, 60 shears, sickles and scythes, 33 razors, 34 saws and other edged carpenter's tools and 34 surgical instruments. The city specialised in high-quality goods, cheaper items being made in the surrounding villages. Forks

59. Court, *Midland Industries, op. cit.,* pp. 234–5.
60. *Ibid.,* pp. 251–3.
61. Berg, *Age of Manufactures,* pp. 271–3.

needed less skill than knives and 20 firms made them outside the city compared with 15 within its boundaries. Around 6,000 workers were employed in the various branches in 1800 and several hundred more in the manufacture of Birmingham-type utensils from the recently developed Sheffield plate.[62]

In the cutlery trades a separation into forging and grinding sections had come about by 1750. Forging was performed by one or two workers, while grinding was done in separate departments of the larger establishments, or else on separate premises known as 'wheels'. The grinding wheels were turned either by water or by boys turning huge fly-wheels. Steam was first introduced to grinding in 1786, but until well into the second half of the nineteenth century the Sheffield trades remained small-scale and dependent on hand skills. After grinding, blades were refined with hammer, emery, whitestone and buffing wheel, with the final processes of building up handles – 'halfting' – being the most skilled of all. The benefits of substituting mechanical methods were limited in a manufacturing system in which goods such as pocket knives were made in a wide variety of types even by single firms. Accordingly the characteristic unit of production remained small, typically in forges attached to the metal-workers' houses. Little capital was required: 'a man with a very small sum of money can employ two, three or four men'. This blurred the line between dependent artisans working at piece rates on put-out materials and small masters producing on a sub-contractual basis, perhaps even for the same merchant capitalist.[63]

With metal-working activity so widespread in eighteenth-century England, it is not surprising that *finished* iron and steel goods, in accounting for almost 7 per cent of the value of British industrial output in 1812, were worth two and a half times the value of iron and steel as raw materials. Such a ratio indicates a substantial manufacturing achievement.

GLASS AND PAPER MAKING

Ranking behind coal, textiles and iron in importance, these two in-

---

62. *Ibid.*, pp. 275–7. The standard work on the cutlery trade remains G.I.H. Lloyd, *The Cutlery Trades: An Historical Essay in the Economics of Small Scale Production*, 1913, new edn, Cass, 1968. For the district around Sheffield, see D. Hey, *The Rural Metalworkers of the Sheffield Region*, Leicester UP, 1972.

63. See Document 6 in Aspinall, *Early Trade Unions*, p. 4.

dustries are representative of those manufactures which had a sustained if unspectacular growth over the period catering for an expanding home market. Both experienced a degree of technological advance. Glass production resembled that of metal in that its new techniques and location depended on coal. The combined output of bottle and white glass almost doubled from 1747 to 1800 from 10,600 to 19,400 tonnes; it was white glass which was largely responsible. The high spot was the opening in 1773 of the Ravenshead works at St Helens to manufacture plate glass using imported French expertise. Otherwise, although London and Birmingham maintained important works, notably for quality decorative glassware, and Bristol used its local coal to good effect in eleven works making white and bottle glass by 1800, the north-east around Newcastle and Stourbridge and Dudley in the Midlands were the main centres. Newcastle produced more window glass than the other centres together in 1800. This illustrates yet again the pull of coal which was needed to fire the reverbatory furnaces; the other essential ingredient, sand, had to be brought all the way from Norfolk. A coastal location helped, for the two essential chemical ingredients of potash and soda were mostly imported. Although Dudley had two large firms and a smaller one in 1796, and a tradition going back to 1713, Stourbridge was the main Midlands centre. It specialised mainly in flint glass and crystal cutting. The growth of glass output therefore reflects several different market developments. The window glass makers reflected the growth of the building industry, while the flint glass makers catered, with their glasses, decanters and cruets, for the expanding market in small household wares. The plate glass from St Helens was used for mirrors and coach windows.[64]

Glass making reveals the importance of coal, but paper making illustrates T.S. Ashton's reminder of the great and continuing importance of water to eighteenth-century manufacturing. By 1700 the number of water-powered paper mills scattered through rural England exceeded a hundred. There was a tendency to concentrate in the south-east. The older process of fermenting rags in water – pulping – was replaced over the eighteenth century by mills which used wooden rollers fitted with knives to destruct the rags, but these 'hollanders' remained water powered. Only one Boulton and Watt steam engine was in use at a paper mill in 1800. Turning the

---

64. Useful accounts of the glass industry are provided in Pawson, *Early Industrial Revolution*, pp. 126–7; Court, *Midland Industries, op. cit.*, pp. 219–23; Musson, *Growth of British Industry*, pp. 126–7.

pulp into paper remained a skilled hand process in which separate sheets were produced with vats and wire-mesh moulds. The paper-making machine invented in 1799 and developed in England by the Fourdrinier Brothers enabled the making of a continuous web of paper on a wire-mesh belt, but it made little progress before 1830. More significant by 1800 were chemical developments in chlorine bleaching, which not only made whiter paper with less labour but enabled coloured rags to be used. Output, as Professor Coleman has shown, increased fairly slowly over the first half of the eighteenth century, then increased three-fold between 1740 and 1800. Over the century 1714 to 1815 tonnage increased from 2,764 to 18,715: almost seven times. By the latter date paper and printing together accounted for around 2 per cent of total manufacturing output, almost equal to silk and a quarter of the share of cotton and of metal.[65]

The great expansion in paper manufacture paralleled one in printing. Technological change was confined largely to the press, with little change in setting where the skills of the compositor remained paramount. Change in the press was slow – *The Times* was the first newspaper to print by steam cylinder press at the end of 1814 – and the progress of the industry is accordingly best revealed in the number of print workers. In 1831 4,000 out of a United Kingdom total of 9,000 worked in London and since the share of the provinces had been increasing since the eighteenth century, it can be presumed that more than half of all eighteenth-century print workers were located in London. There were 2,500 in the capital in 1815 after a rapid expansion over the first decade of the century, so perhaps the national total in 1800 was between 4,000 and 5,000. The book and periodical trades, newspapers and parliamentary printing brought about expanding demand in London as well as creating jobs on a smaller scale for associated trades like book binding and type founding. In the provinces it was above all the appearance of the weekly local newspapers which created the demand for hands to bring out such local institutions as the *Stamford Mercury, Northamptonshire Advertiser, Exeter Flying Post* and *Sherborne Mercury.*[66]

65. The fullest account of paper making is D.C. Coleman, *The British Paper Industry.*
66. Musson, *Growth of British Industry*, pp. 137–8.

OTHER MANUFACTURES

In an age when large industrial establishments were rare, the greatest concentrations of labour were to be found in the royal dockyards. Even the newest of them at Plymouth had passed the thousand mark by mid century – the establishment of 2,033 was only a little below the 2,228 at Portsmouth. Chatham then employed 1,553, Deptford 939 and Woolwich 868. Even the smallest, Sheerness with 439, was by eighteenth-century standards a large establishment. At the height of the French wars in 1813 the workforce at Portsmouth reached 3,582 but fell rapidly with the return of peace to a low of 1,610 in 1822. The Navy's need for ships fluctuated widely. In 1714 it had 247; at the end of the Seven Years War in 1763 it had 432; on the eve of the American war in 1776 only 340, but at its end 617. When the wars with revolutionary France began in 1793 there were 411, but at the height of the naval war in 1810 the fleet exceeded 1,048. By the middle of the peaceful 1820s there were less than 200. Accordingly the establishments at the yards were never stable.[67]

The workforce included many unskilled labourers, but its distinguishing feature was the variety of artisans. Of Portsmouth's establishment of 2,704 in 1803, 900 were shipwrights, 140 sawyers, 200 rope makers, 100 carpenters and 140 caulkers. Skilled workers therefore considerably outnumbered the 350 general labourers. By the end of the eighteenth century these included skilled metal-workers like chain makers, anchor smiths and, with the introduction of copper sheathing, coppersmiths. The shipwright, the true builder of the wooden ship, was the core craftsman and in the flurry of activity at the time of Trafalgar (1805) there were 3,193 of them at work in naval yards. Their skill remained unchallenged until the advent of the iron ship. It was not so with the block makers. Their position was lost under the reorganisation of the yards by Samuel Bentham, brother of the philosopher, who became Inspector General of Naval Works in 1796. Between 1803 and 1809 he introduced a series of machine tools for fashioning blocks. Designed by Marc Kingdom Brunel, father of the more famous engineer, and manufactured by Henry Maudsley, one of the nascent engineering industry's most

67. Dockyard employment figures for 1772 from M. Oppenheim, 'The Royal Dockyards' in *Victoria County History of Kent*, II, Institute of Historical Research, 1926, p. 378; D. Wilson, *England's Apprenticeship*, p. 148; G. and F.L. Harris, *The Making of a Cornish Town: Torpoint and its Neighbourhood*, University of Exeter, extra-mural publication, 1976, p.22; naval shipping statistics from C. Lloyd, *The British Seaman*, Paladin, 1970, p. 261.

successful and innovative entrepreneurs, the machinery enabled ten unskilled men to do the work of more than a hundred skilled ones. In 1849 only nineteen men and nine boys were employed in the making of 37,786 blocks at Portsmouth. Bentham also introduced copper sheathing and in 1797 installed the first steam engine which worked the yard pumps by night and the saw mills by day.[68]

Fond popular memory will always associate the royal dockyards with the building of great ships. In fact, most of their activity was in repair and refitting. With its need for ships so variable, the Navy often preferred to give orders to private yards rather than keep a full establishment at the yards. Most orders went to the Thames yards, but in the American war orders were placed in the north-east for the first time and even on the Solent itself naval ships were often built at Bursledon or Bucklers Hard rather than at Portsmouth. The private yards were much smaller and only those on the Thames were capable of building the larger ships before late in the eighteenth century, although Okill and Co. at Liverpool were building up to 700 tonnes by 1740. Aggregate output vastly exceeded that of the naval yards; even at the height of the naval war in 1810, Britain's merchant fleet of 12,198 was sixteen times the size of the Navy.[69]

By the second half of the century the leadership of the Thames was being challenged. It was still the largest single centre in 1790, but the combined output of the yards in the north-east was greater, and that of the north-west not far behind.

The north-east centres, Whitby, Newcastle, Scarborough, Sunderland and Stockton, had long met the demand for the small ships carrying coal to London along much the busiest of the coastal routes. London continued to build the large East and West Indiamen and the ships for the Levant trade, but its lead in larger vessel construction was dwindling as the century progressed. For much of the time its rival had been not the north-east but the American colonies – as early as 1714 Thames yards were complaining of competition from New England. Up to the Revolution, output from across the Atlantic was increasing: one in four of English merchant ships in 1760, one in three by 1776. MacPherson in his *Annals of Commerce* appreciated which industry benefited most from the war

68. D. Wilson, *England's Apprenticeship*, p. 148; Samuel Bentham hardly deserves to be so much less known than his brother Jeremy. He is a key figure in the history of management. See P. Linebaugh, 'Labour history without the labour process', *Social History*, VII, 3, 1982, pp. 320–2.

69. T.S. Ashton, *The Eighteenth Century*, p. 140.

Table 4.12 Shipbuilding in the years 1790–1, by district

	Tonnage	*No.*	*No. 200 tonnes +*
London	16,372	119	25
East Anglia	7,787	136	2
South coast	15,740	341	7
Bristol Channel and Wales	8,240	145	10
North-west coast	14,945	166	18
North-east coast	40,926	249	88
Total	104,010	1,156	150

Source: R. Davis, *The Rise of the English Shipping Industry in the Seventeenth and Eighteenth Centuries*, David and Charles, 1962, p. 69.

with America: 'A very important advantage was the recovery of the valuable trade of shipbuilding, which had in very great measure been, very impolitically, sacrificed to the zeal for promoting the prosperity of the colonies.'

Earlier naval wars had not led to a great increase in orders because of the successful habit of taking prize vessels. Over the period 1756 to 1763, 1,885 ships had been added to the merchant fleet in this way. However, from the end of the American war in 1783 to the end of the French wars in 1815 there was a 75 per cent increase in the number of ships registered and a doubling of the tonnage. From this significant increase in shipbuilding the north-east was the significant beneficiary.[70]

In 1766 a hundred Cornish tin miners burst into Redruth market and smashed all the Staffordshire earthenware on sale. They went on to Falmouth and repeated their action and were not pacified until a number of prominent citizens promised to do all they could to discourage the use of pottery, indicating their sympathy by bespoking a quantity of pewter dishes.[71] There was irony in the incident, for the white china clays which supplied the surging potteries were increasingly coming from Cornish pits. They had been used in Worcester and Staffordshire porcelain ware for some time before William Cookworthy's Plymouth works began to exploit them more

70. This account has been based on R. Davis, *The Rise of the English Shipping Industry*, Ch. 4.

71. A. Rees, 'Cornwall's place in ceramic history', *Rep. Royal Cornwall Polytechnic Society*, 1935, p. 61.

systematically in 1755. By 1816 Cornish output of china clay and china stone had reached 4,000 tonnes, although it grew even faster over the next decade to 13,000 tonnes by 1826. Perhaps the tinners had a point, for it was obtained from a form of quarrying, which created much less employment than deep mining for tin. Even after a century of growth in 1857 the industry employed only 1,700 men.[72]

Whatever localised fears of unemployment it created in far Cornwall, pottery was one of the success stories of consumer goods production and marketing. As late as 1725 few considered it of much importance or potential, although key techniques had already been learned from the continent including those of making both the lead-glazed 'slipware' and the harder glazed 'ironware'. By 1750, however, London at Bow and Chelsea, Worcester, Derby, Lowestoft and Liverpool as well as Staffordshire had porcelain works. But it was the common Staffordshire ware which was to attain a mass market: 'plate was too expensive, pewter too scarce and porcelain too fragile, to compete with the versatile pot'. Rising population and an increasing ability to purchase 'decencies' as well as 'necessaries' provided an expanding market.[73]

In 1730 even Staffordshire's potters were mostly making from local clays and selling in their own area, but by 1760 the Weaver Navigation was transporting six times as much pottery as twenty years earlier. By then the greatest of the eighteenth-century potters, Josiah Wedgwood, was sending most of his wares to London and by 1795 was selling through Europe and beyond. The 'Potteries', centred on the Five Towns around Burslem, became one of England's best-known manufacturing regions. Burslem had 150 potteries by 1762 supporting a population of 7,000, and John Wesley, who visited then and again twenty years later, commented on how much it had grown in between. Arthur Young visited it in 1771 and remarked on the Potteries' 'late' success, attributing it to 'the inventive genius of Mr Wedgwood'. This was not entirely true – other potters such as Spode and Minton have their place. But it was the celebrated Josiah who most successfully drew together the various threads and experiences of his predecessors and contemporaries. Seizing firmly on the advantages of the division of labour and training

72. Rowe, *Cornwall in the Industrial Revolution, op. cit.*, pp. 48–9, 90, 117.

73. Wilson, *England's Apprenticeship*, p. 309; N. McKenrick, 'The commercialisation of the Potteries' in McKendrick, Brewer and Plumb (eds). *Birth of the Consumer Society*, p. 104. The standard account of the rise of the pottery industry is now Weatherill, *The Pottery Trade and North Staffordshire*.

new hands in highly specialised details of decoration, he closed the gap between quality production and the wider market.[74]

If Wedgwood best represents the new potter, the tea service represents the new product. Nothing contributed as much to the broadening demand for china ware as did the remarkable increase in tea drinking as it percolated downwards through society. Ale tastes fine from a pewter tankard, but tea tastes best from a china cup. Tea consumption increased six-fold over the middle years of the century, then doubled again by its end. Figures are approximate, for tea was a staple of the smuggling trade. If this was pleasing to the makers of Staffordshire teapots, it was not so to the commercial brewers of beer. They had seen off the challenge of the 'Gin Age' – excised spirit consumption peaked at 7,955,000 gallons in 1742 and had fallen back to 2,639,000 by 1780. But tea presented a more permanent challenge as its fall in price changed it from an upper-class luxury stored in locked tea caddies into a daily essential for all social classes. The brewers' response was a new product: porter. Introduced in 1722, it was cheaper to produce and more standard in type than traditional ales. On its sales were based the fortunes of the likes of Whitbread, Barclays and Truman. A dozen large brewers produced a third of London's output by the 1740s and a half by the 1760s. In the provinces firms usually remained small, although things were already coming to a foaming head in the Trent valley, where the establishment of Worthington's at Burton in 1744 saw the beginnings of another of England's best-known industrial locations.[75]

Professor Mathias has shown just how capital intensive large-scale brewing became in the industrial revolution. Outlay was needed for the large copper vats and other utensils, for coal for boiling and, by the 1780s, to raise steam for engines grinding malt. This made the industry exceptional in the food and drink sector (although sugar boiling at Bristol and Liverpool was on a fairly large scale). Harley estimates that the sector as a whole made up 8 per cent of English manufacturing in 1770 and 6 per cent in 1815, although exact statistics are difficult in a sector characterised for the most part by self-employed small producers trading in local markets.[76]

74. Wilson, *England's Apprenticeship*, pp. 309–10; McKendrick, 'Commercialisation of the Potteries', p. 103. The tendency to overstate Wedgwood's importance has been corrected by Weatherill, *Pottery Trade*.

75. Wilson, *England's Apprenticeship*, p. 309.

76. Mathias, *Brewing Industry in England*; Harley, 'British industrialization before 1841', p. 269.

The building industry was by and large similarly structured. Even in 1851, only 70 out of 26,360 employers had a hundred or more men. Around 60 per cent employed only one or two, or worked on their own. Hoffman's index of manufacturing gave the sector 9.2 per cent of total output in 1812, but Harley's more recent estimate is 12 per cent in 1770 and 15 per cent in 1815. Figures for so universal and scattered an industry are guesstimates indeed. Masons, bricklayers, carpenters, plumbers and graziers were found in any town of size, although jobbing 'builders' ready to turn their hands to any task more suited the village economy. When building craftsmen did build on a speculative rather than on a bespoke basis, they often joined together, or else one master craftsman subcontracted others. Mortgage and credit both for supplies and for the wages of labour were characteristic.[77]

No equivalent index to the modern 'number of housing starts' exists for the eighteenth century. The appreciable growth in the number and size of towns means the housing stock must have been very considerably augmented at a rapidly increasing rate over the period. Timber imports increased in value from £121,000 in 1714 to £171,000 in 1750. After 1765 they went up even more sharply from £245,000 to £602,000 in 1815. Excise duties provide a measure of brick output from 1785, when duty was paid on 385.8 million bricks. Over the next twenty years the average output was 646 million, but from 1805 to 1815 it was 866.6 million.

Professor Feinstein's calculations in Table 4.13 reveal the central importance of building to total investment. His figures do not separate agricultural building from total investment in agriculture, but they do for the manufacturing sector. Construction in the transport sector, roads, canals, bridges and docks is not included.

The industrial revolution required a greater investment in bricks and mortar, even without workers' housing, than it did in machinery. Investment in the latter from 1760 to 1820 was on average only around a third of investment in industrial and commercial buildings.[78]

Josiah Tucker, Dean of Gloucester, one of the shrewdest of writers on economic matters in the mid eighteenth century, drew attention in 1757 to the progress of machinery in English manufacturing.

77. Harley, 'British industrialization before 1841', p. 269. The structure of the industry is analysed in C.W. Chalklin, *Provincial Towns of Georgian England.*

78. C. Feinstein, 'Capital formation in Great Britain' in Mathias and Postan (eds), *Cambridge Economic History of Europe*, Pt 1, pp. 40–8.

Table 4.13 Great Britain: gross domestic fixed capital formation

(*Constant [1851–60] prices. £ million p.a. decade averages*)			
	1761–70	*1791–1800*	*1811–20*
Dwellings	1.49	3.35	5.82
Public buildings	0.15	0.33	0.58
Industrial and commercial buildings	0.97	2.20	4.16
Total (per cent of GDFC)	39.3	41.0	51.0

Source: Based on Feinstein in M.M. Postan and P. Mathias (eds), *Cambridge Economic History of Europe:* vol. 7, *The Industrial Economies. Part I: Britain, France, Germany and Scandinavia*, Cambridge, 1982, pp. 40–1.

> Few countries are equal, perhaps none excel; the English in the number of contrivances of their machines to abridge labour . . . the English are uncommonly dexterous in their contrivance of the mechanic powers . . . [they exhibit] a specimen of practical mechanics scarce to be paralleled in any part of the world.[79]

Here is an early example of a modern usage. Thirty years earlier, to Daniel Defoe, 'the guides or masters in handicrafts' and craftsmen in general from weavers to coppersmiths 'are all understood in this one word mechanics'.[80] This broad use remained common until 1815, but association of the word with machinery was developing alongside. The engineering industry grew from several well-developed strands. Pride of place has usually been given to the millwrights. Originally the fitters of wind and water mills, after 1750 they worked increasingly in metal rather than wood in applying their special skill of linking the source of power to its object through shafts and gears. The successful early nineteenth-century engineer Alexander Fairbairn described the eighteenth-century millwright as 'an itinerant engineer and mechanic' who could handle axe, hammer and plane, bore and forge, and cut stone with a skill equal to those who specialised in those trades. It was such men who turned to the manufacture of the early textile machinery, developing a regional specialisation in Lancashire. Traditionally the millwright had carried his tools to work on the spot, but in the late

79. Cited in C. Wilson, *England's Apprenticeship*, p. 311.
80. Defoe, *A Plan of the English Commerce*, 1728, reprinted Oxford 1928, p. 3.

eighteenth century the machine shop began to emerge in engine building. Specialisation increased: pattern makers, iron and brass founders, vicemen, turners, planers, etc. emerged in the place of generalised millwrights, carpenters and blacksmiths. Most of the specialist workers rose from the ranks of those generally known as 'smiths'.

The long-established skills in tool making, especially in Lancashire and those in precision part making and assembly in watch making, have already been noted. There was little wanting in terms of the skills necessary for an engineering industry. Indeed, before their new Soho Foundry opened in 1795, even Boulton and Watt supplied only a supervisor to oversee the erection of their engines on site and arrange for the local supply of labour and materials. The Soho Foundry was the first heavy engineering shop concentrating on producing patterns for castings and on the manufacture of parts which called for special accuracy. Here Watt, concerned about the skill level of his workmen, set about training a body of men, who might well be considered the first purpose-trained engineering workers. Soho was to become a nursery from which engineering skills emanated, as were the later pioneering engineering works such as that of Henry Maudsley established in London in 1798. Development was not dramatic. In 1814 Fairbairn discovered that Manchester shops were still commonly dependent upon hand rather than machine tools and spent a large amount of time chipping and filing. Nevertheless, by then a distinctive engineering industry had clearly come into being: the future was a matter of wider and more rapid skill dissemination and specialisation and a growing use of increasingly sophisticated machine tools.[81]

Arthur Young's much-quoted remark of 1791 that 'All the activity and industry of this kingdom is fast concentrating where there are coalpits' was only a shade hyperbolic. It does not tell the whole story, however. Professor Mathias has suggested that the concentration of steam-powered cotton mills in Lancashire was due as much to the presence of local engineering firms with specialised fitters as to coal.[82] It was the possession of the skills to exploit them which was as critical as the possession of natural resources like coal and iron to the English lead in manufacturing. The localisation of these

81. The emergence of the engineering industry is well described in Berg, *Age of Manufactures*, pp. 269–73, and Mathias, *First Industrial Nation*, pp. 125–7.
82. Young, *Tours in England and Wales*, p. 275; Mathias, *First Industrial Nation*, p. 120.

skills and of those resources explains why the familiar map of nine-teenth-century manufacturing had already taken on much of its shape by the late eighteenth century. The student of the industrial history of eighteenth-century England will note some unexpected presences and some surprising absences, but will not feel like a traveller in a strange country.

CHAPTER FIVE

Forms of Enterprise in Manufacturing and Mining

The extent of manufacturing and mining in the eighteenth-century economy was not more remarkable than its astonishing heterogeneity of form. Possibly the only safe generalisation is that before the last quarter of the century only a small minority of the labour force worked in large units of production or extraction. For most of the eighteenth century there were so few 'factories' that the scattering of precocious examples, such as Thomas Lombe's silk mill at Derby, when chanced upon by travellers, were considered as exceptional as cathedrals, and when occasionally portrayed by artists were depicted hardly less splendidly.

MANUFACTURING

When, by 1807, Robert Southey could write of 'the manufacturing system',[1] it was a comment on the progress of a form of manufacturing which had hardly existed before Richard Arkwright's first water-powered mill began to spin cotton at Cromford in 1771. By the end of the 1790s there were 900 mills spinning cotton by water or, after 1790, by steam power, on either Arkwright-type frames, or Crompton-type mules. Added to at least a dozen silk mills which had followed Lombe's success at Derby, and some factories established in woollen or worsted manufacture (though not yet in spinning or weaving), this suggests that the number of industrial establishments which could be reasonably described as factories in England must have comfortably exceeded a thousand by 1800. It was not the labour of

1. R. Southey, *Letters from England*, 1807, reprinted Alan Sutton 1984, pp. 207, 211.

adult males, however, but mainly that of women and children that they used.

Throughout the period, the royal dockyards remained the largest concentrations of labour. No private employer approached the more than 2,000 employed at Portsmouth. Arthur Young in 1776 thought the great ironmaster Abraham Darby employed around a thousand workers, but that included colliers in his several mines; the number actually working on his Coalbrookdale site was significantly less.[2] This does not mean that large employers did not exist in many areas of manufacturing. Under the putting-out system, merchant capitalists put out materials and collected finished work from a veritable army of dependent out-workers, who were in effect a home-based proletariat. Those who took in work might still be described, in cloth making for example, as *master* weavers. That was a recognition of both the skill they had acquired and the fact that they took apprentices and from time to time might even employ one or two journeymen. However, in the districts where the separation between capitalist clothier and working manufacturer was wide, the ratios are revealing. In two Gloucestershire woollen-producing villages at the end of the eighteenth century, master weavers outnumbered journeymen weavers by two to one. A man could not weave broadcloth without assistance, but for much of his working life that assistance could be provided by the family.[3]

Many putting-out capitalists were substantial employers. A witness in 1802 pointed out that in the West-Country woollen districts a man would not be considered a 'respectable clothier' unless he could 'keep' at least thirty or forty looms. ('Keep' is a revealing usage, for the looms in question were actually owned by the weavers, as were those of a clothier who described himself as 'employing' fifty looms.) The wealth of many of the 'gentleman clothiers' was much commented on. They had virtual control of woollen manufacture by the late seventeenth century, and Defoe was told that it was not unusual for such men to be worth from £10,000 to £40,000. In East Anglian worsted manufacture the controlling capitalists were also merchants rather than manufacturers who, like their Gloucestershire counterparts, affected the style of gentlemen. In some smaller centres of woollen cloth production in-

2. A. Young, *Tours in England and Wales Selected from the Annals of Agriculture*, 1932, p. 275.

3. J. de L. Mann, *The Cloth Industry in the West of England*, pp. 229–30; A. Randall, 'Work and resistance in the West of England' in Hudson (ed.), *Regions and Industries*, pp. 179–83.

dividual clothiers similarly kept many hands at work. In a dispute over apprenticeship at Banbury in 1793, 'everyman working for the same master, amounting to 300, left his work'.[4] In some centres of the Devonshire serge districts, similar organisation was evident. Defoe described the villages around Tiverton as 'full of manufacturers, depending much on the master manufacturers of that town'. But in his time and beyond there were still some master serge weavers who continued to employ a small number of journeymen weavers on their own premises. This was especially true of Exeter, where the Company of Weavers retained something of a guild hold on manufacture. Merchant capital seems only rarely to have mixed with manufacturing in that city. It did, however, largely control the supply of raw materials, the other processing stages like sorting, combing, spinning and finishing, and the merchandising of the cloth.[5]

Mantoux rightly saw that it was through his control of the stock of raw materials and his reach into expanding and spreading markets that the merchant clothier evolved into the pivotal figure in many branches of textile production.

> He bought the raw wool and had it carded, spun, woven, fulled and dressed at his own expense. He owned the raw material and consequently the product, in its successive forms; those through whose hands this product passed in the processes which it underwent were no more, in spite of their apparent independence, than workmen in the service of an employer.

He also drew an apt analogy. In 1765 when a rich Tiverton merchant died without heirs, the town's weavers appealed in a body to the mayor to seek to induce an Exeter merchant to come to the town by offering him a seat on the town council: 'The man's death was for them what the sudden closing down of a factory is for the workmen of today.'[6] T.S. Ashton's description of the merchant clothier capitalists – 'each like a spider at the centre of a vast web, gave out material and drew in finished or semi-finished goods from hundreds, or even thousands of spinners and weavers' – is perhaps a little less flattering than the contemporary likening of a clothier to

4. *Minutes of Evidence before the Committee to whom the Bill respecting the Laws relating to the Woollen Trade is committed*, BPP 1802–3 (95), VII, pp. 37–8; A. Aspinall, *Early Trade Unions*, p. 19.

5. Daniel Defoe, *A Tour through the Whole Island of Great Britain*, 1962, II, p. 17; W.G. Hoskins, *Industry, Trade and People in Exeter*, 1688–1800, 2nd edn, Exeter UP, 1968, pp. 44–53.

6. P. Mantoux, *The Industrial Revolution in the Eighteenth Century*, Methuen edn, 1964, pp. 62, 65.

the sun: 'he scattered life and its supports to everyone around him'.[7]

Not all woollen cloth came from the putting-out system. The most noted exception was the West Riding of Yorkshire where the independent *working* clothiers continued until the coming of the factory. Defoe's description of the manufacture around Halifax in about 1720 has become something of a classic.

> Among the manufacturers' houses are likewise scattered an infinite number of cottages or small dwellings in which dwell the workmen which are employed, the women and children of whom are always busy, carding, spinning etc. so that no hands are . . . unemployed. . . . If we knocked at the door of any of the master manufacturers we presently saw a house full of lusty fellows, some at the dye-vat, some dressing the cloths, some in the loom, some one thing, some another, all hard at work, and full employed upon the manufacture, and all seeming to have sufficient business.[8]

Defoe employed the term 'manufacturer' only when he meant someone actually engaged in the production process; the non-working capitalists of the other woollen districts he called 'master clothiers'. What he is describing is a manufacture going on in the houses of small working masters. One late eighteenth-century estimate gives around 3,240 such men for the West Riding.[9] A witness before a parliamentary committee in 1806 insisted:

> what I mean by the domestic system is the little clothiers living in villages, or in detached places with all their comforts, carrying on business with their own capital . . . in the west of England the manufacturer . . . is the same as our common workman in a factory in Yorkshire, except living in a detached house; in the west the wool is delivered out to them to weave, in Yorkshire it is the man's own property.[10]

The working masters bought the wool from the staplers, and assisted by their wives, children and some apprentices and journeymen, took it through all its stages to the undressed cloth. Contemporary approval of the system rested much on an ideal in which there was little gap between master and man, for not only did they work side by side, but a low capital threshold and available credit meant a real possibility of journeymen advancing to become

---

7. T.S. Ashton, *An Economic History of England,* p. 99.
8. Defoe, *Tour,* II, p. 195.
9. D. Gregory, *Regional Transformation and Industrial Revolution. A Geography of the Yorkshire Woollen Industry,* Macmillan, 1982, p. 115.
10. Cited in Mantoux, *Industrial Revolution,* p. 63 (footnote).

masters. Dr Hudson's recent analysis has explained the factors which enabled this 'domestic system' – or 'artisan system' as she terms it – to survive. These included a favourable position in the credit matrix and the combination of farming with manufacturing.[11]

Even by 1700 these small working clothiers were elsewhere exceptional in the production of woollen cloth and they were hardly to be found in worsted production let alone other textiles. In cotton cloth production, with its imported raw material and early export orientation, merchant capitalists appeared early and rapidly became dominant. As early as 1736 a witness informed a parliamentary committee that he and his brother put out to more than 600 looms, for each of which they also needed four domestic spinners. In 1758 a check maker spoke of employing 500 persons. In 1812 Thomas Kay of Bury was employing 2,500 to 3,000 and Thomas Cardwell of Manchester more than 1,000.[12] A description of Manchester written in 1783 described this development. At first many of the Manchester merchants simply bought cloth from Bolton weavers, who immediately purchased the yarn to make another piece. The merchants soon found that this faced them with problems of supply and quality control: 'To remedy this many of them furnished warps and wool [spun cotton] to the weavers, and employed people to put warps out to the weaving by commission; and encouraged many weavers to fetch them from Manchester.' For a time some merchants even began to give the weavers unspun cotton wool for the weft, requiring them to get the spinning done either in their own household or by paying someone else. Others had been from the start both merchants and manufacturers.[13]

Although the arrival of factory spinning in the last quarter of the century first reduced and then removed the need to put out raw cotton to rural spinners, the increased and cheapened supply of yarn was fed to an army of hand-loom weavers which increased from 75,000 in 1795 to around a quarter of a million by the time factory weaving began to take over in the 1830s. By 1800 Sir Robert Peel needed fifteen depots to serve his out-working weavers from Blackburn in the north to Stockport in the south, and William Radcliffe was distributing warps up to 30 miles from his base.[14]

11. See P. Hudson, 'From manor to mill: the West Riding in transition', in Berg, Hudson and Sonenscher (eds), *Manufacture in Town and Country*, pp. 124–44.
12. Examples from S. Pollard, *Genesis of Modern Management*, pp. 43–5.
13. *Ibid.*, pp. 48–9.
14. S.D. Chapman, *Cotton Industry in the Industrial Revolution*, p. 59.

The putting-out system was to be found in silk weaving as well, but it existed alongside small working masters and loomshops with several journeymen. Sailcloth manufacturers seem to have employed unusually large labour forces. In 1750 a Warrington manufacturer claimed to employ more than 5,000 persons. In the hosiery manufacture of the east Midlands the system was predominant. Here the hosiers not only put out the worsted or cotton yarn to the stockingers but commonly rented them the knitting frames as well. In 1753 the three principal hosiers in Nottingham had 100 frames each, but many of the fifty manufacturers there known as 'putters out' employed fewer, for the total was 1,200. A similar situation existed in Leicester. In 1813 one hosier claimed to have £24,000 invested in frames, another to employ 300 knitters and a third to pay out £200 a week in wages. According to William Felkin, in 1824 there were several manufacturers who had risen to the point of employing more than 1,000 frames.[15]

Of course, the merchant capitalist did not put out directly to or collect from the cottage of the producer. From the workers' viewpoint, this method of organising production must have seemed more like a 'fetch and carry' system. They often had to tramp several miles to warehouses, or from their villages into the towns where the clothier or other merchant capitalist had his premises. This meant a weekly day without pay when, for example, weavers in cotton commonly made 15- or even 20-mile round trips into Manchester. Metal-workers in south Staffordshire made equivalent journeys into Birmingham or Dudley. In the hosiery districts it was said that as much as two and a half days a week might be taken up in getting orders and material, returning finished work and collecting wages.[16]

Since Franklin Mendels in 1972 first popularised the notion of a 'proto-industrial' stage of rural industry preceding modern industrialisation, historians have made an intensive study of the origins and forms of manufacture which spread so widely into the European countryside through the seventeenth and eighteenth centuries. Characteristically, merchant capital organised cottage labour in response to the new opportunities offered by the growth of distant markets. Goods were produced by peasant manufacturers who, at least in the beginning, combined making them with farming. Seeking cheap labour and the evasion of urban guild constraints, merchant capitalists took up the labour slack which existed in the

15. Pollard, *Genesis of Modern Management*, pp. 44–5; F.A. Wells, *The British Hosiery and Knitwear Industry*, reprinted David & Charles, Newton Abbot, 1972, p. 71.
16. Ashton, *An Economic History of England*, p. 102.

households of some agrarian regions. Putting out materials to cottage manufacture kept fixed capital overheads to a minimum, as goods were made off premises by producers who provided only labour and, usually, tools, neither owning the materials nor marketing the commodities they wrought from them.[17]

Studies of proto-industrialisation have certainly increased our knowledge of the processes of capitalist-organised manufacturing in the countryside. Most usefully, they have helped understanding of why it took hold in some areas rather than others, of the importance of the *family* as the unit of production and of the relationship of its emergence and spread to demographic change (see Chapter Two). Their contribution has been to integrate and systematise much that was already known so that the *dynamics* of the putting-out system are better understood. Few have been so accepting as to see a proto-industrial phase as the necessary, or even the likeliest, precursor of industrial capitalism. Some consider that little but jargon has been added to the insights already offered by historians like Joan Thirsk. So far as England is concerned, she had already noted the link between the introduction of cottage manufacturing and labour slack.[18] In her pioneering article of 1961 she argued that rural industry took hold in pastoral, upland or marshland areas, where the soil was too poor for agriculture alone to support growing populations drawn or driven to such areas where extensive commons and weak manorial control offered possibilities of subsisting. Fresh settlement was not prevented – important in explaining not only the origins of labour slack but also how, once manufacturing was introduced, available labour could be not only retained but expanded even beyond its own natural increase. Such regions tended, too, to have partible inheritance, so a generational reduction in holdings increased the need to have supplementary employment while at the same time the retention of some land and, importantly, common grazing rights provided a subsistence cushion allowing the capitalist to pay lower wages than those prevailing in urban manufacturing. This advantage was further enhanced by exploiting the family basis of cottage manufacture. As the labour of women was not usually independently waged but was essential in the production of the piece-rated goods, the larger proportion of

17. For comprehensive discussion of the proto-industrialisation literature, see L.A. Clarkson, *Proto-Industrialisation*, and D.C. Coleman, 'Proto-industrialisation: a concept too many', *Econ. H.R.*, XXXVI, 1983, pp. 435–48.

18. J. Thirsk, 'Industries in the countryside' in F.J. Fisher (ed.), *Essays in the Economic History of Tudor and Stuart England*, Cambridge UP, 1961, pp. 70–88.

the women's labour time went to the capitalist. For household prosperity was tied to the family cycle. With the arrival of young children, the change in the dependency ratio and the greater concentration of the wife on child care brought strain. As the children grew up, things improved, and for a time their adult or near-adult capability brought the family's earning potential to its height. As they left home, the gradual decline into the poverty of old age began.[19]

Dr Hudson has convincingly demonstrated that only through close attention to regional farming variations, levels of manorial control and inheritance differences can we explain the persistence of a woollen manufacture based on the production of small independent working clothiers in one part of the West Riding, and the arrival and rapid spread of a worsted manufacture based on merchant capital and the putting-out system in another.[20] In Leicestershire it was predominantly in the 'open' villages that framework knitting took hold in the late seventeenth and early eighteenth centuries. Levine has shown how the 'unregulated freehold village' of Shepshed developed from the end of the seventeenth century into a manufacturing centre where by 1812 there were 1,000 knitting frames in use in a population of 3,000. Only 15 miles away was Bottesford. Here, 79 per cent of the land was held either directly by the Duke of Rutland or by those appointed by him. Rural industry was kept out. The village's social economy retained its old equilibrium and its population was no larger at the end of the eighteenth century than it had been at the beginning.[21]

As a model, proto-industrialisation has been a limited and imperfect key to the *operating* manufacturing economy of eighteenth-century England – however usefully it has cast light on the *origins* of rural manufacturing in districts where by the eighteenth century it had become well established. As we have seen, access to land had become of restricted and declining importance in the major areas of rural textile or metal ware out-work. Production, even from the countryside, came overwhelmingly from full-time manufacturing workers.

19. The seminal article on the family in proto-industrialisation is H. Medick, 'The proto-industrial family economy: the structural function of household and family during the transition from peasant society to industrial capitalism', *Social History* 3, 1976, pp. 291–315.

20. Dr Hudson's argument is perhaps best approached through her articles 'From manor to mill' *op. cit.*, and 'Proto-industrialisation: the case of the West Riding', *History Workshop Journal* 12, 1981, pp. 34–61. See also Berg, *Age of Manufactures*, Ch. 4.

21. D. Levine, *Family Formation*, especially Chs 5 and 10.

Outside of textile manufacture in its manifold forms, the putting-out system was really prevalent only in the final stages of the iron and non-ferrous metal industries: the production of iron, steel, brass and copper wares. The humblest and most numerous of rural metal out-workers were the nailors. There were about 10,000 of them by the late eighteenth century in the Black Country and perhaps a further 2–3,000 in the iron districts of the north. Heated rods were cut to length on an anvil, placed in a hole and given a sharp tap to head them, which also caused them to fly out ready for the insertion of the next nail. It was a continuous process performed at astonishing speed. An occupation of low esteem, it was carried out by women as well as men. Arthur Young found the road from Birmingham to West Bromwich for 5 or 6 miles 'a continuous village of nailors'. One Black Country iron merchant claimed to put out rod iron to more than a thousand homes. In many cases putting out was organised through a middleman, the 'fogger' who shared some of the risk.[22] Many other items of hardware needing a greater level of skill were made at cottage forges under the putting-out system. Thousands of these were scattered around the Black Country and in parts of the north. The system also existed in brass and copper. One firm in 1767 employed around 2,000 people in brass manufacture.[23] Whether the small manufacturers of metal wares, working often with the labour of only their families or perhaps one or two journeymen, can *in general* be properly considered part of the 'out-working proletariat' alongside the cottage weavers and framework knitters is an important question. Certainly the nail makers can as a group, and in other branches of brass and iron manufacture, chiefly on simpler articles, there were home-based makers who worked on put-out materials. The picture is, however, not that simple. One of the difficulties of taking too proto-industrial a view of the eighteenth-century manufacturing economy is that it tends to suggest firm boundaries between the different methods of organising production and to generalise too readily from the textile industries. It is, for example, true that some cutlery, especially of cheaper quality, was made under the putting-out system in Sheffield itself and to a greater extent in the surrounding rural districts, but the working cutlers of the great centre of edged-tool manufacture

22. D. Hey, *The Rural Metalworkers of the Sheffield Region*, Leicester UP, 1972, pp. 33–6; Young, *Tours in England and Wales*, p. 140; William Hutton, *Life of William Hutton F.A.S.S.*, 1817 edn, p. 110; Ashton, *An Economic History of England*, p. 101; Pollard, *Genesis of Modern Management*, p. 45; W.C.B. Court, *The Rise of the Midland Industries 1600–1838*, Oxford UP, 1953, pp. 193–213.

23. Berg, *Age of Manufactures*, p. 271.

were far from constituting a homogeneous out-working proletariat. Very little capital was needed to set up a small forge. Accordingly, 'little masters' working on their own material existed throughout the period and indeed survived well into the nineteenth century alongside substantial cutlers employing large numbers of workers. Yet the tendency through the eighteenth century was towards increasing capitalist control. The first historian of this manufacture, Lloyd, in 1913 saw himself as writing in the late stages of this process.

> Handicraft passes by small gradations into the domestic system, and many intermediate stages are to be found. One worker may even represent both places simultaneously, producing for a small circle of customers on his own account and at the same time dealing with merchants or other intermediaries.[24]

Even the small working master who purchased his own metal and sold a product rather than labour power tended to become a dependent artisan. He procured his material, usually on credit, from a factor or merchant, and usually 'sold' his finished cutlery to the same merchant, hardly ever on the market. He may have considered his remuneration a 'price' in contrast to the wage he paid his journeyman, but, as Lloyd shrewdly pointed out, his well-being similarly depended on the abundance or scarcity of work allocated by the merchant capitalist. Further, the credit purchase of his metal could tie him to a particular merchant, making that 'independence' so important to his artisan pride more an attitude of mind than a description of reality. It was reported in 1792 that war on the continent was so affecting the market for cutlery that 'the manufactures of Sheffield are sold . . . at the prices given to the manufacturer, the merchant confining his profits solely to what he gains on the raw materials'. The last phrase is highly significant.[25]

A letter to the Warrington ironmonger Peter Stubs in 1794 reveals the same transitional ambiguity even in respect of the lowly nail makers in requesting information on 'the workmen's prices of nails and what they give their masters for iron'. Stubs was especially involved in tool making and many of the smiths and file cutters who worked for him also took orders from others and considered themselves as receiving a price for a product rather than a wage for labour.[26] In contrast, in the Midlands nail makers and some other

24. G.I.H. Lloyd, *The Cutlery Trade*, 1913, reprinted Cass 1968, p. 16.
25. *Ibid.*, p. 15; Aspinall, *Early Trade Unions*, p. 6.
26. Ashton, *An Economic History of England*, pp. 100–1.

rural workers in iron were usually referred to as wage-earning workers. Birmingham, along with other Midland centres of specialist
smallware manufacture like Wolverhampton with its locks, exhibited
fully as much ambiguity as Sheffield. Birmingham, too, was a 'matrix of small workshops'.[27] There were large direct employers of labour, but for every one of them there were a hundred of very small
capital who concentrated on the production of a particular piece of
hardware: 'for one man makes a drawer knob, another a commode
handle, another a bell-pull etc etc'. If the master tried to pay less
than fair journeyman rates, then 'the man has nothing to do but go
and manufacture the article himself'. A finished product might involve several separate craft processes. The gun, lock, stock and barrel on which the 'gun maker' put his plate, was assembled from
components made in nine separate small-scale operations. The putting-out system in the full sense was represented in Birmingham
chiefly in the production of cheap, simple items like buttons where
the home labour of women and children could be exploited, but
there were merchant capitalists who to meet their orders might at
the same time employ some workers directly on their premises, put
out materials to others and pay 'prices' to small masters. But where
merchant capital did not put out, it still underpinned the essential
credit matrix of the town, through the orders it placed determined
the prosperity of small masters who in times of slump 'died like flies
in the night', and could, when trade was less brisk, cut 'prices' just
as direct employers could lower wages.[28]

In every town and in many villages were to be found men who
still fitted the interchangeable meaning of 'artisan' and 'tradesman'. Working with perhaps one or two apprentices and/or journeymen, shoemakers, carpenters, tailors, blacksmiths, wheelwrights
and their like supplied local markets. Even in towns where a specialist manufacture whose product transcended that market was carried
on, this manufacturing group existed alongside them. In some
towns, such as Bath, Oxford or Cambridge, the larger than average
presence of better-off clients extended its size. In larger provincial
centres the range of working tradesmen was extended to supply
rather less often and less widely needed goods: watches, saddles,
furniture or even coaches. For some producers the market was wide

27. D.A. Reid, 'Decline of Saint Monday', p. 77.

28. *Fourth Report from S.C. on Artisans and Machinery*, BPP 1824 (51), V, pp. 319–
20; Berg, *Age of Manufactures*, p. 274; C. Behagg, 'Masters and manufacturers: social
values and the smaller unit of production in Birmingham, 1800–50' in G. Crossick
and H.-G. Haupt (eds), *Shopkeepers and Master Artisans in Nineteenth-Century Europe*,
Methuen, 1984, pp. 142–4.

enough for them to become larger-scale employers, but most remained working masters engaged in small-scale production either bespoken by their customers or retailed locally.

The greatest centre of artisan manufacture was London. In some occupations, such as shoe making, tailoring and watch making, the workers were numbered in thousands. Not far behind were other craft-manufacturing trades like hat making, cabinet making and printing, and then through an astonishing range of smaller trades such as locksmiths, engravers, goldsmiths, brush makers and saddlers to such specialists as the makers of surgical instruments or those of leather shagreen trunks. Some of these trades retained the theoretical guild mobility through which, after apprenticeship and a short period as a journeyman, the fully trained craftsman set up for himself. But the most significant development over the eighteenth century was the emergence in a number of trades of some large employers with the consequential creation of a class of permanent journeymen. Rural proletarianisation through putting out was one part of the accelerating process which justified Adam Smith's generalisation of 1776 that twenty men served under a master for every one who was independent: 'In all arts and manufactures the greater part of the workmen stand in need of a master to advance them the materials of their work, and their wages and maintenance until it be completed.' Another, no less important cause was the growth of the permanent urban journeyman class. In London, according to a recent quantification, only 5 or 6 per cent of the working population could be classified as self-employed craftsmen by 1800.[29]

It was said in 1745 in respect of London's tailors:

> A journeyman is understood to be one, who has by apprenticeship or other contract, served such a portion of his time to that particular business which he professes to occupy, as renders him capable to execute every branch or part of the trade, whereby he is at full liberty, if his ability and condition of life will permit, to set up in the world as a master of his profession; and is only called a journeyman while he continues to serve under the direction of others at certain wages.[30]

It has already been noted that in those cloth-making districts where the putting-out system predominated, only a small fraction of the labour force were described as journeymen. A different situation

---

29. *Smith, Wealth of Nations*, I, pp. 73–4; L.D. Schwarz, 'Income distribution and social structure in London in the late eighteenth century', *Econ. H.R.*, XXXII, 2, 1979, pp. 256–7.
30. Cited in J.G. Rule, *Experience of Labour*, pp. 32–3.

prevailed in several of the craft trades of the capital and to a lesser extent in other large urban centres. The contrast with Sheffield or Birmingham is differently marked, for these journeymen worked for large, not small employers. The condition for their existence was the steady rising of the capital threshold of entry. Wherever capital requirements of setting up were high, entry to the ranks of the employers was likely to be, if not unachievable, at least restricted to a few of exceptional ambition and determination, such as Francis Place. Sometimes, as in printing, the cost of machinery and premises was the barrier, while elsewhere, as in tailoring, it was the cost of renting and maintaining premises in the better end of town, as well as of extending very long credit to upper-class customers. For tailors, as for shoe makers, 'independence' was to be found only at the poorer end of the trade, where it was usually less remunerative than working for wages in the West End. Not that the latter were high. The journeymen tailors of London were described in 1747 as being 'as common as locusts' and 'as poor as rats'. Many were scarcely able to secure regular work. Their wages since 1720 had been fixed by statute on a daily basis and they were called from the inns – 'houses of call' – they were required to frequent to work on their masters' premises as and when they were needed. It was a situation which was already well established by 1714: 'It is a fact that it is the Journeymen, and not the masters, who are the artificers as well as labourers in that trade or calling', and they were 'grievously oppressed' by 'a few purse-proud pretenders, either to ingenuity or labour'. The 'few' preferred to keep things that way. To ensure the persistence of a cheap labour force and discourage independence, they used the law, which required journeymen to undertake any work that was offered at statutory daily rates, to force men to work for them, 'notwithstanding the journeyman may have a prospect of being a master himself, which consequently his master will endeavour to prevent'.[31]

There were many gradations in shoe making, and hundreds of small independent shoe makers still cobbled in garrets. At the richer bespoke end of the trade, however, large employers operated from West End premises and, in the interests of cheapening production, encouraged a division of labour between the 'clickers' who cut out the uppers, the 'closers' who stitched them and the 'makers' who put on the sole and heel. So poor were many of the independent shoe makers, that the trade of leather cutting had grown

31. *Ibid., loc. cit.* for these and other examples.

up, in which large pieces of leather were cut up for those able to afford only enough for one pair of shoes or boots at a time. This trade survived efforts in 1738 by the larger employers to secure a prohibition on the sale of anything less than whole hides, which at that time would have cost £10 each and could probably have been afforded by only around 500 shoe makers in London. Their object was to reduce the independent small makers to journeymen. Such men probably needed to spend around two shillings a week on leather to support their families, but 'the master shoemakers do not care that journeymen should work for themselves'.[32]

By 1777 only around fifty of London's master hatters made up their own materials. When their apprenticeship was completed, most skilled hatters were employed in workshops. There were the so-called 'little masters', but although these worked at home they did so on materials delivered to them by larger hatters. Often they were among the less skilled, brought in by the labour-employing masters only when the press of business was such as could not be met by their regularly employed journeymen. They tended to be looked down on by the latter, whose union prevented them from taking apprentices. Journeymen hatters might have had little prospect of becoming masters but they were a confident body, organised into a union from the end of the seventeenth century, who used control over apprenticeship to create an effective 'closed shop', reflected in the respectable wage of fifteen shillings (75p) a week in 1777. Journeymen compositors in the print trade did even better at £1 a week. Although they complained in 1809 that the capital cost involved in setting up a printworks kept them as journeymen, in stating that this line of advancement was still 'a moral certainty' in 'most businesses' they were making an unwarranted exception of their own situation. It took even more capital to set up as a coach maker, but the condition of journeymen on five shillings (25p) a day was described in 1747 as 'genteel and profitable enough' a description which also covers the calico printers whose London journeymen's airs when they moved to Lancashire after 1780 got them labelled 'gentlemen journeymen'. The role of trade unionism among permanent journeymen will be considered in the companion volume, *Albion's People*, but it can be noted here that by the mid eighteenth century the well-being of many skilled men had come to depend on their ability to limit the overstocking of their trade

32. George, *London Life*, pp. 98–9; R. Campbell, *The London Tradesman*, 1747, reprinted David & Charles 1969, pp. 217–18; *Commons Journals*, XXIII, 1738, pp. 176–7.

rather than on the possibility of setting up as an independent pro-ducer.[33]

Considerable manufacturing also went on in London organised in ways which did not correspond very closely to the pattern in the trades we have just been describing. Shipbuilding on the Thames is one example, but in terms of the nature of the work rather than in the relationships of capitalist employers to a class of skilled jour-neymen whose numbers, as shipwrights and in other trades, fluctu-ated from 2,000 to 3,000 in the late eighteenth and early nine-teenth centuries. Neither did London shipbuilding differ in any sig-nificant way, other than in the size of its five or six yards that coped with building the East Indiamen, from that carried on at Liverpool, Bristol or other centres. The gangs of shipwrights and related crafts-men formed yet another group of well-paid and highly self-esteem-ing journeymen. In London, too, an especially large demand for their product from brewers and shippers placed coopers in a similar situation, although in smaller towns varied local needs could keep the independent craftsman, assisted by journeymen and apprentice, in comfortable employment.[34]

Out-working was especially prevalent in watch making. By 1800 it employed 8,000 men in Clerkenwell and had been organised on a putting-out system for at least fifty years. The division of labour was such that there hardly existed workers capable of making a whole watch. The watch maker had become an assembler, a shopkeeper who put his name to a timepiece, 'though he has not made in his shop the smallest wheel belonging to it'. One 'maker' put his name on 3–4,000 watches between 1795 and 1796, having employed more than 100 out-workers. Although some of these suppliers might have thought of themselves as 'small masters' making parts and offering them for sale, most watch makers perceived themselves as pursuing a respectable trade for an appropriate wage.[35] The putting-out sys-tem was known, too, in the only branch of textile manufacture of significance in London, the silk cloth manufacture located in the Spitalfields district of the East End. But it was far from being the

33. *Commons Journals*, XXXVI, 1777, p. 193; Campbell, *London Tradesman, op. cit.* p. 221; E. Howe (ed.), *The London Compositor: Documents relating to Wages, Working Conditions and Customs of the London Print Trade 1785–1900*, Oxford UP, 1947, p. 143; Anon, *A History of the Combination of Journeymen Calico Printers*, 1807, pp. 13–15, re-printed in K. Carpenter (ed.), *Trade Unions under the Combination Acts*, New York, 1972.

34. I. Prothero, *Artisans and Politics in Early Nineteenth-Century London: John Gast and his Times*, Dawson, 1979, pp. 46–50.

35. Campbell, *London Tradesman, op. cit.* pp. 250–1; George, *London Life, op. cit.,* p. 174.

sole method of production. As Dorothy George has pointed out, into the nineteenth century large and small masters existed side by side, the latter larger in number but the former producing the greater – and increasing – share of total output. Masters employing from ten to forty looms were still common in 1823, but the tendency towards greater capitalisation is revealed in a comment on the effects of slumping trade in 1806: 'Many manufacturers have discharged fifty to a hundred men each and put as many more upon half-work.'[36]

There were a number of manufactures which both were 'new' in the early eighteenth century and had a high capital threshold for the time. In these the separation of labour from capital was marked from the beginning and in most of them there were no journeymen, only hired labourers. Brewing, distilling, sugar baking and soap boiling are representative. Of the last it was remarked in 1747: 'If the master and one man in the house understands the business, the whole work may be performed by labourers.' In the works for manufacturing white and red lead for paint, which were situated in the Whitechapel area, the life-destroying process of manufacture was carried out by 'engines, horses and labourers'.[37]

In other towns and in the countryside too, much manufacturing was not operated under the putting-out system. Those carried out on employers' premises included paper making, brick making, calico printing, glass making, pottery, net making and salt making, as well as examples already mentioned. Indeed, it is hard to think of a single finished good which from raw material to final marketed form was made entirely under an out-working system. The smelting and foundry stages in metal manufacture, as well as many preliminary and finishing processes in textile manufacture, were carried out on employer premises, as was wool combing in worsted production, as well as the wool sorting which had preceded it. In woollen cloth manufacture the same was true of fulling, dyeing and shearing. Workers in these links of production chains were far fewer in numbers than were out-working spinners and weavers, but their contribution was essential. In some cases location was determined by the need for water to power mills, as in fulling or in the silk twisting mills which were the first real factories. In other cases, especially in finishing, employers may simply have preferred to keep supervision for reasons of quality control. A pin manufactory pro-

---

36. George, *London Life, op. cit.*, pp. 178–81, 201–2.
37. *Ibid.*, pp. 160–1; Campbell, *London Tradesman, op. cit.*, pp. 103–4.

vided Adam Smith with his celebrated example of the division of labour.

> One man draws out the wire, another straightens it, a third cuts it, a fourth points it, a fifth grinds it at the top for receiving the head: to make the head requires two or three distinct operations; to put it on, is a peculiar business; to whiten the pins is another; it is even a trade by itself to put them into the paper . . . .[38]

But at the beginning of the century pins had been made by out-workers who purchased their own wire. Being poor, they did so in small parcels from 'second' or even 'third' dealers and relied on selling their pins from week to week at beaten-down prices. Even as late as 1767 not all pins were made in manufactories; one company at that time was putting out to more than 1,200 rural pin makers.[39]

Work on an employer's premises did not usually imply a large concentration of labour. There were exceptions, but workshops were more prevalent than factories. Provincial print works could be very small – a master printer with a handful of journeymen and an apprentice. In London by the beginning of the nineteenth century some of the 200 plus printing shops were much larger, but the normal range of employment was ten to twenty as a total for compositors, pressmen and apprentices. By the mid eighteenth century pottery works employing twenty to forty people were familiar in Staffordshire and elsewhere, even before Wedgwood began his celebrated career. During the best time for journeyman calico printers, in the 1790s before the advent of roller printing encouraged employers to substitute juvenile labour in the guise of apprentices for skilled men, a typical firm employed around thirty journeymen with perhaps ten apprentices. Before the introduction of the shearing frame it took five men to dress and shear a piece of woollen cloth with a boy to assist, learn and clean the teazles. The number of shearmen (or croppers, as they were known in the West Riding) employed would depend upon the scale of operation of the clothier who employed them. Benjamin Gott, one of the largest in Yorkshire, employed eighty in 1809, but as his total labour force was around 1,000, that was an unusually large concentration.[40]

In iron founding by the middle years of the eighteenth century, independent artisan ownership had already passed away. A simple

38. Smith, *Wealth of Nations*, I, p. 8.
39. S. and B. Webb, *History of Trade Unionism*, Longman 1911 edn, pp. 35–6; Pollard, *Genesis of Modern Management*, p. 51.
40. Howe (ed.), *London Compositor, op. cit.*, pp. 36, 54; Musson, *Growth of British Industry*, p. 127.

furnace needed a team of seven men: two founders or keepers, three fillers and two bridge servers (basket fillers). Others, including women and children, were employed in preparatory processes. At the forge at least two finers and hammermen were needed, assisted by an apprentice. The smallest of iron works would therefore have needed around fifteen workers to operate a single furnace and forge. It is not easy to generalise about a norm, average or median number of workers in primary iron manufacture.[41]

In the era of charcoal smelting the typical organisation, according to Professor Pollard, was a 'combine of works in associated ownership, but physically and geographically separated'. Although some of these units represented, for their time, substantial capital investment, few exceeded a hundred workers, even when carters or scattered charcoal burners were included. With the diffusion of coke smelting after about 1750, large, complex units began to appear in locations where coal and iron ore co-existed. Although writers like Arthur Young estimated employees of ironmasters in the 1770s as around 1,000 at Coalbrookdale, several hundreds at Crawley's near Newcastle and 500 at a works in Rotherham, he usually included colliers and out-workers. These were among a small number of exceptional examples, for even in the last decade of the century when the technique of puddling began to spread, the typical size was 200 to 300, except in Shropshire where it was twice as large. Even by the early Hanoverian period the primary side of turning ore into refined metal was already significantly larger in scale than was the final product side. There was, however, the emergence of large casting shops, casting direct from the furnace a growing range of large iron products whose size alone put them beyond the reach of the small forger. Technological developments, especially after 1780, worked in the same direction. Increasing use of slitting and tilting mills meant the necessity of riverside siting. The water-wheels which drove Darby's slitting mills at Coalbrookdale were 20 feet in diameter and of cast iron, while the huge hammer of a tilting mill at Sheffield imparted a 'trembling motion' that could be felt leaning on a gate 'at three perches distance'. With such developments there was an increasing specialisation of labour at the larger works as, alongside the furnace keeper, filler, forgeman and slitter, there appeared the puddler, roller and moulder. In brass founding, too,

41. That is where ironmasters, as they increasingly did, turned their own pig into bar iron. For the relationship between the two stages, see for example Court, *Midland Industries, op. cit.*, pp. 172–80.

by 1770 the all-round founder was being divided into pattern maker, mould maker, caster and finisher.[42]

Large iron works were created by bringing together different processes on a site where water-powered machinery could be operated. (Steam power was first introduced in the 1780s but did not spread very rapidly.) This was equally true of some early 'factory' developments in manufactures which were workshop based. The paradigm presented by the cotton and woollen mills, in which, first in the former textile and then in the second, first in spinning and then in weaving, a hand process was displaced by a machine bringing an astonishing gain in productivity, was exceptional. In several important cases there was a much less radical transformation of work and so-called factories were in effect simply a means of streamlining the links between processes and supervising craft labour. This was true of some celebrated examples. At Etruria Josiah Wedgwood boasted of 'making such machines of men as cannot err', not of replacing men with machines. As Dr McKendrick has pointed out, his success did not come from discovering cheaper methods of production; his pottery sold because he produced to a standard high quality. He responded to the growing demand for new shapes, glazes and clays by training workers in detail – his scheme, as he put it, was 'keeping each workshop separate'. Useful wares were produced not only by different potters from those making ornamental ones, but at separate kilns. Division of labour was pursued to the extent that of 278 persons employed in 1790, only five lacked a specific designation. McKendrick points out that Wedgwood did not destroy skill, he 'limited its field of expression to a particular task, but within those limits he increased it'. A century after Wedgwood, Arnold Bennett could still write: 'no great vulgar handicraft has lost less of the human than potting. Clay is always clay and the steam driven contrivance that will mould a basin while a man sits and watches has yet to be invented.'[43]

Equally famous as an 'early factory' was the Soho Foundry of Matthew Boulton and James Watt built at Birmingham in 1795. This was the first heavy engineering plant. Concentrating on the wide range of parts that went into steam engines, it employed makers in brass as well as in iron. Its historian has fittingly described the shop

42. Pollard, *Genesis of Modern Management*, pp. 94–5; Young, *Tours in England and Wales*, pp. 142, 151, 275; *Northern Tour*, I, pp. 115, 122 and III, p. 9; Berg, *Age of Manufactures*, pp. 38, 291–2.

43. N. McKendrick, 'Josiah Wedgwood and factory discipline', *Historical Journal*, IV, 1961, pp. 33–4, 46.

structure there as a transition between handicraft production and modern mass production. A single craft operation was performed in each shop, although, as at Etruria, they were placed in a systematic order. Like Wedgwood, Watt saw his need as the training up of a new kind of engineer by replacing a 'more general knowledge' with a specialised skill, to remove 'cunning' but leave dexterity. (Once even this application could be achieved with the aid of a machine tool, it becomes appropriate to speak of 'semi-skilled' workers; that, however, is to enter the history of the engineering industry after 1815.) Watt not only tried to keep his craftsmen to the same line of work, he even encouraged them to bring their sons up to it. Some specialised lines at Soho were followed for three generations. In 1800, prior to considering the adoption of an even more systematic arrangement, a description of the existing plan of operations at Soho was drawn up. It identifies ten shops: a heavy drilling shop, a heavy turning shop, a heavy fitting shop, a nozzle fitting shop, a general fitting shop, a special fitting shop for moving parts, a light fitting shop, a pattern making shop, a casting shop and a smith's shop. Engineering works were nowhere very large concentrators of labour. Soho employed 251 in 1831 but probably did not exceed 100 until the 1820s. Henry Maudsley's London works, celebrated for producing the block-making machinery for the dockyards, employed only 80 in 1800. The northern firms who specialised in textile machinery were generally of similar size.[44]

Etruria and Soho have been picked out as the best-known examples of their kind. They were exceptional, but nevertheless were models which received eventual if not especially rapid emulation. For our purposes they serve to demonstrate that there was no single and simple modernisation path in the history of English manufacturing. The achievement of massive productivity gains through the introduction of powered machine processes in place of hand ones – machino-facture instead of manufacture, as Marx described it – of course pointed to the end of much out-working and the re-urbanisation of the central stages of cloth making, though not immediately, for the first spinning mills had to be near the water which powered them.

In fact, some of the pressures which prompted Wedgwood and Watt to reorganise their use of labour could be found within textile manufacture and were drawing a not dissimilar response by the late

44. E. Roll, *An Early Experiment in Industrial Organisation: Boulton and Watt 1775–1805*, 1930, reprinted Cass 1968, pp. 171–3; Berg, *Age of Manufactures*, pp. 271–2; Pollard, *Genesis of Modern Management*, pp. 99–100.

eighteenth century. Even weavers were brought together in 'weaving shops' where expensive yarns were used or where fine quality control indicated supervision. By 1818 the Macclesfield silk maker Henry Critchley had 50 of his 140 looms inside his factory, though he admitted that their weavers were only occasionally under his supervision. The finest kinds of cotton cloth were similarly made in Manchester. In the woollen manufacture of the West Country, a tendency of clothiers to bring weavers into loomshops had developed by 1800 to the point where the cottage weavers tried to revive long-dormant apprenticeship restrictions to limit its spread. In 1806 in the woollen manufacture there was said to exist, alongside the putting-out system of the west and the 'domestic' system of Yorkshire, a third 'mode': 'In the Factory system, the Master Manufacturers, who sometimes possess a very great capital, employ in one or more buildings or factories, under their own or their Superintendent's inspection, a number of workmen, more or fewer according to the extent of their trade.' A similar tendency towards grouping looms in sheds from twenty up to even a hundred in number has been noted in the Lancashire cotton industry, and in any case the weaving of the finer qualities of cotton goods had always been undertaken in Manchester on employers' premises. The clothiers behind such developments were working towards the factory mode, not because of some power-technological imperative but from the related supervisory needs of quality control and the prevention of the embezzlement of raw materials.[45]

For these reasons the water-powered silk-throwing mills were truer precursors of the cotton and woollen mills which came to symbolise the industrial revolution and the factory system than were the workshops or 'proto-factories' which organised hand labour. Taking over an unsuccessful enterprise in 1713, Sir Thomas Lombe's Derwent-powered silk mill at Derby brought together 300 supervised workers, most of them women and children. It was a momentous example, for not only were there a dozen followers in northern centres of silk thread production but it was consciously copied by the first factory masters in cotton spinning. It was a significant emulation. The line between workshop and factory production is an elusive one, but when the organisation of large units of labour, increasingly unskilled, and the concentration of formerly distinct processes under a single roof are added to the adoption

45. *Ibid.*, p. 49; Randall, 'Work and resistance', *op. cit.*, pp. 187–8; quoted in D. Gregory, *Regional Transformation and Industrial Revolution: A Geography of the Yorkshire Woollen Industry*, Macmillan, 1982, p. 53.

of mechanical power, the potential for hugely increased productivity clearly indicates the advent of a new mode of production.[46]

The image of factory spinning dramatically ousting cottage spinning of cotton can be overdrawn. The early spinning jennies were hand, not power machines and could fit into a cottage manufacture. The stages between the first hand-powered small jennies and steam-powered factory mule spinning represented an organisational as well as a technological progression. Nevertheless the transition from domestic to factory spinning still seems in retrospect an astonishingly rapid one in cotton. Arkwright's water-powered mill at Cromford began spinning cotton in 1771, and from then through the first steam-powered spinning mills in Papplewick, Nottinghamshire in 1785 and in Manchester in 1789 to 1816 the labour force in cotton mills expanded to exceed 100,000, less than one in five of whom were adult males. Across the Pennines the making of wools into Yorkshire cloth was being more gradually transformed, even in a district already judged to be the most go-ahead of the woollen regions. The long-staple wools used in worsted manufacture were more suited to machine spinning than were the short-fibred ones of woollen cloth manufacture, but even in this branch there were only eighteen mills by 1800, although by 1820 there was very little hand spinning of worsted yarn. So far as woollens were concerned, outside of the preparatory processes of scribbling and carding, no stage of production was mechanised even at Benjamin Gott's Leeds factory which was capitalised at £397,000 by 1815. Power weaving, which was in its infancy in cotton in 1815, began to make progress in Yorkshire only in the second quarter of the nineteenth century.[47]

MINING

The siting of mines is obviously determined by the location of coal and mineral deposits. Even so, a very considerable range in scale and organisation of enterprise existed in the eighteenth century. At one extreme, the customary rights of the 'free miners' of the Forest of Dean to extract coal and iron were hardly challenged before the

46. Chapman, *Cotton Industry in the Industrial Revolution*, pp. 14–15.
47. Berg, 'Workers and machinery in eighteenth-century England' in J.G. Rule (ed.), *British Trade Unionism 1750 to 1850. The Formative Years*, Longman, 1988, pp. 67–8; N.J. Smelser, *Social Change in the Industrial Revolution: an Application of Theory to the Lancashire Cotton Industry, 1770–1840*, Routledge, 1959, pp. 185, 188; Hudson, *Genesis of Industrial Capital*, p. 29; Musson, *Growth of British Industry*, p. 87.

end of the century. At the other, a few copper mines in Cornwall were already employing a thousand people, raising capital in a sophisticated way from a multiplicity of shareholders, selling their ores through a central marketing agency and colluding in a cartel agreement with Thomas Williams, the 'Copper King' who controlled the briefly abundant ores of Anglesey. By then, all mines of coal or metal of any significance were pumped by steam engines, with all that implied for initial investment and running-cost levels. But throughout the period, small 'independent' mining operations lingered on a shrinking periphery.

Already by 1700 the 'banksman', organising the labour of ten to twenty men and their families at a small pit, had largely disappeared from the north-east, although he could still be found throughout the century elsewhere. The seventy-six men killed in a single explosion in 1710 is vivid testimony to the scale of operation already to be found in the north-east. In 1769 one colliery there had six steam engines, another five having four each. From 1790 even greater expansion began as improved pumping dispelled the old belief that there was a 60-fathom limit to mining. The average labour force of forty-one Tyneside collieries in 1829 was 300 (200 underground). The typical mine in this area was either the property of an active landowner or had been established by a capitalist partnership. In either case an evident feature was the employment of specialist managers ('viewers'). As Professor Pollard has pointed out, with the first widespread miners' strike taking place in 1765, the northern coalfields could be said by then to have become large industrial units of a recognisably modern type.[48]

Not surprisingly the coalfields which touched the coastlines expanded most before the canal era. After the north-east came the Cumberland field, smaller but similarly technically advanced. Here too development had been promoted by a group of landowners: the Lowthers at Whitehaven, the Curwens at Harrington and Workington and the Senhouses at Maryport. The inland coalfields developed more slowly and their mines remained small. The group of collieries around Sheffield probably still employed a total of only 200 men in 1790. The mines on the nearby Fitzwilliam estates also remained small with the largest employing only 112 in 1813. Middleton colliery near Leeds employed 230 in 1803, but thirty years earlier less than 80. In Lancashire the Worsley collieries responded to the needs of nearby Manchester and in 1777 employed

48. Pollard, *Genesis of Modern Management*, pp. 79–81.

100 colliers. After their owner, the Duke of Bridgewater, dug his pioneering canal, numbers increased to 331 by 1783. Staffordshire remained a county of small mines up until the mid nineteenth century when more than 400 Black Country collieries had labour forces of from sixty to seventy men and boys.[49]

Pollard has suggested that coal pits employing six or less men with an annual output of less than 1,000 tonnes probably produced an annual 500,000 tonnes between 1750 and 1850, but this was a fall from 10 to 1 per cent as a proportion of total output. He considers a 'typical medium-sized colliery' around 1800 would have been one with four working shafts and two more being sunk: at twelve men per shaft and with surface and ancillary labour, a workforce of around eighty to a hundred. The great northern field had, of course, left this era behind, it was not 'typical'.[50]

At the end of the seventeenth century a visitor to Cornwall was impressed that there were 'few mines but had twenty men and boys attending'. Undertakings of this size were widespread in the early eighteenth century but a growing number were significantly larger, a trend which increased with the arrival of the copper boom around 1740. In the 1780s few civilian undertakings employed as many hands as did the larger Cornish copper and tin mines. By the end of that decade four or five exceeded the 1,000 mark, with a cluster not far below. The pattern was much like that in coal mining; small undertakings were always to be found. Indeed, there is little evidence that their numbers declined, but their *share* of total output and of the labour force shrank, especially after about 1740. When the first detailed survey was made in 1838, the average labour force of 159 mines was 171. Ninety-five mines even then employed fewer than 100 people each. This, however, amounted to only 12 per cent of the total labour force, 31 per cent of which was employed in the five largest concerns.[51]

In the early eighteenth century few lead mines, in Cornwall or in the two more important centres of Derbyshire and the northern Pennines, employed more than fifty workers. There was some increase in size in the second half of the century, but the largest employers were only middling by Cornish standards. The London Lead

---

49. *Ibid.*, pp. 81–5.
50. Pollard, 'Coal mining' in Feinstein and Pollard (eds), *Studies in Capital Formation*, p. 37.
51. J. Whetter, *Cornwall in the Seventeenth Century*, Lodenck Press, 1974, pp. 68–9; Rule, 'The labouring miner in Cornwall c. 1740–1870', PhD Thesis, University of Warwick, 1971, pp. 13–14.

Company, which had concentrated its mining activities in the northern Pennines after 1780, employed an average of 800 miners and several hundred surface workers at the end of the eighteenth and beginning of the nineteenth centuries, but these were spread over several mines. It mined under lease from the landowner, Greenwich Hospital, but was not the typical lessee. Of thirty-eight other leasing companies, twenty-nine employed less than twenty workers and twenty-one less than ten.[52]

Most glass manufactories, even in 'specialist' areas of production like Stourbridge, Newcastle and Bristol, were still small at the end of the eighteenth century, but larger works were beginning to appear in Birmingham and Dudley, while a notable exception was the 'second start' made by the British Plate Glass Company at St Helens which gave a livelihood to around 400 workers in 1795. Several paper mills employed at around the 200 level, but most were smaller. Even in 1851 only eleven manufacturers exceeded 100.[53]

It is almost axiomatic that one of the distinguishing trends of an 'industrial revolution' is a shift within total investment in manufacturing and mining from circulating to fixed capital – that is, from capital tied up mainly in stocks of raw materials, unfinished goods still in the process of manufacture and unsold stocks of finished goods towards capital in the form of buildings, plant and, in mining the sinking of fresh shafts and the maintaining of existing ones. Such a shift seems evident in the transition from domestic manufacture to the factory system, especially when the displacement of hand manufacture by machine production was taking place. Estimates made by Feinstein suggest that in total investment in industry and commerce the ratio of fixed to circulating capital changed from less than 1 : 1 in 1760 to greater than 3 : 1 by 1860. It would seem, however, that this trend did not become marked before 1800 nor dramatic before around 1830. Its momentum after that date was hastened by the declining necessity of holding large stocks (inventories) as transport developments facilitated speedier and more reliable delivery.[54]

The modern consensus that the 'triumph of the factory' was piecemeal and gradual, and the insistence that cotton's experience was singular rather than representative, would hardly lead us to ex-

52. R. Burt, *The British Lead Mining Industry*, Dyllansow Truran, 1984, pp. 57–8; C.J. Hunt, *The Lead Miners of the Northern Pennines in the Eighteenth and Nineteenth Centuries*, Manchester UP, 1970, pp. 189–90.

53. Pollard, *Genesis of Modern Management*, p. 122.

54. Cited in Hudson, *Genesis of Industrial Capital*, p. 8.

pect a strong shift towards fixed capital during the period covered by this book. Although the volume of circulating capital *per unit* of goods and services did fall, in aggregate terms it undoubtedly increased. In wool production, as Dr Hudson has recently stressed, circulating capital was generally over 50 per cent of total reproducible capital and in some sections and branches nearer 90 per cent. Even in cotton, Edwards found that none of the five firms he examined for 1794–1805 had a fixed capital proportion higher than 21 per cent of total capital invested. This level is also suggested by an example of an early silk-throwing mill at Stockport in 1762 which had £2,800 in fixed capital and £13,800 in circulating capital. Historians have insufficiently noted the exceptionality of Benjamin Gott's first integrated woollen mill, but even in this special case fixed capital in 1801 was valued at only £28,000 compared with a circulating capital of £65,400. Examples such as this seem to suggest that even Professor Pollard's downward-pointing suggestion that in the typical up-to-date mill in the period 1780–1830, fixed capital represented only just a little more than one half of the capital invested, may be something of an overestimate. Of course, the contrast with clothing firms operating purely on a merchant-capitalist putting-out basis, and perhaps getting the more capital-intensive processes like dyeing or fulling done on commission, was both real and growing. J. & N. Phillips, who manufactured cotton small wares at Manchester, had a circulating capital of £4,800, twelve times greater than their fixed capital of £400. The point to emphasise is rather that even in advanced sectors of cloth making, finding circulating capital remained the predominant and pressing need. Even front-line cotton masters needed to fund stocks of raw materials, work in progress, finished unsold commodities, rents, interest and wage payments.[55]

Even in industries like iron making, brewing or coal mining where the need for fixed capital investment tended to be higher, it still did not predominate. Early in the eighteenth century Crawley's iron works founded in 1728 had a fixed capital of £12,000 compared with stocks valued at £93,000, hardly different from the situation in putting-out textile manufacture. As we have seen with the diffusion of coke smelting after about 1750 and the advent a generation later of first water- and then steam-powered rolling, slitting and milling, fixed capital needs in iron making significantly increased. The cost of a typical blast furnace has been put at £3,900

---

55. *Ibid.*, pp. 8–9; Pollard, 'Fixed capital in the industrial revolution in Britain', 1964, reprinted in F. Crouzet (ed.), *Capital Formation in the Industrial Revolution*, pp. 148–9.

in 1760, £4,000 in 1790, £6,000 in 1800 and £9,000 in 1810, and from 1784 the adoption of the puddling process with its superior pig/bar ratio further increased fixed capital needs. Even so, with the exception of a few giants, iron works in 1800 seem to have had a capital worth between £12,000 and £30,000 and to have had normally less than half of their assets in the form of fixed capital.[56]

The shift towards fixed capital within individual firms was hardly emphatic. But the growing number of firms with higher fixed capital ratios in the leading manufacturing sectors, combined with the increasing weight in the economy of the more capital-intensive sectors like coal mining and iron making, aggregated into a significant overall increase in the value of fixed capital over the conventional period of dating for the 'industrial revolution', as well as to an acceleration in its rate of formation. Recent estimates for coal and iron are given in Table 5.1.

Table 5.1 British gross capital formation: coal and iron

Decade ending:	Iron	Coal
	(£'000 p.a.)	
1760	19	83
1780	26	159
1790	43	211
1800	122	351
1810	255	776

Sources: Various.

So far as cotton was concerned, Dr Chapman's careful building on contemporary estimates suggests a total fixed capital investment for knitting and cloth-making branches of £1,856,000 in 1788 and of around £10,000,000 for 1811–12. In the case of wool, as might be expected, figures for the West Riding, the most 'progressive' region, reveal how much more slowly and how much less in total fixed capital investment increased. Nevertheless, change was taking place. Fixed capital stock was only around £5,000 in 1780, had reached £50,000 by 1790 and then entered a period of quite rapid net fixed capital formation to reach £556,000 by 1805 and £751,000 by 1815 – the fixed capital value level of £1 million being attained in the early

56. *Ibid.*, pp. 148–9; R.S.W. Davies, 'The iron industry' in Feinstein and Pollard, *Studies in Capital Formation*, p. 96.

1820s. Since factory spinning had made little headway, and power weaving none at all, this fixed capital was invested largely in mills in scribbling, carding, slubbing, fulling and related processes.[57]

What matters is that rejecting older impressionistic exaggerations of the dimensions of the relative shift from circulating to fixed capital should not lead to underestimating its importance and the need to uncover the processes by which it was enabled. The fact that most expanding firms, whatever the relative position, had to find absolutely larger sums for their everyday working is of great importance. As Pollard pointed out, it was difficulty in this more liquid area which could bring even large and celebrated firms into financial difficulty. Financial resources could not be easily *diverted* from circulating to fixed capital uses. The savings on the amount of raw material stocks and on work tied up in making which accrued from concentrating work in a factory were only marginal and initially at least likely to be offset by taking in increased raw materials to meet a faster output flow. In essence the progressive firm had either to find different sources for its fixed capital investment, or at least free as much of its resources as it could by exploiting whatever 'economising' on its working expenditure was available. What was true for the progressive entrepreneur may have created even more pressing problems for his followers.[58] As Dr Hoppit has suggested, the successful innovator had at least a short-term opportunity to take considerable profits before imitators came in and intensified competition put profit margins under pressure. Contemporaries referred more often to the 'competitive' system than to the 'capitalist' system and for every successful market leader there were a dozen followers forced to find capital to stay in business. That large numbers of them did not succeed in this object is scarcely mentioned in the historiography of the industrial revolution. If 'ploughing back profits' was a mechanism for growth for some, it was a strategy for survival for more.[59]

The role of merchant capital in industrial growth has long been considered important by historians. The familiar image is one of the transfer of commercial gains into the manufacturing sector, and there are good reasons for this. In the expanding economy of the later eighteenth and early nineteenth centuries landowners (from

57. Wool figures based on D. Jenkins, 'The wool textile industry' in Feinstein and Pollard, *Studies in Capital Formation*, Tables 5.1 and 5.3; cotton figures on S.D. Chapman and J. Butt, 'The cotton industry 1775–1856', *ibid.*, especially Table 4.2.

58. Pollard, 'Fixed capital', *op. cit.*, p. 149.

59. J. Hoppit, *Risk and Failure*, pp. 12–13.

the higher rents which came from rising food prices) and merchants (from the boom in overseas trade) are generally thought to
have been the two especially advantaged groups. Following Postan's
enormously influential article of 1935 there was general acceptance
that there was surplus capital enough to meet the investment needs
of the early industrial revolution. The problem as Postan saw it was
to develop the conduits to carry it into manufacturing. The possible
role of landowners will be considered below, but what of merchants?[60]

The model of 'proto-industrialisation' emphasises the role of
merchant capital. It is not only the case that rural manufacturing
under that system was organised and 'owned' by merchant capitalists, but that its dynamics impelled it towards the factory system if
market expansion called for extra output beyond the logistical
reach of cottage-based manufacture. It could become increasingly
difficult to add to the supply of labour, more costly in time and
effort to put out materials and collect goods, and, with supervision
of the workforce impossible, hard to control quality. It is instructive
that many of the early factory owners explained their motives in
these terms, rather than with respect to an anticipated transformation in productivity.

There are many important examples of putting-out merchants
becoming factory builders and owners. Cotton provides a host of
these. Richard Arkwright's pioneering Nottinghamshire mills were
financed largely by his hosier partners Jedediah Strutt and Samuel
Need. The former, indeed, was soon building mills independently
and his business records for the 1780s show that transfer of funds
from his hosiery business was crucial. Merchant-manufacturers from
the Manchester district were active after 1780 – Peter Drinkwater
for example, who built spinning mills at Northwich and Manchester. Better known is Samuel Oldknow, who was already the
country's largest manufacturer of muslins under the putting-out system before he inaugurated a new era with his steam-powered mill at
Stockport. Dr Chapman has shown the general preponderance of
merchant capital in the building of spinning mills in both Lancashire and Nottinghamshire. The situation in woollen manufacture is
less clear-cut. Benjamin Gott built his great Bean Ing mill in 1792
from profits as a cloth merchant and putter out. Dr Wilson's study
of the merchants of Leeds finds that surprisingly few of the cloth
merchants diverted their profits, but if Gott was not typical he was

60. M.M. Postan, 'Recent trends in the accumulation of capital', reprinted in
Crouzet, *Capital Formation*, p. 71.

certainly not unique; he had followers from Halifax and Hudders-field as well as from Leeds. However, even in the more capitalist worsted branch, the transition to the factory was slow with less than a dozen spinning mills operating by 1800, although these were al-most certainly built by capitalists who had previously put out.[61] Nevertheless, as Dr Hudson's major study has recently shown, the sources of the eventual triumph of the factory system in the West Riding were varied, and merchant capital played only a part: 'There is evidence to suggest that the merchant manufacturer, embodying the alliance of merchant and industrial capital, was evolving both from the mercantile and the manufacturing side simultaneously but mainly from the latter.'

Outside of textiles, Matthew Boulton's button and toy making in Birmingham and Peter Stubs' file manufactory in Warrington (1802) are rare examples of merchant manufacturers initiating on-site production of hardware. In both brewing and paper making some movement of merchant capital into manufacturing has been discerned.[62]

Merchants played a much more widespread role in another, and probably more important respect. Neither survival nor expansion was readily achievable without *credit*. The manufacturer had to place himself within a matrix of credit; those who fell out were the input into one of the period's most rapidly growing sectors: bankruptcy. In their extension of credit the merchants eased the capital burden on the manufacturer. Raw materials were provided on credit and although finished goods were sold on credit, advances ahead of final sale were commonly made. Through simple book debts or through 'bills' the manufacturer often paid for his materials, equip-ment and fuel only after his goods had been sold. By the early eighteenth century only the larger Yorkshire woollen manufacturers bought any of their raw wool directly from farmers or factors. While this cut out the profit of the middleman – the stapler – it tied up money in stocks from one annual shearing to the next. Small clo-thiers bought a week's supply at a time, relying on a measure of credit. As the eighteenth century progressed clothiers of all sizes increasingly bought through the staplers. The staplers themselves bought on no or very short credit from farmers or factors but ex-tended longer terms, from one to nine months' credit, to those

61. See Crouzet's own contribution to *Capital Formation*, pp. 168–70, and sources cited therein.

62. Hudson, *Genesis of Industrial Capital*, pp. 16–17, 36, 75, 261–2; Berg, *Age of Manufactures*, p. 290.

who purchased, often in small amounts, from them. In this way the merchant suppliers of raw materials were not only the extenders of crucial credit to manufacturers, they were the main holders of raw material stocks. One large Yorkshire firm, Jowitts, which was dealing with seventy customers in the 1770s, was providing this important service for more than 400 in the 1790s.[63]

The artisan clothiers of the West Riding could not have survived if they had not received much more credit from their suppliers than they extended to their merchant purchasers. For some it permitted more than survival; the net credit gain was sufficient to cover the time for both production and circulation. This, as Dr Hudson has shown, was propitious for the modest rate of capital accumulation necessary for the gradual evolution of larger concerns with relatively greater fixed capital needs. It mattered, too, that the typical working master clothier was also a small land-holder, for land was the best security in general and in particular it enabled the raising of mortgages to meet special investment needs. Even if it was only a matter of participating with other clothiers in the co-operative establishment of carding and scribbling mills, it is clear that domestic manufacturers could play their part in factory building, but it is as evident that it was the support of merchant credit which was the enabling factor.[64]

There were other ways of raising capital. Paying workers in tokens or by truck, usually attributed to the shortage of coin, was a way of extracting credit both from the labour force and from shopkeepers.[65] Few early factories were purpose built; it was cheaper to rent former warehouses or corn mills. For those whose local reputation was sound – and as late as 1850 most exchanges of capital in the West Riding, as elsewhere, took place within a 10- to 15-mile radius and between people known personally to each other – banks and attorneys played an intermediary role in the supply of funds, linking potential lenders to manufacturers as well as to investment in land. In the four wool towns of Leeds, Halifax, Huddersfield and Bradford the number of attorneys increased from fifteen in 1793 to forty-seven in 1815. In Lancashire, too, the central role

63. Hudson, *Genesis of Industrial Capital*, stresses the crucial role of credit in the survival of the small clothiers of the West Riding. She has drawn her argument and findings together in her contribution 'Capital and credit in the West Riding wool textile industry' in Hudson (ed.), *Regions and Industries*, pp. 69–99. Pollard, 'Fixed capital', *op. cit.*, pp. 151–61.

64. Hudson, *Genesis of Industrial Capital*, pp. 127–8, 182, 260, 263, 268.

65. *Ibid.*, pp. 150–1; Ashton, *An Economic History of England*, pp. 207–8; Pollard, 'Fixed capital', *op. cit.*, pp. 157–8.

of attorneys in the eighteenth-century local capital market has been demonstrated by Anderson. Banks would seem to have played a more important role in industrial capital formation than historians have usually allowed. Indeed, many of the private banks in Yorkshire had been founded by textile merchants or manufacturers, having developed as an adjunct to their business dealings. The Brothers Swaine and Co. of Halifax seem from 1779 to have engaged at the same time in both worsted manufacture and trade and banking, and to have hardly considered these as two separate spheres of operation. The extension of the credit network and the shortage of low-denomination currency so increased the use of bills and notes in the developing industrial regions as to make, as Hudson has put it, 'every businessman a banker of sorts'. By being concerned primarily in discounting bills and with shorter-term accommodation, banks complemented rather than competed with attorneys whose local knowledge and acumen could be directed in the main to longer-term loans and the arrangement of mortgages.[66]

In establishing their enterprises, entrepreneurs relied on the support of merchants and wholesalers, but if they expanded their rise could change them from being predominant receivers of credit into significant bestowers of it, especially when they marketed their own goods. In 1810 Josiah Wedgwood had accounts outstanding for £41,000 against a net value of £35,383. Crawley's in 1728 had £87,000 owing, about a fifth of which was bad debt. They owed £26,000 to creditors. Such was not uncommonly the situation of the larger ironmasters, the net value of the Coalbrookedale company in 1796 being £39,383 while it had debts of £50,549. Since they sometimes had excessive amounts of capital tied up in unsold stocks in addition to that financing their customers' debts, it is not surprising that even large firms rocked from time to time. The Cornish Mining Company had £500,000 locked up in copper in 1787, at a time when it was effectively the only significant purchaser of ores from a hundred mines. One of its largest and certainly most frequently complaining customers was Matthew Boulton. The great Birmingham manufacturer had himself been distinctly shaky between 1765 and 1768 when he had so much capital tied up in stocks he could not quickly sell and debts he could not promptly collect that he was greatly stretched to find working capital. The problems of ambitious

66. Hudson, *Genesis of Industrial Capital*, pp. 211–20, 265–7; B.L. Anderson, 'The attorney and the early capital market in Lancashire' in Crouzet, *Capital Formation*, pp. 223–55.

enterprises, rapidly growing in size, have been well explained by Professor Pollard.

> they were both immensely large in relation to their market and intensely ambitious in their initial scale. Not only did their sudden arrival on the industrial scene make it impossible for them to accumulate favourable credit balances in proportion to their turnover as firms growing piecemeal could do, but they were also too large to insert themselves into the circulation of credit. They failed to see that in appearing, fully grown, as whales among the minnows, they would cut themselves off from the mutual support of more equally matched units that was the rule elsewhere. As new arrivals on that scale, they would have, by themselves, to prime the pump of their customers and to pour untold thousands into a seemingly bottomless pit of stocks, consignments and credits granted, without receiving credits on the other side of the ledger in anything like the same proportion.[67]

In effect they needed considerably more capital to sustain a given level of turnover than would a number of smaller firms growing in step with the market.

In the West Riding woollen manufacture it is possible to envisage some of the more developing manufacturers crossing a Rubicon of credit. For most of the eighteenth century the woollen manufacturers had sold their cloth through the cloth halls, although Leeds merchants had been steadily reducing the importance of the London factors at Blackwell Hall. Factors usually allowed their customers twelve months to pay at interest. Small manufacturers could not have survived on this basis, so instead they received a bill drawn on the factors to the value of the goods supplied, the custom of the trade being that bills could be drawn as soon as a transaction for sale was agreed rather than when the factor's customer actually paid. Since 90 per cent of Yorkshire cloth was still passing through the halls, the importance of the credit-extending role of the merchants of the West Riding is clear.[68] It had been so even at the very beginning of the eighteenth century, in the days of Defoe, in inland as well as overseas trade.

> a set of travelling merchants in Leeds . . . go all over England with droves of packhorses, and to all the fairs and market houses over the whole island. . . . Here they supply not the common people by retail . . . but . . . the shops by wholesale or whole pieces, and not only so, but give large credit too so that they are really travelling merchants, and as such they sell a very great quantity of goods, 'tis ordinary for

67. Pollard, 'Fixed capital', *op. cit.*, pp. 152, 157, 159–60.
68. Hudson, *Genesis of Industrial Capital*, pp. 156–9.

one of these men to carry a thousand pounds value of cloth with them at a time.[69]

From 1790 with the marked expansion of exports, a new class of merchant-manufacturer began to appear in the wool cloth sector. Unlike the merchant-manufacturers who had been dominating the worsted branch since the mid eighteenth century, these men began as manufacturers but were beginning to bypass the halls and middlemen. Between 1815 and 1830 such men dominated the manufacture, but their enhanced profits were not without some degree of offsetting cost, for in order to secure customers they stepped over into the ranks of credit givers – in the case of the American market commonly for two years, with the first interest free.[70]

Clearly without merchant credit, even if only in the simple form of a book debt, the many artisanal manufacturers could not have survived and the adventuring few could not have grown. The survival of the independent clothiers of the West Riding as a group is the strongest testimony, but examples can be found in most sectors of manufacturing of enterprises built from small beginnings as well as of successful survival in, for example, the hardware trades of Birmingham or Sheffield. Crouzet has listed a number of prominent cotton-spinning firms built up by entrepreneurs who started as journeymen mule spinners or machine makers, including James McConnel and John Kennedy who, starting in 1795 with a capital of £1,770, had become the largest spinning firm in Britain by 1815. Even in iron making examples exist. The Walker Brothers of Sheffield had a capital of only £600 in 1746, while the great Abraham Darby who set up Coalbrookdale in 1709 began as a metal-worker in Bristol. Isaac Wilkinson set up as an ironmaster in 1740, having previously been a foundry worker. Josiah Wedgwood began as a journeyman potter and entered two short-lived partnerships before setting up on his own in 1759. Capital thresholds were, of course, much lower than they were to become in many industries in the final quarter of the eighteenth century, especially in iron making, but even so it seems unlikely that any of these men of small capital could have built up their businesses so successfully had they been expected to pay cash on the nail for their inputs. Even in the first half of the century such men were hardly typical, and towards its end they were exceptional. As Dr Hoppit has pointed out: 'Thre-

69. Cited *Ibid.*, p. 160.
70. *Ibid.*, pp. 160–1.

sholds of entry into business may have been low by modern standards, but they were high enough for the bulk of the population.' Dr Honeyman has also contested the view that men of 'humble origins' taking advantage of new opportunities were the representative entrepreneurs of the early industrial revolution. She found that the majority of entrepreneurs in cotton spinning in 1787 had been previously engaged locally as manufacturers over a range of textile production: fustian or calico manufacture in Lancashire, silk or hosiery in Nottingham, wool or worsted in Yorkshire. She suggests that the factory masters were much more likely to be 'hereditary manufacturers' who provided a 'continuity of leadership'. The picture was little different in 1811; there was upward social mobility but it was not 'long distance'. Accepting that with low thresholds and with a variety of economising possibilities available, fixed capital requirements were 'unlikely to constitute an insuperable barrier to the determined man of small means', she argues that the greater demands for working capital were in the long term likely to prove fatal for the small man. Successful entrepreneurs came for the most part either from the wealthy or at the very least from men with 'a moderate amount of capital'. Whatever his rank of origin, however, a sound position in the credit matrix was the best safeguard for the manufacturer.[71]

Above the level of, say, the humble shoe maker buying two shillings' worth of leather from the leather cutter to make and sell a pair of shoes a week, credit was usually involved. But there was no uniform outcome. The West Riding clothier was fortunate. He took his raw material on credit from the stapler, while the merchant who took his cloth bore the burden of extending credit to the customer. That permitted his boasted 'independence' – that and his position as a small landowner. Some of the small masters of Sheffield and Birmingham too, for example, prospered and expanded, though usually in a modest way; but not all did. Where the *same* merchant provided the raw material and took the finished goods, things could be different. Small artisanal manufacturers survived but their situation was very close to that of the piece-rate earning out-worker: dependence, not independence, was what the credit nexus brought them.[72]

71. Crouzet, *Capital Formation*, pp. 165–7; Hoppit, *Risk and Failure*, p. 15; K. Honeyman, *Origins of Enterprise*, especially her conclusions summarised on pp. 160–9. Crouzet's recently published *The First Industrialists* generally comes to very similar conclusions.

72. Berg, *Age of Manufactures*, pp. 279–81 for a summary of the credit situation in the metalware trades.

Thus far we have been largely considering manufactures where the entry threshold was fairly low and where investment was not usually 'lumpy', i.e. there was not a lengthy period before it began to yield a return. This was true even of iron making before the 1750s and it was true also of the early cotton mills. In 1809, of sixty-four Manchester firms fifty-two, amounting to 50 per cent of the total capitalisation, had a capital of less than £5,000.[73] The outlawing of joint-stock company formation under the Bubble Act of 1720, which remained in force until 1867, may be considered a constraint, but it is at least arguable that very few manufacturing enterprises would have sought the joint-stock form anyway, not having the same capital needs as international trading corporations or canal projections. Perhaps it would have been a form suited to some mining enterprises, but this sector in any case developed its own means of resourcing capital investment.

> Mining is so expensive in its operations, and so uncertain in its success, that few or none of our Cornish mines are carried on at the risk of one or two persons. Where there are so many blanks to one prize, it would be gaming in the extreme, for any person singly to begin a seeking adventure; or indeed to take up anything of the kind, which is not already discovered and likely to be rendered profitable almost to a certainty: and upon this ground, it generally happens, that the charges of our adventures are borne by many partners, from four to ten, sixteen, twenty-four, and thirty-two.[74]

Thus William Pryce described the mining of tin and copper in Cornwall in his classic *Mineralogia Cornubiensis* of 1778. By then the more important mines were already being drained by Newcomen engines, and the era of Watt was about to begin. Shallow workings had become marginal in total production, so the operating costs of any significant mining enterprise, especially in a county dependent on imported coal, were considerable. But where mining differed from most large operations was in the 'lumpy' nature of initial investment. Before metals or coal could be raised, shafts had to be sunk and levels and drainage adits driven. On mines already operating, further expansion of this kind was carried out alongside the excavation of the 'paying' material. In the Cornish mines two groups of miners were employed: 'tutworkers' who drove the 'dead ground', and 'tributers' who mined the ore. The latter were paid a proportion of the value of the ore they raised, thus ensuring that

73. Crouzet, *Capital Formation*, p. 39 (footnote).
74. W. Pryce, *Mineralogia Cornubiensis*, 1778, reprinted Barton, Truro, 1972, p. 173.

poor results would generally produce a related cut in the wage bill and part of the risk would be borne by the working miner. A similar division was used in lead mines in Derbyshire and the northern Pennines, although in the coal mines the division was less marked, but of course coal seams are very much thicker than mineral veins and the work of driving and excavating accordingly more difficult to separate. It would seem that coal mines did not usually account further sinking as 'capital expenditure', for its predominant cost was in labour, but the historian needs to see it as distinct.[75]

By the time the great boom in copper mining began in Cornwall in the second quarter of the eighteenth century, the tendency towards a more capitalist organisation had long been accelerating in the centuries-old tin mining industry. Working partnerships with small amounts of hired labour were still winning tin – they continued to do so throughout the eighteenth century – but most tin by 1700 came from larger concerns managed on behalf of shareholders. Landowners and merchants were investing heavily in mining by the time of the 'Glorious Revolution'. Even before the Bubble Act of 1720 they did not, however, form joint-stock companies. Instead a system developed known as the cost book system, which was more suited to meet the constantly changing needs of a mining venture from its very beginnings to its eventual exhaustion. A group of adventurers formed a company and agreed a royalty – known as the 'dole' and usually one-sixteenth of the earnings – with the landlord for a mining lease. They subscribed their initial capital relative to the 'share' they had undertaken and profits were distributed at intervals, but when the mine needed development capital or was running at a loss and needed operating funds, 'calls' were made on the adventurers in proportion to their 'share'.[76] This system, which hardly altered over the next hundred years, did not produce the most risk-free investment of the era. Indeed, those who took shares in a fresh venture were in effect prospectors.

> We are out of pocket at this time about £80 to each of our
> thirty-second shares. There was nothing rich discovered in driving the
> adit through Gweal Paul tenement (tho' kindly) but in driving the adit
> further eastward on the course of the lode . . . a promising discovery
> has just been made so that the stocks are now so much advanced that
> 100 guineas have been repeatedly offered this week for one

75. Pollard, 'Coal mining', *op. cit.*, p. 37.
76. For the cost book system, see J. Rowe, *Cornwall in the Age of the Industrial Revolution*, Liverpool UP, 1953, pp. 23–5; R. Burt (ed.) *Cornish Mining*, David & Charles, Newton Abbot, 1969.

thirty-second part though I would gladly have sold mine for less than half that money four months ago, yet I am not willing to sell now at the price offered.

Thus a delighted agent informed his principal in 1795. But not everyone could hold on through the bad times. The same agent later passed on news of a share offered in another mine.

It is . . . judged to be a kindly adventure. But the rock is hard and as the great bodies of tin in the two other mines have been found to be very deep. Poor John, and I fear some other of the adventurers, are getting out of their depth. John went into the concern with a determination of getting himself to be a rich man – but alas! he like many others forgot to sit down and count the cost.[77]

From the perspective of the tin and copper mining industries as a whole, the collective benefit of the system was the success with which it mobilised capital for an expanding but speculative activity. There were many gainers: old landed families, new ones, bankers, lawyers, merchants, shopkeepers were all among them. Much more rarely, even the humble benefited. Sir Francis Basset, claiming Norman descent but whose father had become, according to Lord Hardwicke in 1761, 'full of money, from copper mines', described his contemporary, the county member Sir William Lemon, as the grandson of a miner who had been 'without a shilling'. The father of Davies Gilbert, MP, President of the Royal Society and County Sheriff in 1793, had been a poor clergyman on £35 per annum, but successful adventuring brought him to the position of justice and sent his son to Oxford. Up to the third quarter of the century most of the capital was raised in Cornwall, but thereafter the number of 'out-adventurers' increased: Watt, Boulton, Wedgwood, Wilkinson were among their number.[78]

In the lead mining districts the largest company, the London Lead Company, was a joint-stock company but its origins preceded the Bubble Act, going back to 1692. In any case it became better known after 1704 as the 'Quaker Lead Company', indicating that whatever its form it still belonged to the kin and kindred era of enterprise. For the most part the cost book system took over steadily through the eighteenth century. The lead miners of the seventeenth were independent and have been likened to 'shifting cultivators' working out shallow mines and moving on to break fresh

77. MSS Letterbooks of William Jenkin, County Museum, Truro, letters dated 31 Oct. 1795 and 6 Feb. 1798.
78. R.G. Rule, thesis, University of Warwick, 1971, pp. 196–7.

ground. Even in the early eighteenth century most mines were still small and shallow enough to be within the capabilities of partnerships of working miners leasing from the mineral owners and perhaps receiving some capital participation from local farmers and tradesmen. By the mid eighteenth century the situation had changed, for although very many small miner-owned operations continued, increasingly the main production was coming from larger enterprises, and by the end of the century lead mining was 'no longer an activity appropriate for the small man' who had been displaced by the growing expense. As in Cornwall, capital subscriptions at first came from the region. Dr Honeyman has said that up to 1750 in Derbyshire: 'A list of investors in lead mines reads like a local trades' directory.' After 1750, although landowners remained important, lead smelters and merchants became increasingly predominant.[79]

The Duke of Devonshire opened up a copper mine on his Derbyshire estate at Ecton Hill in 1760 and between then and 1817 raised 66,000 tonnes of high-grade copper from it. But this was an exceptional and singular concentration of copper and the Duke was as exceptional in playing a full entrepreneurial role in its working. In copper, tin and lead mining the role of landlords was essential and went far beyond the permissive one of encouraging exploration and granting appropriate leases. They usually invested as well in the mines which began to operate on their lands. Sometimes they took shares to encourage persistence in exploration or to keep faltering enterprises alive through bad times, for once the pumps stopped only a sharp increase in ore prices would justify reopening. Mostly they sought simply to profit. The Eyns estate near Truro took 44 per cent of its total income from mining between 1727 and 1731 and 40 per cent for 1738–42 against respective outlay percentages of 8 and 23. The Bassetts of Tehidy, near Redruth, were the best known of the mineral lords. Their income from mining was two to three times their estate rentals, but although they built tin-smelting works and a harbour at Portreath to unload coal, even they were not like the coal owners.[80]

Ashton and Sykes, historians of the eighteenth-century coal industry, claimed that because in Britain ownership of minerals was vested in the landowners, this produced an outcome very different from that in countries, like France, where they were owned by the

---

79. Burt, *Lead Mining Industry*, pp. 57–8; Honeyman, *Origins of Enterprise*, pp. 23–6.
80. J.V. Beckett, *Aristocracy in England*, p. 224.

Crown. It led to 'an organisation of coal-mining analogous to that of agriculture'. British landed proprietors took a close personal interest in the exploitation of the coal measures under their estates. A roll call of participating coal owners includes (as well as the Church of England in Durham) the Dukes of Northumberland and Earls of Scarborough on the great northern coalfield as well as gentry families such as Lambton, Bowes, Liddell, Wortley, Clavering, Vane-Tempest and Brandling; in west Cumberland the Lowthers, Curwens and Senhouses; in Yorkshire the Duke of Norfolk and Earl FitzWilliam; in Lancashire the Earls of Crawford and Balcarres as well as the third Duke of Bridgewater, whose colliery interests caused him to inaugurate the canal age; in Leicestershire the Earls of Moira; in the west Midlands the Earls of Dudley and Dukes of Sutherland. Many more lesser-known landowners were at some time or another involved, for early in the eighteenth century most collieries were small, shallow and cheaply worked. They could be taken in the landowner's stride like exploiting timber, lime pits or stone quarries. Twenty landowners were working mines in south-west Lancashire in the 1740s and at least fourteen in Nottinghamshire in 1739. The 'Grand Allies' – Colonel Liddell, the Hon. Charles Montague and George Bowes Esquire – combined in 1726 to buy up or lease as many likely coal measures on the north-eastern coalfield as they could, but could account for less than 60 per cent of the output. Thus in the first half of the century, and for perhaps for the first three-quarters outside of the sea-coast coalfields of Northumberland and Durham and west Cumberland, estate owners could work their coals much as they did their farmlands. That is to say, they could employ agents or stewards (the terms are interchangeable between farming and mining) to work them for their own direct profit, or they could lease them to suitable tenants, usually on leases specifying the manner of their working, just as farming leases were designed to limit the working-out of the land.[81]

Expanding markets, developing technologies and increasingly costly deep working tended over the period to drive out the smaller landlords, leading either to a greater extent of working by capitalist partnerships which tended to remain fairly small and locally subscribed, or to an even greater role for the truly committed landlords who were to form the powerful and distinct group of substantial coal owners so important in the industry until the mid

---

nineteenth century. Sir James Lowther, for example, busied himself during the 1720s and 1730s in buying out smaller men, even extending mortgage facilities to them. There was also a reverse process: landowners who had previously had only limited interest could become more active, especially when adjacent industrial development and improved communications stimulated the inland coalfields in the last quarter of the century. The Duke of Norfolk really began to exploit the coal on his estates near Sheffield only in the 1780s when he brought in an expert from the north-east. In 1805 these mines were leased for £75,000 and had a capital value of £16,500. His neighbour, Lord FitzWilliam, increased his activities around 1800, exploiting coal and iron. By 1820 he calculated that he had spent £122,000 over the preceding thirteen years. He was still well short of the half a million that Sir James Lowther invested in west Cumberland over the first half of the eighteenth century. For the established coal owners, combining to near-monopoly positions on the coastal fields, there was, after a while, usually a capital flow back from coal to land and other property, but beginning serious exploitation of coal deposits could involve finding a substantial inflow of capital. Sir Roger Newdigate borrowed £20,000 in 1777 to reconstruct his Warwickshire collieries, but his land-holding was the essential security for such a loan.[82]

When, after twenty years of direct management, the Duke of Norfolk decided to lease to a consortium of Sheffield businessmen in 1805, it was indicative of a movement that had become increasingly noticeable from 1780, the tendency of coal users to invest in local coal mining. London merchants had contributed to capital formation of the northern field, but with the diffusion of coke smelting and especially after the advent of Cort's puddling and rolling processes in 1784, the most noticeable stream of capital came from ironmasters such as the Darbys, Wilkinsons and Walkers. Ashton and Sykes considered this flow 'one of the outstanding events in the history of the coal industry', but added that its effects were beginning to appear on a large scale only by 1800. What most noticeably emerged were those integrated iron and coal concerns, like Crawley's or Coalbrookedale, where colliers and iron workers appeared side by side in the pay books.[83]

Professor Pollard, noting that some mining enterprises became capitalistic very early, remarks that they began 'to grapple with

82. *Ibid.*, pp. 212–13.
83. *Ibid.*, p. 214; Ashton and Sykes, *Coal Industry*, p. 6.

organisational problems at a time when most of the rest of industry was in the handicraft stage'.[84] In some cases this was not just a matter of internal organisation, for collective attempts were made to restrict output and sales to limit competition and guarantee profit levels. The best-known example of a producers' cartel operating in the eighteenth-century economy was the notorious 'vend' established in 1771 by the north-eastern collieries. These coalfields, because of their coastal proximity, monopolised the coal trade to London; it was an advantageous trading position they sought to exploit. Deliberate limitation of output to hold up prices did not begin with the vend of 1771. Ashton and Sykes documented agreements between sellers in 1711, 1727, 1738, 1741, 1765 and 1766. They note that after a remedial act was passed in 1730, the price of coal at Newcastle fell from 15s to 9s 6d per chaldron. The act lapsed in 1739 and coal rose to 13s, but when a second act was passed in 1744 it dropped back to 11s. A pamphlet of 1739 identifies the role of the 'Grand Allies' in promoting output restriction.[85]

The vend which began in 1771 hardly, then, originated producer collusion. It was partly the result of the opening up of new collieries near Newcastle and on the Wear, and partly the consequence of the adoption of effective screening techniques enabling collieries producing coal of mixed quality to separate their best coals and market them alongside those produced from the better collieries. The coal owners sought to limit the effect which this increase in supply might have on prices. The total vend, based on the volume of the previous year, was allocated between the collieries of the Tyne and of the Wear in the ratio of 3 : 2. Individual quotas were allocated monthly, but mines could overproduce if they paid compensation. Overall the limitation on output was not drastic, for average annual sales for the 1770s exceeded those of the preceding decade. When, however, internal squabbling broke up the vend in 1780, there was a substantial increase in the volume of sales and a price fall of around 13 per cent by 1786. In 1787 another agreement was made and although this was allowed a discretionary lapse in 1799 when a parliamentary investigation into coal prices was getting under way, it was renewed when it was realised that the committee, while it barked a lot, could hardly bite, and it lasted until 1858.[86]

In assessing the effects of the vend, Ashton and Sykes note that the range of price fluctuation at Newcastle was very much smaller

84. Pollard, *Genesis of Modern Management*, pp. 78–9.
85. Ashton and Sykes, *Coal Industry*, pp. 211–12.
86. *Ibid..*, pp. 213–14.

than that at London and conclude that the regulated price was probably not significantly higher than it would have been if producer competition had not been restricted. Coal prices, they suggest, moved in line with other commodity prices. So, of course, they might have; the argument is rather whether, given the gap between the actual and potential supply, they should have *fallen.* They are not surprised that 'the ordinary man of the eighteenth century' wondered at the high price of coal in London, but point out that vagaries of supply due to the weather as well as the activities of dealers at the London end mostly explain this. Be that as it may, it seems fortunate for the early industrial revolution that canal transport unlocked the inland coalfields.[87]

Producers' agreements among the copper mines of Cornwall seem to have existed only for a brief but eventful period. The problem for producers here was that copper ores in themselves cannot be marketed directly to customers; they must first be smelted. Lack of coal in Cornwall meant that this was done by smelters on or near the South Wales coalfield. These were few in number – only ten in 1770 – and it is clear that their buying agents in Cornwall frequently formed 'rings' at the monthly ore sales. It was very difficult to combat this by limits on output, for although the greater part of ores sold came from around twenty mines, more than fifty were responsible for the rest. Any one of these might suddenly break into rich ore and flood a particular monthly sale. Overproduction after the Seven Years War led to a 20 per cent price fall from 1772 to 1774, and recovery was prevented by the arrival on the market of ores from the open-cast mines on Parys Mountain in Anglesey which had been discovered in 1768. These mines were owned by one of the century's most ambitious entrepreneurs, Thomas Williams. He was later to move successfully into copper smelting, but for the time being a combination of smelters looked set to profit from the increase in supply. The defensive reaction was the setting up of the Cornish Metal Company in 1785 to buy the entire output from the Cornish mines. It was headed by the local magnate, Sir Francis Bassett, but its formation had been enabled through the involvement of Matthew Boulton. The great Birmingham businessman had a double interest in the prosperity of Cornish mining: as the partner of James Watt his lucrative premiums based on the coal savings enjoyed by mines pumping with Watt engines depended on

87. *Ibid.*, pp. 22–4.

constant production, while copper was probably the single most important input into his Birmingham manufacturing activities.

The Cornish Metal Company for the seven-year span of its existence was one of the most heavily capitalised enterprises in the whole of the eighteenth-century economy. The initial shareholders subscribed £130,000 at 8 per cent towards an intended capital of £500,000. Marketing effectively as a single producer, the Cornish mines were able to come to an agreement with Williams to share the market with Anglesey in the ratio of 3 : 2 but with no restriction on output. The smelters' ring was broken. The involvement of Boulton, a final user, with the mining companies, initial producers, confirms that this was a strategy aimed at the smelters in the middle, from which the mines hoped to get higher prices and the manufacturer lower ones. The Company closed in 1792, a break-up hastened by differences between Bassett and Boulton, but by then the easily worked ores of Parys Mountain were being worked out and the market was reviving.[88]

88. See Rowe, *Cornwall in the Age of the Industrial Revolution*, pp. 68–88; J.R. Harris, *The Copper King: A Biography of Thomas Williams of Llanidan*, Liverpool UP, 1964.

CHAPTER SIX

Labour in Manufacturing and Mining

WORKING CONDITIONS AND WAGES

Over such a wide range of forms of mining and manufacturing, the experience of labour was inevitably varied. Even within industries this was so, as for example between the 'free' miners of Cornwall and the Forest of Dean and the bonded pitmen of the north-east, or between the working small master clothier of the West Riding and cottage-based out-working weaver in the West Country. The expansion of putting out, the great increase in coal and metal mining and in iron making, the rise of a permanent journeyman class in some sectors of craft manufacture and the emergence of new industries like paper making, commercial brewing and distilling – all emphasised a separation of labour from capital long before the advent of the factory system. By 1776 Adam Smith was able to assert:

> In every part of Europe, twenty workmen serve under a master for one that is independent; and the wages of labour are everywhere understood to be, what they usually are, when the labourer is one person and the person who employs him another.[1]

For Europe generally this is something of an exaggeration, but it is not so for England. The forces creating a waged proletariat were not only stronger there in mining and in manufacturing, but after the mid eighteenth century a distinctive agrarian proletariat had come to characterise the southern and Midland counties. Relations between masters and men were obviously affected by this development. The recognition of a separate interest is, as Adam Smith fully acknowledged, the starting point for conflict.

The wide gulf between the merchant-capitalist clothiers of the West Country woollen district and the out-working weavers they employed

1. Adam Smith, *Wealth of Nations*, I, pp. 73–4.

was frequently contrasted with the bridgeable one in the West Riding between the working clothiers and their journeymen. The former was said to bring industrial conflict, the latter harmony. The very words 'domestic system' implied human relationships and firm rather than oppressive control. In a dialect poem of 1730 on the West Riding the master clothier and his wife appear breakfasting at a common table with their family, a few journeymen, servants and apprentices before setting down to weave together from 'five at morn till eight at neet'. After the working day they sit down to supper and the master sets the tasks for the morrow:

> Quoth Maister – Lads, work hard I pray,
> Cloth mun be peark'd next market-day,
> And Tom mun go tomorn to t'spinners,
> And Will mun seek about for t'swingers;
> And Jack tomorn, by time be rising,
> And go t'sizing mill for sizing,
> And get your web and warping done
> That ye may get it into loom.
>
> Mary – there's wool,- tak thee and dye it . . .

But Mary, the mistress, has something to say about this.

> So thou's setting me my work,
> I think I'd more need mend thy sark,
> 'Prithie who mun sit at bobbin weel?
> And ne'er a cake at top o' th' creel!
> And we to bake; and swing and blend,
> And milk, and bairns to school to send,
> And yeast to seek, and syk as that!
> And washing up, morn, noon and neet,
> And bowls to scald, and milk to fleet,
> And bairns to fetch again at neet!

Her husband knows all this, but she and the servant lass must get up 'soon and stir about and get all done'.

> For all things mun aside be laid–
> When we want help about our trade.

Master and dame then went off to pass time with a neighbour, while the young people sit and talk happily around a good coal fire: 'More free from care than knight or squire'.[2]

Of course, it is an idealisation; an engaging picture of a system of

---

2. Parts of the poem are frequently cited; for the fullest text see *Publications of the Thoresby Society*, XLI, Pt 3, 95, 1947, pp. 275–9.

manufacture which at the beginning of the next century was still being described as 'highly favourable to the paternal, filial, and fraternal happiness – and to the cultivation of good moral and civil habits – the sources of public tranquillity'. The contrast with another poem, this time describing relations in the putting-out system of the West Country, is striking. This poem is entitled *The Clothiers' Delight* and subtitled 'The Rich Men's Joy and the Poor Men's Sorrow'. The first verse concludes:

> We live at our pleasure, and take our delight;
> We heapeth up riches and treasures great store,
> Which we get by griping the poor.
> And this is a way for to fill up our purse
> Although we do get it with many a curse

And the poem ends:

> Then hay for the Clothing Trade, it goes on brave;
> We scorn for to toyl and moyl, nor yet to starve.
> Our workmen do work hard, but we live at ease;
> We go when we will, and come when we please;
> We hoard up our bags of silver and gold;
> But conscience and charity with us are cold.[3]

The poems dramatise the differences between the two systems of manufacturing. But relations between masters and men could be friendly and mutually regarding even under the putting-out system. Samuel Bamford's account of early days in cotton manufacture contrasts the caring attitudes of an older generation of putting-out cotton masters with the harsher circumstances some years later. Nevertheless, the capitalist relations of the putting-out system provided a wide arena for disputes. The emergence of trade unions was only one manifestation.[4]

An embittered West Country clothier complained in 1739 that the only persons who supported the poor were those who did not know of 'the insolence, idleness, debauchery, frauds and dishonesty' of the weavers.[5] He typifies a rhetoric of conflict inherent in the putting-out system. Employers complained of such traits as often and as vehemently as they complained of 'riotous and unlawful combination'. On their part the workers protested over 'oppressions' in the shape of late wage payment, truck, 'stoppages' from pay

3. Quoted in P. Mantoux, *The Industrial Revolution in the Eighteenth Century*, Methuen, 1964, pp. 75–7.
4. Samuel Bamford, *Early Days*, reprinted Cass 1967, pp. 117–19.
5. W. Temple, *The Case as it Now Stands*, 1739, reprinted in K. Carpenter (ed.) *Labour Problems before the Industrial Revolution*, New York, Arno Press, 1972, p. 5.

for allegedly deficient workmanship, of effecting wage cuts by increasing the measure of work expected for a 'price', and of deducting excessive charges for rent of equipment and the supply of essential items, as often as they did of employers' combinations to lower wages.[6]

Accusations that out-workers embezzled materials have to be considered in several contexts: perquisites and wages in kind, the circulation of raw materials to unsupervised manufacturing households and the long delays which often occurred between completing work and receiving payment. The expectation of an exclusively cash wage was developing rather than established, particular rather than general in the eighteenth century. Dr Linebaugh has suggested that much so-called criminal activity on the part of working people was identified in the process of transformation of the wage from a form in which money constituted a substantial part of the wage to one based wholly on it.

> Bugging to the hatter, cabbage to the tailor, blue-pigeon flying to the plumbers and glaziers, chippings to shipwrights, sweepings to porters, red sail docking to navy yard workers, flints and thrums to weavers, vails to servants, privileges to west country clothiers, bontages to Scottish agricultural workers, scrapings and naxers to coopers, wastages to framework knitters, in all these the eighteenth-century labourer appropriated a part of his product or a part of the material of his labour.[7]

Such bits and pieces considered as perquisites could either be disposed of directly or worked up into articles to be sold. The 'vulgar tongue' abounded with colloquialisms suggesting that a particular term conferred a legitimacy which would have been made questionable by a more generalised synonym for stealing. Linebaugh's list is not confined to the putting-out trades, but these did allow a special facility. Invasion of property in the form of the appropriation of put-out materials attracted regular attention as this method of organising manufacture spread. Out-working shoe makers were said to have 'constant opportunities' for defrauding their masters because 'they seldom work in their master's shop'. Clock and watch makers, too, distressed their employers by pawning valuable materials. Sheffield nail makers purloined wire, while in the Black Country iron, lead and brass were easy to dispose of among the thousands of small forges. Employer petitioning secured the passing of a number

---

6. These matters are treated more fully in J.G. Rule, *Experience of Labour*, Ch. 5.
7. P. Linebaugh, summary of a paper in *Bulletin of the Society for the Study of Labour History*, **25**, 1972, p. 13.

of statutes. The swopping of cheap for expensive leathers by shoe makers was dealt with by 9 George I c. 27 in 1722, while 13 George II c. 8 in 1739 dealt with several putting-out trades including iron working, textiles and leather. The hatters were constrained in 1749 by 22 George II c. 27, and the watch makers in 1754 by 27 George II c. 7. The better-known Worsted Acts of 1777 (17 George III c. 11 and c. 56), which set up an inspectorate to work with a prosecuting committee of employers, were described by the Hammonds as a piece of 'class legislation' because they allowed conviction on the oath of the employer who owned the yarn in question and because they empowered extensive searching of weavers' homes. These acts, however, in presuming guilt rather than innocence, were not such a startling departure as the Hammonds thought. The Hatters' Act of 1749, for example, made failure to return surplus material within twenty-one days an automatic instance of guilt.[8]

Spinners could hide appropriated yarn by 'false reeling'. At the next stage weavers or knitters could put some yarn aside and conceal the lightness of the resulting cloth in various ways. A Gloucestershire clothier in 1774 detailed the various forms of theft and deception he had to guard against. His pickers embezzled one pound in twenty and disguised the weight loss by throwing the wool on to wet stones. Scribblers added oil for this purpose, while spinners held wool over a steaming kettle and could conceal the removal of half a pound in every six this way. Weavers got away with five or six pounds from a sixty-pound piece. A search carried out at Frome in 1786 produced several hundredweight of embezzled wool.[9] More interesting was the prolonged and bitter dispute which broke out in Essex in 1757. Colchester clothiers had indicated their intention of prosecuting weavers who did not return the 'thrums', the web ends left in the loom after the cloth had been removed. Retaining these had long been an unquestioned perquisite and trouble began when the clothiers carried out their threat to prosecute and two persons were whipped for theft for failing to return thrums. Clothiers in Baintree and Barking followed suit and demanded the return of thrums from their weavers. In the face of great hostility the clothiers then agreed to pay compensation of threepence a thrum, which suggests some degree of recognition on

8. For a slightly different interpretation of these acts from that of Dr Linebaugh or myself, see J. Styles, 'Embezzlement, industry and the law in England, 1500–1800' in Berg, Hudson and Sonenscher (eds.), *Manufacture in Town and Country*, pp. 182–8; Hammonds, *Skilled Labourer*, pp. 149–50.

9. Examples cited in Rule, *Experience of Labour*, pp. 132–3.

their part that thrums were part of the 'customary wage', whatever the legal position. The weavers valued them more highly, however, and responded with a fourteen-week strike during which they inserted a notice in the *Ipswich Journal.*

> They made a demand of our waste, without offering any allowance for the same; and by degrees did we tamely submit, we should be brought under a yoke, which would have some affinity to that of the Egyptian Bondage. Though we would not presume to deny, but that afterwards through the negociation of the Right Hon. Robert Nugent Esq. they offered us 3d per bay in lieu thereof. The waste is a small perquisite that hath been granted us for several hundred years past, which we are able to prove by our ancient Books of Record, which have been no less than 14 or 15 times ratified and confirmed at the General Quarter Sessions.

The sense of right here goes well beyond the simple assertion of customary practice and is strengthened by the involvement of the local Member of Parliament and the approval of the justices at sessions. More than 500 weavers went on strike in defence of this 'ancient custom', staying out through the winter from November to February before they were reduced to acceptance of the threepence compensation. Thrums were also an expected perquisite in the West Country. A Gloucestershire clothier stated in 1802 that although they 'belonged' without question to the clothiers, their return had never been insisted on.[10]

Contests over perquisites were not confined to textile manufacture. The Earl of Uxbridge attempted to end the coal allowance of his Staffordshire colliers in 1757. His argument was that miners were abusing their personal fuel allowance by removing large amounts to sell. Anything from a half to a third of colliers' earnings was accounted for by an allowance of two draughts of coal a week, and when other Staffordshire coal owners tried to follow the Earl's example, they found their miners demanding threepence a day in compensation.[11] An even longer running battle was fought in the royal dockyards. The Admiralty was sorely agitated by the shipwrights' custom of taking 'chips'. In origin these were scraps of waste wood for fuel, and by the mid seventeenth century they had

10. See A.F.J. Brown, *Essex at Work 1700–1815*, Chelmsford, Essex Record Office, 1969, p. 25; *English History from Essex Sources*, 1952, same publisher, pp. 204–5; *Minutes of Evidence before the Committee on the Laws relating to the Woollen Trade*, BPP 1802/3 (95), VII, p. 320.

11. D. Hay, 'Crime, authority and the criminal laws in Staffordshire 1750–1800', unpublished PhD Thesis, University of Warwick, 1975, pp. 87, 92–3.

grown into a form of wage supplementation. The government became concerned over a growing loss of timber. Workmen were said to be removing loads of so-called chips three times a day, and even to be building huts from waste timber in which to store chips they were unable to carry out at once. In 1753 a rule was introduced that no more could be removed than could be carried unbound under an arm. This does not seem to have succeeded any more than had an earlier regulation that only waste from timber cut with axe or adze was 'lawful', not sawn timber. Clearly these regulations were meant to confine carried-out timber to that fit only for firewood, but in 1792 complaints were still being made of enormous losses of timber through yard workers, who even finished work early to allow themselves time to saw up useful lengths, which they sold at a shilling each. Chips were eventually replaced by a cash allowance in 1805. Whatever the Admiralty's feelings on the matter, the determination of the shipwrights to cling to their perquisite must be viewed in the context of the long delay in paying wages. Royal dockyard workers considered themselves lucky if their pay was only a year in arrears. Recourse to local money-lenders or the 'selling' of future wages was necessary for survival. The value of 'chips', which could be converted into ready cash, is clear.[12]

The workers countered accusations of dishonesty and slipshod working with claims of 'oppression'. *The Clothiers' Delight* is a compendium of them.

> In former ages we us'd to give,
> So that our work-folk like farmers did live;
> But the times are altered, we will make them know
> All we can for to bring them under our bow;
> We will make them work hard for sixpence a day,
> Though a shilling they deserve if they had their just pay.
>
> And first for the Combers, we will bring them down
> From eight groats a score unto half a crown,
> If at all they murmur, and say tis too small,
> We bid them choose whether they will work at all;
> We'll make them believe that trading is bad;
> We care not a pin, though they are ne'er so sad.
>
> We'll make the poor Weavers work at a low rate;
> We'll find fault where there's no fault, and so we will
>   bate;
> If trading goes dead, we will presently show it;

---

12. For 'chips' see Rule, *Experience of Labour*, pp. 128–30 and the sources cited there.

> But if it grows bad, they shall never know it;
> We'll tell them that cloth beyond sea will not go,
> We care not whether we keep clothing or no.
>
> Then next for the Spinner we shall ensue,
> We'll make them spin three pound instead of two;
> When they bring home their work unto us, they complain,
> And say that their wages will not them maintain;
> But if that an ounce of weight they do lack,
> Then for to bate threepence we will not be slack.
>
> But if it holds weight, then their wages they crave,
> We have got no money, and what's that you'd have?
> We have bread and bacon and butter that's good,
> With oatmeal and salt that is wholesome for food;
> We have soap and candles whereby to give light
> That you may work by them so long as you have light.
>
> But if to an alehouse they customers be,
> Then presently with the ale wife we agree;
> When we come to a reckoning, then we do crave
> Twopence on a shilling, and that we will have,
> By such cunning ways we our treasure do get,
> For it is all fish that doth come to our net.[13]

Several forms of exploitation are indicated in these verses: forcing wages down under false pretences – for example by claiming that the market was weak – fining or 'bating' for work wrongly declared underweight, and forcing workers to accept truck instead of due money wages. The persistence of such complaints, which from time to time were endorsed by local persons not connected with the woollen trade, suggests that these 'oppressions' were widespread and long-lasting. Where piece-rate systems were in use, employers tended to cut wages by increasing the quantum rather than changing the price. This avoided the appearance of lowering rates which had often been at a 'customary' level for a generation or more. Gloucestershire clothiers in 1756 'laid the chain four or five yards longer on the bar' and stopped altogether an allowance of two shillings the price which they had been paying for 'stopping' (repairing) the cloth. In 1758 Essex clothiers similarly added to both the length and width of the expected piece.[14] The Sheffield cutlery trades supply an even more glaring example in 1787, when Jonathan Watkinson provoked a strike by insisting on thirteen knives in the dozen.

13. See note 3 above.
14. These and further examples are cited in Rule, *Experience of Labour*, pp. 137–8.

That offspring of tyranny, baseness and pride
Our rights hath invaded and almost destroyed
May that man be banished who villainy screens,
Or sides with big W———n and his thirteens.

And may the odd knife his great carcass dissect;
Lay open his vitals for all to inspect
A heart full as black as the infernal gulf
In that greedy, blood-sucking, bone scraping wolf.[15]

Complaints about payment in kind or in truck were persistent in many parts of the country. Somerset's weavers complained in 1726 of their masters 'paying their wages in goods, and setting extravagant prices on such goods'. In 1739 they complained of being forced to take remnants of cloth as payment. Devonshire weavers were angered in 1743 at their masters 'forcing them to take corn, bread, bacon, cheese, butter and other necessaries of life, in truck as it is called, for their labour'. Around Sheffield this was known as the 'stuffing system' and prices were said to be overvalued threefold. The cutlers rioted against the system in 1756. Watch makers were forced at one time to accept either bread tickets or else take payment in cheap watches which they could sell only at a loss.[16]

Of all workers' complaints, the justice of those over truck seem to have been most widely acknowledged. Even employers who steadfastly denied that they would ever use such a method usually indicated that they knew of those who did. An independent source in the West Country in 1739 thought it 'rare' to find a clothier who paid ready cash unless he also obliged his workers to lay it out again with himself or his friends. As for complaints that employers falsely claimed bad workmanship or embezzlement of materials to deduct fines from wages, even William Temple, an ardent polemicist for the clothiers in a dispute with the West Country weavers in 1727, admitted knowing one clothier who stopped wages 'in a most base and flagrant manner', despite which he became a JP. Temple rejected, though, the weavers' complaint that clothiers in general 'load them with intolerable weights and starve them by stoppages'. Another local 'gentleman' considered, however, that clothiers imposed impossible standards for the closeness of the weave and then extracted arbitrary penalties from the weavers for failing to meet them. Under an act of George I weavers could take their complaints

15. The verses are by Joseph Mather, the radical cutler-poet; see G.I.H. Lloyd, *The Cutlery Trade*, reprinted Cass 1968, pp. 75–7.
16. For sources see Rule, *Experience of Labour*, pp. 138–9.

to magistrates, but Temple himself admitted that such recourse would mark a man and reduce his prospects of obtaining work. It is worth noting that when James Wolfe was sent as a young officer to restore order in the troubled clothing districts of the West Country, his sympathies rapidly shifted to the side of the weavers.[17]

The West Country woollen districts seem unusually well documented on these matters, but there is evidence from other trades. London's hatters complained in 1777 that masters stopped 'hundreds of pounds' for alleged faults, 'when trade has been slack'. On the northern coalfield the rejection of badly filled corves on the grounds that they had been deliberately underfilled – 'they will sometimes be so roguish as to set these big coals hollow at the Corfe bottom, and cover them with some small coals at the top of the Corves, and make it look like a full Corfe' – was a long-running grievance which led to a strike at one mine in 1751. In hosiery manufacture, abatements for alleged negligent or fraudulent work were similarly a frequent cause of friction. Hosiers were accused of making too little allowance for normal waste, so that they could fine knitters whose returned work was lighter than the yarn which had been given out. Some, it was said, even put out silk weighed damp so that when the finished stockings were weighed dry they could claim a deficiency.[18]

The hosiery industry was notorious for the range of deductions employers made from wages. Knitters were pressed to rent the stocking frames and those who owned their own found it hard to get work when times were less busy. The frame rents were not related to their value or to the expected income from their use. They actually rose when second-hand prices were low and wages in decline. The hosier frame owners enjoyed a certain profit from the rent whether or not the knitter was in full work, for it was deducted before wages were paid. Nor was it the only deduction: there were charges for seaming the stockings, for use of a corner of the master knitter's workshop, for needles, candles, oil, coals and for the expenses involved in collecting in work. A wage statement from 1811 shows a total deduction of 4s (20p) from a nominal wage of 13s 3¼d (66p). The coal heavers who unloaded London's seaborne coal were obliged to hire their shovels and other supplies from the undertakers who contracted with the coal vessels and were their direct hirers. Pryce noted that Cornish miners were forced to buy

17. *Ibid.*, pp. 139–41.
18. *Ibid.*, pp. 140–1.

their candles from the mine, and although he did not, in 1778, suggest overcharging, nineteenth-century account books reveal substantial profits being taken.[19]

In 1721 a statute fixed the hours of London's journeymen tailors and divided their day into two half-pay periods. These were not equal, the afternoon session being an hour the longer. The employers took advantage of this and exploited their journeymen by 'letting them play in the morning' and calling them from their 'houses of call' in the afternoon. This not only gave the masters an extra hour's work but saved them having to pay the breakfast allowance of 1½d (0.6p). Time is an aspect of work on which historians have begun to provide an extensive body of literature. They have been especially concerned with the transformation of irregular preindustrial work rhythms into the more ordered day of modern industrial society. Two aspects need consideration: the tendency of workers to lessen their weekly amount of work at times when higher money wages or lower food prices allowed them to meet their customary expectation of comfort from fewer hours of labour, and secondly, the ability of home-based out-workers to control their own pace of work, compensating, if they so chose, for a slack early week with a bout of late-week intensity.[20]

Recently historians have linked these problems to the so-called 'proto-industrial' stage of manufacturing development which spread industrial employment widely into rural districts. The household unit of production, though headed by male weaver or other outworker, was not governed by the object of accumulating a monetary surplus: 'It could not maximise what it could not measure.' Instead it sought an equilibrium, a labour–consumption balance between its economic, social and cultural necessities on the one side and the output of labour by the family on the other. If the returns fell it increased labour output; if they rose it felt no need to do so and opted instead for increased leisure.[21]

To make the poor 'sober, industrious and obedient', asserted William Temple in 1739, the means of idleness had to be removed, and that was high wages. The best goods were made when subsist-

19. F.A. Wells, *The British Hosiery and Knitwear Industry: Its History and Organisation*, reprinted David & Charles, 1972, pp. 63–70; Rule, *Experience of Labour*, pp. 141–2; W. Pryce, *Mineralogia Cornubiensis*, 1778, reprinted Barton, Truro, 1972, p. 180.

20. F.W. Galton, *Select Documents Illustrating Trade Unionism: The Tailoring Trade*, London School of Economics, 1896, p. 56.

21. H. Medick, 'The proto-industrial family economy: the structural function of household and family during the transition from peasant society to industrial capitalism', *Social History*, **3**, 1976, p. 298.

ence was most difficult and workers were 'obliged to work more and debauch less'. Forty years later William Hutton, who had once himself been a framework knitter, wrote that manufactures tended to decay when 'plenty preponderates', for a man who could support his family on three days' labour would not work six. It benefited a manufacturing country to keep provisions at a level which, while within reach of the poor, would still require them to make a full labour commitment.[22] Arthur Young shared his view.

> The master manufacturers of Manchester wish that prices might always be high enough to enforce a general industry; to keep the hands employed six days for a week's work; as they find that even one idle day, in the chance of it being a drunken one, damages all the other five, or rather the work of them.

The great propagandist for agricultural capitalism naturally favoured high cereal prices, but in 1771 he also made the link with high wages, insisting that 'great earnings' caused many workers to offer only four or five days' labour. This was 'a fact so well-known in every manufacturing town, that it would be idle to think of proving it'.[23]

In 1794 wool combers were accused of working only half their time for a wage of 10s (50p) when 25s (£1.25p) was within their reach. Professor Mathias has raised the question of whether such complaints should be viewed as valid description or as opinion indicative of employer attitudes.[24] In fact it has both dimensions. As normative reporting it justified the 'utility of poverty' theory of low wages which was associated with a mercantile concern with low export prices. But it can also be found in the writings of Defoe, who favoured high wages as a stimulant for home demand. The clothier who wrote in 1760 that high wages made his workfolk 'scarce, saucy and bad' was seeking to impress no one, for he entered it in his private diary. Similarly it was in a private letter that a Cornish mine agent wrote in 1793:

> The common tinners continue to be very refractory and insolent: many of them refuse to work, and have not gone underground for three weeks past – They have no cause for it for their wages have been rather

22. Temple, *The Case as it now Stands, op. cit.*, pp. 20, 40; William Hutton, *A History of Birmingham*, Birmingham, 1781, p. 69.

23. A. Young, *A Six Months Tour through the North of England*, 1771, I, pp. 176–7 and III, p. 193.

24. *Journals of the House of Commons*, XLIX, 1794, p. 395; P. Mathias, 'Leisure and wages in theory and practice' in *The Transformation of England*, Methuen, 1979, p. 149.

too high lately than otherwise; the consequence has been too much
brandy drinking and other bad practices.[25]

There is a problem in interpreting this. If workers were spending
their time in this way, they were not only exercising a leisure preference but were consuming a non-essential. There is a conflict between the complaints of a leisure preference coming into play as
soon as wages moved above that necessary to support customary living standards and the accompanying complaints of the 'luxury' expectations of the poor, which were equally used to justify a harsh
attitude to wages. Tea, tobacco, dress styles which aped their bet-
ters, as well as excessive spirit drinking were all roundly condemned
by those who insisted that the poor lived above their station. In fact,
as Mathias has pointed out, employers did not reduce wages when
they wanted an increase in labour. High earning possibilities could
have a compensating effect, for if they increased the 'idleness' of
those already employed, they also drew in new hands. When this
happened, as it did in the golden age of cotton hand-loom weaving
for instance, it could lead to an eventual oversupply of labour and
restore the advantage to the hirer. It seems reasonable to conclude
that the situation described by economists as a 'backward-sloping
supply curve for labour', meaning that contrary to expectations a
higher price produces a decrease in labour offered, was less generally true in the mid eighteenth century than it had been earlier.[26]

When we turn from labour supply to labour intensity, the contrast made by historians is usually that between pre-industrial work
rhythms and those of the factory economy. Edward Thompson has
written of the 'deep-rooted folk memory' resting on 'nostalgia for
the pattern of work and leisure which obtained before the outer
and inner discipline of industrialism settled upon the working
man'. In a seminal article he described the 'characteristic irregularity of labour patterns before the coming of large-scale machine-
powered industry'. This pattern was one of 'alternate bouts of intense labour and of idleness wherever men were in control of their
own working lives'. That the cottage out-worker could control his
own pace seems evident, but the pattern was also to be found in
workshop trades. Hatters were said to have long hours – 'a man
goes early and stays late' – but no fixed hours. Birmingham has

25. See R.C. Wiles, 'The theory of wages in later English mercantilism', *Econ.
H.R.*, XX, 1968, pp. 113–26; J. de L. Mann (ed.), *Wiltshire Textile Trades*, Wiltshire
Record Society, Devizes, 1964, Document 203; cited in Rule, *Experience of Labour*, p.
54.
26. Mathias, 'Leisure and wages', *op. cit.*, p. 161.

been described as a 'matrix of small workshops' forming a 'conducive environment for the survival of immemorial work rhythms'. From Sheffield, with its similar structure of small metal-working forges, comes a revealing song, *The Jovial Cutlers,* written in 1793 and encapsulating the irregularity of artisan labour.

> Brother workmen cease your labour,
> Lay your files and hammers by,
> Listen while a brother neighbour
> Sings a cutlers destiny;
> How upon a good Saint Monday,
> Sitting by the smithy fire
> Telling what's been done o' t'Sunday
> And in cheerful mirth conspire

The cutler's wife enters and indicates, by reference to her ragged attire, that she at least would welcome a little less leisure preference and a little more consumer response to monetary incentive. As she nags, her husband complains of her tongue moving faster than his 'boring stick at a Friday's pace'. Here is the rhythm of his week: Monday a holiday, but Friday needing a furious rate to complete the weekly stint of knives. Obviously such a pattern was affected by price levels and piece rates. Adverse movement in either would lessen the number of hours which could be taken as play, but still would not dictate precisely which hours had to be worked. The response could accompany normal wage times as well as those of high wages.[27]

'Saint Monday' was honoured across the spectrum of trades and in the mines. The year as well as the week was punctuated with holidays. Josiah Wedgwood may have boasted his intent of 'making such machines of men as cannot err' but he could not nail his potters to the floor and was left to fume when they absented themselves for the local 'wakes'. A writer on the Cornish miners in the early eighteenth century complained that because of their 'numerous holidays, holiday eves, feasts, account days (once a month), Yeuwhiddens or one way or another they invent to loiter away their time, they do not work one half of their month for the owners and employers'. Attempts by 'several gentlemen' to end these customs had been of little avail for a complaint of a very similar kind was still being made a century later. Northern coal miners observed a

---

27. E.P. Thompson, *Making of the English Working Class,* 1963 edn, p. 357 and 'Time, work-discipline and industrial capitalism', pp. 49–50; D.A. Reid, 'Decline of Saint Monday', p. 77; *Third Report from SC on Artisans and Machinery,* BPP 1824 (51), V, p. 97; cited in Lloyd, *Cutlery Trade, op. cit.,* p. 181.

long Christmas break and from time to time proclaimed 'gaudy days' on such occasions as hearing the first cuckoo. Every trade took a holiday on the day of its patron saint.[28]

Adam Smith took a more considered view than most commentators. He suggested that a day or so of drunken dissipation was the *result* of a previous period of intense labour. Francis Place, remembering his days as a journeyman tailor, endorsed this view. He recalled the desire for leisure which even the most serious and industrious of workers experienced after a period of constant application, impelling them to 'indulge in idleness'. This was a familiar enough phenomenon, but it is distinct from the *normally* irregular working rhythm of many artisans and out-workers. The author of *The Jovial Cutlers*, Joseph Mather, was himself a working cutler and he wrote for an audience of his fellows.[29]

There was, however, for some of those who worked on their employer's premises, a firmer notion of the working day. The statute of 1721 fixed the hours of London's tailors as from 6 a.m. to 8 p.m. with an hour for dinner. Was this typical? In 1752 the tailors were claiming that it was not and that the norm in most 'handicraft trades' was from 6 a.m. to 6 p.m. However, Campell's authoritative *London Tradesman* of 1747 suggests fourteen hours for breeches makers, carpet weavers, harness makers, coopers, engravers, saddlers, stocking knitters, wool combers and shoe makers. Book binders, broom makers, buckle makers, calico printers, glovers, knife grinders and pin makers all worked an extra hour to 9 p.m. Where daylight was essential, a twelve-hour day was usual except in the winter months. In 1768 the statutory day for the tailors was cut to thirteen hours. Wool sorters at Exeter worked 'from the time of being able to discern the wool until the evening', which amounted to about eight and a half hours in winter and twelve in summer. In the royal dockyards the basic day was twelve hours but it was necessarily shorter in winter, and in summer overtime shifts known as 'tides' were often worked. In paper mills the base for wage calculation was a measure of output judged to occupy eight hours, but paper makers generally worked another four hours' overtime.[30]

Evidence of this kind has led Dr Harrison to challenge the linking

28. N. McKendrick, 'Josiah Wedgwood and factory discipline', *Historical Journal*, IV, 1961, p. 46; Rule, *Experience of Labour*, pp. 56–7.

29. Smith, *Wealth of Nations*, I, p. 92; Francis Place, *Autobiography*, ed. M. Thale, Cambridge UP, 1972, p. 123 (note).

30. 7 George I, c. 13, 1721; Galton, *Tailoring Trade, op. cit.*, p. 52; R. Campbell, *The London Tradesman*, 1747, reprinted David & Charles 1969, pp. 331–40; Rule, *Experience of Labour*, p. 58.

of modern work disciplines to the arrival of the factory system. From a close study of Bristol, not to any great extent a factory town, he argues that regularity was already a feature of urban labour by 1750. In the towns there was by then 'a recognisable working day and working week'. He is insistent on this: 'it is safe to observe, indeed to stress, the following: between 1750 and 1850 almost all employed people, particularly in towns, were to be found at work between the hours of 6 a.m. and 6 p.m., Tuesday to Saturday'.[31] In some ways that is a statement of astonishing banality, for who supposes otherwise? Yet it contains some surprising assumptions. It seems to accept Saint Monday to the extent of being not only general but a 'fixed arrangement' which, added to Sunday, made up a 'weekend'. If Saint Monday was as normal as the modern Saturday, then why was so much fuss made about it? Further, if it is true that later eighteenth-century urban workers had a 'standard' five-day week, albeit of sixty hours, then the factory was to make a very significant difference by insisting on six. As Professor Landes has pointed out, the tolerance of non-factory employers depended on the fact that they did not have to take the running or fixed costs of machinery into account.

There are other problems, apart from the fact that Harrison's evidence dates from 1790 and if there was a regular working pattern in Bristol it may have been of more recent origin than he suggests. His typical working week would be short indeed if he did not consider Saturday as a normal working day – but was it? In many trades it was close to a half-day as well as being pay day. That hours of work were stated for many trades does not mean that they were always worked to the full. Harrison agrees that they were sometimes overworked, but they were as often underworked. The hours of London tailors were fixed by statute, but the journeymen could still complain that the masters called upon them for only half a day, leaving them in their public houses all morning. Campbell in 1747 gave nominal hours of work for hatters, for example, but the men in their evidence in 1777 stated that they measured their day by output, not time.[32] Even if there were regular hours, this says nothing about the intensity of labour. Evidence from a variety of trades, printing, coopering and shipbuilding among them, points to a degree of casualness quite foreign to the machine-dictated rhythms of

31. M. Harrison, *Crowds and History*, pp. 107–8. He first published his argument in *Past and Present* **110**, 1986, pp. 134–68 and drew a sharp response from D.S. Landes in the same journal, **116**, 1987, pp. 192–9.

32. Galton, *Tailoring Trade, op. cit.*, p. 60; *Commons Journals*, XXXVI, pp. 118–19.

factory production. In the latter, fines for simply chatting with work-mates contrast vividly with the drinking customs so often described in the artisan trades. An old potter regretted that machinery did not transform his trade as early as it did that of cotton.

> It would have been better for employers and workpeople if they had been in the disciplinary grip of machinery. . . . A machine worked so many hours in the week would produce so much length of yarn or cloth. Minutes were felt to be factors in these results, whereas in the Potteries hours, or even days at times, were hardly felt to be such factors.[33]

So far as mining is concerned, the long colliery shifts of the nine-teenth century do not seem to have been usual in the eighteenth. Miners in general worked fewer hours than other workers. Young commented that the lead miners of the Dales had finished their underground work by noon or one o'clock. Yorkshire pitmen seem usually to have worked eight hours and sometimes only six. In the lead mines of the northern Pennines shaft sinking and level driving was done on a shift system with each gang working five eight-hour days, or in the Yorkshire lead mines a six-day week of six-hour shifts. Pitmen in Northumberland and Durham were working six or seven hours in 1765 but seem to have been working at least eight by the end of the century, as Whitehaven's colliers had already been doing in 1765. In Derbyshire in 1776 eight hours was usual, save for ex-ceptionally difficult ground when six were worked. Around Leeds in 1787 an eight-hour day was the norm, with no sign yet of the twelve-hour one which had become common by 1842.[34]

In the Cornish mines the tutworkers who opened up the ground usually worked eight-hour shifts, with three shifts over twenty-four hours known by the mid eighteenth century. Tributers, who raised the actual ore, came and went with more freedom. Carew, writing at the beginning of the seventeenth century, had then thought four hours underground was as much as a tin miner could endure, but six- or eight-hour shifts overwhelmingly predominated by the eight-eenth century. According to Pryce in 1778, longer shifts had been experimented with but had been found less productive.

> they were nothing but an excuse for idleness; twelve hours being too many for a man to work underground without intermission.
> Accordingly when a pare of men went underground formerly, they made it a rule, to sleep out a candle, before they set about their work;

33. Charles Shaw, *When I was a Child*, 1903, reprinted Caliban 1977, p. 185.
34. See Rule, *Experience of Labour*, pp. 58–9.

that is if their place of work was dry, they would lay themselves down
and sleep, as long as a whole candle would continue burning; and then
rise up and work for two or three hours pretty briskly; after that have a
touch pipe, that is rest themselves for half an hour to smoke a pipe of
tobacco, and so play and sleep away half their working time: but
mining being more expensive than it formerly was, those idle customs
are superseded by more labour and industry.

In tin and copper mining, as in coal mining, the demands of an
industry becoming increasingly more capitalistic, as mines went
deeper and draining technologies became more costly, meant a
greater commitment from labour. Pryce, for example, assumed that
miners relieved each other in place, but in fact this was in itself an
increased burden on labour which was still being contested in some
mines twenty years later.

A bad custom has prevailed lately in our mines in general which is that
the men work only six hours whereas they used to work eight hours
. . . we entered into a resolution to insist on the men working eight
hours in future, instead of six and relieve in place.

This was in 1785 and by then the major mines were so deep that a
ladder climb to the surface could take an hour. Whether shifts
changed in place or at the surface was thus a matter of some importance. Perhaps employers and miners met part way, for by 1801
the same writer seems to have considered six-hour shifts general.
Early in the nineteenth century, eight hours came to predominate,
although a six-hour shift was even then still worked in exceptionally
hot and difficult mines.[35]

It could be argued that the whole idea of 'normal' hours is inappropriate when applied to out-workers, for it was not so much in
the *length* of the factory day but in its regularity that there was a real
contrast with the weaver's cottage. When, for example, some weaving households were at an adverse point in their family cycles, they
might welcome the chance to work longer hours than the typical
factory shift. One complained in 1802: 'In the factory we can never
work the hours we can at home, nor make the best of our time. We
cannot work above 7½ hours in winter and about 12 in summer.'
With candlelight the day could be stretched from 5 a.m to 7 p.m. in
winter, and in summer daylight permitted working from 5 a.m. to 9
p.m. Asked how such hours could be kept up, the weaver replied:
'As long as God Almighty gives me strength. I have done it for
years. I hardly know anybody but what does; the greatest part of the

35. *Ibid.*, pp. 59–60; Pryce, *Mineralogia Cornubiensis, op. cit.*, p. 173.

inhabitants do.' A Huddersfield clothier concurred. He preferred outwork: 'In a factory you confine them to the hours the master pleases, in the cottage they work very often 15 or 16 hours.' Earlier in the century two broadcloth weavers in 1757 testified that fourteen, fifteen or sixteen hours was the input required to make good wages. Many framework knitters were said in 1778 to work from 5 a.m to 10 p.m. in summer, but this was considered a departure from the more usual start at 6 a.m and finishing at dusk in the winter.[36]

It would seem highly unlikely, except at the times when falling piece rates forced them to, that domestic workers averaged such hours through the week, although they must have worked them on some days, if only to make up for slacker work early in the week. At any particular moment not all weavers had the same choice. Some had large dependent families, while others had teenage children able to make a substantial contribution. During the decline of hand-loom weaving, more and more families were brought under the *necessity* of working longer hours. In cotton weaving rates in 1808 had fallen so low that weavers were reported to be working upwards of fifteen hours, even to twenty, but as an employer remarked it was an impossible situation to sustain and a man would not choose to work eighteen hours if he could live from the labour of twelve. Twelve hours as an average in normal times seems a fair measure. It was what the shearmen in the woollen manufacture, who did not work at home, regarded as usual. At times of high wages or low food prices, out-workers could *opt* for more leisure, but in times of slack trade they might well find themselves unable to get enough work to compensate for falling rates. Workers standing by were not always enjoying a leisure preference; they were sometimes enduring an enforced and hungry idleness.[37]

The hours worked in the early cotton mills varied. Mantoux, on the basis of the enquiry of 1816, instances fourteen, sixteen, or even eighteen hours with a dinner break of forty minutes for the largely female and juvenile labour force. Around Manchester fourteen hours or a shift system with sixteen hours on and eight off, relieving in thirds, was common. Samuel Oldknow was generally regarded as a humane employer, but even he expected his apprentices to work for thirteen hours.

36. *Committee on the Woollen Trade*, BPP 1802–3, VII, pp. 87, 379–80; *Commons Journals*, XXVII, 1757, p. 731, and XXXVI, 1778, p. 740.

37. *Report from Committee on the Petitions of Several Cotton Manufacturers and Journeymen*, BPP 1808 (177), II, pp. 5, 12; *Committee on Woollen Trade*, 1802, p. 115.

But it was not in the number of hours that the factory system brought a new dimension. The first recorded clocking-in system was introduced by Wedgwood at Etruria, backed by a stiff fine of 2s (10p) for any worker coming late. But even in Etruria, although different processes had to be synchronised, the rhythm of labour was still determined by hand work. With power-driven machinery a different pace is dictated by the unvaried and untiring momentum. Dickens likened the piston of the steam engine to 'the head of an elephant in a state of melancholy madness', but even by 1815 it was only a minority of the working population who had as yet been cast in the mould of his 1845 Coketowners who, 'all went in and out at the same hours, with the same sound upon the same pavements, to do the same work, and to whom every day was the same as yesterday and to-morrow'. But it was here, not only in the visual intrusion into a rural landscape, that William Wordsworth saw 'unnaturalness' in reacting to a water-powered spinning mill in 1814. An 'unnatural light' allowed 'never-resting labour' to work at night; labour which had been called to 'unceasing toil' by a bell 'of harsher import than the curfew-knoll / That spake the Norman Conqueror's stern behest'.[38]

Among those thus summoned it was not men who predominated but 'maidens, youths / Mothers and little children, boys and girls'. It has been noted of a pioneer like Arkwright that he had 'to train his workpeople to a precision and assiduity altogether unknown before, against which their listless and restless habits rose in continued rebellion'. Child labour recommended themselves to the early factory masters not only because it was cheap but also because it avoided dependence on adult labour whose traditional work habits were too deeply ingrained. The 'elite' of skilled male mule spinners which was retained seems to have continued to display an artisan-like attitude.

The greater suitability of children for the new tasks was lauded in terms of their 'quickness' and their 'nimble' fingers. The period from the building of the first cotton mills up to a restrictive parliamentary act of 1816 was the era of the factory apprentices – pauper children brought from workhouses all over the country to be indentured to misery. This era of child labour in the factories was the most manifestly exploitative. In the following era, 'free' child workers had been placed there by their families, and not un-

---

38. Mantoux, *Industrial Revolution in the Eighteenth Century, op. cit.*, p. 413; McKendrick, 'Wedgwood and factory discipline', *op. cit.*, p. 56; Charles Dickens, *Hard Times*, 1854; William Wordsworth, *The Excursion*, 1814.

commonly worked with them. In this era discipline could be enforced by fines or dismissal. Apprentices could be sanctioned by neither, and in the general sense it is hardly surprising that resort to corporal punishment was so common.[39]

While the polemics of factory reform tended to publicise the most harrowing cases, it is clear that pauper children uprooted from distant institutions, lodged in dormitories and fed parsimoniously were perhaps the least protected group in eighteenth-century society. Robert Blincoe, born in 1792, was sent at the age of seven with eighty other children from St Pancras workhouse to a Nottinghamshire cotton mill. His later published account describes bad food, hard work over a fourteen-hour day, beatings and injury from unguarded machinery. He once ran away and was flogged on recapture. Compared with the Derbyshire mill of Elias Needham to which he was moved in 1803, this was a good mill. Food was so scarce in Derbyshire that the apprentices had to raid dustbins. The shift was an unbroken sixteen hours and the children were clothed in rags. Easily hidden from the not-too-enquiring eyes of the local magistrates who were supposed to inspect the mill, frightening cruelties were inflicted by overseers whose sadism went unchecked. In Blincoe's view the factory owners were not only aware of this brutality but to a degree participated in it. Of course, such conditions did not disgrace every mill, nor were they wholly absent outside the factory system. Blincoe thought that in centres like Manchester inspection was more thorough; he also felt that by the 1830s cruelties were rare. Nevertheless, his *Memoir* stands as an indictment of the apprentice era. In a measured reconsideration of Blincoe's account, after a modern historian seeking to defend the early cotton masters sought to discredit it, Professor Musson concluded:

> There is no doubt whatever that many children were exploited and ill treated in the early textile mills, that they were used as cheap factory labour, that their hours of work were far too long, that accident, ill-health and deformities were common, and that cruel punishments were often inflicted. There is no doubt that, as the *Memoir* asserts, the owner of Litton Mill [Needham], 'although perhaps the worse of his tribe, did not stand alone'.[40]

Even in his defence of Needham, Dr Chapman admits that at one

---

39. Pollard, *Genesis of Modern Management*, pp. 216–17.
40. *A Memoir of Robert Blincoe*, Manchester, 1832. S.D. Chapman sought to assert its unreliability in *The Early Factory Masters*, David & Charles, 1967, pp. 199–209, but the *Memoir*'s value is convincingly reasserted by A.E. Musson, 'Robert Blincoe and the early factory system' in *Trade Union and Social History*, Cass, 1974, Ch. 9.

mill more than a third of the apprentices died, absconded or had to be returned and only *two* out of 780 apprentices recruited were later employed as adult workers. As for Needham, he 'borrowed' the idea of the 'cage', a basket in which 'serious' offenders were suspended from the ceiling, from the punishment code of the Lancastrian school system. As with his other borrowing, the 'log' – a four- to six-pound weight hung around the child's neck – he was trying 'to copy this progressive idea of the age'. Perhaps the practice of suspending children by their arms over machinery was a refinement of his own.[41]

How extensive was that other form of child labour which shocked Victorian England, that in the mines? The vivid illustrations in the Blue Books of the 1840s could as well have come from the mines of Shropshire in 1770. A contemporary account describes children 'with their hands and feet on the black, dusty ground and a chain about their body, creep and drag along like four footed beasts, heavy loads of the dirty mineral through ways almost impassable to the curious observer'. Boys as young as seven or eight were being employed underground around Newcastle by 1800. For several years their task was to open and close the trap doors which were essential for controlling the circulation of air, then at about the age of twelve they moved on to pushing the underground wagons. For the most part they worked underground with their fathers or other relatives, and, in contrast with the lot of the pauper apprentice, child labour underground for all its burdens and dangers was a first step on the way to the ranks of the hewers. Girls seem to have worked mainly at the surface picking out stones from the coal. Both women and girls appear to have worked underground in some of the Lancashire pits in the eighteenth century but had ceased to do so by 1815. It seems likely that child labour underground increased after 1815 as the greater use of wheeled wagons on rail tracks brought the drawing of coal within their physical capabilities. For this reason, as Ashton and Sykes pointed out, extensive use of child labour in a high ratio to adult male labour underground was a function of technical progress and most marked in the more advanced fields.[42]

Boys, usually related to one or more of the working group, seem to have played their part underground in Cornish mines

41. S.D. Chapman, *Early Factory Masters*, David & Charles, 1967, pp. 170–1, 203–4.
42. Cited in L. Moffit, *England on the Eve of the Industrial Revolution*, 1925, reprinted Cass 1963, pp. 256–7; T.S. Ashton and J. Sykes, *The Coal Industry of the Eighteenth Century*, reprinted Manchester UP, 1964, pp. 20–1.

throughout the eighteenth century, employed chiefly in wheeling barrows of ore. They were far fewer in overall number and in ratio to adult miners than on the northern coalfields, because in metal mining a much smaller volume of excavated material has to be moved. Boys usually went underground at around twelve years of age, having previously worked on sorting and preparing the raised ores at the surface. More were needed for this task than were ever recruited to work underground, and many Cornish youths who worked at the tin 'stamps' as 'buddle boys' never became adult miners. Samuel Drew, who began at the age of eight in 1773 for 1½d (0.6p) a day, was later apprenticed to a shoe maker, while Harry Carter, born in 1749, left the mines at the age of sixteen for the more exciting career of smuggling. Female labour was never used underground in Cornwall and it does not seem to have been much used at the surface either, until the growth of copper mining which rapidly overhauled tin in importance after about 1740. Copper ores needed a considerable labour force to break and sort the ores, and by the 1780s the ratio of female and juvenile labour to adult males had reached 2 : 5. In the lead mines of the northern Pennines the use of young boys underground seems to have decreased after 1750 when mining practice came to favour longer levels, putting the drawing of ores beyond the strength of children. As in Cornwall, however, children and women were employed sorting and dressing ores.[43]

Pauper apprenticeship, like child labour in general, was not a particular novelty of the factory system, although its use in coal mining seems to have developed only in the nineteenth century and to have been largely localised to the Black Country. Under the Poor Law many children found themselves bound to either masters or mistresses who exploited them and at times treated them with great cruelty, while our own age has learned with shame of the extent of ill-treatment even within the family. In free as well as in pauper apprenticeship corporal punishment was allowed within reason, and the treatment of the 'chimney boys' was as notorious as that of the factory children, for in both cases youngsters were being consigned to labour in conditions in which few parents would willingly have placed them. Of the chimney boys, Campbell wrote in 1747:

43. J.H. Drew, *Samuel Drew M.A.: The Self-Taught Cornishman*, 1861, pp. 18–19; J.B. Cornish, *The Autobiography of a Cornish Smuggler 1749–1809*, Truro, 1894, p. 3 reprinted Bradford Barton, Truro, 1971; C.J. Hunt, *The Lead Miners of the Northern Pennines in the Eighteenth and Nineteenth Centuries*, Manchester UP, 1970, pp. 44–5.

the younger they are the better fit to climb up the chimneys; I would not recommend my friend to breed his son to this trade, 'tho I know some masters who live comfortably. I think this branch is chiefly occupied by unhappy Parish children, and may for ought I know, be the greatest nursery for Tyburn of any trade in England.[44]

For living-in apprentices food and comfort could be in scant supply. One, apprenticed to a shoe maker, recalled not a cruel master but a mistress who turned him into a household drudge. William Hutton, apprenticed as a framework knitter, remembered great hunger, and in his case the mistress was his aunt.[45]

Any trawl through the columns of local papers of the time catches a number of cases of cruelty to apprentices which to our age, shocked by revelations of child abuse, suggests the tip of an iceberg. In a period of ten months in 1764–5 the *Exeter Mercury* reported the case of a man, wife, son and daughter-in-law jointly indicted for the murder of a girl apprentice by 'beating and barbarously using her'; the ill-treatment of a thirteen-year-old girl by a master and mistress who branded her on her buttocks, chained her for six hours to an apple tree and then beat her severely before making her work; and a third case, which shows up the vulnerability to sexual abuse of children bound out by the parish, in which a man was sentenced for castrating two eight-year-old boys. In the classified columns of the same newspapers advertisements for the return of runaway apprentices testify as much to harsh treatment as they do to the restlessness of youth, resentful at the constraining nature of apprenticeship.[46]

When, however, contemporaries celebrated the existence of child labour in the pre-factory economy, they hardly ever had the unfortunate pauper children in mind. Their model was the employment of children within the family economy of the domestic system. Indeed, it was one of the great merits of manufacturing to the early eighteenth-century observer Daniel Defoe that it brought increased employment and greater prosperity to a district compared with those which remained wholly dependent on agriculture.

In the manufacturing counties you see the wheel going almost at every door, the wool and the yarn hanging up at every window, the looms,

---

44. Campbell, *London Tradesman, op. cit.*, p. 21.
45. Drew, *Self-Taught Cornishman, op. cit.*, p. 33; William Hutton, *Life of William Hutton, F.A.S.S.*, 1817 edn, p. 95.
46. *Exeter Mercury*, 9 March 1764, 23 March 1764 and 4 Jan. 1765.

the winders, the combers, the carders, the dyers, the dressers, all busy; and the very children as well as the women constantly employed.[47]

It was because he saw them as offering more regular and more worthwhile employment for children than could be found in the agricultural districts, with only seasonal and low-paid needs, that Defoe praised the woollen areas. On Norfolk he remarked that there was not 'any hand unemployed, if they would work; and that the very children after four or five years of age, could everyone earn their own bread'. In the West Riding there was 'hardly anything above a few years old, but its hands are sufficient to itself'. He made similar comments on Taunton and in Essex. When the spreading cotton manufacture extended similar opportunities, Arthur Young wrote of Manchester: 'large families in this place are no incumbrance; all are set to work'. When the West Country clothiers' advocate William Temple wanted in 1739 to point to the advantages of the weavers, he stressed that it was their *family* earnings which lifted them above the condition of the farm worker.[48]

That child labour not only existed in the pre-factory economy but was strongly approved of does not of itself make blinkered sentimentalists of those who reacted so strongly to the 'dark, satanic mills'. Child labour was bound to take on a different quality when removed from the home and, in the case of the pauper factory apprentices, from the locality of upbringing. It has been claimed that the role of parental supervision continued into the early mills. In a limited sense and for a fortunate few who were related to the adult mule spinners with whom they worked, this may have been true. But even in the era of 'free' child labour it can have mollified the condition of only a minority. When it came to removing southern pauper children in large numbers to northern or Midland factories, it can hardly be denied that this, albeit short-lived, stage of the evolution of the factory labour force not only systematised but brutalised child labour.

Child labour in the cottage need not be romanticised. Samuel Bamford remembered winding cotton on to bobbins for his weaver uncle as 'work of cramping, confining and boring nature'. Exasperation often led him into acts of mischief for which he was quickly rapped by his rod-bearing aunt, but the atmosphere in which

47. Daniel Defoe, *A Plan of the English Commerce*, 1728, reprinted Oxford 1928, p. 67.

48. Daniel Defoe, *A Tour through the Whole Island of Great Britain*, Everyman, 1962, I, pp. 17, 62, 266, and II, p. 193; Young, *Tour through the North of England*, III, p. 194; Temple, *Case as it Now stands, op. cit.*, p. 16.

punishment was given and taken was a relaxed one, with his uncle able to laugh at some of his pranks. William Hutton was one of the few who worked in both factory and cottage as a child, for he was first employed in a silk mill in Derby before becoming apprenticed to his framework knitter uncle. He most certainly had few fond memories of the latter employment, but it was the former which caused him to curse his luck at having been born in Derby. From the age of eight he began at 5 a.m. despite being so small that special pattens had to be made to enable him to reach the machinery, and he bore the scars of the corporal punishment inflicted on him there for the rest of his life.

The employers of child workers in the factories were not particular about gender, but what of the employment of adult women in manufacturing and mining? We have already suggested that along with the use of child labour there was little uniformity either chronologically or geographically about the employment of women in coal mines. So far, however, as working underground is concerned, it seems safe to generalise that adult female labour was never widespread and was in decline in the later eighteenth century. The use of girls above ground increased after 1815, but the truth is that we really know very little of the actual numbers of women working in mines. As Dr John has pointed out, women in the smaller coalfields worked as part of a family concern, 'male members utilising the help of their female relatives wherever possible. Since the hiring and payment would be the responsibility of the male collier, women were not usually recorded in colliery accounts.' Their prime task was drawing but, as we have noted, the use of iron tracks about 1770 brought this chore within the capability of even cheaper child labour. On the great northern coalfield they did not work underground after 1780, although to some extent they continued to do so at some pits in Yorkshire, Lancashire and Cumberland. Dr John pointedly contrasts the coal mine with the factory, for in the former technical advances displaced women.[49]

The women who were employed as surface workers at Cornish copper mines were predominantly young and unmarried – that is, unless things had changed very drastically by the mid nineteenth century, for by the time of the 1851 census very few women seem to have continued after their early twenties. Washing lead ores in Derbyshire was undertaken by women throughout the eighteenth century. Defoe met a female lead washer in about 1720, but as the

---

49. A.V. John, *By the Sweat of their Brow: Woman Workers at Victorian Coal Mines*, Croom Helm, 1980, pp. 20–5.

century progressed they seem to have been steadily replaced by boys so that they disappear from the employment records by 1800.[50]

Few women worked in heavy industry. We might note the surprise of William Hutton in 1741 on coming across the women nailers of the Black Country at their small forges.

> In some of these shops I observed one or more females, stript of their upper garment, and not overcharged with the latter, wielding the hammer with all the grace of the sex . . . struck with this novelty, I enquired, 'whether the ladies of this locality shod horses?' but was answered, with a smile, 'they are nailers'.

Hutton was no tourist from the sheltered gentry. He had by this time been child factory worker, apprentice framework knitter and short-term seaman, so his reaction is significant. Nailing was an exception, but women and children were widely employed in the light metal wares of Birmingham. Their nimble dexterity even made them preferred in the manufacture of buttons and in lacquering and japanning, although it did not bring them the wages of skilled male artisans.[51]

In textile manufacture women were first and foremost the spinners. Before the advent of machine spinning it took around six spinners to supply a weaver with yarn, and the putting-out reach of clothiers seeking yarn extended well beyond the perimeter of weaving. Wool from the Devonshire serge makers was sent down to Cornwall for spinning; Norwich wove yarn spun in Cambridgeshire, Bedfordshire and Huntingdonshire. Accordingly in many households women spun, even though the household as a whole was not primarily engaged in textile production. The wives of farmers and farm labourers, of general labourers and of miners are all to be found among their ranks. As it was spinning which was the first textile process to be mechanised, it was women's work which was the first to be taken away by machinery, threatened by the water frame in 1769 and by Hargreaves' spinning jenny in 1770, even before Crompton's mule came into use in the 1780s. All these were pioneered in cotton, but the jenny soon spread to the older fibre. In the West Country woollen region it has been noted that from the 1780s the number of women per cloth fell by 1802 to only 18 per cent of its former level. Protest was immediate and desperate from

50. Defoe, *Tour, op. cit.*, II, p. 162; R. Burt, *British Lead Mining Industry*, p. 136.

51. W. Hutton, *History of Derby*, Nichols, Son and Bentley, 1817, p.158; Berg, *Age of Manufactures*, pp. 310–13.

the wives of farm workers and miners. Jennies were smashed across Lancashire in 1769 and so strongly resisted in the West Country that their penetration in Wiltshire and Gloucestershire was limited before the early 1790s. In Somerset magistrates had to cope in 1790 with 'a lawless Banditi of colliers and their wives, for the wives had lost their work to spinning engines . . . which they suppose, if generally adopted, will lessen the demand for manual labour. The women became clamorous . . . . ' Eden in his survey of the nation's poor described how badly hit the agricultural parishes were in the 1790s. In the textile districts the position was less clear. The first jennies were hand worked and small enough to be operated in the cottages; as Maxine Berg has put it: 'It was part of the domestic system, the machine of the poor.' These jennies were either collected in small workshops or placed out in cottages and seem to have brought increased earnings to many women in the cloth-working families, albeit for a short period until the machines got larger and, more importantly, the largely male-worked spinning mule began to replace the jenny. So far as the throwing of silk into yarn was concerned, whether in water-powered mills or by hand, this was carried out by women and children.[52]

Hand-loom weaving has always been considered a male artisan activity, with the concession that wives from time to time might assist their husbands at the cottage loom. The true picture is more complicated. In both the West Riding and the West Country women seem to have worked more often as weavers than has been assumed, especially towards the end of the century. At times, such as during the long wars with France from 1793 to 1815, they seem to have done so especially to fill the labour gap created by absent men. At times of employment crisis, male weavers organised to exclude them, and in strongly incorporated centres like Exeter they seem to have gained hardly any entry. In cotton country women weavers made coarser cloths, quality pieces remaining a male preserve. Accordingly, when power-looms worked by women began to appear early in the nineteenth century it 'set women against women, especially young women working in the shops or mills against older married women working at home'. In silk weaving the ratio of women

---

52. The best discussion of this issue is Berg, 'Women's work, mechanisation, and the early phases of industrialisation in England' in Joyce, *Historical Meanings of Work*, pp. 64–98; Berg, *Age of Manufactures*, p. 143; Berg, 'Workers and machinery in eighteenth-century England' in Rule (ed.), *British Trade Unionism*, pp. 67–8.

to men weavers was probably significantly higher than in wool or cotton.[53]

None of this has taken account of the overall part played by women in the cloth-making households headed by male weavers or knitters. This work is hidden, as is that of children, for it was not separately waged. Yet, as the historians of 'proto-industrialisation' have stressed, it is the *family* production unit which is the key to understanding the economics of rural manufacturing. There are a few clues which enable us to put a 'value' on some of this labour. For example, if the seaming of stocking was not done at home by the wife, in 1811 a deduction of around 1s (5p) was made from earnings of 13s (65p). Even in craft trades the cost of substituting for a wife could be high: one hatter in 1824 reckoned that if his wife had not picked the coarse hairs out of his material he would have lost from 6s to 9s 4d (30p to 47p) from wages of £2 to £3.[54]

Few of the apprentice-entered trades were specifically female. Campbell's survey of London trades in 1747 describes two: milliners and mantua makers (makers of petticoats, nightgowns, etc.). In both cases the wages of journeywomen were so low that he associates them with prostitution: 'Take a survey of all the common women of the town, who take their walks between Charing Cross and Fleet Ditch, and I am persuaded more than half of them have been bred milliners.' He mentions a third trade – child's coat making – but provides no information other than that women could make 'a good living from it'. More prophetic of the place women were to fill in the sewing trades was his description of those who sewed stays and bodices. The stay-maker proper who cut and shaped the whalebone and canvas was a man, who needed other qualities as well as skill: 'He ought to be a very polite tradesman, as he approaches the ladies so nearly.' He also had to keep secrets, for he knew the real shape of things: 'I am surprised the ladies have not found out a way to employ women stay-makers rather than trust our sex with what should be kept as inviolably as Free-Masonry.' Instead it was the work of stitching which was put out to poorly paid women. Similar work was undertaken by women in shoe-making.[55]

Campbell does not mention women being employed in glove making but they certainly were in the main provincial centres of Oxfordshire, Somerset and Worcestershire, especially from the late

53. Berg, 'Women's work', *op. cit.*, pp. 81–2.
54. *Third Report from the SC on Artisans and Machinery*, 1824, p. 97; Wells, *Hosiery and Knitwear Industry, op. cit.*, p. 68.
55. Campbell, *London Tradesman, op. cit.*, pp. 206–9, 225–5.

eighteenth century when this manufacture along with lace making and straw plaiting expanded rapidly on the basis of cheap female hand labour. Indeed, as Maxine Berg has well explained, a feature of those same closing decades which saw the first cotton mills was the spread of such manufactures.[56] Calico printing provides an interesting example. For most of the eighteenth century the trade had been dominated by an elite group of well-organised journeymen. Their ability to demand high wages was by 1790 causing some employers to dislodge their hold by introducing machinery: 'we are determined to destroy all sorts of Masheens for printing in the Kingdom', runs one of the milder sentences in an anonymous letter from the journeymen received by one employer. However, other manufacturers, including the largest, Sir Robert Peel, found an alternative to both men and machinery by relocating their firms where cheap female labour was available to hand paint the cloth or else to print with wooden blocks studded with thousands of pins instead of the engraved blocks cut by the journeymen. The increasing division of labour in potting pioneered by Wedgwood also used female labour for patterning and decorating. As Dr Berg has noted, even the best paid of such women performing tasks of great delicacy with dexterity were not considered 'skilled' in the full sense, for 'skill' was a male property.[57]

The extent to which women were employed in craft trades is unknowable. Dr Snell has recently suggested that on the evidence of apprenticeship indentures women and girls were bound to a range of occupations in the early and middle years of the eighteenth century from which they were later progressively excluded as capitalistic developments took more work from the home and as population growth accelerated to flood the labour market. In all he found fifty-one trades which received girls as apprentices, many of which paid premiums comparable to those for boys, suggesting that they were to learn the craft. However, it would be dangerous indeed to assume that all these entrants were intended to acquire a full competence in the trade.[58] Work on Essex shows that the skill and training content of female apprenticeships was generally modest, and that they tended to have a different meaning. Historians may have drawn gender lines too sharply, but the view that apprentice-

56. Berg, *Age of Manufactures*, pp. 118, 122–5.

57. *Ibid.*, pp. 148, 152, 256–7; on skill as a 'male property', see Rule, 'The property of skill in the period of manufacture' in Joyce (ed.), *Historical Meanings of Work*, pp. 107–8.

58. K.D.M. Snell, *Annals of the Labouring Poor*, Ch. 6.

ship as serious industrial training towards mastery of a craft was overwhelmingly a path for males is essentially correct. Many widows, however, did carry on their husbands' trade, even in occupations usually considered male. Such women may have been rather running businesses than producing goods in so far as they relied on journeymen. Widows of shipwrights in the royal dockyards had the right to enter apprentices, but could not themselves enter. However, to manage an artisan workshop at very least implies a possession of the knowledge side of a craft if not of the actual making.[59]

Adult males accounted for only 17.7 per cent of employees in cotton mills in Lancashire in 1816 and 18.4 per cent in Nottinghamshire. Even allowing for a slight predominance of boys over girls among children, this still suggests that around two-thirds of the first generation of mill workers were female. This pattern carried on one which already characterised the silk mills that had been set up following the success of the Derby mill. Arthur Young noted of one in Sheffield in 1771 that its employees were chiefly women and children, with the former earning 5–6s (25–30p) a week, five times the earnings of the latter.[60]

WORK AND HEALTH

Crabbe's scorn for pastoral muses who ignored the reality of work on the land – 'alternate suns and showers engage; / And hoard up aches and anguish for their age' – is withering.[61] One can share it and yet recognise that there is justification for contemporary views that work in mines and manufacture had a yet greater effect on health and longevity. To Adam Smith each trade had its 'peculiar infirmity', and the economist was familiar with the widely selling translation of the classic work by Bernard Ramazzini, *De Morbis Artificum Diatriba*, which added to the diagnostic list the question: 'what occupation does he follow? . . . This should be particularly kept in mind when the patient to be treated belongs to the common people.' Manufacturing, declared one pamphleteer, was the equal

59. Berg, 'Women's work', *op. cit.*, p. 75.

60. Chapman, *Cotton Industry in the Industrial Revolution*, p. 70; N.J. Smelser, *Social Change in the Industrial Revolution: An Application of Theory to the Lancashire Cotton Industry 1770–1840*, Routledge, 1959, pp. 185, 188; Young, *Tour to the North of England*, I, p. 123.

61. G. Crabbe, 'The Village' (1783) in A.J. Carlyle and R.M. Carlyle (eds) *Poetical Works*, Oxford UP, 1914, pp. 34–41.

of war in producing 'a mournful procession of the blind and lame, and of enfeebled, decrepit, asthmatic, consumptive wretches, crawling half alive upon the surface of the earth'. That was written in 1782, twenty-three years before Charles Hall indicted the 'new' manufacturing towns for producing 'rickety, squalid, dwarfed, distorted objects'.[62]

The occupational pathology of the eighteenth century is strikingly revealed in a litany which gives us grinder's asthma, grinder's rot, mason's disease, miner's phthisis, stone worker's lung and potter's rot, among others, for dust-caused lung diseases, as well as occupational bursitis in such varying forms as bricklayer's elbow, weaver's bottom, housemaid's knee, hod carrier's shoulder and tailor's ankle. The madness of the hatter was paranoia, one of the several symptoms of poisoning from the mercury used in the trade. Of course, environment, diet and indulgence contributed to the ill-health of many workers, and hours of labour were a major aggravation. Sedentary occupations over the modern working day are a different matter from the twelve or more hours in ill-ventilated workshops which made tailors and shoe makers proverbially consumptive. So, too, was the age at which work began. Charles Turner Thackrah, England's first real specialist in the field, was convinced that shortening hours was the most urgent of improvements.[63]

Work could produce ill-health or early death from a number of circumstances. It could be the result of using or working on certain materials, e.g. lead; of labour in a harmful environment, e.g. damp, ill ventilated, fume or dust filled; of harmful working postures; or of the repetitive use of particular muscles or organs. On top of all these was the risk of accidental injury or death. Ramazzini described the symptoms of poisoning from the lead which was regularly used by house painters, plumbers, glaziers and potters as well as by the extremely short-lived wretches actually employed in lead works: 'First their hands become palsied, then they become paralytic, spenetic, lethargic, cachectic and toothless, so that one rarely sees a potter whose face is not cadaverous and the colour of lead.'[64] Other

---

62. A fuller treatment of the industrial pathology of the eighteenth century is given in Ch. 3 of my *Experience of Labour*. Smith, *Wealth of Nations*, I, p. 91; Bernard Ramazzini, *De Moribus Artificum Diatriba*, 1713, trans. Chicago 1940, p. 3; *Gentleman's Magazine*, LII, 1700, p. 526; Charles Hall, *The Effects of Civilization on the People in European States*, 1805, reprinted New York 1965, p. 21.

63. Charles Turner Thackrah, *The Effects of the Principal Arts, Trades and Professions and of Civic States and Habits of Living on Health and Longevity with a Particular Reference to the Trades and Manufactures of Leeds*, 1831, pp. 118–19.

64. Ramazzini, *De Moribus Artificum, op. cit.*, p. 53.

metals and chemicals had their effects: mercury gave hatters the 'shakes' as well as paranoia; arsenic fumes shortened the lives of workers in copper refining; dyes poisoned calico printers; and soot imparted a particular cancer to chimney boys.[65]

The white faces of miners reflected years of working in poor air and extreme temperatures, while their lungs, like those of Sheffield's grinders, were wrecked by dust. Dust took a toll also among coal heavers, masons, quarrymen, bricklayers and even bakers and hairdressers. Intense heat and charcoal fumes from their stoves ensured that few wool combers reached the age of fifty. Cramped working positions were a fact of life for miners in the narrow seams, but other trades too complained of cramps and 'craft palsies' including saddlers, sawyers and nail makers. Eyestrain from working at close stitching in artificial light was endemic in the 'needle' trades. Long hours of standing over benches by the lock makers got part of the Black Country known as 'Humpshire'. Long hours of sedentary work were linked to the consumption which made the poor tailor the 'wretched emblem of death'. Physical injury was frequent, not only in notoriously dangerous places like mines, where gas explosions added to the threat of rock falls, gun powder mishaps and shaft falls, but in grinding where the huge wheels sometimes shattered into flying slivers.[66]

Health risks were matters of acceptance for the most part by employers and workers alike. Wedgwood insisted on hygiene practices to limit the danger from lead used in pot glazing, and some Sheffield masters chained a protective guard over their wheels, but these were exceptional.[67] Nor was there any real notion of wage compensation. There was no need. Workers did not choose these employments. Miners became miners because they lived in Cornwall; grinders became grinders because they lived in Sheffield. The comfortable classes could take it for granted that such conditions were the lot of the working classes: sad but normal. Such extraordinary conditions as prevailed, for example, in the lead works at Whitechapel amounted to a virtual death sentence. Only the truly needy or desperate would undertake them. Those at the bottom of the pile could expect little better; workers in the 'dishonourable' trades were stigmatised by degeneracy and evident inferiority. They had no real chance of attention, let alone remedy or compensation.

65. Rule, *Experience of Labour*, p. 79.
66. *Ibid.*, pp. 82–3.
67. McKendrick, 'Wedgwood and factory discipline', *op. cit.*, pp. 30–5; Young, *Tour through the North of England*, I, pp. 123–4.

In this environment it is perhaps surprising that the early factories should have received such hostile criticism. However, they concentrated labour, largely that of women and children, in a more visibly exploitative mode. It would not be easy to see how a case could be made that factory employment was an especially health-destroying occupation for adult males. Conditions in cottage industry were hardly rosy; work space competed with living space in dark and damp habitations. Nevertheless, there was immediate access to fresher air and open skies, while the less intense and stressful rhythms of manual production gave some opportunity for recreation. There *were* significant differences, for the factory system not only took child labour outside of the home, it placed it in an inferior overall environment. Long, regimented hours, more formal discipline and danger from unguarded machinery all imply differences in form and intensity which were not hidden from medical men who were familiar with the early factories. The Manchester doctor Thomas Percival reported on a 'confinement' which 'either cut them off early in life' or rendered them sick and feeble. A report on Manchester mills in 1784 condemned their low ceilings and floors overcrowded with machinery as well as noting the effects of cotton dust and friction-heated oil. At night great numbers of candles added their heat and smoke. John Aiken, who wrote in 1797, was also a doctor and he described apprentices brought in batches from distant workhouses to toil in 'injurious' air by day and night. Temperatures were extreme and epidemics rife. The evidence produced by the major enquiries which took place between 1816 and the 1840s has been variously treated by historians, but what little evidence there is for the earlier mills seems uniformly bleak.[68]

Although conceding that manufactures were in many respects deserving of the 'high encomiums' bestowed upon them, a pamphleteer of 1782 went on to remark:

> Scarcely are we fed, lodged, clothed, warmed, without sending multitudes to their grave. The collier, the clothier, the painter, the gilder, the miner, the maker of glass, the workers in iron, tin, lead, copper, while they administer to our necessities, or please our tastes and fancies, are impairing their health and shortening their days.[69]

At a time when we are exhorted to esteem the 'entrepreneurs', we should not overlook those who bore the burden as well as those who took the 'risks'.

68. Moffit, *England on the Eve of the Industrial Revolution, op. cit.*, pp. 256–9; J. Aiken, *A Description of the Country from Thirty to Forty Miles around Manchester*, 1795, reprinted New York 1968, pp. 219–20.

69. *Gentleman's Magazine*, 1782, *loc. cit.*

CHAPTER SEVEN

Roadways and Waterways

> Having walked all day at a great pace . . . we descried towards
> evening, to our inexpressible joy, the waggon about a quarter of a mile
> before us . . ..

With only a slight quickening of their pace, Roderick Random, the
eponymous hero of Smollett's 1739 novel, and his companion
caught up with the carrier wagon and for a shilling were taken to
the next inn on their journey from Newcastle to London. Only the
better-off could afford to travel at more than a walking pace in
eighteenth-century England – unless, that is, they had access to a
riding horse. True, the number of stage coaches increased significantly as the century progressed and became even more numerous
and faster in the early years of the nineteenth century, but their
number hardly kept pace with a rising population. For the vast majority rapid travel was unavailable before the railway age. Even
money could not buy a quick passage through some of the conditions met with on the unimproved roads of the early eighteenth
century. Around 1720 Daniel Defoe witnessed a splendid triumph
of determined old age over adversity near Lewes.

> I saw an ancient lady, and a lady of very good quality, I assure you,
> drawn to church in her coach with six oxen; nor was it done in frolic
> or humour, but mere necessity, the way being so stiff and deep [with
> mud], that no horses could go in it.[1]

The invention of the wheel may be one of the landmarks of the
forward march of humankind, but there were still parts of eighteenth-century England where it was of scant practical value. Passengers had perforce to ride, and goods were carried on the backs
of packhorses or mules. Trains of animals, each carrying 5 or 6

---

1. Daniel Defoe, *A Tour through the Whole Island of Great Britain*, Everyman edition,
1962, I, p. 129.

hundredweight, crossed the wilder stretches of the country or plodded along the narrow paved causeways that were to be found on both sides of the Pennines and as far south as Derbyshire. Sheffield, for example, had a weekly link of this kind with London. The expanding copper and tin mines of west Cornwall depended on mule trains until the second quarter of the nineteenth century. An advertisement from 1813 reads:

> To be let by tender . . . all the copper ore raised from Crinnis Mine, near St Austell . . .. The number of mules necessary to carry the said ores is supposed to be from 25 to 30.[2]

Until the 1790s the ore was carried in single sacks of 3 hundredweight, but so many carriers were injured in lifting these across the backs of the mules that the load was then divided between two sacks. Except for the hilliest areas and the West Country more generally, pack animals had dwindled by 1800 with road improvements bringing even relatively remote places into the expanding network of timetabled stage-wagon services.

Roderick Random need not have elected to travel from Newcastle to London by road. In fact he had been advised to take cheap and expeditious transit on one of the small four-crewed colliers that sailed from Tyne to Thames, which journey, depending on wind and tide, took less time. But so far as the economy was concerned, lack of reach was a much bigger problem than lack of speed. Only in the most favourable circumstances could towns away from the coast or navigable rivers grow to much of a size, a condition emphasised by Adam Smith.

> by means of water carriage a more extensive market is opened to every sort of industry than what land carriage alone can afford it, so it is upon the sea coast and along the banks of navigable rivers that industry of every kind naturally begins to subdivide and improve itself.[3]

A twenty-strong animal pack-train could carry only around 3 tons and even a wagon, hauled at walking pace by six or eight horses, was restricted to 3 tons up to 1765 and 6 thereafter. Wagons could carry most things, but their slowness was hardly offset by cheapness. The cost in horses and men was heavy, and the feeding of the former a significant outlay, especially when corn prices were high: 'Robert Russell, proprietor of the daily fly wagons which set out

---

2. E. Pawson, *Early Industrial Revolution*, pp. 136–7; *West Briton*, 12 March 1813.
3. Smith, *Wealth of Nations*, I, p. 3.

from London . . . to Falmouth, feels much pleasure in being able, owing to the blessings derived from the late harvest, to reduce the advances he lately made on carriage.'[4]

Even a cursory glance at the operating economy of the early eighteenth century suggests that the supply and efficiency of transport services were the most widespread and basic limitations on its growth, for it is on that sector that both the supply of raw materials and the size of the market depend. Professor Mathias has stressed that rising output and improving productivity will lower the average costs of a commodity 'only if the goods can be cleared to a widening market . . . Improvements in both water carriage and roads were an important pre-condition for the evolution of the home market in its manifold aspects.'[5] Final commodity prices will fall to an even greater extent than the actual saving in carrying costs if improved transport also breaks down local monopolies. Overseas markets too are affected, for only if they can reach ports at reasonable cost and efficiency can goods be readily exported. Adam Smith's view of the great significance of transport developments in increasing the wealth of the nation has been much quoted.

> Good roads, canals and navigable rivers, by diminishing the expense of carriage, put the remote parts of the country more nearly upon a level with those in the neighbourhood of the town. They are upon that account the greatest of all improvements.[6]

Writing this in 1776, he was pleased enough with what was happening; had he been able to look back from 1815 he would have seen his optimism largely vindicated. In the judgement of two recent historians of British transport, the increased supply and quality of road and waterway transport over the eighteenth century are 'perhaps the most important part of the build-up of the general facilities of the economy – what economists call its infrastructure – and are therefore to be regarded as a preparation for general economic advance'.[7] It is to the details of transport developments before 1815 that we must now turn.

4. H.J. Dyos and D.H. Aldcroft, *British Transport*, pp. 77–8; Pawson, *Early Industrial Revolution*, p. 141; *West Briton*, 4 Feb. 1814.
5. P. Mathias, *First Industrial Nation*, p. 97.
6. Smith, *Wealth of Nations*, I, p. 165.
7. Dyos and Aldcroft, *British Transport*, p. 52.

ROADS

Defoe, who travelled more of the roads of the country than most of his contemporaries, was inclined to see himself in the foothills of a better transport age – the equal of the fabled Roman achievement. The instrument of resurrection was to be the turnpike.

> this custom prevailing, 'tis more than probable, that our posterity may see the roads all over England restored in their time to such a perfection, that travelling and carriage of goods will be much more easy both to man and horse than ever it was since the Romans lost this island.

He wrote as someone perceiving a breakthrough.

> turnpikes or toll-bars have been set up on the several great roads of England, beginning at London, and proceeding thro' almost all those dirty deep roads, in the midland counties especially; at which turnpikes all carriages, droves of cattle, and travellers on horseback are obliged to pay an easy toll . . . in no place is it thought a burthen . . . the benefit of a good road abundantly making amends.

The economic advantage gained would be significant.

> as for trade, it will be encouraged by it every way; for carriage of all kind of heavy goods will be much easier, the waggoners will either perform in less time, or draw heavier loads, or the same load with fewer horses; the pack-horses will carry heavier burthens, or travel further in a day . . . all which will tend to lessen the rate of carriage, and so bring goods cheaper to market.[8]

From the Middle Ages the responsibility for road repair had rested on the parish and the provision of statutory labour. From the end of the seventeenth century, turnpike trusts set up under private acts of parliament began to appear. After fifty years there were 143 of them, responsible for the upkeep of 3,400 miles of roadway from the tolls parliament allowed them to levy. Individually the trusts were small, usually maintaining only about 20 miles of road, but as they were formed and linked, the basis for a coherent road network was being established. During this first period (up to 1750) of relatively slow and uneven growth, trusts were set up at a rate of only eight a year and were concentrated largely around London, radiating especially to the north and west and into the Midlands. Away from the capital, however, turnpikes had crossed the Pennines, and indeed linked in an almost continuous line along the Great North

8. Defoe, *Tour*, II, pp. 113–32.

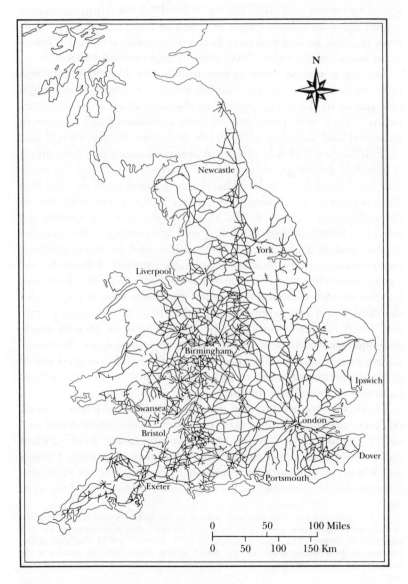

Figure 7.1 The turnpike road system in 1770

Road to the border. Their second phase from 1750 to 1772, when the annual rate of formation exceeded forty a year, was one of rapid spread over most parts of the country, at the end of which more than 500 trusts repaired more than 1,500 miles of the roads of England and Wales. The success of turnpiked stretches had inspired extension and cross linking. After 1772 the 'turnpike mania' settled down in a long steady progress to an eventual 22,000-mile peak in 1836, accelerated only in the widespread speculative investment booms of the early 1790s, 1809–12 and the mid 1820s.[9]

Averaging around thirty miles a trust in the mid eighteenth century, the turnpike trusts were an outstanding example of the major role played by the parliamentary enablement of local economic initiatives. They were promoted by local landowners and farmers or industrial and commercial interests and even by the clergy, and their active promoters in groups of around a dozen ran their affairs at monthly meetings, employed the paid surveyors and labourers and contracted for repairs. The few in existence up to 1706 had their administrative authority vested, as in the continuing case of the public parish roads, in the justices of the peace at quarter sessions, but from that date, beginning with acts relating to two stretches of the road to Holyhead, in Bedfordshire and in Worcestershire, independent trustees took over the administration of the tolls and the responsibility for road maintenance. After 1720 the form had become so well established that new turnpikes were set up under the clauses of a general public act, rather than by individual private acts. Their original term was to be twenty-one years, though extension was usual, and few restrictions were imposed on the trusts' powers of raising capital on the security of the tolls, on their use of it, or on the appointment of toll gatherers, nor on the freedom to contract out the tolls at auction.[10]

There was opportunity for maladministration in terms of both efficiency and peculation. Forty years after Defoe's enthusiastic welcome, another great traveller, Arthur Young, made some strident criticisms of several toll roads. The 'infernal road' joining Preston and Wigan, he knew not 'in the whole of language, terms sufficiently expressive to describe', as he negociated its four-foot-deep ruts.

9. For summaries of the rate and pattern of turnpike formation, see Pawson, *Early Industrial Revolution*, pp. 141–2; Dyos and Aldcroft, *British Transport*, p. 69; and especially W. Albert, 'The turnpike trusts' in D.H. Aldcroft and M. Freeman (eds), *Transport in the Industrial Revolution*, pp. 36–44. Two essential full-scale studies of the turnpikes are Albert, *Turnpike Road System in England*, and Pawson, *Transport and Economy*.

10. Albert, 'Turnpike trusts', *op. cit.*, pp. 33, 45.

The 'execrable' turnpike from Altrincham was even worse.[11] His powers of description were yet again exceeded by that from Dunholm to Knutsbridge, but of all 'the cursed roads that ever disgraced this kingdom' the nadir was the turnpike from Billericay to Tilbury.

> It is for nearly 12 miles so narrow, that a mouse cannot pass by any carriage . . .. The ruts are of an incredible depth. The trees everywhere over-grow the road, so that it is totally impervious to the sun, except at a few places. And to add to all the infamous circumstances which concur to plague a traveller, I must not forget the eternally meeting with chalk-waggons; themselves frequently stuck fast, till a collection of them are in the same situation, and twenty or thirty horses may be tacked to each, to draw them out one by one.[12]

He did travel some good roads. The turnpike from Salisbury towards Romsey was the best and earned high praise for the trustees, whose management he judged responsible, for he had met with other roads whose materials were as fine but 'never with any that were so firmly united, and kept so totally free from loose stones, ruts and water'. It was broad enough for three carriages. After this he ranked the great road north to Barnet, then that to Kent and those to Chelmsford and Uxbridge.[13]

Turnpikes were not always better kept than parish roads. A traveller in 1798 found the latter in Middlesex to be 'hard and clean in every sort of weather; so much so, that gentlemen may ride along them, even directly after rain, and scarcely receive a splash'. On the other hand, despite an annual county aggregate of £30,000 in tolls, the turnpikes were 'generally very bad'. Instead of scraping them, a heavy expenditure was incurred on pumps, carts and hired labour to keep down dust levels by watering: 'the mud indeed is so very deep all the winter and so fluid after rain, as to render it unsafe to meet horses, owing to their feet throwing the mud not only over an horseman's clothes but also into his eyes'.[14]

The 'uncommon' road from Salisbury to Romsey had the advantage of running through flint-laden chalk. It was on the heavy clays around London and in the Midlands that the most serious problems occurred as the burden of traffic increased. The turnpike out

11. A. Young, *A Six Months Tour through the North of England*, 1771, IV, pp. 580–85.
12. Young, *A Six Weeks Tour through the Southern Counties of England and Wales*, Strahan, 1768, p. 27.
13. *Ibid.*, pp. 248–9.
14. J. Middleton, *View of the Agriculture of Middlesex*, G. Nicol, London, 1798, pp. 393–7.

through Tyburn to Uxbridge bore more broad-wheeled wagons than any other, and in the winter of 1797–8 was reduced to a single six-foot-wide muddy track. In such conditions, with clays deep and clinging enough to bog down a regiment of horses, the real issue was not one of scraping versus watering but of radical improvement in methods of building and repair.[15] The significance of the turn-pike system was that, eventually, in the hands of concerned trustees, it could provide the financial means of employing the talents of a generation of road builders who pioneered techniques which re-mained the basis of road making into the twentieth century. 'Blind Jack' Metcalfe (1717–1810) emphasised the importance of a firm foundation under a smooth convex surface, running off the water into side ditches below road level. His road-contracting business em-ployed up to 400 men. John McAdam (1756–1836) concerned him-self less with the bed of the road and more with drainage. He stressed consistency and proper and regular supervision. His basic method became a generic term in the English language, and his special contribution was to develop an economical way of bringing and keeping existing roads up to scratch. Thomas Telford (1757–1834) was renowned as a bridge-builder, but he produced roads of great solidity through the intermeshing of small, angular stones. Only the wealthier trusts could afford his standards, but if they did so they purchased a road good for more than a century.[16]

In assessing the advantages of the turnpikes, a balance has to be struck between contrasting contemporary opinions, and account taken of real possibility and unlikely occurrence. Arthur Young's noisy criticisms have been more noted than his frequent, but quieter, content. The latter reaction was clearly predominant in the writings of the men who toured the country writing reports for the Board of Agriculture in the last decade of the eighteenth century. Perhaps, as Dyos and Aldcroft have suggested, Englishmen's expec-tations were rising, for foreign vistors were usually impressed.[17] Adam Smith did not deny that there were bad examples within the 'system of repairing the highroads by tolls', but in 1776 thought this was because the system was not then of long standing. Experience and the 'wisdom of parliament' could be expected soon to prevent the appointment of those 'mean and improper persons' who were too frequently appointed trustees and to develop a proper system of checking accounts and controlling toll levels. While he did not dis-

15. *Ibid., loc. cit.*
16. Dyos and Aldcroft, *British Transport*, pp. 83–4.
17. *Ibid.* p. 74.

pute that in many cases money had been levied that was twice what was necessary for satisfactory repair, and even then that the work carried out had been slovenly or even not done at all, the great *laissez-faire* economist had been convinced by the turnpikes that so far as public works 'for facilitating commerce in general' were concerned, 'the greater part may easily be so managed as to afford a particular revenue sufficient for defraying their own expense, without bringing any burden upon the general revenue of society'. This was only fit and proper.

> When high roads, bridges, canals etc, are in this manner made and supported by the commerce which is carried on by means of them, they can be made only where that commerce requires them, and consequently where it is proper to make them. Their expense too, their grandeur and magnificence, must be suited to what that commerce can afford to pay. They must be made consequently as it is proper to make them.[18]

The historian with the gift of hindsight might wish to counter-assert the greater benefits brought by well-planned public infrastructural investment. That was not an alternative in eighteenth-century England. The contribution of the turnpikes must be measured not against the prescriptions of later ages but against the possibilities of their own. Enabled by the willingness of parliament to facilitate local economic improvement, the turnpike trusts succeeded in injecting resources into the improvement of a road network which might otherwise have remained much worse.

The contribution of the turnpikes as a transport service

The turnpikes can be reasonably considered the leading edge of road improvement, although at no time did ordinary roads not outnumber them by five to one. In assessing their contribution it should be borne in mind that many parish roads were improved while many turnpikes were neglected. Above all the turnpike era saw a marked expansion in the volume, speed and reliability of wheeled traffic. By 1800 wagon services were numerous enough in most parts of the country to be timetabled. Long-distance wagons journeyed in stages. Canvas covered and drawn by up to eight horses, most of them moved along at walking pace, but some lighter vans or 'fly wagons' with more regular change of horses were faster. Historians have tended to overlook the possibilities of more rapid

18. Smith, *Wealth of Nations*, II, pp. 245–6.

transit where the cargo concerned was profitable enough to merit it. Even fresh sea fish, the most perishable of commodities, could be rushed to markets, although only the prime varieties, turbot and sole, justified the cost. By the 1780s Bath and Bristol as well as London were the receivers, via Exeter, of the 500 vanloads a year which were sent from Brixham in Devon. At times when the winds obliged, Torbay smacks sailed their catches to Portsmouth for a shorter van-haul to the capital. Even more inventive was the route by which early-season mackerel reached London, for the price dropped rapidly once the shoals began their seasonal movement up the English Channel. They were caught off Scilly by the Mounts Bay luggers, effective fish catchers but not rigged for speed. Accordingly the fast-sailing Brixham smacks arrived to purchase the fish and race them to Portsmouth.[19]

The journey of a normal wagon from London to Manchester took around four days carrying an astonishing range of commodities and the odd passenger. The freight rate was around a shilling (5p) per ton-mile. National carriers like Pickfords, with their own warehouses and regular clientele, soon emerged and contributed to an aggregate load which was prodigious, though unmeasurable. By 1700 stage wagons were a common sight in southern England and were usual through the Midlands by 1750. Leicester, for example, had weekly services to London, Leeds, and Manchester, Birmingham, Bristol and beyond by 1770. Over the next twenty years its hosiery products and other goods were utilising around twenty wagon services to Bristol, Birmingham, Northampton, Stamford and Cambridge as well as more than 200 serving surrounding districts. Even in the north the turnpike enabled the wheeled wagon to push the pack-train to the fringes. Chester by 1780 had only one packhorse service, to North Wales, while it had wagon and coach services to a large number of English towns. Towns all over the north of England and into Scotland were served by wagon from Newcastle, sometimes weekly or even two or three times a week.[20]

Parliament regulated the weight wagons might carry, the width of their wheels and the number of horses. The General Highway Act

19. J.G. Rule, 'The home market and the sea fisheries of Devon and Cornwall in the nineteenth century' in W.E. Minchinton (ed.), *Population and Marketing: Two Studies in the History of the South-West*, Exeter UP, 1976, pp. 131–3.

20. Dyos and Aldcroft, *British Transport*, pp. 77–8; J.A. Chartres and G.L. Turnbull, 'Road transport' in Aldcroft and Freeman, *Transport in the Industrial Revolution*, pp. 80–3; Pawson, *Early Industrial Revolution*, p. 137.

of 1767, for example, restricted wagons with six-inch wheels to a six-horse team but allowed those with nine-inch wheels to add a further horse. The act was a considerable relaxation of earlier limitations and indeed, the progressive relaxation over the period seems to be as much a testimony to the improved load-bearing of the roads as an accommodation of the expanding volume of goods traffic. One estimate, derived from directory listings of carrier services to and from London, is that there was a ten-fold increase in their number between 1715 and 1840 and, given increases in capacity and speed, a thirty-four-fold increase in terms of ton-miles. However, there is a great risk in counting from directories because a route might allow the listing of several destinations as though they were separate journeys, and the increase, although undoubtedly substantial, may have been much smaller than it appears.[21]

Goods traffic is more fundamental to a developing economy than is that in passengers or mail, but these are also important. The improvement in the speed and comfort of coach travel over the eighteenth and early nineteenth centuries was very striking, although overshadowed by the even more dramatic later impact of the railways. By 1705 London already had 180 departing coach services; by 1836 it was to have 342. In the provinces, because the starting point was much lower, the rate of increase was even faster. Early in the century the state of the roads meant that many coach services had to be suspended in winter, but by 1770 improved conditions allowed exact year-round timetabling of faster, safer journeys. The journey from London to Bath took forty hours in 1720 but only half as long in 1770. By 1815 it could be done in fifteen hours. The equivalent figures for the trip to Manchester were eighty, forty-five and less than thirty hours. The single daily coach from London to Birmingham in 1740 had become thirty by 1783. Leicester in the 1760s had a daily crossing of coaches on runs from Manchester or Leeds to London; by 1815 more than thirty left the town each day for London and other major population centres in the Midlands and north.[22] By the time of Waterloo, for those few who could afford the coaches, passenger travel was perhaps four times as fast as it had been in 1750 between major centres and twice as fast elsewhere. Inside fares by 1800 were from 4d to 6d (1.5p to 2.5p) a

21. The estimates made by Chartres and Turnbull, 'Road transport', *op. cit.*, have been challenged in D. Gerhold, 'The growth of the London carrying trade 1681–1838', *Econ. H.R.*, XLI, 3, 1988, pp. 392–404.

22. Dyos and Aldcroft, *British Transport*, pp. 78–9; Chartres and Turnbull, 'Road transport', *op. cit.*, pp. 64–73.

mile. Even those prepared to sacrifice comfort for hair-raising economy still had to find 2d or 3d (1p or 1.25p) a mile.

> Persons to whom it is not convenient to pay a full price, instead of the inside, sit on the top of the coach, without any seats or even a rail. By what means passengers thus fasten themselves securely on the roof of these vehicles, I know not; but you constantly see numbers seated there, apparently at their ease, and in perfect safety.[23]

This traveller's account from 1783 considered that outside, 'the company is generally low', but with fares equal to a fortnight's wages for even a skilled craftsman, that must be considered a relative judgement on status. The increased seating capacity which would be provided by even an extra fifty coaches leaving a town over ten to twenty years, at a time of rapid urban population increase, points to how tiny a fraction of the population ever travelled by stage coach.

Of wider significance was the effect on postal communication. The system of posting-horses introduced by Ralph Allan in 1720 held on until his death in 1762, but by then passenger stage coaches were travelling faster on most major roads. The mail coaches which were introduced in 1783 went at around 8 miles an hour, 2 miles faster than the riding horses. Economic intelligence is a vital ingredient in a progressing economy and its rapid spread was aided not only by the post, but also by the increasing reach of the provincial press, with its purveying of market information and its advertising of investment opportunities. Twenty-eight weekly newspapers based in English towns in 1758 seems a sparse enough provision, but their circulation could be extensive. Pawson has shown that the *Newcastle Journal* in 1739 was distributed to agents as far south-west as Preston, south-east as Ripon, north as Eyemouth and west as Whitehaven.[24] At the other end of the country, by the 1770s the *Sherborne Mercury* was read from Salisbury to Penzance.

> my father was chiefly employed in what was called 'riding Sherborne'. There was at that time, scarcely a bookseller in Cornwall; and the only newspaper known among the common people, was the *Sherborne Mercury*. . . . The papers were not sent by post, but by private messengers, who were termed *Sherborne men*. . . . Between Plymouth and Penzance were two stages on the main road, each about forty miles. . . . My father's stage was from St Austell to Plymouth. He

23. C. Moritz, *Travels in England in 1782*, cited in J. Sambrook, *English Life in the Eighteenth Century*, Macmillan, 1940, pp. 12–13.
24. Pawson, *Early Industrial Revolution*, pp. 154–5.

always set off on his journey early on Monday morning, and returned on Wednesday.[25]

Such links were part of a transformation which Eric Pawson has summed up: 'many townspeople who at the start of the century had never, or rarely, seen a wheeled vehicle, were setting their time pieces by the arrival of the daily coach at its end'.[26]

SEA CARRIAGE

The growth in value and volume of overseas trade will be discussed in the next chapter, but it is appropriate to consider here the provision of shipping and of port facilities. Increases in the volume of shipping are usually accommodated for some time by existing docks and harbours before the pressure on them leads to a heavy capital investment in fresh and usually lengthy building. Improvements in the slower-growing economy before 1780 were not insignificant. Harbour commissions, like so many other improving economic institutions of the time enabled by act of parliament, undertook a steady upgrading and extension. The first purposely constructed wet-dock was completed at Rotherhithe in 1700 and was followed at Liverpool (1709) and Bristol (1717). Improvements had already been made at Bridlington and Whitby, important as refuges as well as fishing stations, by the time the coal ports of Sunderland, Whitehaven and Maryport were improved. On the south coast Newhaven and Littlehampton in the 1730s and Shoreham in the 1760s provided new harbours, while Ramsgate, designated as a port of refuge in 1749, consumed £600,000 between then and 1816, during which period almost 40,000 vessels took shelter there.[27]

As Gordon Jackson has pointed out, it was only after the great growth period in foreign trade began from 1783 that the real improvement in receiving and handling facilities gave birth to the modern port.[28] Harbour improvements continued alongside the thriving coastal trade, but the biggest investment necessarily came in those few ports which dominated overseas trade. Ships in this

25. J.H. Drew, *Samuel Drew: The Self-Taught Cornishman*, Ward and Co., 1861, pp. 36–7.
26. Pawson, *Early Industrial Revolution*, p. 156.
27. *Ibid.*, p. 151.
28. G. Jackson, 'The ports' in Aldcroft and Freeman, *Transport in the Industrial Revolution*, p. 177.

sector were larger, needed deeper water and took longer to turn around. Further, because raw material imports rose through the eighteenth century while those of manufactured goods fell, there was an even more marked increase in volume than in value. With almost as much of an increase in the volume of exports and an even greater one in that of re-exports, ports engaged in foreign trade were, as a group, handling four times as much cargo in 1800 as they had been in 1700, and perhaps two and a half times as much as in 1750.

The impact fell heavily on a small number of ports. Of seventy-four listed ports in 1772, 59 had less than 500 registered tons active in foreign trade, while the seven who exceeded 10,000 tons accounted for 81.7 per cent of the total. Nor did this distribution change much as the level of trade accelerated. In 1785 nine ports exceeded 10,000 tons and now accounted for 86.5 per cent. Thus it was at London, Bristol, Liverpool, Hull and Glasgow in the last years of the eighteenth and beginning of the nineteenth century that a 'lagged response' to the great increase in trade was concentrated. The most fundamental need was to increase the area of water by the provision and enlargement of wet-docks and basins, the total acreage of which doubled over the last quarter of the eighteenth century as a prelude to a much greater expansion between 1800 and 1830.[29]

There was no dramatic increase in the total volume of shipping using British ports over the first half of the eighteenth century, but there was a relative shift away from London to provincial ports. Bristol, linked via the Severn valley to an exceptionally productive hinterland, was second in 1700, but with an inconvenient 7-mile approach up the Avon and with congestion making for a slow turnaround, limits to its expansion were already becoming visible. Its problems began to be solved only with the digging of a new 2-mile course in 1802. The rising northern port of Liverpool was much more dynamic. Its commerce was increasing perhaps four times as fast as the rest of the country between 1716 and 1800. A new tidal basin was opened in 1743, a second wet-dock (Salthouse) in 1753, and three more between 1771 and 1796. The largest, the Prince's Dock, was begun in 1811 and on its completion in 1821 the total dock acreage had reached 37 (though this is put into perspective by a seven-fold increase over the next sixty years). Liverpool was in

29. *Ibid.*, p. 188.

'everyway exceptional in the eighteenth century', but Hull too was enlarging with 10 acres of wet-dock built in 1775–8.[30]

As for London, a three-fold increase in tonnage cleared did not lead very quickly to a solution to the severe congestion of the Pool, on which was concentrated a cargo handling facility employing 120,000 men. Things were made to stir in 1793 when the Committee of West Indies Merchants precipitated what has been described as the 'first dock boom' by threatening a remove. Eventual development was to follow the vision of William Vaughan which roamed beyond the Pool to embrace Wapping, the Isle of Dogs and Rotherhithe. A parliamentary select committee managed to delay things somewhat, but the new era was inaugurated with the West India Dock Act of 1799. That dock was completed in 1806, by which time so were the London Docks.[31]

What permitted the concentration of foreign trade in a few ports was the complementing of overseas trade by coastal trade. Bristol no more needed a direct link with Hamburg than Hull needed one with Ireland, while London could, as Jackson has put it, 'perform for Britain the entrepot functions which Britain was later to perform for Europe'. The large increase in coastal shipping after 1760 was built on a transport facility which had already proved itself over a long period among the most valuable of the country's natural assets. Inevitably London, the greatest centre of mass and conspicuous consumption, dominated with its tremendous appetite. Between 1670 and 1750 the capital's intake of seaborne coal from the northeast averaged an annual half a million tons. Although the number of vessels engaged in the trade shrank somewhat, the sailing colliers which had been around 100 tons in the seventeenth century were averaging 312 by 1730. After fuel came food and drink. Corn imports were already exceeding 1.5 million quarters by 1700, while Faversham sent 353 ships in 1728 loaded with the hops and malting barley to be brewed with Newcastle coal. Wines and spirits were usually received trans-shipped from Southampton or Bristol. Outwards from London went colonial imports like tea and sugar, as well as an astonishing range of manufactured goods.[32]

Without ever approaching that with the metropolis in magnitude, coastal trade between provincial ports probably increased at a faster rate. The greatest traffic flow was along the east coast. Just

30. *Ibid.*, pp. 193, 200–8; Dyos and Aldcroft, *British Transport*, pp. 57–9.
31. *Ibid.*, pp. 59–62.
32. G. Jackson, 'The ports', *op. cit.*, p. 180; J. Armstrong and P.S. Bagwell, 'Coastal shipping' in Aldcroft and Freeman, *Transport in the Industrial Revolution*, pp. 142–3.

over half of the 97,000 tons of English coastal shipping in 1709 belonged to the ports of Scarborough, Whitby, Newcastle, Yarmouth and King's Lynn – fishing, coal and corn. The more hazardous nature of voyages along the west coast, especially from south to west, was a deterring factor. Seventy per cent of coal shipped from Newcastle was London-bound, but half of the residue went to the two East Anglian ports of Yarmouth and King's Lynn, from which corn formed the return cargo. Tonnage engaged in English and Welsh coastal shipping increased from 101,475 tons in 1760 to 160,931 tons in 1780, an increase of 58.6 per cent in just twenty years.[33] The continued domination of the east coast ports is shown in Table 7.1.

Table 7.1 Ten leading provincial ports in English coastal trade in terms of tonnage of coastal shipping

| | 1760 | | 1780 | |
	Rank	*% of total*	*Rank*	*% of total*
Newcastle	1	26	1	44
Sunderland	2	21	2	22
Scarborough	3	12	3	8
Whitby	4	11	6	5
Great Yarmouth	5	7	8	4
Hull	6	5	4	6
Maldon	–	–	5	5
King's Lynn	7	5	7	4
Poole	8	4	–	–
Lymington	9	4	–	–
Harwich	10	4	–	–
Cardigan	–	–	9	4
Beaumaris	–	–	10	3

Source: Armstrong and Bagwell in D.H. Aldcraft and M. Freeman (eds), *Transport in the Industrial Revolution*, Manchester UP, 1983, pp. 150–1.

Of southern and western ports, Weymouth was ranked tenth in 1765 and ninth in 1770 but was not ranked in 1775; St Ives was eighth in 1765, fourth in 1770 and tenth in 1775; Gloucester was ninth in 1765. Western ports did play a part in shipping corn to London, in some years at least, the capital's swallow reaching as far as Exeter and beyond to Cornwall. Bristol, too, took in a whole

33. *Ibid.*, pp. 143–4.

range of seaborne food supplies. Some of the more interesting links along the west coast were those involving manufacturing inter-relationships. An advertisement for a china-clay pit in 1817 stressed that it was only 3 miles from the purpose-built clay port of Charlestown. Those 3 miles were the only ones the clay would have to travel by road on its journey via Liverpool and the Trent and Mersey canal to Wedgwood's canalside Etruria. (The flints the potteries needed came from the south, along the east coast via Hull.)[34]

Coal for the pumping engines on the Cornish mines came from Swansea, and the copper ore went back to be smelted in South Wales. Such a convenient exchange of heavy cargoes was ideal for the coastal trade, but in general spare capacity on return sailings explains some very cheap transit costs. From London to Newcastle the rate was only 3s (15p) a ton. Among industries whose early growth depended upon the coastal trade were iron, tin, copper and lead processing, the leather trades, brick making and building, especially for timber and for specialist materials like Portland stone (via Weymouth). Coal, however, between 1779 and 1784 absorbed around 40 per cent of total carrying capacity, the 1.5 million tons carried on coasting vessels in 1779 having trebled by 1814. Grain continued to be next in importance and exhibited a very different pattern in linking very many small despatching ports to a handful of receiving ones like Liverpool, Bristol, Hull, Newcastle and, of course, London. Livestock was also carried, but especially from Ireland, so that it could be considered a true food import rather than a coastal one. Bulk cargoes were not the whole story. Files from Warrington, for example, were sent to Glasgow for only a sixth of the cost by road. Passengers were also carried, though only those who were not over-particular about their time of arrival.[35] Greater regularity was, however, in sight by the last years of the century, with a glimpse into a future of more rapid transport. In 1815 the inhabitants of the west Cornwall port of Hayle crowded to see the arrival there of a 'vessel worked by steam'. Constructed 'on a large scale', she was *en route* from her birthplace in Scotland to London, and had steamed the 120 miles from Milford Haven against a head wind at an incredible 10 knots. Early experiments had begun in 1788, and by 1812 nine steamboats carried passengers on the Clyde, followed by links between London and Gravesend and between

34. *West Briton*, 9 May 1817.
35. Armstrong and Bagwell, 'Coastal shipping', *op. cit.*, p. 155.

Newcastle and Shields. Only six years after Waterloo there were already 20,028 tons of steam shipping around the coasts.[36]

NAVIGABLE RIVERS

The reach of the sea up estuaries and along the great rivers was much extended over the late seventeenth and early eighteenth centuries. The Humber – into which flowed the Trent, Calder, Aire, Don and Yorkshire Ouse – the Severn, the Cambridgeshire Ouse and the Thames were all major highways for much of their lengths. The Severn had the longest uninterrupted stretch, and its 20- to 80-ton open barges carried down coal from Shropshire and salt from Droitwich, as well as agricultural produce, and brought up iron from the Forest of Dean for the Midlands metal makers, and a whole range of goods and groceries from Bristol. Oxford could be reached by boats of similar size, but further up the Thames cargoes were taken over by 'lightening' boats. Most river barges had sails but also relied on the muscle power of horses, or even of the 'halers', working gangs of men. Acts to enable river navigations to be improved, necessary because the building of locks, new cuts or dredging often affected the interests of local landowners, farmers and especially millers, went back as far as the sixteenth century but were consolidated in a veritable spate of river improvement after the Restoration. By 1721, with a noted concentration in 1719–21, acts had been secured for, among others, the Stour, Wye, Medway, Great Ouse, Colne, Tone, Aire and Calder, Trent, Bristol Avon, Dee, Derwent, Douglas, Idle, Kennet, Weaver, Mersey and Irwell. By this time, according to Dyos and Aldcroft, most of the potential for river improvement had been exhausted and the time had come for the deliberate making of waterways, a step which, though it was a natural development from a learning process on the rivers, was yet one of great import.[37]

CANALS

On a sound towpath a horse could pull up to 50 tons. That is equal to the carrying capacity of as many as sixteen wagons up to 1741

---

36. *West Briton*, 9 June 1815; Pawson, *Early Industrial Revolution*, p. 151.
37. Dyos and Aldcroft, *British Transport*, pp. 37–45, 85.

when the statutory load restriction was 3 tons, and as eight wagons when the limit was increased to 6 tons in 1765. On the basis of 2.5 cwt per animal, it would have needed 400 horses or mules. Such ratios serve to show the very great importance an extension of the waterway network had for the movement of heavy and bulky materials. By the time of the spread of the railways in the second quarter of the nineteenth century, the industrial map of Britain was in its main outlines already drawn – a sequence unique in the history of industrialisation and the clearest of testimonies to the role of canals.

The canal age effectively began in south-west Lancashire where it developed naturally from improvements to the river navigations serving Liverpool and Manchester. The River Weaver had been improved in 1733, but the improvement of the Sankey Brook Navigation from the coalfield around St Helens in 1754–7 was especially significant in that it involved several new cuts. The historic moment, however, came in 1761 with the Duke of Bridgewater's famous canal from his mines at Worsley to Manchester. The 'Canal Duke's' vision and determination and his employment of the self-taught engineering genius James Brindley combined to produce a true 'deadwater' link over a completely new route. Involving aqueducts and tunnels, it was a demonstration of engineering potential of transforming importance. It pointed to a future in which the hitherto limiting relationship of water transport to the economy could be inverted: now waterways could be *brought* to favourable sites: 'The controlled application of water to industrial and commercial purposes was indeed the basic and most potent technology in Britain's early economic advancement.'

The new canal was symbolic in a further sense: it was built to carry coal. It was above all in the transport of this vital material that the canals came to play a crucial enabling role in the development of industrial Britain. Before the Duke's canal was completed in 1765, coal had sold in Manchester at double its pit-head price; thereafter it was halved to threepence farthing a hundredweight.[38]

Over the next generation the first phase of the opening up of inland industrial Britain proceeded. Of fifty-two acts for inland waterway improvement passed by 1774, thirty-three were in the Midlands and north and a further five in the Scottish lowlands. Most of the residue of fourteen for the rest of Britain were concerned with river improvement. As Professor Duckham has pointed out, the

38. *Ibid.*, pp. 85–91.

combined mileage was not great until after 1790 (up to then it was well under a thousand miles) but in terms of strategic linking they were already beginning to turn the 'golden key . . . to unlock the riches of the inland coalfields'.[39] Great promotional activity until the financial slowdown of 1772 secured in an astonishingly short time a linking of the major English river systems: the Severn, Thames, Great Ouse, Trent, Humber and Mersey. The links were often circuitous, narrow and made more difficult by differing levels. It was, however, becoming possible to foresee local initiatives developing into a network which, although unlike the railways was never to become a truly national system of transport, would link the main industrial regions back to their sources of supply and, to a lesser extent, forward to their outlets. If the inland waterways came even close to being a nation-serving system, this was more a matter of outcome rather than of preconception. Canal building responded to regional economic needs, above all for the carriage of coal. If eventually it became possible to access most of the major manufacturing and mining regions, that was a secondary, although welcome development, not a primary intent.

To offer a perhaps extreme example, the Gloucestershire clothiers who celebrated the completing in 1779–82 of the Stroudwater Canal had been trying since 1730 to intercept the coal supplies moving down the Severn from the pits of the Midlands. Their venture had been from start to finish 'planned by the woollen interests, financed from the profits of that trade and built predominantly for the needs of the woollen industry.' It was a local canal planned by local men with local capital for local reasons.[40] An extreme example perhaps because it was on the periphery of the network, but in general few canals were cut with other than local economic benefits in mind. Accordingly, the full network took almost a century to emerge. Mantoux's verdict – 'in less than thirty years the whole face of England was furrowed with navigable waterways. In this there was a concerted movement' – is misleading, and is in fact contradicted by the map (Figure 7.2).[41]

Canals were not built in pursuit of a grand national design, although Brindley clearly saw the possibilities for expansion and a

39. B.F. Duckham, 'Canals and river navigations', in Aldcroft and Freeman, *Transport in the Industrial Revolution*, pp. 101–3, 105–6, 128.

40. M. Hanford, 'Coal, clothiers and the navigation to Stroud 1730–1780' in H.E.S. Fisher and W.E. Minchinton (eds), *Transport and Shipping in the West Country*, Exeter UP, 1973, p. 5.

41. P. Mantoux, *The Industrial Revolution in the Eighteenth Century*, Methuen, 1961, p. 126.

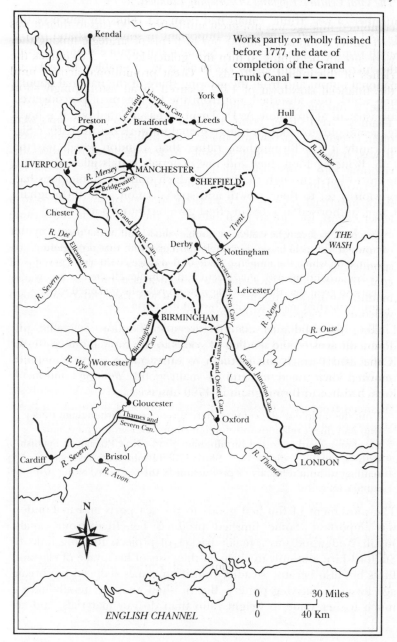

Figure 7.2 Navigable waterways in the centre and north of England at the end of the eighteenth century

number of key 'trunk' canals had been cut. Thus for much of the period after 1760, canals were important in some areas and over a small number of major routes. National importance stemmed from the increasing contribution these areas were enabled to make to national output and from the growing share of the national population which they absorbed, not from the fulfilment of preconceived infrastructural provision. As Dr Turnbull has pointed out, it is hardly meaningful to talk of a trans-regional network before 1810.[42] Significantly it was Birmingham rather than London which was the hub. Bringing food, fuel and raw materials canals allowed inland towns to burst through the bounds which transport limitations had previously set to their growth and specialisation. The Birmingham Canal, authorised in 1768, in effect gave birth to a port.

> The port, as it may be called, or double canal head in the town crowded with coal barges is a noble spectacle, with that prodigious animation which the immense trade of this place could alone give. I looked around me with amazement at the change effected in twenty years; so great that this place may now probably be reckoned with justice, the first manufacturing town in the world.[43]

Linking the Midlands manufacturers to London by canal undoubtedly assisted the sending of goods to the capital, but conversely the canals which linked them to other major ports sometimes removed their need to send as many goods *through* London. A French visitor to Birmingham in 1790 observed:

> Until the middle of the century there was not one Birmingham trader who had direct relations with foreign countries: London merchants warehoused and exported Birmingham goods. Now Russian or Spanish firms order . . . direct . . .. Since 1768 Birmingham has been sending without difficulty its production to the sea ports, owing to canal traffic.[44]

The movement of finished goods to the sea ports and to London was important. Some finished products benefited from canals. Josiah Wedgwood was a major backer of projects forming links to Staffordshire, not only to cheapen the costs of his intake of clay and flints but also because steadier transit on canals reduced the breakage losses in carrying pottery. But finished goods generally have a much higher value to weight ratio than do raw materials, and ac-

---

42. G. Turnbull, 'Canals, coal and regional growth', p. 541.
43. Cited *ibid.*, p. 544.
44. Dyos and Aldcroft, *British Transport*, p. 114.

cordingly it was on the transit costs of the latter that canals had their most marked effect.

Wedgwood would have been interested even without the special needs of his product. The Grand Trunk Canal promoted by him and his merchant associate Thomas Bently was set afoot in 1766 after the Duke of Bridgewater had already moved the line of his Runcorn cut to meet up at its northern end and complete the joining of the Trent and Mersey. His famous Etruria works were built on the canal and the carriage costs of coal and raw materials from Liverpool, including the vital china clay shipped to the Mersey port from Cornwall, fell to a rate of 13s 4d (67p) per ton compared with the old road carriage rate of £2 10s (£2.50). As well as engineering this link, James Brindley also built the Staffordshire and Worcestershire (or Wolverhampton) Canal connecting at the other end with the Severn. Other prominent industrialists were involved in canal promotion, though as a group they seem to have provided only a small part of the necessary finance. The Darbys and Reynolds, ironmasters of Coalbrookdale, were active in getting the Shropshire Canal built (1788–92), and Richard Arkwright subscribed to the Cromford Canal (1789) which served his pioneering spinning mills in Nottinghamshire. The industrial bias of canal building can be readily perceived by looking at Figure 7.3. From the beginning down to the railway age, the concentration in the industrial Midlands, the north-west and the West Riding was emphatic.[45]

In the north the greatest achievement was the crossing of the Pennines.[46] This process began in the 1770s when the Leeds and Liverpool Canal, eventually to be the most important link, commenced its 127-mile journey via Wigan and Burnley and on through Skipton to Shipley, linking there in 1774 to the Bradford Canal. It then rested when finances ran out before resuming in 1790 and reaching its intended link with the Aire and Calder and Don navigations in 1816 and thence to the Humber estuary. Less extended in its construction was the Rochdale Canal, completed between 1794 and 1804; it had needed only two short tunnels. The Huddersfield Canal, planned in 1774, did not reach Ashton-under-Lyne for another thirty years, through a 5,456 yard tunnel and seventy-four locks, sixty-four of which were in flights.

Outside these regions, canals were fewer and cross linking much

45. Duckham, 'Canals and river navigations', *op. cit.*, pp. 120–1; Dyos and Aldcroft, *British Transport*, pp. 94–6.

46. The crossing of the Pennines is well described in Dyos and Aldcroft, *British Transport*, pp. 97–9.

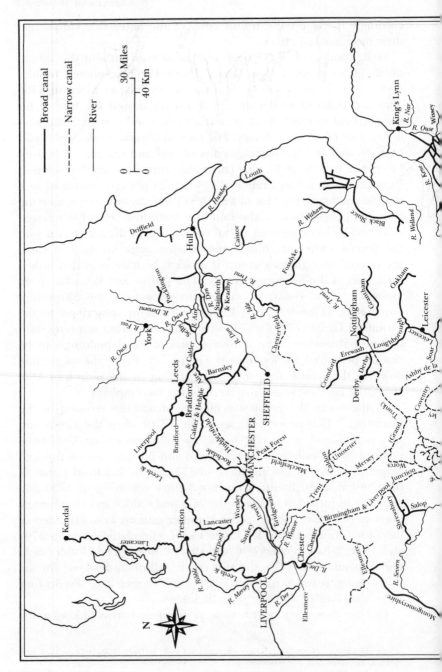

Figure 7.3 The principal waterways of England and Wales *c.* 1830

less developed. Some were not without importance. The Thames and Severn, begun in 1783, was six years later passing thirty-ton barges into the Thames at Inglesham, but even so the river itself remained largely unimproved and in the 1790s manufactured goods from Birmingham for London were still being carried overland from the end of the Oxford Canal. That problem was remedied in 1805 when the completion of the Grand Junction Canal, 93 miles long, even avoided use of the narrow and circuitous Oxford Canal and took an astonishing 131 miles off the journey. It is noticeable that from this time wagon services between London and the Midlands did not expand as did those to other parts of the country. The link from London across to the Severn estuary reached its best-known stage with the completion of the Kennet and Avon Canal between 1794 and 1810 – the only major canal across the south. It paid well enough, especially the small link from the Somerset coalfield, but as Dyos and Aldcroft point out, at their busiest the inland waterways of southern England carried only 15 per cent of total traffic and never rewarded those who invested in them in the way those of the industrial Midlands and north did.[47]

The great inland coal reserves of England awaited full exploitation, first as fuel and then as energy. Tapping them was the achievement of the canals. That this began to happen only after 1760 and to be anywhere near completion only after 1790 has perhaps rather less to do with the availability of investment funds, or the level of engineering knowledge, than with the overall pace of industrialisation, urbanisation and demographic increase. Only coal could have fuelled the growth of towns and allowed them to concentrate labour to such a degree, and in addition the canals brought building materials and food supplies. As such their contribution was crucial to the related locational changes in economic activity and in population which became so important from the third quarter of the eighteenth century.[48]

It was claimed in 1803 that no less than 90 out of 165 canal acts obtained since 1758 had been concerned primarily with coal carriage, while a further 47 had been linked to iron or non-ferrous metal works or mines. By 1815 the canals may have been carrying in excess of 10 million tons of coal, not only more cheaply – on average coal prices (and those of other bulky materials) fell by between 50 and 70 per cent in larger urban centres with the opening of a canal – but also over an extended reach. Reading, by the early nine-

47. *Ibid.*, p. 101.
48. Turnbull, 'Canals, coal and regional growth', p. 545.

teenth century, was receiving coal from the Midlands via the Oxford Canal and from the Forest of Dean via the Kennet and Avon, but the main beneficiaries were the inland coalfields themselves and the areas adjacent to them.[49]

Canals may have performed a general price-lowering function in, to use Professor Mathias's phrase, 'cracking open' local monopolies, but it should not be forgotten that they were in themselves monopolies, even though canal companies hardly ever operated carrier services and confined themselves to earning from tolls. The Duke of Bridgewater was exceptional in keeping to his promise of enabling coal to be brought cheaply to Manchester, and on his death in 1803, rates doubled. The large dividends paid by the more successful companies incorporated a substantial element of monopoly profit. Furthermore, costs in handling cargoes, the transfer complications brought about by different lock widths and the supplementary road haulage costs, however short the distances, mean that the simple ton-mile difference between quoted road and canal rates represents a gross rather than a net saving. The latter was, however, sufficient to transform the economic potential of England's industrialising regions.[50]

It was not for this reason alone, fundamental though it is, that Phyllis Deane has written of canals that they were 'of the essence of the industrial revolution'. Their role in capital formation will be discussed below, but their role in the advancement of practical civil engineering needs to be noted. Pawson has pointed out that in building the canals, British engineers had for the first time 'to grapple with large scale civil engineering problems'. This was the main contribution of their construction phase, for they were not much involved, as the railways later were, with mechanical engineering, nor did their building consume large quantities of iron. James Brindley, by common consent of contemporaries and historians, was a practical genius, but it seems he was unable to spell 'navigation'. Others, however, were better able to 'school' a profession. Thomas Telford was as great a canal builder as he was road maker, and in 1818 became the first president of the Institution of Civil Engineers. William Jessop, John Rennie and Thomas Green all made contributions, while John Smeaton, better remembered as a builder of lighthouses, was almost certainly the leading civil engineer of the canal era. The pioneering work of these men provided a bedrock of

49. Dyos and Aldcroft, *British Transport*, p. 111.
50. Mathias, *First Industrial Nation*, p. 97; Dyos and Aldcroft, *British Transport*, pp. 114–15.

knowledge and experience without which the later railway system could not have been constructed with such astonishing speed.[51]

Of the men who actually dug the canals we know less. But these 'navigators' did, of course, bequeath their expertise to those who built the railways. From the later period of canal cutting to the early one of railway building there was clearly a link in the inheriting of a core of toughened labourers and foremen who, even if posterity has chosen to present them as the antithesis of skilled, at very least knew what they were doing when it came to tunnels, cuts and embankments. As an operating system the canals never became a large-scale employer like the railway companies, whose 'servants' as well as engineers and trackmen on the 'permanent way' included the new 'uniformed working class'. That is hardly surprising. Canals did not create new towns; those built up by the railway companies, such as Swindon, Crewe or Eastleigh, being concerned with the building of locomotives and rolling stock, had no parallel. Neither did the very many railwaymen who were concerned with passengers, nor, since the canal companies did not usually operate as carriers, did they employ anything like the same number of men in handling freight. Indeed, a common complaint in their early days was that they caused unemployment. One writer in 1766 even went so far as to propose that canals be required to end short of their planned destinations.

> If a manufacturer can have a certain conveniency of sending his goods by water carriage within four miles of his own home, surely that is sufficient, and profit enough, considering that other people must thrive as well as himself; and a proportion of profit to each trade should be the biasing and leading policy of this nation.[52]

In this way, he reasoned, the ruin of the numbers supported by horse carriage would be avoided.

It is usually argued that fixed capital increasing projects, even if they cause local and short-term unemployment, actually increase total employment through permitting significant increases in output. It is a smug axiom whose general applicability is doubtful, but, it is almost certainly true in the case of the canals. The expanding volume of traffic not only brought into being the colourful and idiosyncratic travelling labour force of the canal boatmen but also

---

51. P. Deane, *First Industrial Revolution*, p. 78; Pawson, *Early Industrial Revolution*, pp. 150–1; Dyos and Aldcroft, *British Transport*, pp. 108–9.

52. W. Cunningham, *The Growth of English Industry and Commerce in Modern Times: The Mercantile System*, Cambridge, 1925 edn, p. 534 (note).

increased the need for short-haul overland carriage, more expensive in cost per mile than long-haul and needing just as much muscle in loading and unloading. Indirectly the permitted industrial expansion must have created extra employment; this effect on the inland coalfields alone was, though impossible to compute, very considerable. After all, among the activities that most benefited from the canals were many in which labour-displacing technologies had hardly developed. This was true of coal mining, of hardware manufacture and of pottery in all of which increased output still depended on increasing the labour force.

TRANSPORT AND INVESTMENT

After 1760, with the acceleration in turnpike trust formation and the advent of the canal age, investment in transport came to account for a substantial fraction of total capital investment in Britain. From then until 1820 it represented above a fifth of gross domestic capital formation (GDCF). Although with the building of the railways its share reached a third (35 per cent in 1841–60), the 1760–1820 contribution was equal to that in manufacturing and trade in 1761–90, and not so far behind it, or agriculture, in 1791–1820.

Table 7.2 Sectoral shares in GDCF, per cent

	1761–90	*1791–1820*	*1841–60*
Agriculture	33	25	12
Industry and trade	22	26	33
Transport	23	20	35
Residential and social	22	29	20

Source: Based on Feinstein in M.M. Postan and P. Mathias (eds), *Cambridge Economic History of Europe.* Vol. 7, *The Industrial Economies. Part I: Britain, France, Germany and Scandinavia,* Cambridge, 1982, pp. 40–1.

In terms of annual capital spending on transport, there was a surge in the late eighteenth century. Investment in canals and inland waterways peaked at around £1 million per annum in the canal mania of the 1790s, while outlay on the steady expansion and improvement of turnpiked roads averaged half a million pounds between 1760 and 1810 and thereafter doubled to £1 million. By 1820 investment in shipping, docks and harbours was also around the million mark, and there were similar trends in bridge building. To these must be added the continuing high level of expenditure on parish roads, while the construction of new roads during enclosures must be acknowledged even though it cannot be calculated. Total expenditure on transport services around 1750 probably exceeded £1.25 million a year; by 1800 it was probably over £3 million, and by 1815 may have been approaching £5 million.[53]

The one-fifth of GDCF provided by investment in transport almost certainly understates its importance. Transport is usually considered as the key component of the provision of social overhead capital. That is, it is infrastructural and confers a public benefit, from which enterprises in general will gain. Accordingly investment in this sector probably led more than it followed investment in agriculture or manufacturing.

The initial capital for canals and turnpikes came from local sources. While it is true that without the transport sector's contribution, the overall rate of investment in the economy would not have exceeded 10 per cent of national income by 1815, concentration on such macro-economic data tends to obscure the fact that the financing of improvements in transport was above all an example of regional capital formation.

> virtually all the early canals and probably a majority of the later ones, were overwhelmingly local in both promotion and finance . . ..
> Promotion committees were normally closely integrated groups of local interests and worthies, who sought stable financial commitment from men of known substance and probity.[54]

Even in the case of ventures of the scale and celebration of the Trent and Mersey, Oxford and Leeds and Liverpool canals, most of the initial investment flowed from the territories they traversed. From the scholarship of J.R. Ward,[55] a great deal has been learned of the structure of this regional capital employment. Table 7.3 is based on his analysis of 29 per cent (£5 million out of £17 million) of the traceable capital supplied between 1755 and 1815.

---

53. C. Feinstein, 'Capital accumulation and the industrial revolution' in Floud and McCloskey (eds), *Economic History of Britain*, pp. 133–4.
54. Duckham, 'Canals and river navigations', *op. cit.*, p. 114.
55. J.R. Ward, *Finance of Canal Building*, p. 74, *passim*.

Table 7.3 Investment in canals: percentage of nominal capital invested

	1755–1815	*1755–80*	*1780–1815*
Peers, gentry, etc.	22	41	22
Farmers, graziers, etc.	2	1	2
Commerce, merchants, traders, tradesmen, etc.	39	27	40
Manufacturers	15	8	15
Professions (including clergy)	16	16	16
Women	6	8	6

Source: Armstrong and Bagwell in D.H. Aldcraft and M. Freeman (eds), *Transport in the Industrial Revolution*, Manchester UP, 1983, p. 119.

The predominance of the first group in the first phase of the canal era is explained largely by one individual – the Duke of Bridgewater – although Buckingham, Grafton, Clarendon, Exeter and Spencer were also noticeable among his peers. The 'Canal Duke' also illustrates another important point: it was as coal owner, not as agricultural landlord that he committed himself. Although the gentry did invest in canals through rural hinterlands in the later phase, it is evident that agricultural savings were not noticeably tapped. Despite the interest of some well-known industrialists, manufacturers as a group seem to have contributed only in proportion to their weight in the population. In contrast to the merchants and traders, they had an increasing need to concentrate on investment in fixed capital in their own enterprises, and indeed, with canal carriage reducing raw material costs and quite possibly releasing capital tied up in inventories, on their ability to increase their stock of fixed capital.[56]

If we assume that some investors within each group were 'not interested' in an activity made more profitable by the construction of a canal but only in dividends or, after 1790, in speculative profit, and that this was almost wholly true of women investors, substantially so of the clergy and of the majority of those from the professions, then it is clear that overall at least a quarter of investment in canals was drawn from a net cast unprecedentedly widely.[57] Oppor-

56. See Duckham's summary and analysis of Ward's researches in 'Canals and river navigations', pp. 118–23.

57. G.R. Hawke and J.P.P. Higgins, 'Transport and social overhead capital' in Floud and McCloskey (eds), *Economic History of Britain*, pp. 230–4.

tunities to invest in other sectors were not equally available to all those ranks in society able to save. Without prior purchase there was little opportunity to invest in land, except for those 'professionals' tapping its rising value indirectly through offering mortgages. Very few manufacturing enterprises reached beyond family resources, ploughed-back profits or local banking sources. Government stock was safe, but for much of the period offered poor return and no speculative incentive. Many urban tradesmen, especially those connected with the building industry, seem to have invested in a small way in housing for rent, but there can be little doubt that the special facilities in raising capital conferred by acts of parliament on turnpike trusts and canal companies enabled them to become the recipients of a flow of capital from sources which would not otherwise have been drawn so directly towards economic improvements.

Such investors tended to come in when stocks were exchanged rather than present themselves at the moment of initiation. The Duke of Bridgewater's 'small waterway empire' on the borders of Lancashire and Cheshire was exceptional. Most ventures were undertaken by a joint-stock company authorised by act of parliament to raise a capital sum from a share issue and supplementary capital by borrowing. With the Bubble Act still in force, such a form of enterprise was permitted only through specific parliamentary enablement. Accordingly, canals offered the only widespread opportunity of investing in £100 ordinary shares. As Pawson has suggested, it was they, before the railways, who 'introduced the better-off to the marketable share, and the chance to invest savings and earn dividends'. This is an aspect of canal finance for recognition rather than exaggeration, for at no time did total investment in waterways approach the sum in the 'funds'. While a canal was being built, ownership tended to remain with 'interested' locals, and indeed, with operating profits as yet ungenerated, recourse was frequently had to local banks for short-term working capital – the Kennet and Avon had an overdraft of £60,000 in 1815. Once built, share dealings increased the diffusion of ownership, both socially and geographically. Most of the original £300,000 for the Leeds and Liverpool Canal in 1777 had been raised in the two counties, but by 1800 37 per cent was held in London and the Midlands. The Truro banker William Praed invested £19,400 in the Grand Junction, and even if it was on behalf of clients, it still represented the mobilisation of savings from a county 300 miles from the canal.[58]

58. Pawson, *Early Industrial Revolution*, p. 150; Duckham, 'Canals and river navigations', pp. 114–18; Dyos and Aldcroft, *British Transport*, pp. 103–8.

These tendencies became especially marked in the canal mania of the 1790s when, according to an enthusiast in 1796, 'perseverance having vanquished prejudice, the fire of speculation was lighted and canals became the subjects of general conversation'. Fifty-one canal acts were secured between 1791 and 1796, peaking in 1793–4. Their initial capitalisation totalled £7.5 million. As with most booms, this one was based on proven results and justifiable prospects. The Birmingham Canal paid a dividend of 23 per cent in 1789 and in 1792 a single £140 share was sold for £1,250; another for £130 in the Staffordshire and Worcestershire fetched £1,100. Grand Trunk shares traded at around three times their nominal value. Such returns were enticing, but exceptional. However, on the whole most of those who invested in canals in the industrial Midlands and north did well enough. The average dividend of eighty canals in 1825 was 5.75 per cent, but the top ten were averaging 28 per cent. The thirty-seven canal companies who in 1825 were barely meeting their expenses were situated mostly in the south, in which region most of the unwise ventures of the boom period were concentrated.[59]

The enthusiasm for canal stock in the 1790s may have been the greater because the yield on Consols had not been very gratifying between 1784 and 1792. But suggestions, notably that by T.S. Ashton, that trends in canal investment generally followed changes in the interest rate have not found favour with more recent historians. Before the war of 1793 the long-term interest rate reached neither heights sufficient to deter nor depths sufficient to arouse. In any event, most of the holders of government stocks lived in the Home Counties, removed from the centres of canal enthusiasm. Dr Ward suggests instead that canal construction was more generally related to the level of economic activity, slackening with the economy for example from the mid 1770s to 1782. This is to be expected given that most of the initial investors were actively involved in the regional economy and anticipated wider gains.[60]

So also with turnpike trust formation. While it was marked in years when interest rates were low, there is, as Dr Albert has indicated, no evident correlation with the main turning points. Interest rates had already been low for twenty years when the turnpike mania began in 1750 and remained low after it ended in 1772. They must be accorded a permissive rather than a causal role. In

59. Dyos and Aldcroft, *British Transport*, pp. 103–8.
60. Duckham, 'Canals and river navigations', pp. 103–5.

the early 1790s, however, like canals, the trusts did feature in a general investment boom, as they did again in 1809–12.[61]

Turnpike trusts were formed to keep up and improve the 'King's Highway'. It seemed more suitable to employ the legal form of the trust than to set up private joint-stock companies to 'own' the roads. They could not issue shares but were enabled by act of parliament to borrow against future tolls. Since repair rather than fresh building was their prime rationale, they did not need to raise an initial capital comparable to that needed for constructing a canal – estimated by the Duke of Bridgewater to be £10,000 guineas a mile. What the trust offered was the opportunity to invest in interest-bearing mortgages. Up to 1750 the most significant group of investors was made up from gentlemen, landowners, yeomen and tenant farmers. After that time there was increasing participation from merchants, manufacturers, artisans, shopkeepers and also from widows, spinsters and clergymen, whose concern was limited to a return averaging around 5 per cent by 1800.[62]

The bulk of capital continued, however, to be supplied by the landed interest whose resources and local initiatives did most to provide the improved road network. Those who lent to the turnpike trusts were even more localised than those who bought canal stock. In the case of trusts based on prosperous urban centres, there was a considerable increase in the participation of smaller savers. Dr Buchanan has shown this to have been the case with the Bath Turnpike Trust where it had become crucial by the end of the eighteenth century when the share of the landed interest had dropped below 10 per cent. Seventy per cent of the £12,000 capital raised in the 1750s was sold in the secondary market within twelve years, while the placing of advertisements is significantly indicative of a developing movement towards soliciting funds from unknown clients.[63]

Investment in coastal shipping yet again reveals how local the process of capital formation in transport was. There is little detailed information for the eighteenth century, but the geographical pattern of investment was probably even more circumscribed than that revealed by an analysis for 1825 of 315 ships. These aggregated 31,782 tons, 42 per cent of which was owned within the port of registration and a further 48 per cent within a 20-mile radius of it.

61. Albert, 'The turnpike trusts', pp. 36–9.
62. *Ibid.*, pp. 53–4.
63. B.J. Buchanan, 'The evolution of the English turnpike trusts – lessons from a case study', *Econ. H.R.*, XXIX, 2, 1986, pp. 223–43.

In terms of occupations, at least three-quarters of the tonnage was owned by merchants, mariners or persons connected in other ways with shipping.[64]

CONCLUSION

What stands out about the development of transport in England between 1700 and 1815 is the creation from privately supplied capital of a system which, though not preconceived, was to prove sufficiently complementary in its supply and its operation to accommodate a modernising economy with a growing range of activities. It was a 'social provision' in the most obvious sense that many more gained from it than ever directly drew dividends. It was because the economy was as yet exhibiting a modest rate of overall growth (by modern standards) that investment could be undertaken on a private and regional basis with the state's role confined to that of legal enablement. As two econometric historians have succinctly expressed it: 'Those who were the beneficiaries of the uncaptured social gains were the residents of the geographical area served by a particular canal . . . and the same groups constituted the main recipients of private returns.'[65] Although, as we have seen, shareholding tended to become somewhat more diffused over time, it remains very largely the case that those who promoted and initially financed canal companies and turnpike trusts, were those who expected to benefit from them. Accordingly, perception of a gap between social and private returns was not a major handicap to investment.

The limited, but in permissive terms essential, role of government in the supply of what later ages were to know as 'social overhead capital' must be seen in the context of the close identification the political nation made of the public interest with that of property owners. Dr Albert has described turnpike trusts as 'an administrative innovation brought into being by a small section of the community in what it saw as it own best interests'.[66] Created by those with social, political and economic power, they redefined a previous property relationship. Just as enclosures divided the countryside

64. Armstrong and Bagwell, 'Coastal shipping', *op. cit.*, p. 165.
65. Hawke and Higgins, 'Transport and social overhead capital', *op. cit.*, pp. 249–50.
66. See M. Freeman's Introduction in Aldcroft and Freeman, *Transport in the Industrial Revolution*, pp. 12–15.

with hedges, so toll gates divided its roads and a communal institution was replaced by a cash-based one. It is not very surprising that turnpike proposals were opposed not only by some who saw a threat to their local economic interest but also by others, like the coal miners from Kingswood near Bristol, who destroyed toll gates in 1749 which they saw as infringing their right of free movement.

Overwhelmingly, improvements in roads and waterways happened in response to existing economic pressures and prospects. That is to say that they were demand led, except perhaps in their respective 'manias' when a number must be viewed as having been undertaken ahead of a demand. Of course, once a new or improved transport link was in operation, fresh entrepreneurial opportunities might be spotted, but for the most part promoters anticipated specific rather than general gains. A canal, as the Duke of Bridgewater explained, had 'to have coals at the heels of it'. This large degree of regional economic responsiveness served the developing economy well, in that the outcome was a provision whose components were complementary. Before the railway no single transport innovation offered instant betterment in terms of speed, regularity, reach and all-weather, all-round capacity. Canals, for example, were not *generally* superior to roads. They were better in moving bulky and heavy materials from concentrated locations and their direct water linkages with major ports facilitated the export of manufactures. But so far as the growing and diversifying domestic market for manufactured goods was concerned, improved road transport was far more important a means of distribution, for here speed and reliability were often sought above cheapness. Canals were appreciably slower and the advantage of improved roads actually increased in this respect. True, barges and wagons alike were drawn by horses, but the latter did not have to negotiate flights of locks (the Rochdale Canal had ninety-two locks in only 33 miles), and until the advent of 'fly boats' at the very end of the canal era there was no night working, with the canals open only from sunrise to sunset. In contrast, night work was becoming common on the roads after 1780, and by 1800 scheduled wagon services often departed at dusk. Seasonal conditions which inhibited or prevented travel on the roads have been made much of by historians, but the mushrooming growth in scheduled services after 1760 is testimony to a substantial improvement in this respect. On the other hand, as Dr Freeman has pointed out, the shortfall of canals in this respect is often overlooked. Winter freezing closed the Trent and Mersey Canal for five weeks in 1814–15, and Freeman has calculated that on the canals of the Lancashire plain there must have been twenty-day stoppages in thirty of the winters between 1771 and 1831 and thirty-day stoppages in ten of those. Perhaps as important was time lost through 'short-water working' in dry spells. Eighteenth-century data are scarce, but the problem is indicated by the fact that the Huddersfield Canal lost thirty-nine days in 1818.[67]

Speed and reliability were important to dealers in manufactured goods who wanted to catch rising markets abreast with or ahead of their competitors. Freeman has given the example of a West Riding firm which despatched its woollen goods entirely by road, and it was the customers who paid carriage. By the last years of the eighteenth century the stage coaches were conveying a growing traffic in samples. Contemporary 'conservatives' could feel unease as they glimpsed a 'social revolution' of which the turnpikes were harbingers. A pamphleteer in 1762 foresaw that more frequent trips to London would put increasing numbers of country gentlemen 'in the mode'. They would 'get fine clothes, go to plays and treats, and by these means get such a habit of idleness and love of pleasure, that they are uneasy ever after'. John Byng in 1781 saw the revolution as reaching rather further down the social scale: 'I wish with all my heart that half the turnpike roads of the kingdom were plough'd up, which have imported London manners, and depopulated the country – I meet milkmaids on every road, with the dress and looks of Strand misses. . . .'[68]

We have already noted how improved roads permitted the spread of the newspaper. If there was a 'consumer revolution' in eighteenth-century England, it must have owed a very great deal to an improvement in road transport which, according to one writer, allowed 'our very carriages to travel with almost winged expedition'.

> There was never a more astonishing Revolution accomplished in the internal system of any country than there has been within the compass of a few years in that of England. . . . Journeys of Business are performed with more than double expedition . . . .. Everything wears the face of despatch; every article of our produce becomes more valuable; and the hinge upon which all these movements turn is the reformation which has been made in our public roads.[69]

When Henry Homer wrote this in 1767 the canal age was in its infancy, but he predicted that not only by the turnpikes but with the aid of 'an even more valuable project of increasing inland navi-

67. *Ibid.*, pp. 17, 25–6.
68. Cited in R. Porter, *English Society*, p. 209.
69. Cunningham, *The Mercantile System*, p. 539.

gation, a facility of communication is soon likely to be established from every part of the Island to the sea and from the several places on it to each other'. Of all the economic 'advances' retrospectively labelled by historians, those in the transport sector were the most evident to contemporaries.

CHAPTER EIGHT

Markets

DOMESTIC MARKETS

The Malthusian debate is concerned with the way in which, through the centuries, economic growth has first induced and then restrained population growth. Great significance has been attached to the 'break with the past' at the end of the eighteenth century, when critical economic changes for the first time allowed *sustained* population growth. However, there is another important perspective from which population growth can be seen as a precondition in some circumstances for economic growth and, possibly, economic transformation. Population growth not only increases the supply of labour; in favourable conditions it increases the demand for both food and manufactured goods.

An 'optimum' rate of population growth could be considered one which while it increases the labour supply, is not so fast as to outgrow the supportive powers of the economy and prevent income per head from rising. It has often been asserted that England was favoured in just such a way on the eve of her industrial revolution. Other historians, inclined to supply-side explanations, have been sceptical about the role of expanding demand. Supply, they insist, with all the force of their born-again classicism, creates demand. 'The demand for things in general,' according to Professor McCloskey, 'is income itself which is determined by the resources and technology supplied to the nation.'[1] There is indeed a degree of circularity about simple models which explain industrialisation primarily in terms of a mass-production response to an expansion of the home market induced by population growth in favourable circumstances.

1. D.N. McCloskey, 'The industrial revolution 1780–1860', in R. Floud and D.N. McCloskey (eds), *Economic History of Britain*, I, p. 20.

In the belief that what matters is the interaction of supply and demand, I will examine the range of market-based explanations which have been proffered by historians, while seeking to avoid an assertive list on either the demand or the supply side. The general proposition that an increase in demand was central to the industrial revolution was given its best-known exposition fifty years ago by Elizabeth Gilboy. She sought to redress both the neglect by historians of 'changes in the nature of demand' and their concentration on labour as a factor of production rather than as constituting 'the major portion of the consuming public'.

> Obviously the factory system with its complicated industrial mechanism cannot function profitably without a large and growing demand ready and willing to absorb its products as fast as they are produced.[2]

If we resist the temptation to place the factory *system* too far back into the eighteenth century and consider the factory mode alongside other prior and parallel methods of manufacturing, it seems hard to deny that there was something of a supply-side response to an increase in demand. Several historians have employed variants of market expansion to explain the primacy of British industrialisation. Most notably, a 'consumer revolution' had taken a place alongside those other economic 'revolutions' which dominate the textbooks. Of course, there is no simple maxim of 'rising population equals rising demand'. At other times in other places demographic increase has led to falling living standards, even to the extent of pushing large numbers of the population to the margin of subsistence. Professor Perkin has stressed how favourable Britain's situation was.

> Industrialism requires a very delicate adjustment of demographic growth: not too fast; because that will lower wages and thus both consumer demand and the incentive to labour saving investment; not too slow, for that will raise wages so high as to entrench on profits and the capacity for investment. In the last quarter of the eighteenth century British population hit the critical rate of growth squarely in the middle, slow enough to maintain, or even slightly improve real wages and yet to encourage labour saving innovation, fast enough to keep down labour costs and yet to expand aggregate demand for food and mass consumer goods.[3]

Perkin's placing of the critical moment in the last quarter of the eighteenth century does not mean that a new demand for manufac-

---

2. Gilboy, 'Demand as a factor in the industrial revolution', pp. 121–2.
3. Perkin, *Origins of Modern English Society*, pp. 100–3, and *The Structured Crowd*, Harvester, 1981, pp. 42–3.

tured goods suddenly made an impact on the British economy around the time of the American Revolution. Increasing resort to factory production is a late step in matching output to a rising market. Dating a 'consumer revolution' suggests a beginning at least a generation earlier. Indeed, Dr Thirsk has suggested that even before the end of the seventeenth century new consumer goods were absorbing an increasing share of the nation's economic resources.[4]

Population growth accelerated only after 1750. Historians have to explain how it was that slower increase up to then permitted an expansion of the home market which the later faster rate of population increase did not reverse. Perhaps we could start by banishing that anachronism with which otherwise good arguments have been blemished, and not refer to *mass* consumption of manufactured goods before the twentieth century. What took place was a widening and deepening of consumption so that goods previously confined to the wealthier classes came to be purchased next by the middle-income ranks and then, to some degree, by the lower. Goods once considered luxuries became 'decencies': essential demarcations between a tolerable standard of living and deprivation. Hence, if there was a 'consumer revolution' it was a matter of stages, with different roles played by different social groups at different times. For example, the first rise in expectations of the lower orders would be for more and better food before manufactured goods. This in turn could have brought higher incomes for farmers, and, since they constituted a significant section of the consuming population, a consequent increase in *their* demand for manufactured goods. Yet in the first half of the eighteenth century population growth was too slow to have had this effect. Why, then, might the demand for manufactured goods have nevertheless increased?

In fact, by a process almost of inversion. Professor John in a seminal article stressed the great importance of the coincidence of a modest rate of population growth, putting no general pressure on a food supply expanded by a generation of agricultural improvement, with the bounty of a long period of good harvests. Output of cereals in fact exceeded home demand. This configuration was, John argued, propitious for the overall growth of the economy. Foodstuffs fell in price, especially in the southern wheat-consuming counties. On average prices were around 25 per cent lower between 1720 and 1780 than they had been between 1660 and 1680. This shifted the terms of trade between the manufacturing and agricultu-

4. J. Thirsk, *Economic Policy and Projects: The Development of a Consumer Society in Early Modern England*, Oxford UP, 1978.

ral sectors in favour of the former. Large sectors of the population were left with an increased disposable income after paying for their food. The effect was most noticeable on middle-income groups. Because the extra spending had been released by falling food prices, manufacturing employers did not lose their relative advantage by having to pay higher money wages. Consequently, social groups down as far as the craftsmen and artisans developed 'an appetite for mass-consumption' which survived the impact of faster population growth in the second half of the century.[5]

Since John wrote, Wrigley and Schofield's calculation of the consumption–production ratio has pointed to this period before the industrial revolution as having been 'very fortunate' in that the age structure meant a smaller dependency burden of non-working children than was to become the case in the late eighteenth and early nineteenth centuries. They share John's view that slow population growth from the mid seventeenth to the mid eighteenth century sustained high per capita incomes among the labouring population and thus boosted the output of commodities other than necessities. This earlier eighteenth-century boost to manufacturing was crucial for the future development of a range of important industries.[6]

While some of the gains to the economy were eroded after 1750 with the return of population pressure once again testing the ability of the economy to provide essentials, critically there was no *overwhelming* erosion of the living standards of the general population. Such stagnation as there was in income per capita was offset by the increase in numbers. The paradox of this maintained demand, despite the return of higher food prices and periodic scarcities, needs explanation. Grain prices between 1750 and 1800 not only were higher on average than those of the preceding fifty years but conceal years like 1766, 1773, 1795–6 and 1800–1 in which harvest failures brought widespread hunger and food rioting. A Malthusian crisis threatened late eighteenth-century England. At times it came very near but, narrowly and not without some years of great misery for most of the labouring population, it was averted.

In the outcome there was no long-term crisis of subsistence, but living standards in many parts of the country did fall. Yet there was no check to the expansion of the market. For some, entering the market as consumers had more to do with necessity than with a

5. A.H. John, 'Aspects of English economic growth', pp. 360–73.
6. E.A. Wrigley and R.S. Schofield, *Population History of England*, pp. 444–8.

growth in personal income. For several reasons more people had come to depend on the cash purchase of goods. Self-sufficiency, payment in kind and living-in service were all shrinking. As Dr Berg has put it: 'Certainly the home market grew in the eighteenth century, but its expansion was based on changing social relations and not on a national trend of rising living standards.'[7]

Thus the forces operating to maintain and even continue expanding the home market were multi-directional, in that market dependency can increase irrespective of income levels. Professor Hoskins perceived the compulsion under which labourers might enter the world of the money wage and the cash purchase when he assessed the impact of 'agricultural improvement' on the village of Wigston in Leicestershire.

> No longer could the peasant derive the necessaries of life from the materials, the soil, and the resources of his own strong arms. The self-supporting peasant was transformed into a spender of money, for all the things he needed were now in the shops. Money which in the sixteenth century had played merely a marginal, though a necessary part, now became the one thing necessary for the maintenance of life. . . . His Elizabethan master had needed money intermittently, but he needs it nearly every day, certainly every week of the year.[8]

In his survey of the condition of the labouring poor in 1797, Eden contrasted the persistent degree of self-sufficiency in the north with an almost total market dependence on the part of southern labourers. He considered the advantage to lie with the former. Bought clothing in the south had none of the hard-wearing qualities of northern home-spun. Southern bread, bought because of the scarcity of fuel, was more expensive and less wholesome than home-baked, while ready-brewed beer was poor stuff indeed.[9] In short, Eden did not consider market dependence to indicate prosperity; rather it was an impoverishing imperative. If even farm labourers in the south and Midlands were beginning to be market consumers as a consequence of becoming a waged proletariat, the tendency was even more marked among other sections of the working population whose numbers were growing more quickly, the urban population and those who manufactured in the countryside. The market dependence of the latter group is attested by their proclivity for food rioting, as is that of miners, while urban expansion obviously increased the role and reach of the market.

7. M. Berg, *Age of Manufactures*, p. 99.
8. Cited *ibid.*, p. 98.
9. F.M. Eden, *The State of the Poor*, B. & J. White, 1797, I, p. 555.

That growing sectors of the labouring population were pushed into the market falls short of telling the whole story of its expansion. Much is explained by the growth of purchasing power and consuming propensities among the middle ranks of society. It is not wise to write, as some have done, of an expanding middle-class market for an ever-widening range of manufactured goods, for 'middle-class' is a nineteenth-century usage and too restrictive for the eighteenth century. In eighteenth-century England there was, in comparison with other countries, a large section of the population which could be described as neither rich nor poor, ranging from the prosperous shopkeeper or yeoman farmer to the skilled artisan in full employment.

The growth in the number of those with a margin to spend after subsistence enables concepts like 'rising expectations' or even 'social emulation' to be applied quite widely to eighteenth-century English society. A demand thus based could further expand both from the increasing prosperity of the middle-income groups and from their increasing numbers, absolutely and proportionately, in the population. Both were happening and enough English people came to live in sufficient comfort to maintain the demand for manufactured goods through the eighteenth century, even though food prices rose steeply and in sharp contrast to the deep and widespread poverty of much of the labouring population.[10]

But what was the bottom income line above which recipients can be presumed to have enjoyed at least the modicum of comfort above subsistence and simple 'decency'? Professor Eversley has stressed that it need not be drawn very high and points to the importance of groups at the margin, who used soap to wash with and wore some cotton instead of home-spun linen: 'what seems necessary for growth is that the very exceptional expenditures should become a little less so'. In fact, that expenditure on what Nassau Senior termed 'decencies' – between necessaries and luxuries – should increase. On the basis of Gregory King's survey, Eversley suggests that growth and the changing structure of the economy drew around 3 million of the population above the line over the eighteenth century. Their incomes aggregated into the £30,000,000 that Arthur Young considered to be the value of the home market for manufacturing and mining in 1800. That the expansion of exports falls well short of absorbing the growth in manufacturing output suggests that something of this kind must have happened, as does

10. For an emphasis on the role of social emmulation, see especially Perkin, *Origins of Modern English Society*, pp. 91–5.

the fact that the nature of the new products does not allow for explanation in terms of extra spending on luxuries by high-income earners.[11]

The expansion of middle-income purchasing power owes a great deal to England's unique rate of urban growth. Towns emphasise the switch to money incomes and, as Adam Smith well knew, in general to higher money incomes. They also provide the context for the emergence and multiplication of the better-paid and more specialised trades. Even towns which were associated with particular manufactures did not have more than half of their occupied populations employed in them. Using data from directories, Dr Corfield has shown how urban growth 'spawned an immense range of specialist jobs'. From her sample she recorded 1,964 separate job descriptions in the 1770s and 1780s, yet lists from the late seventeenth century designate only a few hundred. She considers this multiplication to have been especially marked in the later eighteenth century. Many of these 'specialists' were engaged in merchanting and warehousing an astonishing range of commodities from oil stoves through Newcastle glass ware and Wedgwood china to wines and ostrich feathers. Many others made up the array of artisan manufacturers, either as independent masters or, increasingly, as waged journeymen. Still others were engaged in the supply of basics like food, housing and clothing, or in carrying. They interacted in ever more complex and expanding networks of economic activity and not the least input into the broadening of consumer demand came from those who were themselves employed in meeting it. In part, the producers of manufactured goods and the providers of urban services were the market.[12]

Those who worked in rural manufacturing, retained only a marginal self-supporting ability and entered the market for most of their needs. Their purchasing power as households was usually greater than that of families in agriculture. More specifically, several branches of rural life experienced, at different times, 'golden ages' when consumption of non-essentials became conspicuous. The framework knitters enjoyed such a time between 1755 and 1785, continuing to some extent to 1804, and William Radcliffe described such age for cotton hand-loom weavers from 1788 to 1803. When machine-made yarn brought a great demand for their labour, the weavers entered a 'higher state of wealth, peace and godliness'.

11. Eversley, 'Home market and economic growth', pp. 211, 214.

12. A preview of the findings of Dr Corfield's major research project was provided in *The Times Higher Education Supplement*, 13 Sept. 1985.

Their dwellings and small gardens were clean and neat, their families well clothed. Each man had a watch, while the women's dresses became 'fancy' rather than 'homely'. Homes were well furnished with clocks, Staffordshire tea services, silver-plated sugar tongs and a range of utensils and ornaments to display. Country weavers and knitters were to become better remembered for the long sad days of their early nineteenth-century decline, but they had happier days when they consumed the products made by their fellow artisans in Burslem, Sheffield and Birmingham. London artisans, too, had their good times. In his famous survey of 1849 Henry Mayhew found that the memory of the sawyers reached back through better days up to 1826 before the saw mills proliferated, to the even more lucrative times of their fathers, when sawyers could earn £1 a day.[13]

Much of the 'extravagant' expenditure of the lower orders so bemoaned by contemporaries went on imported 'groceries' – tea, sugar and tobacco – but consuming these also involved consuming the products of growing home manufactures. Josiah Wedgwood built his fortune on tea as surely as did investors in the East India Company. Many of Birmingham's population of artisans were occupied in producing trays and caddies, as well as snuff boxes for Virginia tobacco. From Black Country kettles to Sheffield plate, the consumption of imports led directly to new opportunities for home manufacturers. Imported raw cotton was the basis for the emergence of the most dynamic of the 'new' manufactures, but as late as 1776 Adam Smith omitted cotton goods from his argument for a sustained expansion and downward spread of consumption of nonessentials over the 'course of the present century', and still found examples enough for his purpose.

> The great improvements in the coarser manufactures of both linen and woollen cloth furnish the labourers with cheaper and better clothing; and those in the manufacture of the coarse metals, with cheaper and better instruments of trade, as well as with many agreeable and convenient pieces of household furniture.

Supply creating its own demand? Perhaps so, but the great economist also saw it as confirming evidence of improving real wages.

> The common complaint that luxury extends itself even to the lowest ranks of the people, and that the labouring poor will not now be

---

13. For the importance of such 'Golden Ages', see my Introduction to the 1979 Longman edition of Hammonds, *Skilled Labourer*, pp. xiv–xv, and Rule, *Experience of Labour*, pp. 203–4.

contented with the same food, clothing and lodging which satisfied them in former times, may convince us that it is not the money price of labour only, but its real recompense, which has been augmented.[14]

Smith was writing as the era of good harvests and cheap food was ending and before the onset of demographic acceleration. It would be less wise to attribute the continuing importance of the home market in the latter part of the eighteenth century and in the early nineteenth to a general improvement in real wages. Nor can it be wholly explained by the employment changes which were pushing greater numbers of people into the market irrespective of wage trends. Neil McKendrick has said of his 'consumer revolution' that the rich led the way in the 1760s and 1770s with an 'orgy of spending' on their magnificent houses. The rich, however, also expanded the market for more modest goods than silks, Chippendale furniture and ornate carriages, for they also purchased uniforms for their servants and furniture for the servants' hall, as well as the utensils for their great kitchens. When the quality took to watering at Margate they travelled overland in their gilded carriages, but their servants and baggage were the mainstay of the passenger-carrying sailing hoys plying the Thames in increasing numbers.[15]

Even if the real earnings of adult males stagnated, household consumption could still have improved if there was an increase or improvement in the employment available for its other members. McKendrick has suggested that such earnings were able to add a significant number of extra families to the 'middling ranks' earning above the £50 a year bottom line suggested by Dr Eversley. He thinks that expanding opportunities, especially in manufacturing, meant that in some districts the earnings of women and children were able to double family income – perhaps enough to add the extra 150,000 households Eversley considered were needed to explain the leap in home demand between 1750 and 1780.[16] There were certainly regions where this situation was developing – the new cotton districts of south Lancashire for example, and in the Potteries where females unknown in the industry before 1760 could earn from 12s (60p) to £2 a week by the end of the century. The household of the skilled potter became in income terms the equal of that of the lower clergy.

But how extensive were such developing opportunities? The new

14. Smith, *Wealth of Nations*, I, p. 87.
15. N. McKendrick, 'The consumer revolution of eighteenth-century England', in McKendrick, Brewer and Plumb, *Birth of a Consumer Society*, pp. 10–11.
16. McKendrick, 'Home demand and economic growth', pp. 184–90.

cotton-spinning mills created opportunites for some women after the mid 1760s, but in many rural districts the loss of cottage spinning reduced family earnings. The recent researches of Dr Snell point to a net decline in earning opportunities in southern England, brought about not only by the decline of cottage manufacturing but also by changing work practices in agriculture. It seems clear that for women as well as for men, the expanding employment and rising incomes provided by manufacturing growth were a markedly regional phenomenon.[17]

The availability of higher wages did not necessarily produce a commensurate increase in consumption. As we have seen, many eighteenth-century workers chose extra leisure instead. This was the constant complaint of Arthur Young, among others,[18] and the great sociologist Max Weber later put its link to consumption very clearly.

> He did not ask: how much can I earn in a day if I do as much work as possible? but how much must I work in order to earn the wage which I earned before and which takes care of my traditional needs? . . . A man does not by nature wish to earn more and more money, but simply to live as he is accustomed to live and to earn as much as is necessary for that purpose.[19]

To the extent that this 'pre-industrial' attitude prevailed, earnings and expenditure were forgone. It seems likely, however, that there was some relative shift away from a traditional leisure preference over the eighteenth century. It has been argued recently that by 1750, urban workers especially were working 'a very disciplined, formalised, surprisingly regular and long working week'.[20] Perhaps so, but according to employers, Saint Monday still had far too many devotees.

How can we sum it all up? Higher earnings and increased opportunities for earning by women and children were characteristic of some regions. Some trades and crafts prospered generally, while others had noted periods of prosperity. In the first half of the eighteenth century low food prices and slight demographic pressure may have allowed an aggregate increase in spending on non-essentials, even if the relative elasticities meant that more and better foodstuffs were the likely first call on extra income. Even though more rapid

17. K.D.M. Snell, *Annals of the Labouring Poor*, Ch. 1.
18. A. Young, *A Six Months Tour through the North of England*, 1771, I, pp. 176–7, and III, p. 193.
19. Max Weber, *The Protestant Ethic and the Spirit of Capitalism*, Unwin, 1965, p. 59.
20. Harrison, *Crowds and History*, p. 106.

population growth and poorer harvests occurred after mid century, by then the changing structure of employment was accentuating the trend towards wage-dependency, which had already reached a level quite exceptional compared with that in other countries. Urbanisation both emphasised this trend and widened spectacularly the range of urban trades, professions and manufactures bringing increasing numbers into the 'middle ranks' of income earners. Taken together all these can explain the existence in England of a home market for manufactured goods which was both wider and more dynamic than that offered anywhere on the continent. Contemporaries were well aware of this: 'Were an inventory to be taken of household goods and furniture of a peasant or mechanic in France and of a peasant or mechanic in England, the latter would be found on average to exceed the former in value by at least three to one.'[21]

Exactly how wide and deep the market expansion ran is hardly knowable. As Professor Stone has pointed out, while the growing demand for goods and services is a central feature of eighteenth-century England and provides 'the most striking evidence of the rise of the "middling sort" ', the really hard evidence comes from the supply side, from the output growth of the goods and services in question. From its nature it cannot do much to provide an answer to the key question: who were the consumers? As we have seen, to consider them to have been the labouring people in general is, in the face of the evidence of stagnating living standards over much of the country, hopelessly optimistic. In any case, as an explanation it is not necessary. Household inventories contain some clues but as a source are seriously limited by their accidental survival and their social unrepresentativeness. It is those who had no proclivity towards will making about whom we most wish to know. Dr Weatherill has been investigating probate inventories for the late seventeenth and early eighteenth centuries. She has discovered that a boundary line for consumption of non-staple household goods existed even across the bequeathing classes, and has cautioned against accepting much contemporary opinion that the 'luxury' market had reached well down the social scale.[22]

21. McKendrick, 'Home demand and economic growth', pp. 191–2.

22. Lorna Weatherill, 'Consumer behaviour, the ownership of goods and early industrialization' in *ESRC Working Group on Proto-industrial Communities*, University of Warwick, 1985, pp. 161–4. See her recent *Consumer Behaviour and Material Culture in Britain*, 1660–1760, Routledge, 1988.

However, as McKendrick has pointed out, increased spending on a greater volume and range of consumer goods does not need to have been general or even typical. To underwrite a sound basis of domestic demand for the growth of eighteenth-century manufacturing after 1760 it is necessary only to add 'an elite section of the labour force' to those in receipt of middling incomes and to continue the trend towards wage-dependency. Nor need this group have been composed of the same households throughout: as the fortunes of different employments fluctuated so different groups could have been included at different times. Eversley has stressed that too much should not be claimed for such a class. It is enough that there should have been growing pockets of households within the income range £50 to £200 a year, sufficient to have amounted to around 15 per cent of the population in 1750 and 20 to 25 per cent by 1780. If, he argues, the misery of large numbers of the agricultural and manufacturing proletariats at the end of the eighteenth century had been the general condition of the labouring population throughout the century, then industrialisation could not have taken place for it depended on 'the home sales of articles of everyday life to a section of the labour force which was neither very poor nor very rich' but which wielded an effective purchasing power in the face of many difficulties.[23] The point is echoed by McKendrick who argues that as well as 'the many who suffered during the late eighteenth century, and even more in the later stages of industrialisation, there were those who gained'.[24]

Even Professor Mokyr, who considers that the determination of 'when, where and how fast' so far as the industrial revolution is concerned should be sought first and foremost in supply factors, accepts that the sustaining of demand was important in maintaining the momentum of economic growth.[25] That demand did not, of course, come entirely from the domestic market. Some of the fastest-growing sectors of the late eighteenth-century economy, most notably cotton, owed their extra dynamism to Britain's pre-eminence in foreign trade, and it is to the growth of overseas markets that we now turn.

---

23. Eversley, 'Home market and economic growth', pp. 258–9.
24. McKendrick, 'Home demand and economic growth', p. 173.
25. J. Mokyr, 'Demand versus supply in the industrial revolution' in Mokyr, *The Economics of the Industrial Revolution*, Allen & Unwin, 1985, pp. 109–10.

OVERSEAS MARKETS

Foreign trade is the most visible of economic activities and those who engage in it usually the most vociferous of interest groups. Over the long eighteenth century there was a remarkable expansion in the volume and value of British overseas trade. It is not surprising that historians have frequently sought to link the growth of the economy directly to it. The impressive, though erratic performance of exports certainly encourages this approach, for overall the rate of export growth was ahead of that of output and of that of the population. As Professor Hobsbawm has put it: 'Home demand increased but foreign demand multiplied.' There is, however, a counter-tendency on the part of some historians to stress the home market and to share the scepticism of contemporaries such as MacPherson, who considered overseas markets to be only one-thirtieth as important for the growth of industrial output as home demand. That was something of an exaggeration, but any emphasis on the rate of growth of manufacturing generally must take account of the weight of particular export-inclined industries in total output.[26]

Some statistics will illustrate the point. At the beginning of the eighteenth century domestic exports accounted for around 7–8 per cent of national output, through its middle years perhaps 10 or 12 per cent and at its close peaking around 17 per cent. All in all, exports did not take up more than a fifth of the increase in the output of the economy as a whole.[27] A good deal is concealed by such broad statistics. Up to mid century grain was exported. Thereafter the situation changed fundamentally and, despite the interference of the Corn Laws, grain came to figure high on the list of imports in years of bad harvest. After 1750 domestic exports were made up predominantly of manufactured goods. Even so, recent re-estimates of their weighting suggest a degree of caution in evaluating their contribution. In 1700 only 7.5 per cent of industrial output other than woollens was exported and as late as 1831 only 7.7 per cent of output other than that of all textiles (with cotton now well ahead of wool) and of iron. This introduces an important perspective, but since cotton and iron were experiencing a productivity growth ahead of most other industries, their importance exceeds their weighting. To the extent that spectacular productivity gains were being achieved through technological

26. E.J. Hobsbawm, *Industry and Empire*, Weidenfeld and Nicolson, 1968, p. 32; Mokyr, 'Demand versus supply', *op. cit.*, p. 99.

27. W.A. Cole, 'Factors in demand', in Floud and McCloskey, *Economic History of Britain*, I, pp. 38–9.

advance, a demonstration effect was present for later imitation and emulation.[28]

These are matters to which we must return, but first we need to examine more closely the trends and patterns of overseas trade. Official trade figures need careful handling, but those who specialise in this area generally agree over what they reveal. This is that industrial output increased four-fold over the eighteenth century, home consumption of it three-fold and exports six-fold. The outcome by 1800 was that around a fifth of manufacturing output was exported compared with a third in 1700, and that whereas manufactured goods had then up to a third of imports, by 1815 they hardly figured at all. The trends towards these outcomes were not unbroken. There were periods, notably 1720–40 and 1760–1770, when home consumption increased more quickly than exports, but as Professor Cole has pointed out, exports over the century as a whole could well have accounted for 40 per cent of the increase in industrial output. Exporting to this level clearly offered a significant expansion of the market for manufacturers, an offer which was taken up to different degrees by different industries.[29]

In 1700 British trade was still directed largely towards Europe. Imports from the continent valued £3.9 million, with linen, wine, timber, naval stores and bar iron prominent. This was almost balanced by domestic exports of £3.8 million to which £1.8 million of re-exports were added. Woollen cloth led but was increasingly supplemented by a wider range of manufactured goods as well as by re-exports of tobacco, sugar and dyes. The most evident change as the eighteenth century progressed was the relative decline in the importance of Europe. By 1800 less than a third of English imports came from the continent and only a fifth of her exports went there. Europe was being displaced by the colonies. In 1700 North America and the West Indies together took only 11 per cent of domestic exports and re-exports while supplying 20 per cent of imports. By 1815 trade with them had increased more than six-fold, with over a third of imports coming from the North and Central American colonies. Exports to them had increased by 200 per cent and they were taking more than half of British exports.[30] Colonial trade enabled Britain to pay for continued imports of linens, wines and timber from

28. N.F.R. Crafts, *British Economic Growth during the Industrial Revolution*, p. 144.

29. Cole, 'Factors in demand', *op. cit.*, pp. 39–40; R. Davis, *Industrial Revolution and British Overseas Trade*, p. 36.

30. R.P. Thomas and D.N. McCloskey, 'Overseas trade and empire' in Floud and McCloskey, *Economic History of Britain*, I, pp. 90–1.

Europe with re-exported colonial products, which had been paid for by the export of domestic manufactures.

Import substitution tended to close down markets in northern and western Europe, but for the first sixty years of the century southern Europe, especially Portugal, filled the gap and in itself provided a link between the old and new geographies of trade. In trading with Portugal, Britain was indirectly trading with the Americas. The two countries had enjoyed a special relationship since the Methuen Treaty of 1703. Professor Davis has calculated that over 75 per cent of the growth in English exporting over the first half of the eighteenth century depended on either southern Europe or the Americas. Dr Fisher has clearly demonstrated that the export of manufactures to Portugal was closely bound to their subsequent re-export from Lisbon to Brazil: 'The business that English merchants drove to the English colonies in this period was in fact complemented by substantial indirect trades to the Iberian empires in America.' The expansion in manufactured exports to Portugal was the result of sixty years of prosperity in the gold mines of Brazil. When that prosperity ebbed in the 1760s, so too did the tide of English exporting to Portugal. Exports had doubled from 1700 to 1740 to a value of £1,164,000 which generally held steady until the 1760s. What made this trade especially useful was the small extent to which it depended on re-exports and the very great extent to which it brought markets for English manufacturers, especially in woollen and worsted textiles of the lighter and cheaper kinds. Hats and stockings featured too, as did iron wares, though only to the extent of an annual £20,000 by the 1750s. In return England took its favourite wine, some oranges, some figs and a bullion surplus of around £1 million a year in the 1750s.[31]

By the time the Portuguese trade passed its peak in the 1760s, a more than adequate substitute had developed, with special rapidity after 1740. This was the direct trade with Britain's own North American and West Indian colonies, especially with that part of the former which was to become the United States. Products from these colonies, notably tobacco and sugar, had joined those from Asia to make up the re-export trade which had been balancing Britain's payments since the Glorious Revolution of 1688. The earnings of those who provided them pushed things a step further. They opened up a market of huge potential for English manufacturers in the New World. The natural advantages of established manufacturing

---

31. See H.E.S. Fisher, 'Anglo-Portuguese trade, 1700–1770' reprinted in Minchinton (ed.), *Growth of English Overseas Trade*, pp. 144–64.

in England, reinforced by the artificial ones provided by the Navigation Laws and related manifestations of the 'colonial system', ensured that the high incomes of West Indian and Virginian plant-ers created a growing market. In the case of North America this was further emphasised by a generally high wage level. For all the pioneer ideology of frontier self-sufficiency which came to surround the early Americans, increasing in both numbers and wealth, they provided a market for consumer goods by 1740 which was not unlike that which had emerged in England itself. Exports to North America increased eight-fold between 1770 and 1773 and moralists on the eastern seaboard were beginning to echo the condemnation of a tea-drinking, fashion-wearing, luxury-wallowing populace which had become so strident in England. Home-spun goods, attractive enough as a symbol of frontier self-sufficiency, can become wasteful of time and energy. Close study of rural households in Massachusetts has suggested that home-making was by no means commonplace in an eighteenth-century America which was experiencing 'a steady commercialisation of economic life'.

As the population of the mainland colonies rose to 2.25 million by the time of the revolution of 1776, it suffered no decline in per capita income. The increasing numbers of white Americans of 1773 purchased British goods to the equivalent of £1.20p per person, compared with £1 in 1700. Professor Breen has suggested that the American consumer market took off in the 1740s. He argues that a demand which emanated from the earnings of export staples became itself the driving force behind even greater efforts to balance the increasing import of desired English manufactured goods. As a New York merchant expressed it in 1762: 'Our importation of dry goods from England is so vastly great, that we are obliged to betake ourselves to all possible arts to make remittances to the British merchants.'[32]

Charles Wilson has pointed out that it was the increased incomes of the landed which began the consumer revolution in England. In a similar way it was the growing wealth of the planters which first drew English manufactures to the American colonies. The tobacco planters of Virginia enjoyed a golden age between 1734 and 1756. Notoriously, they hardly changed their spending habits when it ended. South Carolina rice growers boomed after 1730 and reinforced their fortunes from indigo after 1750. In the 1790s came

32. See T.H. Breen, 'An empire of goods: The anglicisation of colonial America, 1670–1776', *Journal of British Studies*, XXV, 4, 1986, pp. 467–99.

cotton and a crop of 2 million lb in 1791 had reached 182 million by 1821. The sugar prices received by the West Indian planters rose steadily from 1713, and this too was translated into a demand for manufactured goods. West Indian plantations also provided a growing demand for fish, grain and timber which was met by North America. The urban merchants of Boston and other eastern ports who grew rich from it were no less avid in their conspicuous consumption of English goods.[33]

In North America consumer expectations moved quite rapidly down the social scale, drawn by high wages and less marked social rigidities. Tea consumption had reached the poor Philadelphia house by 1766. Tea drinkers need cups, fine enough to taste from and strong enough to hold very hot liquid and these qualities were apparently not achievable by colonial potters. As the range of English consumer goods expanded, Staffordshire and Worcester wares were joined by glass and metal wares including, in huge numbers, the humble nail. Even where local products could be bought, so superior were English goods presumed to be that place of origin marks on goods of colonial manufacture were often falsified.[34]

Direct trade with Africa was comparatively small, although the export of trade goods and guns to secure slaves for the New World plantations expanded rapidly after 1780.[35] The notorious Atlantic trade in black Africans has received the extensive and controversial attention of historians, and that is as it should be, for it was a shameful traffic for which apologetics are quite out of order. Human beings were wrenched from their homeland and crammed into the airless stinking holds of vessels to provide, if they survived, the slave labour of the plantation economies of the West Indies and the southern states of North America. Just how many made the passage is a matter of considerable argument, but a figure of around 2 million will do.[36] It is, however, possible to exaggerate the contribution which slaves as a commodity made to the overall value of British trade. By 1714 there was no longer any monopoly of the slave trade. Three English ports – London, Bristol and Liverpool – participated to a measurable degree, although the capital's role de-

---

33. C. Wilson, *England's Apprenticeship*, pp. 283–4; W. Miller, *A New History of the USA*, Paladin, 1971, pp. 75ff.

34. Breen, 'Empire of goods', *op.cit.*, pp. 488–9, 497.

35. Minchinton (ed.), *Growth of English Overseas Trade*, Introduction, pp. 30–1.

36. For the number of slaves see the discussion in C.J. Robinson, 'Capitalism, slavery and bourgeois historiography', *History Workshop Journal* **23**, 1987, p. 133.

clined significantly over the eighteenth century. The total number of vessels engaged in the trade from the three ports fluctuated.

Table 8.1 Vessels engaged in the slave trade:
London, Bristol and Liverpool (total)

1710	46
1725	150
1730–9 (av.)	85
1750–9 (av.)	82
1772–5 (av.)	161

Source: W.E. Minchinton, 'The British slave fleet 1680–1775. The evidence of the Naval Office Shipping lists' in *De la traité à l'esclavage*, Nantes, 1985, p. 398.

At Bristol and Liverpool slavers did make up significant proportions of the merchant fleets. At the former, however, they never formed more than 15 per cent. At the latter, over the third quarter of the eighteenth century, slavers rose from a quarter to a third of the merchant fleet.[37] Their importance to the level of employment at the port was recognised by the journeymen carpenters who in 1792 let it be known that if the slave trade were abolished they would riot and pull down the houses of leading abolitionists.[38] The black trade was not ended until 1807, but after 1800 was offering small returns. Up to then, however, on Dr Anstey's figures the profits made were at least the equal of most other areas of investment, with 9.5 per cent being the aggregate decennial average from 1761 to 1807.[39] The slave trade cannot be considered in isolation from the whole Atlantic economy. It was, as is well known, a triangular trade, taking out trade goods from England to Africa, carrying the hapless Negro slaves to the West Indian and southern state plantations and returning with American cargoes. Without slave labour the plantations of sugar and cotton could not have been as rapidly developed.[40] Dr Eric Williams' famous thesis linking the rise of capitalism to the slave trade probably overstated the extent to which capital derived from the infamous traffic fed into the growing

37. These figures are derived from: Minchinton, 'The British slave fleet 1680–1775: the evidence of the Naval Office Shipping Lists' in *De la traité à l'esclavage*, I, Actes du colloque international sur la traité des Noirs, Nantes, 1985, pp. 395–427.
38. A. Aspinall (ed.), *Early English Trade Unions*, p. 2.
39. R. Anstey, *The Atlantic Slave Trade and British Abolition*, Macmillan, 1975, p. 47.
40. Minchinton, *Growth of English Overseas Trade*, Introduction, p. 31.

industrial sector of the expanding English economy, but in pointing out that abolition came only when the slave trade was rapidly losing importance he can hardly be far from the truth. The decline of the West Indian sugar economy, and the near-complete ability of the US cotton economy to supply its own black labour through the re-production of its gender-balanced slave population, lessened the vested interest which might otherwise have held off the evangelical/humanitarian reformers rather longer.[41]

The East was no great consumer of English manufactures; rather it was a major, if contentious source of imports. These, including tea brought in by the East India Company from China, grew from around £500,000 in value in 1700 to almost £2 million by 1770. Throughout, exports met only about half of their cost. Attempts to reduce the balancing outflow of bullion were having some effect by the 1760s and 1770s, however. The share of woollen goods exported to Asia was 2.5 per cent in value in 1720, but 5 per cent by 1770. For other manufactures the shares at the respective dates were 2 per cent and 12 per cent.[42]

Apart from the East India Company, which kept its monopoly until 1813, the domination of English trade by the great chartered companies had dwindled by the eighteenth century. The rise of the outports and the parallel increase in the importance of the Irish and Atlantic trade had emphasised the growing role of the individual merchants and of small trading partnerships. The East India Company survived. Its monopoly of the Asian trade was still its reward for being one of the main holders of the national debt, and after Robert Clive's victory over the French at Plessey in 1757 it was the virtual ruler of Bengal. The great company received a fluctuating benefit from this situation. The costs of ruling an 'empire' were high, but for a time in the 1760s the revenues of northern India were almost self-supporting, with no bullion being exported in 1767–8. Thereafter, and notably from the 1780s, the company had to make recourse to fresh stock issue not so much to raise fresh working capital but to release it from debt. As a recent historian has expressed it, 'The transition from trader to sovereign was uncomfortable and largely unsuccessful.' The financial rationale of the great companies had been the way in which they had enabled a generation of investors, most of whom were substantial, to become merchants by proxy. Even in the merchant activities of the outports,

---

41. E. Williams, *Capitalism and Slavery*, University of North Carolina, 1944. Robinson's article (note 36 above) is an important reassessment of this influential thesis.

42. Minchinton, *Growth of English Overseas Trade*, Introduction, pp. 30–1.

however, a great number of people were taking shares in trading ventures, and from much further down the social scale than was the case with the East India Company, only 1.6 per cent of whose investors held less than £100 in 1764. It seems probable that the Atlantic trade mobilised capital far more effectively, and equally probable that in aggregate it did so to a greater extent, if the East India Company's heavy non-trading interests are first discounted.[43]

Table 8.2 Geographical distribution of English trade by value, per cent

	1700–1		1750–1		1772–3	
	Imports	*Domestic exports*	*Imports*	*Domestic exports*	*Imports*	*Domestic exports*
Europe	66	85	55	77	45	49
North America	6	6	11	11	12	25
West Indies	14	5	19	5	25	12
East Indies and Africa	14	4	15	7	18	14

Source: W.E. Minchinton (ed), *The Growth of English Overseas Trade in the Seventeenth and Eighteenth Centuries*, Methuen, 1969, p. 27.

When the cotton trade began to boom in the 1780s, Africa and Asia took between them a fifth of cotton goods exported, with Europe and America sharing the rest almost equally. The share of Africa and Asia then plummeted to less than 2 per cent by 1815, although it doubled in value. Thereafter, however, their share increased steadily until by 1850 this market was more important than either the European or North American market, in both of which home cotton manufacture had become significant.[44]

Apart from Indian raw cotton in the early days of cotton manufacture, England took no industrial raw materials of significance from the East. Indirectly, however, that region contributed importantly to the re-export trade which balanced essential imports from Europe. Re-exporting of tropical and semi-tropical products had boomed in the later seventeenth century and although expansion was less rapid thereafter, it held firm through the first three-quar-

43. The pattern of shareholding is analysed in H.V. Bowen, 'Investment and Empire in the later eighteenth century: East India stockholding, 1756–1791', *Econ. H.R.*, XLII, 2, 1989, pp. 186–204.

44. For the 'push' of cottons into the Asian, especially Indian, market, see Davis, *Industrial Revolution and British Overseas Trade*, pp. 19–21.

ters of the eighteenth century. By providing around a third of total export value, re-exporting to Europe helped to offset the saturation of the market for woollens in northern and western Europe. In the first fifteen years of the nineteenth century re-exporting still accounted for between a fifth and a quarter of total exports. To this, Asian tea and to a lesser extent textiles and dyes can be added alongside West Indian sugar, rum and coffee and North American tobacco and rice.[45]

Table 8.3 Percentage share of value of re-exports

	1784–6	1794–6
Tea	11	5
Sugar	6	16
Tobacco	15	3
Dyestuffs	6	8

Source: Based on data in appendix to R. Davis, *The Industrial Revolution and British Overseas Trade*, Leicester UP, 1979.

There is little question that overseas markets, by and large the trophies of war, were of great value for the growth of English manufacturing over the eighteenth century. That is not to say that without them growth would have been *seriously* less. The peculiar framing of econometric questions and counterfactuals may posit alternative arrangements in which, in theory, growth would have been as good or even better. It is quite proper that it should, for assertions of indispensability are dangerous. The historian's first and final duty, however, remains the explanation of the world that was, rather than the one that might have been. The eighteenth-century English economy both shifted an astonishing percentage of its working population away from agriculture and came to rely on importing many of the raw materials it required. The permissive context for this was an expanding foreign trade. Dr Lee has recently pointed out that although the resources which went into the exporting industries *could* have been channelled elsewhere, the return would almost certainly have been less: 'An eighteenth-century economy without resource to trade would have been smaller, less

45. Minchinton, *Growth of English Overseas Trade*, Introduction, p. 26; P. Deane, *First Industrial Revolution*, p. 57.

diversified and must have generated less growth even than the modest rate of increase actually achieved.'[46]

England's eighteenth-century manufacturing growth may not have been in any full sense 'export led', but foreign trade did nevertheless have a significant and dynamic role. A different allocation of resources might also have produced growth, but diverting them merely to the home market would have substituted only on the assumption that resources were already being fully utilised there. This seems denied by the evidence of unemployment and underemployment and the general cheapness of labour.

To a considerable extent manufacturing expansion over the first three-quarters of the eighteenth century came in response to increasing demand, with overseas markets substantially supplementing the opportunities at home. This remained the case. The North American market was to surprise contemporaries by its continuing importance after the revolution brought an end to British rule. During the wars themselves there had been considerable disruption, but by 1785 trade had fully recovered. It was worth on average more than £2 million a year from 1786 to 1790 and £2.5 million in the following quinquennium.[47] Yet this was also the period during which the United States became the main supplier of the hugely increasing need for raw cotton. Professor North has suggested that the booming of the specialised plantation economy in the southern states was the key factor in the growth of a pattern of dynamic regional specialisation which allowed the north-eastern states to cradle an American industrial revolution by 1830.[48] Up to then, however, it was primarily British manufactures which met the needs of the new republic. A parliamentary enquiry of 1812 revealed the persisting importance of the American market to hardware manufacturers. One claimed in 1808 that of 50,000 people, excluding 20,000 nailors, engaged in hardware production in Birmingham and the surrounding district, as many produced for American consumption as did for the home market. A Sheffield manufacturer suggested that 6,000 men, women and children in his district similarly depended on the American market for their employment. Exports of traditional 'smallware' metal goods was increasing, while alongside them metal wares of a new kind, including machinery

---

46. C.H. Lee, *British Economy since 1700*, pp. 118–19.

47. P. Mathias, *First Industrial Nation*, p. 91.

48. D.C. North, 'Industrialization in the United States' in M. Postan and H.J. Habakkuk (eds), *Cambridge Economic History of Europe*, Vol. VI, *The Industrial Revolutions and After*, Cambridge UP, 1966, 2, pp. 673–704.

and steam engines, were beginning to show up, although by 1820 the value of this last group was still only £250,000.[49]

Prospect and actuality were closer in the case of cotton. Professor Hobsbawm considers that the rise of the cotton industry marks a fundamental change in that mechanised factory production resulted in such rapidly diminishing unit costs as to be 'no longer dependent on existing demand, but to create its own market'.[50] This point has been emphasised by other writers. It is essentially that the technological and organisational changes accompanying the factory system were to invert the previous relationship of supply and demand. Professor Davis noted that the industries which expanded before 1780 did not transform themselves in the dramatic way we have come to know as an industrial revolution. Following the lead of cotton the later changes revolutionised production. Cotton was new not only in its methods, but in its product. Before the advent of machinery, English hand workers could not spin to the requisite fineness to rival Asian calicos. Machinery overcame this skill deficiency, and did so while bringing constantly falling costs. The market expanded enormously at home, in Europe and in America. The negligible export of cotton goods in 1770 was transformed into half of all British exports between 1800 and 1850. Its example was followed, although more slowly, by woollens.[51]

At first the cotton industry had found its outlet at home, where a latent demand for a cheap, durable, light textile had long existed. After two decades cotton came to account for a third of the increase in manufactured exports from 1784–6 to 1794–6. By 1815 Britain was exporting 4 yards of cotton cloth for every 3 used at home, and between 1794–6 and 1804–6 cotton goods accounted for 84 per cent of the increase in manufactured exports. During that decade of major war, Britain's near-monopoly of factory industry was sustained, and after 1815 she entered a new era of economic history in which the mutual influences of industrialisation and trade expansion could work freely, and in which, as Professor Thomas has expressed it, 'trade was the child of industry'. From the late eighteenth century the rise of the cotton industry not only reversed the long relative decline in the importance of textile exports but

49. Committee on the Orders in Council, BPP 1812, III, cited in A.E. Bland, P.A. Brown and R.H. Tawney (eds), *English Economic History: Select Documents*, Bell, 1914, pp. 689–91.

50. Hobsbawm, *The Age of Revolution*, Weidenfeld, 1962, p. 32.

51. Davis, *Industrial Revolution and British Overseas Trade*, pp. 9–10, 14; Mathias, *First Industrial Nation*, p. 93; Deane, *First Industrial Revolution*, pp. 65–6.

pushed the first industrial nation, if not in an entirely new direction, at least up a much steeper path.[52]

'King Cotton' spearheaded a new, dynamic but at first narrowly based surge in manufactured goods capable of creating as well as meeting market demand. In recognising this we must not underestimate the contribution made to the industrialising economy by the earlier expansion of manufacturing in response to home and overseas demand. Firstly, persuaded by Crafts, Lee and others, we have learned to shift the relative weighting of the traditional and the transformed industries before the early nineteenth century quite sharply towards the former. Secondly, the cumulative impact of less than spectacular modifications in methods of production and organisation on productivity in long-established manufactures was significant, as Maxine Berg and others have shown. Thirdly, in Britain the dynamic industries surged ahead not of a generally underdeveloped economy but of one which was in no real sense 'pre-industrial'. That is why Britain largely escaped enclave development and why we must augment Hobsbawm's assertion that the home market 'provided the broad foundations for a *generalised* industrial economy', by adding that in this provision it was materially assisted by an overseas market for manufactured goods of a kind possessed by no other economy.[53]

52. Thomas and McCloskey, 'Overseas trade and empire', *op.cit.*, pp. 100–2.
53. Hobsbawm, *Industry and Empire*, *op.cit.*, p. 32.

CHAPTER NINE

Money Matters: Debt, Taxes and Currency

DEBT

> Let it be supposed that according to the usual methods of borrowing
> and funding, the Public Debts, during the present war, should encrease
> to no greater degree than they did in the last war; which was about 30
> millions: And let it be supposed, according to past experience, that in
> ten or twelve years after a peace; we should be plunged into a fresh
> war; which might encrease the debts of the nation 30 millions more,
> and that afterwards we should have another breathing time of ten or
> twelve years, and that according to custom a third war should ensue, no
> less expensive than each of the former two; these three wars will swell
> the national debts to the amount of 170 millions, and that in little
> more than fifty years. For if we have no reason to believe that any more
> of the debts will be paid during the intervals of peace, than have
> hitherto been: Nay the whole of the Sinking Fund, by such an
> increased debt, becoming absolutely anticipated, together with
> numbers of additional oppressive taxes, we have less reason to expect
> any of the old debts to be discharged, as we go on contracting of new.[1]

Writing this in 1757, at the beginning of the Seven Years War,
Malachi Postlethwayt may have failed to prophesy the exact sequence of war and peace, but he perceived clearly enough the interactions between war, debt and taxation which largely determined
the public policy of Hanoverian England. In fact he underestimated
the level the national debt would reach; by the beginning of the
war with France in 1793 it had reached £242,900,000. The advent of
Dutch William in 1688 may have brought a Protestant ruler, but it
brought one already embroiled in war with Louis XIV, and ended a

---

1. M. Postlethwayt, *Great Britain's True System*, 1757, reprinted Gregg 1968, pp. 1–2.

period in which the offshore island had played small part in the struggles of continental Europe. For more than half of the years between 1689 and Waterloo in 1815 Britain was at war, mostly with the French. The longest period of peace was the twenty-six years between the end of the War of Spanish Succession in 1713 and the outbreak of that of the Austrian Succession in 1739. That celebrated interlude is associated with the strong preference for peace of Sir Robert Walpole. Especially from the Seven Years War in 1757, the wars in which Britain was involved may have been European and dynastic in origin, but so far as her struggle with France was concerned, they were global in breadth. Naval superiority succeeded in winning control for Britain of an empire from the Americas to the Indies.

Wars were never cheap, but they were fought over such a span that they became progressively more costly. Government both borrowed and taxed to finance them. It borrowed so heavily that the greater part of its peacetime revenue was mortgaged to service and repay its debt. Financing the industrial revolution was small beer compared with the cost of waging war. In 1785 it cost £63,174 to build the 100-gun ship *Victory*. That was five times greater than the fixed capital value of Ambrose Crawley's celebrated iron works – one of the industrial wonders of the age. Professor John Brewer has recently pointed out that the capital value of the fleet at the end of the eighteenth century was perhaps five times greater than the £402,651 at which the West Riding woollen manufacture was valued in 1801. With refits and repairs the upkeep of the fleet by 1750 probably exceeded £500,000 a year, and the wartime floating population which had to be provisioned exceeded that of any town save London. Only a modest proportion of government expenditure went on civil matters, while between 75 and 85 per cent of annual expenditure went either on current spending on the Army, Navy and ordnance, or else to the service of war debts.[2] Wars became ever more expensive, and with them the national debt rose to heights that to contemporaries seemed awesome (see Table 9.2).

The bearing of such a burden, as one historian has recently remarked, suggests that in moving from lightweight to heavyweight in the European balance of power while simultaneously acquiring an overseas empire, Britain owed as much to her clerks and administrators as she did to her soldiers, sailors, generals and admirals.[3] Making possible success on land and at sea was Europe's most efficient

2. J. Brewer, *Sinews of Power*, pp. 34–6.
3. *Ibid.*, p. xvi.

Table 9.1 Military expenditure as a percentage
of total expenditure and of national income

	% of total expenditure	% of national income
1739–48	64	
1740		10
1756–63	71	
1760		14
1775–83	61	
1780		12.5

Source: J. Brewer, *The Sinews of Power*, Unwin, 1989, pp. 40–1.

taxation system. The British government borrowed sufficiently and cheaply enough because its reputation for efficient tax gathering allowed anticipated revenues to provide the security for its present borrowings. This was the principle of the funded debt, which was the basis of a credit system in which, in response to government's borrowing needs, banking and stock and security exchanging developed into a mechanism capable of serving the needs of the developing economy as well as those of the state. Underlying confidence was such that the system survived the extraordinary madness of the South Sea Bubble in 1720, so well that, once the vapour had cleared, it became possible to talk of beneficial outcomes from history's most infamous bursting.

Many men played a part in building this system: leading ministers such as the confidence-rebuilding Walpole and the quietly reforming Henry Pelham, and beneath them the officials and clerks. They established and operated a revenue system which, if far from pure, was less venial and more efficient than that of any other European state: 'The ability of government administrators to establish the routine by which revenues were collected, money raised and supply requisitioned could make the difference between victory and humiliation.'[4]

Outside of government the success of public credit depended upon the interest, skills and self-interested cooperation of the financiers of the City, especially on those of the three great corporations who controlled so much of the national debt stock: the Bank of

4. *Ibid., loc. cit.*

Table 9.2 The logistics of war, 1689–1784

War	Average annual personnel			Average annual expenditure	Average annual tax revenue	Debt	
	Navy	Army	Total			Begin	End
1689–97 Nine Years War	40,262	76,404	116,666	5,456,555	3,640,000	–	16,700,000
1702–13 War of Spanish Succession	42,938	92,708	135,646	7,063,923	5,355,583	14,100,000	36,200,000
1739–48 War of Austrian Succession	50,313	62,373	112,686	8,778,900	6,422,800	46,900,000	76,100,000
1756–63 Seven Years War	74,800	92,676	167,476	18,036,142	8,641,125	74,600,000	132,600,000
1775–84 American War	82,022	108,484	190,506	20,272,700	12,154,200	127,300,000	242,900,000

Source: J. Brewer, *The Sinews of Power*, Unwin, 1989, p. 30.

England, the East India Company and the South Sea Company. Successful borrowing and taxing were different sides of the same sound coin of reputation, but their relationship can best be understood if we look at the pattern and structure of each in turn.

Borrowing financed 31 per cent of spending in the War of Spanish Succession (1702–13) and over 40 per cent of that in the American war (1776–83). In more than half of the years between 1713 and 1785 debt service took up more than 40 per cent of total revenue. At the end of the American war it even reached 66 per cent.[5] The debt which George I took over in 1714 was of two main kinds: short-term unfunded and long-term funded. The main concern over the century was to shift as much as possible from the first to the second form. With each war came a flood of short-term credit in the form of exchequer, Army, Navy or ordnance bills with lengthening repayment periods creating a public credit crisis. The solution sought was the conversion of as much of the debt as possible into long-term funded redeemable debt, as in 1763 at the end of the Seven Years War when £3,670,739 worth of Navy and ordnance debt was converted into a 4 per cent stock funded on 'earmarked' tax revenue. Here is one obvious link between borrowing and taxation: each new issue of funded stock depended upon either the introduction of a tax or the rescheduling of an existing one. With indirect taxes more favoured the burden fell on the consuming population at large, but from the point of view of the government, if such conversions did not shrink the national debt, they at least made it more controllable. In no Hanoverian war did the unfunded proportion of the debt exceed 20 per cent, and it was rarely that high.[6]

The moving from fixed-term to redeemable stock was necessary to secure lower interest rates, and such stock predominated in issues after 1714. However, there was still a large legacy to service. In 1714 more than a third of the debt was in the form of fixed-term annuities, most of which had been floated before 1710 and which cost an annual £800,000 to service. Fixed-term stock did imply that the national debt would have to be repaid, one day, but for most of the eighteenth century control of the cost took priority over reduction of the principal. Walpole, it is true, kept out of wars and was able to cherish the prospect of reduction from the Sinking Fund established in 1717. In the ten years after 1727 he managed to redeem £6,500,000 worth of annuities and South Sea stock but after

---

5. *Ibid.*, pp. 114–16.
6. *Ibid.*, pp. 116–19.

that the fund was 'raided' for purposes other than liquidating the public debt. Success now was of the kind associated with Henry Pelham, who during his time at the Treasury from 1749 to 1757 rescheduled almost 90 per cent of the 4 per cent debt, down to 3.5 per cent in 1750 and down again to 3 per cent by 1757. It was as well, for the Seven Years War, which cost £82 million of which £60 million was borrowed, was about to begin a period of widely contested expensive wars. The national debt surged from its 1756 level of £74.6 million to reach £231 million by the end of the American war in 1783 and £820 million by the time of Waterloo.[7]

Despite this immense burden, only one episode disrupted the generally sound managing of the public debt – the South Sea Bubble of 1720. Several things interacted to produce that infamous fiasco. The South Sea Company had been formed under a Tory administration in 1710. Ostensibly it was to prosper from a monopoly of trade with Spanish America, which would be bestowed upon it by the government in return for taking over the entire £9 million worth of unsecured national debt. The holders of this would receive the company's stock at par. In addition the government would pay an annual sum equivalent to 6 per cent interest on the transferred stock. But, however genuine the prospects of trade with the South Seas might have seemed, especially when enhanced by the right to sell slaves to the Spanish colonies granted at the Treaty of Utrecht in 1713, it is clear that so hugely capitalised a new incorporation was also intending to contest with the 'big two' – the Bank of England and the East India Company – for the profits which came from dealing in the national debt. The outbreak of war with Spain soon removed even the façade of trade as its main purpose, yet it had royal support and between two and three thousand shareholders. In 1715, in return for writing off two years of annuity payments worth something over £1 million, the government permitted it a fresh share issue which brought its capital up to £10 million, about half of the entire joint-stock capital in the country. By 1719 its absorption of so much of the unfunded debt was suggesting to ministers that they might also shift a proportion of the funded debt its way. This hope had been inspired by events in France, where the financier John Law, exiled after a fatal duel, was perceived to be achieving a spectacular unloading of the public debt.

In England the funded debt selected were the annuities stemming from a lottery loan of 1710. The company was to be allowed to

7. *Ibid.*, pp. 122–3. (figure for 1815 added).

increase its capital by £1,150 for every £100 p.a. worth of annuity offered to it by holders up to £2.5 million. The Exchequer would pay 5 per cent on the new stock and would have reduced its service cost by almost half. The authorised capital of the company would reach £12.5 million. Switching the public debt on to the company appealed to the country gentleman's prejudice against public indebtedness, and, feeling sure of parliamentary support, the government went further and sought to shift a total of £31 million of debt, almost equally split between redeemable and irredeemable stock, wrapping it into a single huge annuity on which the company would receive 4 or 5 per cent. Of course, the holders of irredeemable stock were not obliged to exchange it for South Sea stock, but as fast as they did so the company would issue an equal amount of its stock. It was a time of speculative fever burning over western Europe, and debt holders not only rushed to exchange, many of them quickly put the stock back on to a soaring market where others rushed to take it up. The effect was the unloading of a mountain of stock on to a market which was becoming overheated. By June the total capital of companies floated in a single week reached £224 million, and South Sea stock, floated at 110, had reached an astonishing peak of 1,050, spearheading a speculative mania of spurious company flotation.[8]

Sir Robert Walpole summed up the motives which had persuaded the government to enable the debt transfer by the South Sea Act (6 George I c. 4) of 1720.

> to consult the landed and trading interest of the nation, by lessening its incumbrances and public debts, and putting them in a method of being paid off in a few years; which could not have been done, unless a way had been found to make the Annuities for long terms redeemable; which had been happily effected by the South-Sea Scheme, without a breach of parliamentary faith.[9]

With the conversion achieved, the Sinking Fund might, with the lower interest charge, redeem the public debt over twenty-five years. The government was not to be a real loser. In September, South Sea stock, which had dropped over August, collapsed, in tune with what was happening in Paris and in Amsterdam. A financial panic ensued, as frantic as the earlier boom. By the time the next session

---

8. My account of the South Sea Bubble is based largely on P.G.M. Dickson, *Financial Revolution*, pp. 90–200, and the very readable general account by John Carswell, *The South Sea Bubble*, Cresset, 1961. A succinct account is provided in C. Wilson, *England's Apprenticeship*, pp. 315–17.

9. Cited in Dickson, *Financial Revolution*, p. 97.

of parliament began in December, the stock stood at 191. Walpole, who had kept his hands almost clean, began the task of rebuilding, a task that was possible only with the cooperation of the Bank of England and the East India Company in taking up some of the over-issued stock. The South Sea Company was to be excused payment of sums of £4.1 million, but not the £1 million due on Exchequer bills. In return £2 million of its capital and a proportionate part of the interest which the government paid the company was to be cancelled. Dickson has described Walpole as the man who applied 'the harsh cautery of common sense to the soaring dreams and megalomaniac expectations of the South Sea year'.[10] The company had to give up the surplus stock it had accumulated at the expense of the public creditors and rescind its claims to be paid in full for the amount it had sold, but the real victims were the public creditors, who had to reconcile themselves to drastic losses in income and capital.

Historians generally agree that the outcome was favourable to the government. It had managed to convert most (over 80 per cent) of the termed annuities into South Sea stock, thus paving the way for reductions in interest and capital under Walpole and Pelham. As Brewer has put it:

> The scheme, disreputable and corrupt as it was, succeeded in its chief aim of changing the structure of the national debt. In 1717 the annual charge of terminable annuities to public expenditure was £1,870,000. Five years later it had been reduced to £212,000.[11]

Professor Charles Wilson views the effects of the Bubble as 'salutary', but considers that the taking over of so much of the South Sea Company's excess stock by the Bank of England and East India Company perpetuated into the 1730s the situation in which more than half of the national debt was held by the great corporations.[12] The *fund-holder*, later typical, was still dwarfed. Nevertheless, the trend towards a greater number of holders was a persistent one. In 1720 there were 30,000, and by 1757 there were twice as many. Not only did this dilute the power of the incorporated companies, but there was no replacement by an equivalent power, for the larger and more amorphous body of investors was hardly as able to lobby against interest reductions or other schemes to lessen the weight on government. When government stock issues had been taken up pre-

10. *Ibid.*, p. 176.
11. Brewer, *Sinews of Power*, pp. 125–6.
12. C. Wilson, *England's Apprenticeship*, p. 317; Dickson, *Financial Revolution*, pp. 290–302.

dominantly by the triad, there had been little need for anything much in the way of a 'market'; but the change in the structure of debt ownership led inevitably to the emergence of broking and job-bing practices which were to become institutionalised into the Stock Exchange. Increasingly underwriters took blocks of stock which they moved on to clients. Men like Samuel Gidion made the City's lar-gest fortunes from dealing in government loans. Although Henry Pelham managed a successful open subscription, much government stock was still moved through intermediaries in the form of closed subscriptions. In 1758 the Duke of Newcastle was forced to work through 'the most knowing people in the City' in raising a huge loan of £8 million. It was underwritten by twenty-two financiers who included governors of the Bank of England, East India Company and South Sea Company. Now, however, they were not taking up corporate subscriptions for their institutions but tapping the resour-ces of their friends and contacts. By 1750 the buying and selling of government stock had become a straightforward routine.[13]

Purchasers or those seeking to collect interest, or their agents, had simply to attend the offices of the Bank of England, the East India Company or the South Sea houses of the Exchequer on the appropriate day. By mid century, however, most of those attending regularly were 'known to be jobbers' and their presence, together with that of the brokers, was a clear pointer to the development of a speculative stock market. Not allowed into the Royal Exchange, the dealers had taken to meeting at Jonathon's Coffee House near the Bank, which was to become known in 1773 as the Stock Ex-change. The familiar modern terminology was already in use: 'bull' already described a dealer who bought stock and sold it ahead of having to pay for it, while 'bear' applied to those who contracted to sell stock they had yet to obtain. Contemporaries distrusted them in the belief that they brought an unsavoury speculative element to the market in stocks. The modern Exchange, with its dealing in industrial and other company equities, still lay well in the future. It awaited the great mobilisation of savings that railway construction elicited and the parallel arrival of limited liability, but, as Professor Wilson has pointed out, 'by advertising the opportunities of the stock market' the dealers of 'Change Alley' helped in the long run 'to widen the circle of investors as well as of speculators, by creating habits of investing rather than of hoarding and possibly levelled out

13. C. Wilson, *England's Apprenticeship*, pp. 321–2.

extremes of fluctuation by increasing competitive bidding for stock'.[14]

Up to the end of the American war the public credit system supported the burden placed upon it. Ironically for a quarrel which had arisen as a result of a revolt against the colonial taxation imposed to increase the revenue and retrench some of the expenditure on the Seven Years War, the American war doubled national expenditure from £131 million in 1775 to £245 million by 1783. Britain's resulting debt burden was in fact greater than that of the French, whose consequent indebtedness has been linked to her political crisis of 1788–9. Yet there was only a small increase in taxation. The land tax took its usual wartime hike, to 4s (20p) in the pound; the malt tax rose from 9½d (4p) to 1s 4½d (7p) on the bushel, and duties were imposed on wine and tobacco. Borrowing was pushed to the limit, but nothing broke. As Professor Mathias has pointed out, on the British side there was resort neither to penal levels of taxation nor to promiscuous paper-money inflation. The British relied upon 'an immaculate credit rating'. This was guarantee enough to secure loans which left the government in the peacetime year of 1786 paying 55 per cent of its net expenditure in interest on the national debt, compared with a level of 45 per cent before the war.[15]

Subsequent developments in public finance derived from the realisation that a limit had been reached. The ratio between tax yields and borrowing levels needed to be narrowed, both by extra revenue and by reducing the size of the debt. Concern swung away from programmes designed to reschedule a reduction of service costs, back towards the earlier aspiration of redemption. In this respect the arrival of William Pitt the Younger at the Treasury in 1784 was significant. He commenced by stemming the revenue loss resulting from smuggling by reducing duty levels to lower its profitability, as well as by strengthening the preventative service. By 1790 the yield from wine duties had increased by 29 per cent, that from spirits by 63 per cent and that from tobacco by 89 per cent. Two years later Pitt claimed to have added £1 million to the annual revenue from customs duties, £1 million from new taxes, notably on windows, and £2 million from additional excise rising from increased domestic consumption of excised goods. In that year revenue was 47 per cent

---

14. *Ibid.*, pp. 324–7; Dickson, *Financial Revolution*, Ch. 20.

15. P. Mathias, 'The finances of freedom: British and American public finance during the War of Independence' in *The Transformation of England*, Methuen, 1979, pp. 286–8.

higher than it had been in 1783. A surplus of £1.7 million displaced a deficit of £10.8 million, largely because, although he was no great fiscal innovator, Pitt taxed cleverly and efficiently.[16]

So far as the debt was concerned, the first success was in converting most of the short-term, high-interest credit which had stemmed from the wartime issue of government bills to a funded 5 per cent stock in 1784–5. The most noteworthy development, however, was the re-establishment of a Sinking Fund in 1786. This was made possible by the return to a revenue surplus, diversion of part of which rapidly decreased the debt by the repurchase of £10.25 million of government stock. The Sinking Fund can be considered a success up to the point when the outbreak of the 'Great War' of 1793 removed any likelihood of a revenue surplus.[17]

The debt at the end of the American war had been sixteen to seventeen times the revenue, and prophets of doom were widely heard amid the financial gloom. Yet Pitt during his first eight years managed to raise annual revenue from £12.5 million to £18.5 million. He even managed to get an extension of the unpopular excise to cover first wine, then alchohol generally. His whole system was to be tested to its limits when a war with France began in 1793 which lasted, with only brief intermission, for more than twenty years. Costs were unprecedented. Britain's most significant land battle in the Seven Years War, at Minden in 1759, had involved 4,400 infantry. At Waterloo in 1815, Wellington had 21,000. By the summer of 1809 on land and sea, 786,000 men were serving – one in ten of the adult population. The government raised £1,500,000,000 from loans and taxes, while the national debt leapt from £242,900,000 in 1793 to £744,900,000 in 1815. Furthermore, almost all of this debt had been raised from British creditors. Up to the mid eighteenth century, foreign holdings, predominantly Dutch, amounted to around a fifth of the debt. By the 1780s it was only half as much and by 1807–10 only £20 million out of more than £500 million of government stock was held abroad.[18]

16. For Pitt's financial policy, see the recent generally approving survey of P.K. O'Brien, 'Public finance and the wars with France', pp. 165–85. Figures cited in E.J. Evans, *The Forging of the Modern State: Early Industrial Britain, 1783–1870*, Longman, 1983, pp. 24–5.

17. *Ibid.*, pp. 25–6; I.R. Christie, *Wars and Revolutions, Britain 1760–1815*, Arnold, 1982, pp. 187–8. For emphasis on importance and novelty of the Sinking Fund, see O'Brien, 'Public finance and the wars with France', pp. 175–6.

18. D.A. Jarrett, *Pitt the Younger*, Weidenfeld, 1974, pp. 99–101; C. Emsley, 'The impact of war and military participation on Britain and France, 1792–1815', in Emsley and J. Walvin (eds), *Artisans, Peasants and Proletarians 1760–1860*, Croom Helm, 1985, pp. 59–60; Dickson, *Financial Revolution*, pp. 322–3.

The only major crisis in public finance came in 1797. Up to then borrowing had not been difficult, although the cost was high. A 'loyalty loan' at the end of 1796 had produced a subscription of £18 million in less than sixteen hours. Problems were, however, building up. Loanable funds were not in total short supply, but the same growing and diversifying economy which could provide them also created competition from private borrowers and investors. One consequence was that Pitt had to float special government loans at high discounts, because he could not secure a sufficient sum from the 'market'. This would have commanded high interest rates but these might, on precedent, have been subsequently lowered. Thus by the beginning of 1797, discounting contributed to a situation in which the adding of £200,000,000 to the debt secured an effective loan of only £108,000,000.[19]

This was perhaps the most directly inflationary aspect of Pitt's financial management, and the bridging of the gap between income and expenditure was not helped by his stubbornly sticking to the idea of the Sinking Fund. It was now that the gold backing of the currency came under strain and, pushed over by fear of invasion, actually broke. The Bank of England in 1795 had held around £8 million in specie. Most of this made its way to the government, so that by February 1797 it had been run down to less than a sixth of this level. The arrival of a French fleet off Ireland brought a further request to the Bank for a loan of £1,500,000 to assist the Irish government. Increasing invasion paranoia had already started a withdrawing of specie from country banks, who in turn drew on London. So by the time an actual (although as it turned out farcical) landing took place in North Wales on 25 February, there was little gold in the chest to meet massive withdrawing.[20]

There was now little choice. The Privy Council on 26 February authorised the Bank to refuse cash payments, and the country banks had to follow suit by tendering Bank of England notes in the stead of gold. The suspension was initially to be rescinded within four months, but it was to be renewed up to 1821. That duration testifies to the substantial fact that for all the alarm the crisis produced, the British financial system had reached a level of sophistication and general confidence which enabled it to live through a moment which in earlier times would have seemed the harbinger of doom. Pitt's great parliamentary opponent, Charles James Fox and

19. Christie, *Wars and Revolutions, op.cit.,* p. 237.
20. Emsley, *British Society and the French Wars 1793–1815,* Macmillan, 1979, p. 57.

his supporters roundly condemned his profligacy in loans to foreign powers, an obvious but overestimated cause of gold drain, and accused him of bringing the country to the point of bankruptcy. Meanwhile, according to the *Annual Register*, petitions against the suspension of cash payments came in from all corners. That from the nobility, gentry, clergy, yeomanry and freeholders of Middlesex considered the action both illegal and arbitrary as well as threatening to the very concept of private property: 'the pretended necessity of reserving for the public service the specie deposited by individuals in the Bank . . . may be pleaded at any time, and applied, with equal reason, to any private property whatsoever'. In fact, as an eminent Scottish banker remarked looking back from seven years on, it was remarkable, 'after the first surprise and alarm was over, how quietly the country submitted, as they still do, to transact all business by means of bank notes for which the issuers give no specie'.[21]

At least two reasons account for this, besides general confidence. In the first place, although non-convertible bank notes may have been a new element, many – perhaps most – commercial transactions had long depended on paper bills rather than value-for-weight coin. In the second place, the Bank of England issued its paper money with a restraint which inflated the money supply steadily rather than drastically. A recent review of the period has concluded that the 'opportunities' presented by the Restriction Act, as it was known, were abused neither by the government nor by the Bank.[22]

Nevertheless, the events of 1797 suggested that there was a limit to public confidence, and contributed to a significant shift in the pattern of war finance. Of the extra revenue raised to fight wars from 1739 to 1783 the proportion obtained from taxation stayed at around 20 per cent; for the long French wars it was 58 per cent.[23] Most attention has been focused on Pitt's introduction of income tax in 1798–9, but indirect taxation also rose significantly. Those on luxuries such as carriages and servants were trebled in 1797. Sources of income and wealth had rapidly diversified as the economy developed over the long eighteenth century, so a graduated tax on incomes was a logical development to collect revenue from a merchant and manufacturing class which had hardly been as heavily burdened as either the landowners or the poor consumers. Pitt

---

21. *Ibid.*, pp. 57–8.
22. I.P.H. Duffy, 'The discount policy of the Bank of England during the suspension of cash payments, 1757–1821', *Econ. H.R.*, XXXV, 1, 1982, p. 69.
23. O'Brien, 'Political economy of British taxation', p. 4.

managed to collect only half of the £10 million he had anticipated in 1799, but better results were to be achieved when Henry Addington took over the Treasury and reshaped the taxation of incomes in his budgets of 1803 and 1804. At first Addington had linked the coming of peace in 1802 to the repeal of the hated tax which 'should not be left to rest on the shoulders of the public in times of peace, because it should be reserved for the more important occasions, which he trusted, would not soon recur'. The Treaty of Amiens in 1802 brought a brief peace, and by June 1803 Addington was again presenting a war budget. In that, and in his budget of 1804, the one-time tax repealer, in Professor Christie's words, 'far outdistanced' Pitt as a successful tax gatherer. He needed to. Not only was maintaining the British war effort imposing an ever-increasing burden, but subsidies to allies seriously inflated that burden. Of the total of £66 million, all but £9.2 million came after the Amiens interlude.[24]

Addington's form of income tax introduced the novel principle of deduction at source, which enabled much better anticipation of outcome than had Pitt's own assessments. His tax, known as a property tax, worked better because it realised that efficient assessment and collection were more important than raised levels. His top rate, on incomes of £150 or more, at a shilling in the pound was half that imposed by Pitt. On incomes between £150 and a threshold of £60, a graduated levy beginning at 3d was imposed. The wartime earnings of most skilled shipyard workers, for example, would have exceeded £60 a year, and with the Admiralty deducting at source and paying over to the Treasury, yields came much nearer to expectation. Deduction at source was hardly possible with other than government employees, nor on the recipients of rents and interest, but Addington's division of his tax into five schedules, A to E, was not only a major step in the direction of obtaining accurate assessments but remained the basis of income taxation into our own time. The five schedules were on: land and buildings; the produce of land; interest of fund-holders; profits from trades and professions and on salaries; and incomes from offices, annuities, pensions and stipends. The closeness of yields to estimates was impressive: an actual £4.76 over £4.5 million in 1803 and £4.9 over £4.8 million in 1804. Pitt had been a critic of both the principle of deduction at source and the rescheduling, but they proved their worth and he retained

24. Emsley, *British Society and the French Wars,* op.cit., pp. 93–4; Christie, *Wars and Revolutions,* op.cit., p. 262; Evans, *Forging of the Modern State,* p. 76.

them when it was his turn to present a budget in 1805. Addington, rather than the Younger Pitt, can therefore be regarded as the father of modern British taxation.[25]

To administer and collect income tax a new arm of administration had to be created comprising experts, officials and clerks: an 'army' which in terms of its efficiency and rapacity came to be the equal of the long-esteemed Excise. Indeed, it was the quality of the latter revenue department, as much as opposition to income taxation in principle, which had inclined eighteenth-century governments towards using indirect taxes on consumption alongside the traditional land tax. As we noted, Hanoverian wars had always, in the end, been financed by taxation; the novelty of the French war years was the attempt to defray the greater part of their cost from *present* rather than *deferred* revenues. We must now turn to examine the pattern of taxation upon which the success of public borrowing depended.

TAXATION

The Hanoverians inherited a system of taxation which was already shifting away from the taxes on land and immovable property that had provided almost half of government income under the later Stuarts. By 1793 they provided only a fifth. Thus, even before the arrival of income tax the relative role of the land tax was shrinking relative to that of indirect taxes. Only after Addington's budgets of the first decade of the nineteenth century did direct taxation, albeit in a much altered form, begin to recover its share.

In the beginning the land tax had itself been somewhat 'revolutionary'. Its granting by parliament in 1692 had meant that the king was no longer expected to 'live of his own' even in peacetime. Possibly, as Dr Beckett has suggested, nothing radical had been intended, but nevertheless high-yield, permanent direct taxation had come into being. It rapidly became a conservative fiscal base – an unchanging standby for governments unable to come up with alternative ways of assessing a national wealth that was not only growing but was substantially changing in form. Financial survival without pushing the burden of the land tax to intolerable levels was in fact possible though the milking of commercial expansion by indirect

25. Emsley, *British Society and the French Wars, op. cit.*, p. 106.

taxation. As Dr O'Brien has recently pointed out, in effect British governments between 1714 and 1815 constructed a revenue system from component parts which enabled them to increase tax revenues per head from Europe's most rapidly growing population much more successfully than the French from the end of the eighteenth century, despite having been less heavily taxed up to then.[26]

The main feature of this system was the relatively small and, on trend, declining proportion of public revenue which came from direct taxation. Although the land tax assessment could at times be stretched to include houses, windows, servants, hair powder, non-working horses, carriages and playing cards, and although in times of war the 10 per cent peacetime limit was pushed twice as far, there was no fundamental revaluation and in many parts of the country assessment levels were nominal. In political terms this failure forced heavy dependence on indirect revenue sources. A latent macro-economic effect was that the social groups most likely to save bore a relatively light burden – important, perhaps, for the financing of economic growth. Most forms of capital other than land escaped, while the real burden on land itself was, according to O'Brien and Mathias, 'light and diminishing'. If the doubled level of wartime was a more significant imposition, it was to a degree offset by greater farming profits.[27]

A worsening distribution of income in eighteenth-century England was hardly unrelated to the low tax burden on the richest groups, which was not high to begin with and which was to fall overall as the burden on consumption increased. Custom and excise revenue already formed 57 per cent of total tax income by 1750 and rose to more than 70 per cent before Addington's direct tax gathering of 1803–15 reduced it to 60 per cent. With the ending of income tax after 1815, indirect sources yet again rose above 70 per cent. Of the two sources, excise revenues outweighed those from customs duties by a usual ratio of 2 : 1. While stamp duties of various kinds played a useful role in wartime, especially when they could be attached to particular loans, their total importance was slight. The excise fell heavily on the production and consumption of alcohol: on home-produced spirits, beer, malt and hops. Walpole in the mid 1730s was deriving as much as a third of the annual

26. J.V. Beckett, 'Land tax or excise? The levying of taxation in seventeenth and eighteenth-century England', *English Hist. Rev.* C, 1985, p. 286; O'Brien, 'Political economy of taxation' pp. 4–7.

27. *Ibid.*, pp. 18ff; Mathias and O'Brien, 'Taxation in England and France', p. 616.

revenue of £4.5 million secured from indirect taxation from malt and beer. By 1760–5 these two were providing £3 million out of £4.8 million, and by 1800 £4.6 million out of £11 million. In addition, import duties were levied on wines. As O'Brien points out, in many years of the eighteenth century the nation's drinkers were the single most important sustainers of public revenue.[28]

As well as these taxes, the consuming masses paid excise on bricks, starch, glass, salt, printed fabrics, paper, soap, candles, leather and, in London, coal. Customs duties on imported alcohol were producing more than 60 per cent of a total duty yield of £7 million in 1800, although this was in part because Pitt's reforms had cut the duties on tea. Other import duties fell on sugar, tobacco, timber, silk, iron bars and, in some years, grain. Indirect taxation was usually regressive in effect, the more so since the households of the rich were commonly self-suppliers of some excisable goods, such as beer. Tax gatherers and political economists usually subscribed to a rhetoric of taxing 'luxuries', but sufficient aggregate yields can hardly be secured from imposing only on the consuming habits of the well-to-do. The net has to draw in a least some widely consumed articles: gin and beer, the 'curses of the working classes', had to be included alongside wines and fine brandy. Silk, especially after the revolution in the supply and cheapness of cotton, was a luxury, but tobacco was widely indulged in. Salt was a necessity, tea and sugar rapidly becoming so. If not necessities, soap and candles were at least 'decencies'. Increasing the cost of bricks, timber and glass did not do much to lift the housing standards of the poor.[29]

Stamp duties, which did fall on the luxury consumption of the better-off, made up only 13 per cent of indirect taxation in 1800 and less than half as much of total revenue. In general there appears little to challenge the important conclusion of Mathias and O'Brien that the main economic incidence of British taxation was on the level of effective demand, for the majority of the taxpayers were not savers. Just what macro-economic inference is drawn from this depends on the relative importance ascribed to supply and demand in explanations of the increased growth of the economy after mid century. The main point to be taken, however, is that by then, even if not yet dramatic, the growth of the economy was strong enough for per capita tax yield to rise with the growing population. This was the permissive factor which allowed the military needs of

28.   *Ibid.*, pp. 617–18.
29.   O'Brien, 'Political economy of taxation', pp. 12–13.

Table 9.3 Sources of taxation, 1665–1810

Five-year averages centring on	Excises and stamps levied on domestic productions and services		Customs duties levied on retained imports		Direct taxes levied on manifestations of wealth and income	
	£m	%	£m	%	£m	%
1665	0.3	23	0.4	31	0.6	46
1670	0.2	14	0.2	14	1.0	72
1675	0.5	31	0.5	31	0.6	38
1680	0.4	28	0.5	36	0.5	36
1685	0.4	36	0.6	55	0.1	9
1690	0.9	30	0.7	23	1.4	47
1695	0.8	27	0.8	27	1.4	47
1700	1.7	35	1.2	25	1.9	40
1705	1.8	34	1.5	28	2.0	38
1710	1.9	36	1.3	25	2.1	40
1715	2.4	44	1.5	28	1.5	28
1720	2.8	46	1.7	28	1.6	26
1725	3.1	53	1.6	27	1.2	20
1730	3.0	49	1.6	26	1.5	25
1735	3.2	55	1.6	28	1.0	17
1740	3.2	52	1.5	24	1.5	24
1745	3.1	48	1.3	20	2.1	32
1750	3.5	51	1.4	20	2.0	29
1755	3.8	54	1.7	24	1.5	21
1760	4.1	49	1.9	23	2.3	28
1765	5.5	55	2.2	22	2.3	23
1770	6.0	57	2.6	25	1.9	18
1775	6.3	58	2.6	24	1.9	18
1780	6.6	56	2.6	22	2.6	22
1785	7.8	57	3.3	24	2.7	20
1790	7.5	43	6.3	36	3.6	21
1795	8.9	44	7.2	36	4.0	20
1800	11.5	36	11.5	36	8.8	28
1805	19.4	41	16.4	35	11.2	24
1810	22.9	36	18.8	30	21.2	34

Notes: Where possible the figures refer to net receipts available for expenditure by the central government. They are five-year averages rounded to the nearest £100,000. Minor branches of taxation (including post office, hawkers and peddlers, hackney coaches, alienation, first fruits and tenths, salaries and pensions, etc.) have not been included.

Source: P.K. O'Brien, 'The political economy of British taxation.' *Econ. H.R.*, XLI, 1988.

Table 9.4 The burden of taxation: France and Britain

	France, 1715–1808			Britain, 1715–1812	
Year circa	Tax revenue per head in livres at prices of 1721–45 Index 1715 = 100		Year circa	Tax revenue per head in £. at prices of 1700 (4 + 5) Index 1715 = 100	
1715	7.1	100	1715	0.82	100
1725	8.8	124	1720	0.90	110
1730	9.2	130	1725	0.83	101
1735	11.0	155	1730	0.93	113
1740	8.8	124	1735	0.89	109
1745	10.2	144	1740	0.82	100
1750	8.1	114	1745	1.02	124
1755	9.5	134	1750	1.00	122
1765	9.8	138	1755	0.90	110
1770	7.5	106	1760	1.08	132
1775	8.8	124	1765	1.05	128
1780	10.3	145	1770	1.03	126
1785	9.4	132	1775	0.96	117
1790–1	10.6	149	1780	1.11	135
1803–4	10.8	152	1785	1.18	144
1807–8	13.7	193	1790	1.36	166
			1800	1.45	177
			1803–12	2.12	259

Source: P. Mathias and P.K. O'Brien, 'Taxation in Britain and France, 1715–1810.' *Journal of European Economic History*, V, 1975, pp. 604–5.

the state to be met from the indirect taxation of a wide range of consumer goods, which in turn funded the wartime borrowing needs of a country taking an increasing part in the state system of Europe.[30]

Within indirect taxation there were sound reasons for favouring excise over customs duties. The most important of these, the sheer efficiency of collection, was also the reason why Walpole found such political and popular resistance in trying to move towards an excise-based system, although over the century most of the commodities he would have included in his general excise did find their way into its embrace. By 1780 the Excise had watch over 33,000 brewers and

30. Mathias and O'Brien, 'Taxation in England and France', pp. 621–3.

victuallers, 36,000 publicans, 35,500 tea and coffee dealers and several thousand chandlers, as well as smaller numbers in such trades as calico printing and paper making. By the end of the American war its establishment, which had been 2,738 in 1714, had risen to 4,910 – twice as large as the rest of the financial administration. Backed by summary jurisdiction applied by local justices in the provinces and by the excise commissioners in London, its ability to secure conviction against evaders was, by eighteenth-century standards, astonishing. In 1789–90 the conviction rate in London was 79 per cent and in the provinces 85 per cent. No wonder the great common lawyer Blackstone was of the opinion that 'the rigour and arbitrary proceedings of excise laws seem hardly compatible with the temper of a free nation'.[31]

Be that as it may, the efficiency of the Customs service was much less regarded. That department was less professional, more full of placemen and more frequently evidenced corruption and bribery. Apart from this, its task of dealing with widespread coastal smuggling was very much harder than that of the Excise in detecting inland evasion. Furthermore, while economic historians might assess in retrospect the effects of excise on levels of consumption, or by implication on the level of savings, customs duties in their own time were never seen solely from the point of view of the revenue but always as an important instrument of economic regulation. From the time of Walpole they developed into a system of encouraging home manufactures and food producers while disadvantaging competitors. Indeed, as the path of economic development over the eighteenth century moved the composition of retained imports away from manufactured goods towards raw materials, the possibility of increasing revenue without harming the productive side of the economy narrowed steadily. Reforms, like those carried out by the Younger Pitt, were impressive in their own terms but could do little to diminish the greater role of the Excise.[32]

Taxation can be redistributive without being progressive. That is to say, it can merely shift income from one better-off section to another. When eighteenth-century gentlemen complained that the landed classes were being taxed to the gain of others, it was not the poorer classes they had in mind. The process was perceived as a simple one. The government taxed to finance the national debt,

31. Data and quotation from Brewer, *Sinews of Power*, pp. 102–14.
32. O'Brien, 'Political economy of taxation', pp. 23–6.

which debt was held by the new upstart class of City men and merchants. As one jaundiced critic put it in 1733: 'A set of brocaded
tradesmen cloathed in purple and fine linen, and faring sumptuous-
ly every day, raising to themselves immense wealth, so as to marry
their daughters to the first rank, and leave their sons such estates as
to enable them to live in the same degree.'[33]

In 1757 Postlethwayt went so far as to argue that the national
debt had had the effect of transferring property to the 'money-mon-
gers' at such a pace that, 'Since our debts have taken place, not
near one tenth of the land of England is possessed by the posterity
or heirs of those who possessed it at the Revolution.' He went further: with the rise in *dealing* in government stock, true merchants
were changing into something else.

> . . . while Men's Heads are busied with the arts of money-jobbing
> between the Exchange and the Exchequer, they will be drawn off from
> the solid arts of honourable traffic; which alone can prove nationally
> and permanently lucrative. But if we convert our traders into
> stock-jobbers, who is to carry on the commerce of the kingdom?[34]

Hyperbolic perhaps, but Dr Dickson's analysis of the structure of
debt holding confirms that some degree of transfer from taxpaying
land-holders to a class of debt-holding financiers was a characteristic
of the public finance system. It was qualified by the extent that financial gains found their way back into land, and by the role that
stock holding played in providing a source of secure income for
pensioners, widows and orphans (the Court of Chancery was one of
the largest holders). Landed proprietors generally did not much invest in the funds, although some individual peers had substantial
holdings. In the mid eighteenth century only 10 per cent of holders
lived outside the Home Counties, the majority of ordinary holders
being members of the London bourgeoisie or petit bourgeoisie:
merchants, bankers, brokers, jobbers, clergymen, doctors, lawyers,
shopkeepers, artisans and sometimes even servants. Dr Dickson, on
whose research our knowledge of the structure of debt holding depends, has analysed the pattern for Bank of England, South Sea,
East India and government 4 per cent stock around the time of
Pelham's reduction of interest in 1749–50. There were around
30,000 public creditors. Holders of less than £500 formed around
21 per cent of the total number of accounts in both Bank and East
India stock, 38 per cent of holders of the 4 per cent stock and more

---

33. Dickson, *Financial Revolution*, p. 27.
34. Postlethwayt, *Great Britain's True System, op.cit.*, p. 21.

than half of the holders of South Sea stock, but in all four cases this group held less than 10 per cent of the total stock. Holders of £500 to £1,000 worth formed 31.4 per cent of the East India stock holders, 22.9 per cent of the Bank's, 18 per cent of the South Sea Company's and 19 per cent of the 4 per cent's. The proportion of stock they held was, respectively 11.5 per cent, 6.3 per cent, 10.2 per cent and 7.7 per cent. Much more significant in this respect were holders of £1,000 to £5,000, who held respectively 42 per cent, 47.5 per cent, 25.8 per cent and 35.4 per cent of accounts in proportions of 50, 42.8, 41.8 and 43.3 per cent of stock. At the top of the scale those whose holdings exceeded £5,000 formed from 3.5 to 8.1 per cent of account holders but held from 35 to 48.5 per cent of total stock. Dickson concludes that: 'Tory fears of the great world of wealth and influence, which they hated with the intensity of the excluded, were based on something more solid than ignorance and prejudice.'[35] If there was a redistributive aspect to funding of the national debt and its associated taxation, it was largely one which operated within the ranks of the better-off. The redistributive aspects of *local* taxation, however, were quite different.

Although the statistics are hardly firm, it would seem that by the end of the eighteenth century county rates, used mostly for gaols, criminal prosecution, constables and, to a smaller extent, bridge repair, aggregated only around £300,000, but the levying of the *parish* rate for the relief of the poor was of much greater import. Here, as Professor Mathias has pointed out, aggregated receipts were at levels comparable to those of the government for civil expenditure. Just under £750,000 in the mid eighteenth century, they rose through £5.3 million in 1803 to more than £8 million by 1813.[36] As population grew and harvests failed more often, attitudes towards the rate-receiving poor hardened, especially after the food crisis of 1795–6 when even firmly rising rents were outpaced by the soaring poor rate. Landlords not only were assessed on their directly occupied land but were constantly calling for relief for tenants, for whom increasing poor rates were setting a ceiling for rents. Contemporaries such as Joseph Townshend who, in his *Dissertation on the Poor Laws* in 1786, referred to the poor rate throughout as a tax, were in no doubt that the landed interest, from landlords through the gentry to large and smaller tenants and owners, bore the main brunt of the poor rate: 'Monied men have greatly the advantage

35. Dickson, *Financial Revolution*, pp. 290–8.
36. Mathias, *First Industrial Nation*, p. 46.

over the owners and occupiers of land, as being free from those heavy taxes, which the latter pay to the King, to the church, and to the poor.'[37]

At no time was this 'advantage' more glaring than when putting-out capitalists contracted or suspended their activities in rural manufacturing districts, throwing workers on to the parishes. It seems reasonable to accept the contemporary view that in rural England, albeit with much variation in the pattern between parishes, a significant transfer of income took place towards the poorer members of society. The view, increasingly held, that the pre-1834 Poor Law was a far from ineffective mechanism in this respect, rests on the recognition that until the sums needed for relief inflated so hugely in the later eighteenth century and especially after the crisis of the mid 1790s, extreme disgruntlement was not often expressed, as a sense of community support and involvement led to a fairly general acceptance of the obligation which rested on the better-off. It rests also on the insight that income 'transferred' by this means was not used only for the minimum relief of destitution, for the old, widowed, orphaned and infirm, but also for the purchase of some 'decencies', for the supplementation of the earnings of the under-employed as well as the relief of the involuntarily unemployed, and for the apprenticing of the children of the poor. There is strength in the argument that poor rates, viewed as a form of local taxation, were wholly different from national taxation in their redistributive effects.

INSURANCE, BANKING AND CURRENCY

Insurance is one of the longest established of British financial activities. Its marine branch was developed in the sixteenth century, although Lloyd's Coffee House became its focus only from 1698, producing its first 'List' in 1734 and its Register from the 1750s. Odd instances of life insurance contracts have been found from the same period, while fire insurance was known in seventeenth-century London. In the period following the Great Fire of London in 1666 several companies were floated, but the real expansion came with the increase in urbanisation of the late eighteenth and early nine-

---

37. Joseph Townshend, *A Dissertation on the Poor Laws*, 1786, reprinted University of California Press, Berkeley, 1971, p. 31.

teenth centuries. The sums involved in fire insurance quadrupled between the mid 1780s and the late 1820s. This branch was controlled by incorporated companies based in London – a dominance still marked in the first decade of the nineteenth century when City-based firms were responsible for 90 per cent of sums insured. In 1806 a handful of major companies – the Sun Fire Office (1710), the Royal Exchange Assurance (1721) and the Phoenix Fire Office (1782) – between them still transacted 60 per cent of fire insurance. According to the leading present-day authority on this sector, Professor Supple, it was over the course of the eighteenth century that it assumed its modern form and structure, with agencies and branches, inter-company coordination of premium rates and policy conditions, and averaging of claims.[38]

Life insurance developed alongside, but did not really take on its modern form until the last decades of the eighteenth century. Policies were issued from the 1720s by both Royal Exchange Assurance and the London Assurance – the only two survivors of the South Sea Bubble – but these were few in number, rarely issued for more than a year at a time and based on uniform rather than on age-related premiums. Supple considers the modern form to have originated with the Society for Equitable Assurances on Lives and Survivorships in 1762, but its example was not followed by the Royal Exchange for another twenty years and only two new life companies were formed before 1800. Indeed, in insurance the eighteenth century was generally a period of establishment rather than of rapid growth. The inflationary stimulus of the war saw the promotion of fifteen offices between 1793 and 1815, but twenty-nine were to come into existence between 1815 and 1830 and fifty-six between 1830 and 1844.[39]

The underwriting activities of insurance companies are important in both economic and social contexts, but their link with the financial revolution lies in the raising of investment funds. Like the Bank of England and the great chartered companies, the London Assurance Company and the Royal Exchange Assurance Company received their monopoly status in 1720 in return for lending considerable sums to the government. These companies and others, such as the Sun Fire Office, through their accumulated resources became major sources of investment. Sun Fire around 1800 had an

38. B. Supple, 'Insurance in British history' in O.M. Westall, *The Historian and the Business of Insurance*, Manchester UP, 1984, pp. 3–6.

39. C. Wilson, *England's Apprenticeship*, pp. 334–5; Supple, 'Insurance in British history', *op. cit.*, p. 5.

investment income of £30,000 per annum compared with under-writing profits of £12,000. It also held East Indian bonds, and the fact that it gave substantial mortgages on land has led Dickson to suggest that to an extent it was diverting funds derived from indus-try and trade towards the landed interest. Certainly insurance com-panies, however widespread their operations may have become, were in important respects City institutions. As late as 1790, less than a fifth of shareholders in Sun Fire lived in the provinces.[40]

The setting up of the Bank of England in 1694 was a major step in the foundation of a sound system of public credit, but the sec-ondary effects of its establishment were at least as important for the development of the eighteenth-century economy. As Professor Deane has put it, there took place, mainly in the first half of the century, 'a series of developments in the money market, an expan-sion in the number, range and efficiency of English financial in-stitutions which amounted in all to a financial revolution'. Key elements of the financial system grew up around the Bank, such as insurance, partnership banks, chartered trading companies and the Stock Exchange. What the Bank got in return for its public lending services were paper assets which ranged from Exchequer and Navy bills to longer-term consolidated stocks. With these it 'further lubri-cated the channels linking savings and investment by creating a large stock of negotiable paper assets which new savers could buy whenever existing lenders wanted to realise their loans'. At the same time the Bank took the lead in securing regular deposits suffi-cient both to underwrite and to secure and expand private credit. Not only this, for the trusted promissory notes of the Bank easily became a form of paper money. With the establishment of a safe market in claims to money and credit, a large and expandable stock of liquid assets was fed into the economy, easing transactions and short-term trade credit.[41] In short, as Dickson has put it, the rise of a regular security market in London had the effect of 'making debts that were permanent for the state, liquid for the individual'. Trusted paper became both a collateral for short-term credit and an immensely important medium of exchange. The issuing of cheques or bank notes on the security of withdrawable deposits enabled the creation of a paper currency which was central to the financial rev-olution and crucial for the growth of commerce and manufactur-ing. What emerged over the first half of the century was a financial

40. Lee, *British Economy since 1700*, pp. 58–9; Dickson, *Financial Revolution*, p. 292.
41. P. Deane, *First Industrial Revolution*, pp. 183–5.

system which, if limited by comparison with what was to develop over the next two centuries, was capable of mobilising substantial funds and of providing most of the essential services needed by a diversifying economy growing both in output and in sophistication.[42]

Whether it is appropriate to talk of a 'national banking system' by the mid eighteenth century is debatable. Certainly one was emerging, and its embryonic form was increasingly dominated by London. This tendency, as Professor Joslin pointed out, accelerated once the landed classes came to appreciate both the security and the convenience of lodging a substantial part of their incomes with London banks. This flow was paralleled by remittances to the City of customs and tax revenues from the district collectors. As well as the clear dominance of overseas and inland trade by London, it was becoming increasingly common for transactions between separate provincial places to be effected through it. In important respects, however, the Bank remained, as Clapham termed it, the 'Bank of London'. In terms of note issue, for instance, its volume was more than equalled by that from country banks, although this in part reflected its own increasing specialisation in discounting.[43]

The number of institutions in London which can reasonably be considered private banks seems to have doubled in the fifty years between 1725 and 1775 to reach fifty-two. Some of these were small; others like Childs, Hoare, and Barclay, were to become major names in the world of finance. All must be presumed to have been somewhat limited in potential, for the Bank of England's sole right to joint-stock banking constrained the others into the 'partnership' form. The Bank, however, hardly competed vigorously for private accounts before mid century. Its holdings were dominated by the great trading companies, especially the East India Company. In any case, the clear separation of *the* Bank from all others was well enough indicated by Lord North in 1781 when he referred to it as 'a part of the constitution' and 'to all intents and purposes the public exchequer'. As well as its management of the floating debt, it had increasingly taken over the handling of the service payments on the funded debt, and it held the balances of many departments of state as well as of provincial tax gatherers. In the private sector its notes were the main medium of exchange for London transactions;

42. Dickson, *Financial Revolution*, p. 457.
43. D.M. Joslin, 'London's private bankers', pp. 340–1, 348; T.S. Ashton, *An Economic History of England*, p. 179.

circulation reached £6 million in 1785, backed by a sizeable fraction of the country's bullion stock.[44]

The banks who held the great majority of private accounts were divided by Joslin into two groups. The first, in the West End, had as its clients the peerage and gentry rather than the mercantile classes. These depositors were less likely to make sudden substantial withdrawals, which allowed for lower cash reserves: profit without risk, especially since lendings were usually secured on land mortgage. Banks like Childs and Hoares received the rents from the estates, made investments in stocks and collected dividends for their landed clients. It may have been this group Professor Ashton had in mind when he drew attention to the way in which London banks played a role in making available the 'savings of agriculturalists' to provide 'much of the investment in manufacture'. It seems more likely, however, that the banks who received income from the landed re-lent within that class and contributed more to agricultural than industrial progress. In so far as they purchased stocks for their clients, that was, if an important redirection of resources, hardly an immediate switch between sectors.[45]

If we view this group as 'conservative', the same is not true of the distinct world of the Lombard Street banks whose depositors were the true mercantile and financier groups of the City. Yet after 1750 this group came to acquire a special connection with the provinces through its links with the country banks. Increasingly these came to employ London banking houses as agents to honour their bills drawn on London and to cash their notes payable in the City, either investing the realised funds or remitting cash into the country. The London banker either charged a commission or profited from the use of his clients' cash deposits. It was the City banks with mercantile connections, rather than the West End houses used by the landed classes, who moved into this relationship – less surprising than it seems, for, as Joslin pointed out, the country banks had themselves most often grown from country merchant or manufacturing activities. A list of 1797 provides the information that the 25 per cent of London's banks who did not act as agent to even one country bank included most of those in the West End but only a few of the older of the Lombard Street group. Most of the latter group's banks did so act, some holding as many as ten agencies. Of these extreme pluralists, only Barclay's had been established before the banking boom of 1769–73. It is clear, then, that

44. Joslin, 'London's private bankers', pp. 346–8.
45. *Ibid.*, pp. 348–55; Ashton, *An Economic History of England*, p. 185.

the independent rise of country banking had, after about 1770, a major impact on the structure of London banking, bringing a new and risky business which needed greater commercial knowledge and expertise. A clear symbol of the growth of a banking *system* was the establishment in 1773 of the London Clearing House to cope with the huge increase in inter-bank payments. Thirty-one out of thirty-six City banks joined in this key venture and it was also from their group that the practice of banks holding accounts at the Bank of England and re-discounting through it developed towards the end of the century. This looked forward to the main role of the Bank as the bankers' bank and, eventually, to the normal settling of inter-bank debts through it.[46]

The relationship of the development of London banking to the industrial revolution must be sought in the interactions of the macro-economy rather than directly. Historians have, however, been shown to have underestimated the role in this respect of the country banks. Ashton pointed out that the late rise of formal banking in the country was due in part to the fact that it grew naturally out of the financial activities of men who 'were content to describe themselves simply as merchants or traders, retailers or even innkeepers'. To his list we could add attorneys and even local receivers of taxes, six of whom appear in a list of country bankers drawn up in 1784. Later manufacturers such as Matthew Boulton entered the ranks, though at the same time being himself, through his close involvement with Cornish mining, an account holder with Elliot and Praed of Truro, whose rise and activities were closely linked to that industry. If country banks were a product of the latter half of the eighteenth century, country *banking* functionally defined has a longer history, despite the fact that only a dozen institutions formally known as banks were in existence before 1750. A list of 1797 records 334, which number had doubled by 1810. Like their London counterparts, their institutional and individual development was limited by the Bank of England's monopoly of the joint-stock form.[47]

In rural districts the banks' main purpose was the receiving of bills brought in by local traders and farmers. These were sometimes directly discounted for coin or notes but, as we have seen, were increasingly sent on to the London agent for collection. Demand for funds was more likely to exceed supply in manufacturing dis-

46. Joslin, 'London's private bankers', pp. 355–7.
47. Ashton, *An Economic History of England*, pp. 180–3.

tricts, and country banks in this situation drew on their correspond-ents in the City by sending in immature bills. As Ashton has pointed out, to the extent that the London recipients discounted these from the balances of rural banks, capital was being moved from areas of oversupply to those of greater demand.[48]

Many country banks lent in their own notes, but others did so only in coin or in Bank of England notes or bills and drafts. Most of those in rural districts were note issuers, as we know urban banks in Newcastle, Norwich, Bristol, Sheffield and Birmingham to have been. It seems, however, that few notes were issued in Lancashire and in parts of the West Riding. More favoured here was the use of promissory notes and bills of exchange in large volume and down to low denominations. Indeed, until acts of 1775 and 1777 intro-duced bottom limits of £1 and £5 respectively, some north-western manufacturers issued promissory notes to facilitate the payment of wages for denominations as low as a shilling. These were taken by local retailers, who accumulated them for exchange against larger bills drawn on London.[49]

Currency

In Fielding's *Tom Jones* a poor beggarman who finds a pocket-book is at first well pleased with his reward of a golden guinea, until he learns that the piece of paper it contained was a bill for £100, which 'a Jew would have jumped to purchase . . . at five shillings less than £100'. Bemoaning his ignorance, the beggar curses his par-ents: ' "for had they", says he, "sent me to charity-school to learn to read and write and cast accounts, I should have known the value of these matters as well as other people".' The episode is a double reminder: firstly of the fact that in an age when the propertied had a not unreasonable fear of highwaymen and footpads, bills repre-sented security in more than one sense; secondly, that however im-pressive historians may find the range of accepted paper in use in the eighteenth-century economy, for the bulk of the population money still meant coin, and that was short in quantity and poor in quality.

In principle the eighteenth-century pound sterling was, as its name implies, based on silver. The problem was in maintaining both an adequate supply and a full face value. With the Mint paying

48. *Ibid.*, pp. 184–5.
49. *Ibid.*, pp. 185–7.

less for silver than it would fetch abroad, especially in the Far East but also in Holland, Norway, Denmark and Sweden, new coins of the great recoinage of 1696–8 had soon disappeared from circulation. By the mid eighteenth century there was little silver coin in circulation except for a quantity of worn shillings and sixpences. In effect England was by then on the gold standard with the guinea better esteemed than the twenty-one shillings it officially represented, although gold was not formally declared the standard until 1816.[50]

Complaints both of an absolute shortage of coin, especially of small denomination, and of the deficiency in weight of those that remained in circulation were frequent, bitter and widespread. When the government first faced up to this problem in 1717, on the advice of Sir Isaac Newton, it decided to lower the silver price of gold by reducing the guinea from 21s 6d in silver to 21s and prohibit the payment or receipt of gold coins at any higher rate. However, although this restored the ratio of exchange to general European levels, it was still above that of the Far East, so exportable silver bullion still brought a premium over silver bought for coinage, allowing a profit still to be made from importing gold, turning it into guineas and exchanging these for silver coin which could be melted and sent abroad. The inefficiency of the Mint, with the monopoly of coining bullion, is a potent reminder that not all the institutions of the eighteenth-century 'City' operated efficiently and assisted economic development. Undervaluation not only led to an export of silver, it also discouraged its import for coining. From 1717 to 1760 only £500,000 worth of silver was offered to the Mint, and during the last forty years of the century only negligible amounts were coined. The rising population of a leading commercial economy had, in the words of T.S. Ashton, 'to make shift with shapeless and debased pieces'. Without doubt the shortage of silver coin was both a major handicap to the retail trade and a burden that the wage-earning population had especially to bear. It was remarked in 1759 that bankers commonly offered a premium for silver coin so as to be able to meet the demands of their customers, which were especially high at harvest time when wage bills were at their peak.[51]

50. For the coinage, see Ashton, *An Economic History of England*, pp. 167–77, and J. Styles, 'Our traitorous money makers: the Yorkshire coiners and the law, 1760–82' in J. Brewer and J. Styles (eds), *An Ungovernable People. The English and their law in the seventeenth and eighteenth centuries*, Hutchinson, 1980, pp. 172–7.

51. *Ibid.*, p. 176.

By the 1770s even the supply of gold guineas and half-guineas was being diminished as merchants and manufacturers selected the heavier coins for sale to bullion dealers and exchange brokers. At this point Adam Smith summed up the failure of the Mint: 'The mint was employed, not so much in making daily additions to the coin, as in replacing the very best part of it which was daily melted down.'[52]

Sweating down and clipping were widespread, so that the gold coins which were in circulation were commonly deficient in weight. In 1773 £16,500,000 worth were called in and replaced with new full-weight coins. How long these might have survived is unclear, for the outbreak of the great wars with America and then revolutionary France raised the prices of bullion to irresistible heights. Of even greater concern was the poor state of the coins used in everyday small transactions. Copper halfpennies and farthings had an official approximation to face value as legal tender for sums below sixpence, but had become so deficient that traders accepted them only by weight. Despite the growth of cash transactions of the population and of the waged labour force, no new copper coins were minted between 1754 and 1794 except for a small issue in 1771–5. The new technologies of Matthew Boulton at Birmingham were employed by the government from 1797 to produce new copper coins of twopence, a penny, a halfpenny and a farthing of such a good approximation to face value that the penny served as an ounce weight. The end of the 1790s, however, brought a rise in the price of copper of sufficient magnitude to produce an official enquiry, and the twopenny and penny coins were melted into the fate which awaits all coins whose metal content significantly exceeds their face value. A new and lighter issue in 1806 met the same fate as the price of copper rose yet again, and from 1807 no new copper coins were minted until 1821.[53]

How did the everyday economy cope with such a dearth of usable coin? In parts of the north and west the shortage of coin was especially acute and merchants were said to waste much time riding in search of small coin to pay their manufacturing workers. There was much settlement in kind, often bitterly resented by the recipient. Long pay periods became common, with some miners and manufacturing workers being paid monthly. Samuel Oldknow paid his poor spinners fortnightly in coin, but his better-off employees were

52. Smith, *Wealth of Nations*, II, p. 60
53. Ashton, *An Economic History of England*, p. 173.

paid monthly and in bills from which local shopkeepers deducted threepence in the pound for conversion. The bills he drew up on his own shop, set up in 1793, seem to have attained the status of a local currency and were passed from hand to hand. The ironmaster John Wilkinson even bought up supplies of the depreciated paper money of the French Revolution and used them, after countersigning by his clerk. This was soon prohibited, but in 1797, when a ban on the issue of small bills was lifted, he began to print cards for amounts as small as threepence and paid in these. Other manufacturers issued token coins, although this had been technically illegal since 1672. Both John Wilkinson and the copper magnate Thomas Williams produced copper coins for local circulation, some of which were actually bought for their use by other manufacturers. So many manufacturers produced token coins that by 1792 the country was said to have been 'flooded' with this unofficial local currency – for that is what it sometimes amounted to when large numbers circulated widely without ever being presented for redemption. The practice was ended in 1821, but it is hard to deny that improvised currencies played a crucial part in permitting the everyday economy to continue functioning. Doubtless forgers and clippers helped too at a time when, as Ashton put it, 'England was short of hard money and labour was underemployed.'[54]

Some historians have tended to take rather literally the designation 'service' sector and in examining its growth have accorded it little autonomy. At times, like Ashton, they tend to see the success of the service sector evidenced largely in its permissive relationship to the growth of physical output; in short, the 'financial revolution' is viewed as one of the preconditions for the 'industrial revolution'. Other historians see the growth of a service sector as an outcome of the greater national wealth, for which manufacturing is given the main credit, while yet another approach singles out financial services and esteems their success in providing the level of public borrowing necessary for British success in the international power game. Dr Lee has recently suggested that neglect of the service sector is 'one of the curiosities of historiography of British economic development'. However, it is perhaps not so much a matter of absolute neglect as one of persisting to see its role as ancillary or derivative.[55]

54. *Ibid.*, pp. 174–6, 186. For token coins generally, see Mathias, 'The people's money in the eighteenth century: the Royal Mint, trade tokens and the economy' in P. Mathias, *The Transformation of England*, Methuen, 1979, pp. 190–208.

55. Lee, *British Economy since 1700*, p. 98

Crafts has shown that only over the first three decades of the nineteenth century and in the period between the two world wars of the twentieth century was the contribution of the service sector to national income growth below that of manufacturing. Over the eighteenth century the service sector was consistently comparable in its contribution to aggregate growth. While this does not necessarily point to an autonomous contribution, the later dependence of the British economy on 'invisible' earnings to balance international payments suggests that the role of the service sector, most especially of its financial component, may have been undervalued. The recent textbook by Dr Lee is an attempt to redress this.[56]

Linkages are not to be denied nor undervalued, but there was already coming into existence in the eighteenth century a metropolitan economy which 'represented not only a structurally different type of economy, as well as a geographically separate one from the industrial regions, but in terms of size and wealth was probably the greater'. It is reasonable to suppose that the demonstration by Rubenstein and others that it was in this 'economy', rather than by manufacturers, that the greatest fortunes were made in the nineteenth century holds at least partly true for much of the eighteenth. The service sector was not in any sense purely a dependent one.

> The service sector was able to respond to a number of very potent sources of demand in both the eighteenth and the nineteenth centuries. The growth of the City of London as a major European financial centre in the eighteenth century, developing into the major international financial centre in the Victorian period, was the most obvious stimulus to such growth.[57]

Britain became the workshop of the world in the nineteenth century. She also became its insurer, banker, commodity broker, and easily its single most important overseas investor. There was clearly a degree of interdependence between the two roles, but equally there was still room for a significant autonomous financial function.

---

56. N.F.R. Crafts, *British Economic Growth during the Industrial Revolution*, pp. 34–5.

57. Lee, *British Economy since 1700*, p. 103. For the pattern of wealth-holding in Britain, see W.D. Rubenstein, 'Wealth, elites and the class structure of modern Britain', *Past and Present*, **76**, 1977, pp. 99–126.

CHAPTER TEN

The Vital Century?

The hundred years separating the Hanoverian succession from Waterloo witnessed changes which in the economic sphere at least were more profound and significant than those which can be located in any earlier period of similar length. These may have been dwarfed by the huge changes associated with the triumphant industrial capitalism of the nineteenth century, but many were anticipated or even set in train during the 'vital century'. Scholars will not cease arguing as to whether these changes amounted to a 'transformation' or marked the 'transition to the modern world', but their cumulative and ultimately determining impact is hard to deny. By 1815, having doubled its population, England had the demographic base for industrialisation, which it had not had in 1714. Even if revised estimates of its ability to outpace that population surge with growing output suggest a more faltering performance at the end of the eighteenth century, it cannot be denied that the onset of rapid demographic increase after about 1750 did not, in the event, turn out to be yet another optimistic start destined to crash into a Malthusian trap. Estimates of agricultural output confirm that by the end of the century England could not feed herself to the level and standard the population expected, but she nearly could. That in itself was an achievement when mouths had doubled while the proportion of the occupied population engaged in agriculture had fallen to a third. Such an occupational structure was hardly the European norm; in France a third of the population still farmed in 1914. The significance of the fact that Britain was already dependent on exchanging manufactured products for food imports by 1815 and yet had exported grain up to the mid eighteenth century is surely an historical turning point to note.

Economic development was underwritten by a major infrastructural extension and modernisation in transport. So marked was this, and so impressive the improvement in speed and reliability, that contemporaries spoke of a 'revolution' in transport. They would have been even more astonished had they been able to see what the railways were to offer. But the impact of the turnpikes and the canals was real enough – so much so that when the railways came to nineteenth-century Britain, they did not *provide* the industrial map but fitted into it.

In concluding his classic study *The Industrial Revolution in the Eighteenth Century*, Paul Mantoux was not so carried away as to see its accomplishment by 1800, but he did consider that the transition to industrial society was well under way.

> Nevertheless the modern industrial system did already exist with all its essential features, and it is possible to detect in the developments which had taken place at that time the main characteristics of the great change. . . . We know that there were machines before the era of machinery, 'manufacture' before the formation of industrial capitalism and of the 'factory proletariat'. But in the slow-moving mass of society a new element does not make itself felt immediately. And we have not only to note its presence but its relation to its environment, and, as it were, the space it occupies in history. The industrial revolution is precisely the expansion of undeveloped forces, the sudden growth and blossoming of seeds which had for years lain hidden or asleep.[1]

After the beginning of the nineteenth century, the arrival of the factory system was clearly visible. 'System' was the keyword. Robert Southey referred in 1807 to the pernicious effects of the 'manufacturing system' and was using 'manufacturing' in a very different sense from the early eighteenth-century usage of Defoe. By 1815 Robert Owen was building a social philosophy around the 'manufacturing system' which had 'so far extended its influence over the British Empire, as to effect an essential change in the general character of the mass of the people'.[2]

As we have seen, recent revisions of macro-economic data, notably by Professor Crafts, suggest that the kind of surging growth rates associated with new technological and organisational forms which mark the classic 'industrial revolution' should be placed in the early nineteenth century rather than the later eighteenth. Crafts, however, still emphasises the exceptionally early and marked shift away from agricultural employment.[3] Others have pointed out

1. P. Mantoux, *The Industrial Revolution in the Eighteenth Century*, Methuen, 1961 edn, pp. 475, 477.
2. Robert Southey, *Letters from England*, 1807, ed. J. Simmons, Alan Sutton, 1984, p. 267; Robert Owen, *A New View of Society and Other Writings*, Everyman, 1927, p. 121.
3. N.F.R. Crafts, *British Economic Growth during the Industrial Revolution*. Crafts' measurement is itself now being criticised; see for example J. Hoppit, 'Counting the Industrial Revolution', *Econ. H.R.*, XLIII, 2, 1990, pp. 173–93.

the slowness with which other industries followed the technological pace-setters like cotton and iron, stressing that the typical manufacturing worker even by 1851 still worked in a small-scale workshop rather than a factory.[4] This does not mean, however, that away from the cotton mills productivity was static. It has been roughly calculated that the number of operative hours needed to process 100 lb of cotton had been around 50,000 with hand spinning. In the pioneering Arkwright mills in the 1770s and in the first steam-powered mills it was in the range 250 to 350 hours.[5] But do such huge productivity gains have to become universal before we can talk of an 'industrial revolution'? In most manufactures progress was more modest, but it was measurable, widespread and significant. There were the changes in tooling, unlinked to power, which typified Birmingham's workshop trades but were far from confined to that town.[6] Adam Smith had seen the key to improved productivity in the increasing division of labour, and even with the retrospect of another hundred years behind him, Karl Marx had similarly stressed the importance of the workshop era of the 'period of manufacture'.[7] New techniques, new materials, new divisions of labour, all these could produce productivity gains of two, three or even ten times. By implying an historically inappropriate definition of what should be understood by 'industrial revolution', some modern writers seem to be throwing out more than the bath water.

The 'factory proletariat' may have been small in 1815, but wider changes in the organisation of manufacturing and agriculture had been accelerating the growth of a wage-dependent proletariat throughout the 'vital century'. Indeed, this is one of its most significant features. There was a 'proletariat' in England well before the factories of Charles Dickens' 'Coketown' began to send up their 'interminable serpents of smoke'.[8] It was a social consequence of economic change which was itself the cause of further changes. The extent of wage-dependency in Hanoverian England had implications not only for the reach and growth of the market and through its effect on the birth rate, but also for the mechanisms of social control and on the forms of popular protest.

4. For strong arguments against traditional views of an 'inevitable' progress to the factory system, see: M. Berg, *Age of Manufactures*; C. Sabel and J. Zeitlin, 'Historical alternatives to mass production: politics, markets and technology in nineteenth-century industrialisation', *Past and Present* **108**, 1985, pp. 133–76.
5. S.D. Chapman, *Cotton Industry in the Industrial Revolution*, p. 20.
6. Berg, *Age of Manufactures*, pp. 265–86.
7. Karl Marx, *Capital*, Everyman edn, 1930, I, Ch. 12.
8. Charles Dickens, *Hard Times*, 1854.

'Continuity versus change' has become a trite and overworked dichotomy in recent approaches to the eighteenth century.[9] Of course, there were sectors in which the former was much more marked than the latter, and even more in which aspects of both are to be found. Consider, for example, the huge and varied range of processes which were needed to make a piece of worsted cloth. Cumulative change, gradual and uneven, does not impress itself to a marked degree on those who experience it. How does one perceive, for instance, a population increase of 1.5 per cent a year? Is there a perceptible tightening of the labour market, or a gradual rise in the price of food? Probably not. Short-term factors like the closing of a market for cloth through war or a change in fashion were more evident harbingers of unemployment, and bad harvests a more obvious and dramatic cause of dear food. The varied experiences of war, above all those of the great French wars from 1793 to 1815, are considered by Clive Emsley to have been more important to contemporaries than any cluster of economic changes lumped together as an 'industrial revolution'.[10] While historians should not slip into anachronism but try to understand an age in its own terms, they also have the responsibility of placing it in longer-term significance by employing a perspective denied to contemporaries. Professional historians cowed by the fear of being accused of a 'Whig interpretation' risk leaving important areas of historical explanation to amateurs.

In 1815 most English people still lived in the countryside, but a third were living in towns. This was a significant proportional increase over 1714 and in aggregate terms trebled the urban population from 1 to 3 million. This does not overstate the growing urbanisation of eighteenth-century England. It takes a baseline of 5,000 inhabitants for towns and no account of the fact that many of those living in the countryside had at one time or other lived and worked in towns, for the population contained a large youthful mobile element. The England of 1800 was in many ways nearer to that of 1851, when the urban and rural populations were officially measured as equal, than it was to 1750.

9. The most recent history of the eighteenth century has put the emphasis once more on change. Dr Paul Langford declares a welcome intent 'to emphasise the changes which occurred in an age not invariably associated with change'. In particular he stresses the growing importance of 'a broad middle class' (P. Langford, *A Polite and Commercial People: England 1727–1783*, Oxford, Clarendon Press, 1989, p. xi).

10. C. Emsley, *British Society and the French Wars 1793–1815*, Macmillan, 1979, and see generally the classic study by T.S. Ashton, *Economic Fluctuations in England, 1700–1800*, Oxford UP, 1959.

On the continent any increases in aggregate urban populations which did take place were explained largely by the further domination of sprawling capital cities. That was not the case in eighteenth-century England, where provincial towns set the pace. London's share of the total population remained unchanged from 1700 to 1800 at around 11 per cent. By 1750 the combined population of the provincial towns matched it and by 1801 their population was almost double that of the capital. Not all towns grew; smaller market towns especially suffered. There was a fall of 18 per cent in their numbers between 1690 and 1792. But their decline was more than matched by the growth of others: regional centres, manufacturing towns, ports and spas. English urban growth was, as Dr Corfield puts it, 'multi-centred, not focused on a single city'.[11] This wider spread reflected the intimate links of the towns with surrounding regional economies, as well as the growing specialisation of some, for even those normally considered manufacturing centres were in reality multi-functional.

The dual economy was not marked in England, where towns were hardly 'islands of modernity'. Far from it, they were 'pace-setters for rural England', the leading edge of a developing economy. Professor Daunton has rightly contended that in eighteenth-century England, towns were no longer 'parasitic' but had become engines of growth.[12] Following his work and that of Peter Clark and Penelope Corfield, the dynamism of urban England is now effectively contrasted with the paralysis affecting continental towns. According to Professor Clark, 'both older and newer towns gave significant, if sometimes indirect impetus to economic growth: they were a vital lead sector in the wider modernising processes affecting English society'.[13]

Historians such as Arnold Toynbee and T.S. Ashton who stressed the idea of industrialisation dating from a particular breakpoint in the eighteenth century associated it with a change in ideology as well as in manufacturing practice. Toynbee wrote in 1884:

> Side by side with the revolution which [has been] effected in the methods and organisation of production, there has taken place a change no less radical in men's economic principles, and in the attitude of the state to individual enterprise. England in 1760 was still

11. Corfield, *Impact of English Towns*, p. 10.
12. *Ibid.*, p. 186; M.J. Daunton, 'Towns and economic growth in eighteenth-century England' in P. Abrams and E.A. Wrigley (eds), *Towns in Societies. Essays in Economic History and Historical Sociology*, Cambridge UP, 1978, pp. 245–77.
13. P. Clark (ed.), *Transformation of English Provincial Towns*, p. 14.

to a great extent under the medieval system of minute and manifold industrial regulation. That system was indeed decaying, but it had not yet been superseded by the modern principle of industrial freedom.[14]

It was a change which filled the socially concerned Toynbee with apprehension. While recognising its force, he could not approve it with the enthusiasm that Professor Ashton was to radiate fifty years later.

Many old privileges and monopolies were swept away and legislative impediments to enterprise removed. The State came to play a less active, the individual and voluntary association a more active, part in affairs. Ideas of innovation and progress undermined traditional sanctions: men began to look forward.[15]

To such historians, the great moment was the publication in 1776 of Adam Smith's *Wealth of Nations*, the greatest intellectual and ideological justification for the system of free enterprise, stressing political economy which was to become known as 'liberal capitalism'. According to the advocates of *laissez-faire*, government best served the developing economy by leaving it alone. In fact, it served the economy well by doing a very great deal. Parliament was the great enabler. Its generation of permissive legislation in the form of private acts to allow enclosures, turnpike building, town improvements, harbour construction or canal excavation was colossal – and these were only the best-known examples. Government regularly obliged employers with laws against trade unions and statutes to deal with workers who embezzled materials. Faced with Luddism, it made it a capital offence to break machinery. Above all it fought wars successfully enough to provide the overseas empire, without which the economic expansion of the eighteenth century would have been more modest and differently patterned.

The *tendency* over the latter half of the vital century was towards the curtailment and constraint of a paternalist role. It was a definite, but slow and uneven process. There was little left in the area of price control. Campbell, writing in 1747, warned that baking was not one of 'the most profitable trades; he is so much under the direction of the magistrate, that he has no great opportunity of making himself immensely rich; however he has a living profit allowed him by law'.[16] He was referring to the Assize of Bread

14. A. Toynbee, *The Industrial Revolution of the Eighteenth Century in England*, Longman, 1908, pp. 50–1.
15. Ashton, *The Industrial Revolution 1760–1830*, Oxford UP, 1962 edn, p. 2.
16. R. Campbell, *The London Tradesman*, 1747, reprinted David & Charles, 1969, p. 275.

under which local justices could set prices. It was not abolished until 1815, but its use had long been on the wane in most localities. The clauses of the Statute of Artificers of 1564 which had allowed them to make wage assessments was not repealed until 1813 but had fallen into disuse in most counties well before then. Yet as late as 1792 the government had extended the reach of the Spitalfields Act of 1773, fixing wages in London's silk manufacture, to mixed-weave cloths. The act was not repealed until 1823.[17]

From the acts of the 1720s banning trade unionism on the part of tailors and woollen workers, the several statutes passed against combinations in specific trades had all been balanced by including a wage-fixing clause. This relic of paternalist concern was not included in the act of 1796 following strikes of journeymen paper makers. It had been deliberately removed at the bill stage. This act was to be the model for the general prohibition of trade unions in 1799.[18] Trade unionism was even more weakened by the repeal of the apprenticeship clauses of the Statute of Artificers in 1814. A number of London's artisans had sought to use this legislation to preserve control over entry to their crafts, but they had awakened a sleeping dog. Government, responding quickly to the employers' lobby, put the poor old beast down. Apprenticeship regulation and the closed shop it provided had long been surviving in a full sense only where workers' combinations were strong enough to enforce it. Even the common lawyers admitting it to be statute law took care to indicate that it was an obsolete survival and a hindrance to commerce, and restricted its operation in case law decisions. Parliament had refused its extension to the new cotton manufacture in 1756 and exempted dyers from its requirements in 1777. Specific statutes controlling apprenticeship in hat making and in woollen manufacture were rescinded in 1777 and 1809 respectively.[19]

So far as inland trade was concerned, local customs and prohibitions had long ceased to hinder the growth of a national market, which, after the union with Scotland in 1702, was probably the largest free-trade area in Europe. Ireland was another matter. Those who favour the recent suggestion that Hanoverian England was an 'ancien régime' might well consider that it took the revolution of 1789 to bring about this market situation in France, while in Ger-

---

17. J. Moher, 'From suppression to containment: roots of trade union law to 1825' in J.G. Rule (ed.), *British Trade Unionism 1750–1850. The Formative Years*, Longman, 1988, pp. 78–80.

18. *Ibid.*, pp. 80–1.

19. For the apprenticeship issue, see Rule, *Experience of Labour*, pp. 95–119.

many it was a development of the middle nineteenth century. In respect of international commerce very little progress was made towards free trade, for all its central role in Adam Smith's thought, its later close association with Britain's nineteenth-century domination of trade in manufactured goods and its centrality in the ideology of liberal capitalism. The polemic delivered in *The Wealth of Nations*, against the policies Smith called 'mercantilist', had not moved many people of influence by 1815 and had made no impact at all on the great propertied who insisted on their protective Corn Laws down to 1846.

Loosely expressed, 'mercantilism' means little more than 'the belief that the economic welfare of the state can only be secured by government regulation of a nationalist character'.[20] Applied to foreign trade, since there was no belief in the possibility of a significant increase in aggregate consumption of manufactured goods, protection was considered necessary to maintain employment at home. There is little need here for a detailed examination of British policy over the first half of the eighteenth century. That has already been provided in another volume in this series by a master of the subject, Professor Charles Wilson. The policy of industrial encouragement, even if it meant lower revenues, reached its apogee under Sir Robert Walpole, who began by removing whatever duties there were on manufactured exports and on imported raw materials. Export of raw materials, especially of wool, was prohibited, as was that of machinery and the emigration of skilled artisans. Coal could be exported only over a duty which was increased in 1714. Duties res-trained the imports of goods such as silks and linens, to enable English producers to compete. At a time of emerging industrial prowess, Walpole's strategy probably served the interests of manufacturing growth better than a policy of free trade would have. In it were embodied ideas of national economic purpose.

> Walpole's reforms in 1721 and later years completed a long process. To the abolition of export duties was added a series of bounties to stimulate industry positively; on whale fishing, linen, sailcloth, paper etc. Protective duties on competing manufactured imports were multiplied. The pattern was consistent. . . . The relatively ordered framework of duties and laws called by Adam Smith, 'the mercantile system' provided the matrix within which continued economic expansion went forward. It was not without anomalies, even scandals, and in due time it would outlive its usefulness. But that it did in time

20. Definition from Unesco *Dictionary of the Social Sciences*, cited by D.C. Coleman in his Introduction to *Revisions in Mercantilism*, Methuen, 1969, p. 1.

do so does not destroy its claim to have been effective in the early stages of growth. . . . Its fundamental assumption – that the economic plant may be induced to grow in apparently infertile soil – embodied a truly dynamic view of economic growth.[21]

Chronology does not in fact allow any other system to be associated with Britain's rise to world manufacturing leadership. As Professor Davis has pointed out, the foreign-trade policy criticised by Adam Smith in 1776 as 'mercantilism' was very far from being long established. Indeed, it was still extending at the time *Wealth of Nations* was being written. Reform in the direction of free trade had to wait until the second quarter of the nineteenth century, for it was a policy best suited to the maintenance of industrial leadership rather than to the assisting of economic development. Once Britain had become the 'workshop of the world', free trade could become a self-serving ideology. That is why it had such a short history as an internationally preferred policy.[22]

Briefly in the 1780s William Pitt the Younger, who was the first prime minister to become a follower of Adam Smith, tried to move trade policy away from mercantilist assumptions. The loss of the American colonies necessitated a new relationship with a major and potentially even more important market. But Pitt failed to persuade parliament to agree to a free-trade relationship with the new republic. He failed even to get agreement to remove restrictions on trade with Ireland, whose colonial administration was in many respects even more repressive than that which had caused the Americans to revolt. His hopes of a European-wide liberalisation of trade led only to the Anglo-French Treaty of 1786, a single agreement which he actually considered a step backwards. His reductions in the duties on tea and tobacco proved his point that revenue would increase if smuggling were made less profitable, but this was his only triumph. Professor Ashton suggested that had the long wars with France not begun in 1793, 'One is left wondering what peaks might have been reached, both in commerce and human liberty if the war could have been avoided.'[23] Arguably it would have made little difference so far as free trade was concerned. Vested interests were opposed and pragmatists unconvinced. There is little sign of a general readiness to make an ideological leap into the 'new world' of Dr Adam Smith.

21. C. Wilson, *England's Apprenticeship*, p. 267.
22. R. Davis, 'The rise of protection in England, 1669–1786', *Econ. H.R.*, XIX, 2, 1966, p. 313.
23. Ashton, *An Economic History of England*, p. 166.

In this, as in some other respects, such as the continuing political hegemony of the landed elite, the eighteenth century can seem less than dynamic, but in seeking to maximise employment later mercantilism defines itself as, for its time, a growth-promoting rather than a revenue-dominated policy. Just such a distinction, according to Sir John Hicks, marks the arrival of a modern political economy.[24] The eighteenth century was not rushing towards the nineteenth. Still less did it arrive there in a great bound from a take-off point somewhere in the 1780s. The pace was varied, usually gradual and sometimes faltering, but in terms of direction, changing structures and the revelation of a transforming potential for the output of material goods and the harnessing of resources for that end, the recognisable beginnings of the modern economy must be sought in the 'vital century'.

24. J.R. Hicks, *A Theory of Economic History*, Oxford UP, 1969, pp. 22–4.

Select Bibliography

This is a select listing of recent secondary works. The page foot-notes contain full details of all works used and cited in the text. Titles are listed only once, so the assignment between categories is somewhat arbitrary.

GENERAL

Ashton, T.S., *An Economic History of England: The Eighteenth Century*, Methuen, 1955

Clark, J.C.D., *English Society, 1688–1832; Ideology, Social Structure and Political Practice during the Ancien Régime*, Cambridge UP, 1985

Deane, P. and Cole, W.A., *British Economic Growth 1688–1959*, Cambridge UP, 1969

Digby, A. and Feinstein, C. (eds), *New Directions in Economic and Social History*, Macmillan, 1989

Floud, R. and McCloskey, D. (eds), *The Economic History of Britain since 1700*, Vol. I, *1700–1860*, Cambridge UP, 1981

Langford, P., *A Polite and Commercial People: England 1727–1783*, Clarendon Press, Oxford, 1989

Malcolmson, R.W., *Life and Labour in England 1700–1780*, Hutchinson, 1981

Mathias, P., *The First Industrial Nation: An Economic History of Britain 1700–1914*, Methuen, 2nd edn, 1983

Pawson, E., *The Early Industrial Revolution: Britain in the Eighteenth Century*, Barnes and Noble, New York, 1979

Perkin, H.J., *The Origins of Modern English Society, 1780–1880*, Routledge, 1969

Porter, R., *English Society in the Eighteenth Century*, Penguin, 1982, revised 1990

Rule, J.G., *Albion's People: English Society 1714–1815*, Longman, 1992

Rule, J.G., *The Experience of Labour in Eighteenth-Century Industry*, Croom Helm, 1981

Rule, J.G., *The Labouring Classes in Early Industrial England, 1750–1850*, Longman, 1986

Wilson, C., *England's Apprenticeship 1603–1763*, Longman, revised 1984

POPULATION

Chambers, J.D., *Population, Economy and Society in Pre-Industrial England*, Oxford UP, 1972

Drake, M., (ed.), *Population in Industrialization*, Methuen, 1969

Flinn, M.W., *The European Demographic System 1500–1820*, Harvester, 1981

Flinn, M.W., 'The population history of England, 1541–1871', *Econ. H.R.*, XXXV, 1982

Glass, D.V. and Eversley, D.E.C., *Population in History: Essays in Historical Demography*, Arnold, 1965

Levine, D., *Family Formation in an Age of Nascent Capitalism*, Academic Press, 1977

Levine, D., 'Industrialization and the proletarian family', *Past and Present*, **107**, 1985

Rotberg, R.I. and Rabb, T.K. (eds), *Population and Economy*, Cambridge UP, 1986

Wrigley, E.A., 'The growth of population in eighteenth-century England: a conundrum resolved', *Past and Present*, **98**, 1983

Wrigley, E.A. and Schofield, R.S., *The Population History of England 1541–1871*, 2nd edn, Cambridge UP, 1989

ECONOMIC GROWTH

Crafts, N.F.R., *British Economic Growth during the Industrial Revolution*, Oxford UP, 1985

Deane, P., *The First Industrial Revolution*, Cambridge UP, 2nd edn, 1979

Harley, C.K., 'British industrialization before 1841: evidence of slower growth during the industrial revolution', *Journal of Economic History*, XLII, 1982

Hartwell, R.M., *The Industrial Revolution and Economic Growth*, Methuen, 1971

Hoppit, J., 'Counting the industrial revolution', *Econ. H.R.*, XLIII, 1990

Jackson, R.V., 'Growth and deceleration in English agriculture 1660–1790', *Econ. H.R.*, XXXVIII, 1985

Jackson, R.V., 'Government expenditure and British economic growth in the eighteenth century: some problems of measurement', *Econ. H.R.*, XLVIII, 1990

Jones, E.L., *Agriculture and Economic Growth in England 1650–1815*, Methuen, 1967

Lee, C.H., *The British Economy since 1700: A Macroeconomic Perspective*, Cambridge UP, 1986

O'Brien, P.K., 'Agriculture and the industrial revolution', *Econ. H.R.*, XXX, 1987

AGRICULTURE

Beckett, J.V., 'English landownership in the later seventeenth and eighteenth centuries: the debate and the problems', *Econ. H.R.*, XXXIII, 1977

Beckett, J.V., 'The pattern of landownership in England and Wales, 1660–1880', *Econ. H.R.*, XXXVII, 1984

Beckett, J.V., *The Aristocracy in England, 1660–1914*, Blackwell, 1986

Bonfield, L., 'Marriage settlements and the rise of great estates', *Econ. H.R.*, XXXII, 1979

Chambers, J.D. and Mingay, G.E., *The Agricultural Revolution 1750–1880*, Batsford, 1966

Clay, C., 'The price of freehold land in the later seventeenth and eighteenth centuries', *Econ. H.R.*, XXVII, 1974

Clay, C., 'Marriage, inheritance and the rise of large estates in England, 1660–1815', *Econ. H.R.*, XXI, 1968

Habakkuk, H.J., 'English landownership, 1680–1740', *Econ. H.R.*, X, 1939–40

Hammond, J.L. and B., *The Village Labourer, 1760–1832*, 1911, reprint Longman, 1978

Havinden, M.A., 'Agricultural progress in open-field Oxfordshire', *Agricultural History Review*, IX, 1961

Holderness, B.A., 'The English land market in the eighteenth century: the case of Lincolnshire', *Econ. H.R.*, XXVII, 1974

Kussmaul, A., *Servants in Husbandry in Early Modern England*, Cambridge UP, 1981

Martin, J.M., 'The small landowner and parliamentary enclosure in Warwickshire', *Econ. H.R.*, XXXII, 1979

Mingay, G.E., 'The eighteenth-century land steward', in E.L. Jones and G.E. Mingay (eds), *Land, Labour and Population in the Industrial Revolution*, Arnold, 1976

Reed, M., 'The peasantry of nineteenth-century rural England: a neglected class?', *History Workshop Journal*, **18**, 1984

Snell, K.D.M., *Annals of the Labouring Poor. Social Change and Agrarian England 1660–1900*, Cambridge UP, 1985

Thirsk, J. (ed.), *The Agrarian History of England and Wales*, Vol. V, *1640–1750*, Cambridge UP, 1984–5

Thompson, F.M.L., 'The social distribution of landed property in England since the sixteenth century', *Econ. H.R.*, XIX, 1966

Turner, M.E., *English Parliamentary Enclosure*, Dawson, 1980

Turner, M.E., 'Agricultural productivity in England in the eighteenth century', *Econ. H.R.*, XXXV, 1982

Turner, M.E., *Enclosures in Britain, 1750–1830*, Macmillan, 1984

Turner, M.E., 'Parliamentary enclosures: gains and costs', *ReFRESH*, **3**, 1986

Wordie, J.R., 'Social change on the Leveson-Gower estates, 1714–1832', *Econ. H.R.*, XXVII, 1974

Wordie, J.R., 'The chronology of English enclosure, 1500–1914', *Econ. H.R.*, XXXVI, 1983

Yelling, J.A., *Common Field and Enclosure in England 1450–1850*, Macmillan, 1977

MANUFACTURING AND MINING

General

Berg, M., *The Age of Manufactures 1700–1820*, Fontana, 1985

Berg, M., Hudson, P. and Sonenscher, M. (eds), *Manufacture in Town and Country before the Industrial Revolution*, Cambridge UP, 1983

Burt, R., *The British Lead Mining Industry*, Dyllansow Truran, Redruth, 1984

Chalklin, C.W., *The Provincial Towns of Georgian England: A Study of the Building Process, 1740–1820*, Arnold, 1974

Chapman, S.D., *The Cotton Industry in the Industrial Revolution*, Macmillan, 1972

Coleman, D.C., *The British Paper Industry 1495–1860. A Study in Industrial Growth*, Clarendon, 1958

Davis, R., *The Rise of the English Shipping Industry in the Seventeenth and Eighteenth Centuries*, David & Charles, Newton Abbot, 1962

Edwards, M.M., *The Growth of the British Cotton Trade, 1780–1815*, Manchester UP, 1967

Flinn, M.W., *The History of the British Coal Industry*, Vol. II *1700–1830, The Industrial Revolution*, Clarendon, 1984

Harris, J.R., 'The employment of steam power in the eighteenth century', *History*, **175**, 1967

Harris, J.R., 'Skills, coal and British industry in the eighteenth century', *History*, **202**, 1976

Harris, J.R., *The British Iron Industry, 1700–1850*, Macmillan, 1988

Harte, N.B. and Ponting, K. (eds), *Textile History and Economic History*, Manchester UP, 1973

Hudson, P. (ed.), *Regions and Industries: A Perspective on the Industrial Revolution in Britain*, Cambridge UP, 1989

Hyde, C.K., *Technological Change and the British Iron Industry 1700–1870*, Princeton UP, 1977

Mann, J. de Lacy, *The Cloth Industry in the West of England from 1640 to 1880*, Oxford UP, 1971

Mathias, P., *The Brewing Industry in England, 1700–1830*, Cambridge UP, 1959

Musson, A. E., *The Growth of British Industry*, Batsford, 1978

Riden, P., 'The output of the British iron industry before 1870', *Econ. H.R.*, XXX, 1977

Wadsworth, A.P. and Mann, J. de Lacy, *The Cotton Trade and Industrial Lancashire 1600–1780*, Manchester UP, 1931

Weatherill, L., *The Pottery Trade and North Staffordshire, 1660–1760*, Manchester UP, 1971

Investment and organisation

Clarkson, L.A., *Proto-industrialisation: The First Phase of Industrialisation?*, Macmillan, 1985

Crouzet, F. (ed.), *Capital Formation in the Industrial Revolution*, Methuen, 1972

Crouzet, F., *The First Industrialists*, Cambridge UP, 1985

Feinstein, C. and Pollard, S., *Studies in Capital Formation in the United Kingdom, 1750–1920*, Clarendon, 1988

Honeyman, K., *Origins of Enterprise: Business Leadership in the Industrial Revolution*, Manchester UP, 1982

Hoppit, J., *Risk and Failure in English Business 1700–1800*, Cambridge UP, 1987

Hudson, P., *The Genesis of Industrial Capital: A Study of the West Riding Wool Textile Industry, c. 1750–1850*, Cambridge UP, 1986

Mathias, P. and Postan, M.M. (eds), *The Cambridge Economic History of Europe*, Vol. VII, *The Industrial Economies: Capital, Labour and Enterprise*, Part I, Cambridge UP, 1978

Pollard, S., *The Genesis of Modern Management*, Penguin, 1968

Labour

Aspinall, A. (ed.), *The Early English Trade Unions*, Blatchworth, 1949

Hammond, J.L. and B., *The Town Labourer*, 1917, new edn, Longman, 1978

Hammond, J.L. and B., *The Skilled Labourer*, 1919, new edn, Longman, 1979

Harrison, M., *Crowds and History: Mass Phenomenon in English Towns 1790–1835*, Cambridge UP, 1988

Joyce, P.K. (ed.), *Historical Meanings of Work*, Cambridge UP, 1987

Reid, D.A., 'The decline of Saint Monday 1776–1876', *Past and Present*, **71**, 1976

Rule, J.G., *The Experience of Labour in Eighteenth-Century Industry*, Croom Helm, 1981

Thompson, E.P., 'Time, work-discipline and industrial capitalism', *Past and Present*, **38**, 1968

Thompson, E.P., *The Making of the English Working Class*, Penguin, 1968

TRANSPORT

Albert, W., *The Turnpike Road System in England, 1663–1840*, Cambridge UP, 1972

Aldcroft, D.H. and Freeman, M., *Transport in the Industrial Revolution*, Manchester UP, 1983

Dyos, H.J. and Aldcroft, D.H., *British Transport: An Economic Survey from the Seventeenth Century to the Twentieth*, Penguin, 1974

Gerhold, D., 'The growth of the London carrying trade 1681–1838', *Econ. H.R.*, XLI, 3, 1988

Pawson, E., *Transport and Economy: The Turnpike Roads of Eighteenth-Century Britain*, Academic Press, 1977

Turnbull, G., 'Canals, coal and regional growth during the Industrial Revolution', *Econ. H.R.*, XL, 4, 1987

Ward, J.R., *The Finance of Canal Building in Eighteenth-Century England*, Oxford UP, 1974

MARKETS

Davis, R., *The Industrial Revolution and British Overseas Trade*, Leicester UP, 1979

Eversley, D.E.C., 'The home market and economic growth in England, 1750–80' in Jones, E.L. and Mingay, G.E. (eds), *Land, Labour and Population in the Industrial Revolution*, Arnold, 1967

Gilboy, E.W., 'Demand as a factor in the industrial revolution', 1932, reprinted in R.M. Hartwell (ed.), *The Causes of the Industrial Revolution in England*, Methuen, 1967

John, A.H., 'Aspects of English economic growth in the first half of the eighteenth century', *Economica*, 1961, reprinted in E.M. Carus Wilson (ed.), *Essays in Economic History*, II, Arnold, 1962

McKendrick, N., 'Home demand and economic growth: a new view of the role of women and children in the industrial revolution', in McKendrick, N. (ed.), *Historical Perspectives: Studies in English Thought and Society*, Europa, 1974

McKendrick, N., Brewer, J. and Plumb, J.H., *The Birth of a Consumer Society: The Commercialization of Eighteenth-Century England*, Hutchinson, 1983

Minchinton, W.E. (ed.), *The Growth of English Overseas Trade in the Seventeenth and Eighteenth Centuries*, Methuen, 1969

FINANCE

Brewer, J., *The Sinews of Power*, Unwin, 1989

Dickson, P.G.M., *The Financial Revolution in England – A Study in the Development of Public Credit 1688–1756*, Macmillan, 1967

Joslin, D.M., 'London's private bankers, 1720–1785' in E.M. Carus Wilson (ed.), *Essays in Economic History*, II, Arnold, 1962

Mathias, P. and O'Brien, P.K., 'Taxation in England and France, 1715–1810', *Journal of European Economic History*, V, 1975

O'Brien, P.K., 'The political economy of British taxation, 1660–1815', *Econ. H.R.*, XLI, 1988

O'Brien, P.K., 'Public finance and the wars with France, 1793–1815', in Dickinson, H.T. (ed.), *Britain and the French Revolution 1789–1815*, Macmillan, 1989

TOWNS

Borsay, P. (ed.), *The Eighteenth-Century Town*, Longman, 1990

Clark, P. (ed.), *The Transformation of English Provincial Towns*, Hutchinson, 1984

Corfield, P., *The Impact of English Towns, 1700–1800*, Oxford UP, 1982

George, M.D., *London Life in the Eighteenth Century*, Penguin, 1966

Index